THE ORIGINS OF LOGIC
One to Two Years

DEVELOPMENTAL PSYCHOLOGY SERIES

SERIES EDITOR

Harry Beilin

Developmental Psychology Program
City University of New York Graduate School
New York, New York

A complete list of titles in this series is available from the publisher.

THE ORIGINS OF LOGIC
One to Two Years

Jonas Langer

Department of Psychology
University of California
Berkeley, California

1986

ACADEMIC PRESS, INC.

Harcourt Brace Jovanovich, Publishers

Orlando   San Diego   New York   Austin
London   Montreal   Sydney   Tokyo   Toronto

ACADEMIC PRESS, INC.
Orlando, Florida 32887

United Kingdom Edition published by
ACADEMIC PRESS INC. (LONDON) LTD.
24–28 Oval Road, London NW1 7DX

LIBRARY OF CONGRESS CATALOGING-IN-PUBLICATION DATA

Langer, Jonas.
    The origins of logic.

    (Developmental psychology series)
    Bibliography: p.
    Includes index.
    1. Reasoning in children.   2. Logic.   I. Title.
II. Series.
BF723.R4L36   1985   155.4'22   85-11064
ISBN 0-12-436555-8 (alk. paper)
ISBN 0-12-436556-6 (paperback)

PRINTED IN THE UNITED STATES OF AMERICA

86 87 88 89   9 8 7 6 5 4 3 2 1

Contents

Preface

This is the second installment of our research on how children begin to construct their cognition. The first objective of the research, undertaken in *The Origins of Logic: Six to Twelve Months*, is to discover the elements of cognition during infancy. The objective, initiated in this volume, is to determine how infants' elementary cognition evolves into full-fledged knowledge.

The period from 1 to 2 years bridges the transition from infancy to childhood; it is the age when children begin to speak and when their knowledge becomes representational. Yet, relatively little is known about this crucial period of cognitive development. The present work seeks to fill this lacuna by investigating children's conceptual, symbolic, and linguistic development at ages 15, 18, 21, and 24 months.

Our prime focus is on children's developing logicomathematical cognition. Part of studying logicomathematical cognition involves comparing and contrasting it with physical cognition, especially causal and spatial cognition. Our expectation is that infants progressively construct necessary logicomathematical relations during their second year, such as quantitative equivalence between their compositions of objects. This development is expected to be paralleled by infants progressively constructing contingent (possible and impossible) physical relations, such as experimenting with tilting a block to see if it will remain upright or fall over. It is further expected that infants' developing logicomathematical cognition progressively introduces necessity or certainty into their physical constructions; conversely, infants' developing physical cognition progressively introduces contingency or uncertainty into their logicomathematical constructions.

This analysis is coupled with an examination of how infants' elementary logicomathematical and physical cognition becomes representational during their second year. To determine how infants develop representational cognition, we investigated the symbolic as well as the conceptual aspects of their evolving knowledge. Therefore, the present volume continues our report on how infants begin to symbolize in action (e.g., gestures and play) and in language, and on the developing relation between their language and thought.

While most theories of cognitive development assume that infants' developing symbolization, particularly their acquisition of language, ushers in their representational cognition, we make no such assumption. Just as we previously proposed that infants do not need to symbolize in order to form their elementary cognition during their first year, so we now propose that they do not need language in order to develop representational cognition during their second year. Our thesis is that infants construct representational cognition by mapping elementary cognitions onto each other. Infants develop representation by constructing cognitions upon cognitions previously constructed.

Elementary Cognition 1

The elements of cognition are constructed by infants during their first year. In the present view, these elements are precursors of the representational cognition that originates during the second half of infancy. In turn, representational cognitions are transitional to, and are the expected progenitors of the operational cognition that begins during middle childhood.

So, determining the structures of infants' and young children's constructive interactions with their environments is crucial to analyzing the origins, development, and organization of their knowledge. This endeavor entails three overall objectives. The first, which was taken up in a previous volume, is to determine infants' precursory logicomathematical and physical constructions, labeled proto-operations and protofunctions, respectively (Langer, 1980).

The second objective is to determine how proto-operations and protofunctions are transformed into representational operations and functions. The aim is to determine how representational cognition originates and develops during infancy. This is the focus of the present volume.

Constructing representational cognition during infancy and early childhood is necessary in order to generate basic and relatively well-established cognitive structures, particularly concrete operations and functions, during middle and late childhood (e.g., Beilin, 1975; Davidson, 1983; Inhelder & Piaget, 1964; Piaget, 1972; Piaget, Grize, Szeminska, & Vinh Bang, 1977). These first two research goals are therefore necessary so as to understand how children's logicomathematical and physical cognition during middle and late childhood develop out of their infantile proto-operational and protofunctional foundations, via their transitional representational forms. This is the third objective of our research program.

Realizing these objectives requires formulating a theory that embraces three components. The first is analyzing the basic primitive elements that make up cognition. Accordingly, we have proposed that part–whole transformations are basic to constructing logicomathematical cognition, and means–ends transformations are basic to constructing physical cognition.

The second theoretical requirement is postulating the structures of infants' constructive part–whole and means–ends interactions, and their products, that entail or embody logicomathematical proto-operations and physical protofunctions. The model proposed comprises three base or foundational structures, their organization, and their products. The first are combinativity proto-operations of composing, decomposing, and reforming; also included are their derivatives, such as recomposing and attaching, which construct pragmatic elements and sets. The second are relational proto-operations of addition, subtraction, multiplication, and division. They are applied to the products of combinativity; for instance, they construct pragmatic ordered series. The third are exchange, correlational, and negation proto-operations. Exchange comprises replacing, substituting, and commuting elements, sets, and series. Correlation includes both one-to-one and one-to-many correspondences between elements, sets, and series. Negation includes both inversion and reciprocity between elements, sets, and series. These generative structures are sufficient to produce three fundamental elements of cognition: quantitative and qualitative equivalence, ordered nonequivalence of magnitudes, and pragmatic reversibility between proto-operations and between protofunctions.

The third theoretical requirement is determining the structural developmental processes or mechanisms by which proto-operations and protofunctions are transformed into full-fledged operations and functions. A crucial transitional step in this process, investigated in this volume, is their initial representational transformation during the second year of infancy. Our basic hypothesis, elaborated in Section III is that infants construct their representational cognition by mapping their elementary mappings, proto-operations, and protofunctions onto each other.

In brief, these are the theoretical bases for investigating the precursors of logicomathematical cognition during infancy and their development during early childhood. Our main focus is on part–whole logicomathematical structuring, but causal and spatial, means–ends physical structuring is also examined. The origins, initial organization, and development of the first four stages of precursory logicomathematical and physical cognition during infants' first year have already been reported (Langer, 1980, 1981, 1982a, 1983). They are reviewed in this chapter as a preparation for the rest of the volume, which investigates the subsequent representational transformation and four stage progress of cognition during infants' second year. As we shall see, they are the developmental derivatives of Stages 1–4 that evolve during infants' first year. The sequence of stages that develop during infants' second year are thus numbered Stages 5–8.

Part–whole constructions are at the heart of all operational structuring and therefore constitute prime data for studying the development of logicomathematical cognition. Accordingly, the experimental preparations do not have any built-in physical goals, problems, or solutions. The preparations are not designed to evoke means–ends transformations, although they do not preclude such structuring by children, as is noted in the section on functions.

The subjects in the study are simply presented with small objects, either singly or in small sets. All of the subjects' manipulations of objects, and the transformations that these interactions produce, are recorded audiovisually. Interactions and transformations are analyzed into microunits while preserving the sequence and context in which they occur. So the data are quantitative measures of subjects' spontaneous manipulations of, and constructions with, objects, as well as qualitative observations. The results of experimenter-provoked manipulations and of counterconditions supplement these spontaneous measures. The precise details of the research design, including the kinds of objects presented to subjects and the testing procedures, have already been fully described (Langer, 1980, pages 15–23 and Appendix) and are summarized in the Appendix to this volume.[1]

The objects presented either embody logical class predicates (e.g., two additive classes of four square rings and four triangular rings) or they do not (e.g., controls comprised of all different objects). There are no built-in tasks and no instructions in the spontaneous manipulation conditions. Hence, it is possible to construct part–whole transformations with these preparations, including the intensive (predicate) part–whole structures of those conditions that embody classes. But there is nothing in the procedures that requires this construction from the subjects.

All the procedures are nonverbal, thus permitting comparable testing of subjects from ages 6–60 months in the research program. These procedures also facilitate comparative research without most of the usual communication problems one finds when testing children in different cultures (Jacobsen, 1984) and special children such as autistic children (Slotnick, 1984). Consequently, some of the central results reported in Langer (1980) and in the present volume have already been replicated with (a) Aymara Indian infants living in rural, basically impoverished settings at high altitudes in the Southern Peruvian Sierras, and (b) Quecha Indian infants living in Azango, a small Peruvian town of about 6000 inhabitants (Jacobosen, 1984).

The structural–developmental model briefly outlined above posits that operations—such as composing, substituting, and negating—and their products—equivalence, nonequivalence, and reversibility of elements, sets, and series—are

---

[1]Appreciation is due to Melanie Killen for testing subjects, to Caroline Bennett and Colleen Galloway for audiovisual transcription, and to Emily Reid for drawing the illustrations. Subjects were drawn from the nursery school enrollment application lists of the Harold E. Jones Child Study Center, University of California, Berkeley.

irreducible or minimal forms of logicomathematical cognition. These primitives should therefore be manifest in precursory form as soon as infants begin to interact pragmatically (with any systematicity) so as to construct part–whole transformations. The data, some of which we now review, confirm this expectation (see Langer, 1980, for detailed reports).

I. Operations

Part–whole transformations of objects and events are basic mapping forms by which children structure their functional interactions with the environment. *Mappings* are functions that express the transformational consequences of applying actions to the environment, with or without objects (see Langer, 1980, for detailed discussions on mappings and their development from ages 6–12 months). Mappings are therefore our basic unit of analysis because they capture the interactive transformations in both the subjects' and the environment's processes and products. In short, mappings characterize subjects' constructions.

Part–whole structuring may be invariant. If so, the mappings that subjects generate are universally applicable because (a) they are possible with all types of objects, whether discrete (nonmalleable), quasi-continuous (malleable), or conglomerate (part nonmalleable and part malleable); and (b) they produce identical part–whole transformations in all types of objects. The principal transformations are (1) the uniting of objects into compositions of objects, (2) the reuniting of compositions into derivative variants (including coordinating compositions with each other to form second-order constructions), (3) the separating of compositions into related subcollections, and (4) the separating of compositions into related objects.

Part–whole structuring may vary with the type of object being transformed. The mappings subjects generate are therefore not universally applicable because they are possible with only those types of objects with which they produce unique part–whole transformations. Only the part–whole structures of quasi-continuous malleable objects can be transformed from (1) one form of composite object into another by rearranging the parts (e.g., from a ring into a solid and vice versa), (2) a single object into a collection by taking apart the whole, and (3) a collection into a composite object by putting together the elements into a whole. Two other part–whole transformations are unique to structuring conglomerate objects that combine discrete (nonmalleable) with quasi-continuous (malleable) objects. These are (1) the adhering of malleable to nonmalleable objects to form conglomerate wholes, and (2) the taking apart of conglomerate wholes into malleable and nonmalleable parts.

Infants' part–whole interactions at age 6 months usually comprise single consecutive mappings of the transformative consequences of having applied their actions to the environment. Some mappings involve manipulating single objects before going on to other mappings with or without other single objects. Among other transformations, these interactions already map the rudiments of pragmatic matching (i.e., ordered pairs) that are necessary to produce quantitative equivalence. For instance, infants construct one-to-one correspondences frequently and two-to-two correspondences infrequently (such as banging hand or block on table twice, pause, repeat). Infants' interactions also already map pragmatic addition and subtraction, which is sufficient to produce the beginnings of an ordered nonequivalence not exceeding the minimal 2-point magnitude series (e.g., banging hand or block on table once, then twice). Perceptual data (Starkey & Cooper, 1980; Starkey, Spelke, & Gelman, 1983) are consistent with this minimal quantitative matching and ordering and may already be manifest by infants during their first week (Antell & Keating, 1983), although the authors of this study question the adequacy of their methods.

A substantial proportion of infants' interactions involve uniting objects into collections (see also Hetzer, 1931; and Vereeken, 1961). At least as early as age 6 months, infants consistently compose objects together. They spontaneously generate between four or five compositions of objects per minute. Moreover, the rate of composing does not vary as a function of the preparation (e.g., whether the materials contain similar or dissimilar elements).

Most compositions unite the minimal number of objects possible: two objects. Still, 15% already include more than the minimum; most of these comprise three objects while four-object compositions are rare. The number of objects infants manipulate in order to construct these compositions is also usually minimal: one object (e.g., bringing one object into contact with another object sitting on the table). Even so, more than a third are already constructed by infants manipulating two or more objects (e.g., bringing two objects into contact with each other).

Compositions tend to be labile (see Werner, 1948). More than half are mobile (kinetic) compositions. Typically, these mobiles comprise two objects produced by infants directly manipulating only one of the objects, but so that there is momentary contact between both objects. For instance, one held object is pushed into another so that they both move together for a moment. Still, two-fifths of infants' constructions are already stabile (static) compositions. Most of these stabiles, however, are also transient two-object compositions produced by infants manipulating only one of the objects composed (e.g., infants hold one object on or near another object for a moment).

Single collections characterize infants' constructions. One-third are generated in temporal isolation from any other collection. The other two-thirds are generated consecutively, one immediately after the other. Effectively, infants this age never construct two collections in either partial temporal overlap or at the same time. Still, generating consecutive collections permits recomposing as well as composing. One-third of subjects' constructions are variant recompositions of their initial compositions.

Even relatively labile combinativity operations restricted to composing single collections plus some recomposing of these collections begin to provide minimal elements for protological structuring. Indeed, the elements of relational and conditional operations that structure discrete magnitudes are already manifest by age 6 months. Consider some of the main operations that are representative of infants' precursory logicomathematical structuring:

1. Adding and subtracting produces single ordered series. Objects are usually added and subtracted within two-object compositions, but sometimes within as many as three-object compositions. Increasing and decreasing series of elements are generated in this way by half of the subjects.

2. Correlations are structured within single collections. But they are incomplete. One-to-many, but not many-to-one, correspondences are generated with three objects (e.g., tapping one object to two objects). Most correlations, however, produce equivalence by one-to-one correspondence within two-object compositions (e.g., aligning two triangular rings symmetrically so that their bases are matched to each other).

3. Exchange by replacing, substituting, and commuting produces equivalence within single collections. One-third of the subjects substitute one object for another in two-object compositions that they have constructed. These infants just begin to produce equivalence between consecutive versions of two-object collections. Parallel initial replacing and commuting are also generated by infants within two-object compositions that they have just constructed.

4. Classification is by negation. Infants consistently couple together different objects into single collections (discrimination measures yield consistent results; see Bornstein, 1981, and Cohen & Younger, 1983, for recent reviews). This does not vary according to class conditions (i.e., whether the preparations embody additive, multiplicative, or disjoint class structures). To illustrate, when presented with an additive preparation, such as two blue square and two blue triangular rings, infants consistently compose a square with a triangular ring rather than two square or two triangular rings.

Part–whole structuring of quasi-continuous (malleable) objects parallels that of discrete objects. In addition, infants' interactions with quasi-continuous objects already map some unique transformations upon them. The two main ones are deforming and decomposing objects. Putting together two or more objects to form one larger whole is never generated. Reversible structuring is absent with the sole exception of one infant's recomposing of previously decomposed object parts. Furthermore, only the extensive (quantitative) properties of the initial whole are reconstructed; the intensive (form) properties are not.

These unique combinativity operations provide further elements for relational and conditional operations. Only those unique to quasi-continuous objects need be considered here. Focusing on deforming only is sufficient for this purpose, particularly since it is the most frequent transformation of quasi-continuous objects generated by infants.

Ordered deforming is generated frequently. Both increasing deformations (e.g., progressively elongating a PlayDoh strand) and decreasing deformations (e.g., pressing on a piece of PlayDoh ball so that it becomes progressively thinner at that spot) produce ordered nonequivalence within single objects. These ordered nonequivalences are seriations of continuous quantities. As such, they complement and parallel the ordered series of discrete quantities by adding and subtracting which infants begin to structure with nonmalleable objects.

Infants also begin to construct equivalence between continuous quantities by deforming malleable objects. This includes generating several corresponding deformations into single objects at the same time (e.g., by several fingers pressing into a piece of clay at the same time so that several matching indentations are made). Thus these constructions, like those just mentioned of ordered nonequivalences, complement and parallel the equivalences between discrete quantities by one-to-one correspondences that infants begin to structure with nonmalleable objects.

Infants' mappings are relatively complex, differentiated, and integrated by age 12 months. Two temporally overlapping mappings are generated about as frequently as single consecutive mappings. Some contemporaneous mappings include manipulating one or two objects, but rarely three objects (e.g., one hand touches a cylinder on a column held by the other hand). Even three overlapping mappings begin to be generated; these may involve manipulating one or more objects (e.g., one hand rotates a cylinder on which the mouth is sucking while the other hand pushes a column on the table). Simultaneous but split constructions are now clearly within infants' competence; they can attend to and generate two unrelated things at the same time.

There are concomitant advances in the protological constructions generated by these relatively developed transformative interactions. They are manifest in infants' pragmatic matchings that produce quantitative equivalence. For instance, the mapping of two-to-two correspondences is no longer exceptional; and the mapping of three-to-three correspondences is already generated infrequently (such as banging hand or block on table three times, pause, repeat). Parallel manifestations are found in infants' pragmatic addition and subtraction, which produces ordered nonequivalence. These manifestations now include 3-point magnitude series as well as 2-point series (analyses of sensorimotor seriation by Mounoud & Hauert, 1982, provide corroborative evidence, as do findings of perceptual discrimination by Strauss & Curtis, 1981).

Developments in combinativity operations by age 12 months are numerous, and we therefore sketch only some of those that are central to constructing elements for developing relational and conditional operations. The production of more extensive compositions does increase. Most of infants' compositions still include the two-object minimum, yet one-fifth to one-third of their compositions unite more than the minimum number of objects, and most of these are three-object compositions. Furthermore, over half of the compositions are constructed by infants directly manipulating two or more objects in order to unite them.

Static stabiles are generated as frequently as kinetic mobiles. These compositions are less transient; they are preserved for longer periods of time (e.g., infants place two objects on or near each other for some time). Thus, there is a decline in the lability of compositions and a reciprocal increase in their stability.

Almost all infants' constructions continue to be single collections (as also found by Forman, 1982; Hetzer, 1931; and Sinclair, Stambak, Lezine, Rayna, & Verba, 1982, using different objects). But the shift is away from temporally isolated collections; these are now reduced to between one-eighth and one-fourth of infants' constructions. The shift is toward consecutive collections that increase to three-quarters of infants' constructions. Furthermore, two-fifths of these collections are variant recompositions of infants' initial compositions. A very small but potentially important proportion, from 5% to 10%, begins to comprise two collections constructed in temporal overlap. This proportion includes the origins at this stage of decomposing one larger collection into two smaller ones.

Progressively stable combinativity operations provide an enlarged and enriched source of discrete elements or constant givens for protological elaboration. All relational and conditional structures are thus now in place, as is evident from a quick review of how infants' precursory structuring of discrete quantities (outlined on page 6) develops by this stage.

1. Adding and subtracting objects within collections forming three-point increasing, decreasing, and bidirectional series are generated with ease. In addition, many infants generate four-point ordered series of objects (first discovered by Hetzer, 1931, with seriated objects). Especially significant is the origin at this stage of associative adding and subtracting to form flexible three-point increasing and decreasing orders.

2. Correlation structures are now complete. Many-to-one as well as one-to-many correspondences are generated and with as many as four objects (e.g., tapping one object on three objects). One-to-one correspondences are expanded to produce equivalence within three-object compositions (e.g., uprighting three blocks in parallel so that their placements are matched to one another).

3. Exchange by replacing, substituting, and commuting is elaborated to produce both equivalence in expanded collections and pragmatic identity by reversibility. All infants generate multiple and reversible substitution in the two-object compositions that they have constructed (e.g., by placing one block next to one ring, substituting a second ring for the block, and then substituting the same

block for the second ring). Multiple substitutions preserve quantitative equivalence in the collections while transforming them. When they are reversible at the same time, they also produce intensive (predicate) identity sets by inversion. Half of the subjects extend substitution to producing quantitative equivalence in three-object collections. Some of these include reversible substitutions that produce three-object identity sets by negation. The development of replacing and commuting parallels that of substitution.

4. Classification is shifting away from negation. Infants consistently unite different objects into single collections in only one out of the six class conditions—the most complex class condition tested (i.e., eight-object multiplicative). The primary shift is toward random classification. Infants' collections are marked by inconsistent classificatory features in three out of the six class conditions tested (i.e., fluctuation between uniting identical, similar, and different objects into single collections). Classification by affirmation originates at this stage. Infants consistently unite identical objects into single collections in two of the six class conditions—the simplest class conditions tested (i.e., four-object and eight-object additive). Thus infants begin to couple identical objects together into very small single compositions (somewhat different procedures and analyses by Nelson, 1973; Riccuiti, 1965; Starkey, 1981; and Sugarman, 1983, yield comparable results).

The development of part–whole structuring of quasi-continuous objects parallels that just described of discrete objects. Some unique mapping transformations with malleable objects not yet manifest by age 6 months originate by this stage. So, the complete range of unique, as well as universal, part–whole structuring of quasi-continuous objects is now constructed.

The principle additional direct combinativity operation that infants generate is the putting together of two or more objects to form one larger whole; but such composing should not be overestimated, because it is still generated by only half of the subjects even at this age. Furthermore, all the main direct combinativity operations are becoming reversible. Reforming objects they have deformed back into their initial form (thereby producing an identity operation) is generated by one-third of the subjects. Recomposing the extensity of objects that they had decomposed by putting the parts back together to produce quantitative equivalence of the whole is produced by one-sixth of the subjects. They still do not recompose the intensity (form); this action would produce an identity operation. Redecomposing objects previously composed is generated by one-fourth of the subjects.

These augmented combinativity structures provide an enlarged and enriched source of continuous elements for progressive relational and conditional structuring. Even a cursory examination of the data reveals that infants' precursory logicomathematical structuring of continuous quantities, outlined on pages 6 and 7, develops significantly by this stage. As we did with infants' precursory constructions at age 6 months, we limit our considerations to how these structures develop (a) the relational operations of adding and subtracting that produce ordered nonequivalence of continuous quantities, and (b) the conditional operations of one-to-one correspondence that produce equivalence of continuous quantities.

The most striking advance in producing ordered nonequivalence is the construction of geneological series, even though it is still generated by only one-fourth of the subjects. These infants generate sequences of decomposing that construct asymmetrical geneologies of descendant parts out of single larger wholes. To illustrate, a PlayDoh ring is decomposed into two parts: One part is decomposed into two smaller parts, one of these parts is again decomposed into two smaller parts, and so on. The products are ordered series of objects decreasing in magnitude.

Deforming continues to be the most frequent combinativity operation infants generate with quasi-continuous objects. Producing equivalence between continuous magnitudes by corresponding deformations is expanded to include more objects. When generated simultaneously, matched deforming does not usually exceed equivalent transformations of two objects (e.g., by poking index fingers into two PlayDoh balls at the same time). When generated consecutively, matched deforming may be generated with as many as five or six objects. Thus, this developing structure of continuous quantities, like that of ordered nonequivalence, complements and parallels infants' progressive structuring of discrete quantities with nonmalleable objects.

These multiple advances in infants' part–whole transformations by age 12 months permit drawing some general conclusions about the initial organization and early development of logicomathematical cognition. Both the constitutive (coordinations) and the constituted (products) structures by this stage are continuous with, and discontinuous from, those out of which they develop and which they, in turn, integrate. By age 12 months the constitutive structures of logicomathematical cognition are fairly complete and complex combinativity, relational, and conditional proto-operations. These structures are embodied in infants' mappings, in objects, and in infants' mappings with objects. Their constituted structures are relatively powerful constructions of equivalence, ordered nonequivalence, and reversibility of both discrete and continuous magnitudes. Their elements, however, do not usually exceed relations between infants' mappings, between objects, within single sets, and within single series. The exceptions are important, as can be seen in Section III of this chapter.

The precursory constitutive structures out of which the relatively advanced structures at age 12 months evolve are already present by age 6 months. They are primitive and incomplete combinativity, relational, and conditional proto-operations. Their constituted structures are minimal constructions of equivalence, ordered nonequivalence, and reversibility. Yet, as we have seen, these primitive and incomplete foundational coordinations and constructions at age 6 months provide sufficient precursory organization to generate progressive logicomathematical development during infants' first year. How logicomathematical cognition continues to develop out of these precursory foundations during infants' second year is investigated later in this volume.

II. Functions

The origins, organization, and early development of physical cognition parallels that of logicomathematical cognition. Physical cognition, like logicomathematical cognition, is structured by children's interactions with their environment. At the beginning, at least, physical and logical constructions share common elements. These elements are the coordinative products of infants' own mappings and combinativity operations (i.e., actions, objects, and collections).

Unlike logicomathematical cognition, physical cognition does not entail structuring part–whole transformations with these basic elements. Instead, it requires structuring means–ends transformations with them. The constructed physical relations are co-ordinated dependencies or functions, not operations.

Unlike part–whole transformations, means–ends transformations are generated by children when they are creating, orienting to, or solving some goal, object, or problem. Means–ends transformations range from maintaining or reproducing an interesting or desired event to performing an experiment (see Piaget, Grize, Szeminska, & Vinh Bang, 1977, for related theoretical analyses). For instance, the means–ends relation between a desired object that is moving away from an infant (the end) and an instrumental organ such as the hand that is at rest (the means) is transformed when the organ gropes or searches after the objective.

This research program was designed to study part–whole transformations. As already noted, none of the procedures was designed to evoke means–ends transformations. Even so, the procedures allow subjects to spontaneously map two fundamental forms of physical means–ends coordinations. The first are causal functions. To illustrate, the means–ends relation between two proximal objects is transformed from causal nondependency to dependency when subjects propel one with the other. The second forms are spatial functions. To illustrate, the means–ends relation between two proximal objects is transformed from spatial nondependency to dependency when subjects stack one object on the other.

The development of causal means–ends functions is central to the cognition of physical phenomena. Two primitive and primary types of causal functions are already generated by age 6 months. One type begins with infants constructing, replicating, and observing minimal effects that are directly dependent upon rudimentary causes (and which are also characteristic of Piaget's, 1954, sensorimotor stage 3 secondary circular reactions). For instance, subjects use one object as a means to push or bang on another object several times in a row while observing these causal constructions. Perceptual discrimination data (Leslie, 1982, 1984) are consistent with this causal type, although the author of these studies questions the adequacy of his methods.

The other, complementary type of function begins with infants anticipating and observing minimal effects that directly influence their subsequent rudimentary causal constructions. For instance, subjects use one object as a means to block and stop another object that is rolling in front of them while observing the effects of their causal predictions and constructions. Their causal blocking is directly dependent on their predictions of their targets' trajectories; otherwise they would miss their targets, which would then continue rolling away.

The construction of both types of direct causal functions progresses markedly by age 12 months. At this stage infants already semisystematically vary the action and object components of causal relations. Subjects generate small ordered series of causal actions that produce seriated effects. For instance, they push objects harder and harder, observe the differential results, and sometimes replicate them (which now characterizes Piaget's, 1954, sensorimotor stage 5 tertiary circular reactions). Dependent partial variables or semivariables (i.e., variations in effects) are becoming direct functions of independent semivariables (i.e., variations in causes).

This advance in the first type of causal function is clearly mediated by developments in infants' relational operations of adding and subtracting. It requires at least minimal coordination between constructing ordered nonequivalence and causal dependency. Indeed, such coordination between operations and functions marks the origins of any logic of experimentation. This coordination supports our structural developmental hypothesis that while they are different structurally, operations and functions come to share more than common elements with which to construct either part–whole or means–ends transformations. They progressively interact to form a hierarchical organization of structures in which they may facilitate each other's development.

This hypothesis is further corroborated by the development of the second, complementary type of causal function. Infants' anticipations or predictions of effects semisystematically direct their causal constructions. For instance, subjects select causal objects so as to predetermine the results. To illustrate, they increasingly push only one kind of object (cylinders) that will roll away and not others (square columns) that will not. Here, too, it is apparent that infants' developing logicomathematical operations, in this instance, classification, are engaged. These operations inform and support the development of causal functions.

The structures of means–ends transformations vary depending upon whether infants construct causal or spatial dependencies. Causal functions represent dependent energy relations. As far as infants are concerned, causal dependencies take the form of generating transformations such as propulsion (e.g., pushing something) or amplification (e.g., banging something). Spatial functions represent dependent placement relations. As far as infants are concerned, spatial dependencies take the form of generating transformations such as alignment (e.g., contact between things), envelopment (e.g., container–contained relations), or translation (e.g., inverting or rotating things through one or more planes).

Notwithstanding these formal differences, the development of spatial functions parallels those of causality during infants' first year. Primitive and primary spatial dependency functions are already generated by age 6 months. The alignments infants construct are little more than momentary contact between objects. Alignments of two objects are the norm, but exceptional three-object alignments are already constructed, such as that of each hand displacing a rectangular ring toward each other and a doll that forms a ring, doll, ring alignment. This example is unusual in one other way: It is generated by manipulating two objects to construct a composition. Thus, the generative displacements, plus the placements they produce, are symmetrical (see Forman, 1982).

This example is typical in two respects. First, almost all spatial dependencies are constructed in one dimension. Second, most are also constructed in the horizontal plane on a surface such as a table top; they are rarely constructed in the air by infants, for example, holding two objects together. Some spatial dependencies are already constructed in the vertical dimension, including two-object stacks or heaps that share the common structure of the top object balancing properly on the bottom object and therefore constituting a spatial function defined by this spatial dependency relation.

Envelopment is unusual (even though it is expected to be precocious by Piaget, 1980; Piaget & Inhelder, 1967). Precursory labile forms just begin to be generated with discrete objects (e.g., by knocking over a doll that lands in a rectangular ring so that the doll is contained in the ring). It is not yet generated with quasi-continuous or conglomerate objects. Negating envelopment of conglomerate objects is already common (i.e., by pulling the nonmalleable object out of the malleable object in which it is partially embedded). But enveloping nonmalleable in malleable objects (e.g., by poking one into the other) is not yet attempted.

The spatial translations that infants construct are already comparative. While they do not change their own point of view, subjects vary the view of objects, partially but semisystematically. Subjects repeatedly turn objects over and over, side to side, backward and forward, and so on (see also, Piaget, 1954). At the same time they visually sight or tactually explore the objects. The comparative spatial perspectives subjects thereby construct are dependent upon, or vary as a function of, the changing views of the objects that they themselves generate.

All spatial functions progress by age 12 months. Alignments are progressively stable and lasting, and they no longer require a surface on which to be constructed. While most alignments are still based upon contact between objects, some involve proximal alignments. Additionally a small but growing minority are constructed in two intersecting dimensions. These comprise alignments of objects at right angles to each other in the horizontal plane or alignments of objects constructed in both the horizontal and vertical plane (e.g., a bridge structure). They also comprise symmetrical designs (e.g., proximal placement of two spoons at opposite vertices of a cross ring). Vertical alignments increase to one-third of infants' constructions. These include an increasing number of stacks or heaps in which a balancing function or dependency is constructed (see also Halverson, 1931, and Hetzer, 1931).

Envelopment has become common (as also found by Hetzer, 1931, and Sinclair *et al.*, 1982). Subjects contain as many as four to six objects in single receptacles. Some envelopment already includes constructing reciprocal dependencies between the container and the contained. Both the receptacle and the objects are transformed in reciprocal relation to each other (e.g., one hand pushes a receptacle toward the other hand, which throws an object into the receptacle). Envelopment begins to include multiple containing or embedding of objects into one another. The maximum consists of upside-down embedding of four plastic cups into one another to form a stack. Envelopment also begins to include insertion with discrete objects (e.g., touching a spoon into the center of a ring or into a cup) and with conglomerate objects (i.e., embedding nonmalleable objects into malleable objects).

Comparative translations remain internal to the objects with which infants interact. By now, subjects systematically vary the view of objects; they still do not systematically vary their own point of view. There are at least two additional noteworthy advances. First, spatial perspectives are expanded to the comparison of small numbers of objects; sometimes this includes two or three objects at the same time (e.g., each hand rotates an object while the subject looks back and forth from one to the other). Second, construction of translations or perspectives within objects is expanded to exploration inside of the objects themselves or of the containment features of space (e.g., by tilting cups in order to see what is inside them).

Like logicomathematical proto-operations, then, elementary physical proto-functions are coordinative constructions that originate and develop during infants' first year. Here, too, the constitutive (e.g., coordination by repetition) and the constituted (e.g., equivalence semivariable) structures are both continuous with, and discontinuous from, those out of which they develop and which they, in turn, integrate. How causal and spatial categories of physical cognition continue to develop out of these precursory foundations during infants' second year is also examined in this volume.

III. Representation

Several genetic epistemological assumptions underpin the theoretical distinctions made here between logicomathematical and physical cognition (see also Langer, 1985; Piaget, 1981, 1983; and Turiel & Davidson, 1985). One assumption is that developing logicomathematical constructions become progressively necessary. It follows that the roots of cognizing logical necessity are to be found in infants' elementary part–whole transformations or first-order proto-operations (e.g., correspondences, substitutions, and classifications) that construct equivalence, nonequivalence, and reversibility.

A second, complementary assumption is that developing physical constructions become progressively contingent. Possible and impossible physical phenomena are progressively differentiated from, and coordinated with, one another. It follows that the roots of cognizing physical possibility and impossibility may be traced to infants' elementary contingent means–ends transformations or first-order causal and spatial protofunctions.

A third, superordinate assumption is that logical necessity is progressively differentiated from, and hierarchically integrated with, physical contingency. This development is expected to be paced by progress in infants' operations and functions. During infants' second year, it is expected to be influenced particularly by operations and functions becoming representational.

The conditions forming representation during infants' second year is an open question. The usual hypothesis is that symbolizing not-here and not-now phenomena is the hallmark of representation (Cassirer, 1953; Piaget, 1951; Vygotsky, 1962; Werner & Kaplan, 1963). A corollary is that representation is marked by the origins of language and that language becomes the main instrument of thought (Bruner, Olver & Greenfield, 1966; Luria, 1961). While subscribing to this hypothesis, Piaget (1952a) adds that representation also requires the origins of deductive calculations, though these are still preoperational or syncretic, fluctuate between the particular and the general, are figurative, and so forth.

Our thesis, explored in this volume, is that representation is formed by infants combining their elementary cognitions. By combining mappings, infants form mappings of mappings and composite mappings, or what we call *routines*. Mapping proto-operations upon proto-operations transforms them into representational logicomathematical cognition. Mapping protofunctions upon protofunctions transforms them into representational physical cognition. The thesis is that these second-order applications form representational cognition. Second-order applications raise cognitive structures to the second degree.

In this view, symbolization is not the hallmark of representation. Nor is language essential to the origins of representational cognition. Mapping first-order cognitions onto each other produces representational cognition. Core conceptual cognition, then, comprises mappings, operations, and functions, but does not include language.

Mappings begin to be combined with each other to form routines toward the end of infants' first year and at the beginning of their second year (Langer, 1983). It is expected that routines will develop the syntactic structure of pragmatic propositions, including subjects or agents, actions, and objects or patients. Typically, routines are sequences of mappings that infants combine both in parallel and in series, such as one hand picking up and storing an object while the other hand sets another object upright that is thereafter knocked over with the stored object. Furthermore, such protosyntactic routines may be replicated several times, varied semisystematically, interrupted without disruption, and so on.

Especially important to the progressive development of protosyntactic routines is the expected elaboration of equivalence classes of subjects, actions, and objects. These classes may be combined with each other to form different permutations upon the initial routine (see von Wright, 1963, for an attempted formal analysis). In the illustrative routine this means, for example, that different objects may be substituted for the agent that initiates the action and for the patient that suffers the action. The action may be varied on a continuum centered around "knocking over" (e.g., from gently to violently and from accidentally to intentionally) or it may be negated (e.g., by replacing the knocked over object in an upright position).

Protosyntactic mappings or routines are expected to provide the necessary conditions for the development of symbolization during infants' second year. Three essential ingredients of symbolization are therefore expected to originate and progressively feature a subset of infants' pragmatic propositions during the second year. These ingredients augment the process of detaching mappings from their objects of interaction that initiates protosymbol formation by infants during their first year (Langer, 1980).

The first ingredient is the development of substituting subjects, actions, and/or objects of routines. These routines "stand for" or map other mappings not being generated at the moment. As such, they progressively become symbols for referents that are "not-here and not-now." Infants need not be cognizant of the "standing for," or mappings of mappings relations, in order to construct them. Once they have constructed them, however, infants provide themselves with the necessary elements for becoming progressively cognizant of "standing for" or mapping relations, thereby setting the preconditions for both (a) generalizing or transferring them to other media, such as language, and (b) anticipating or comprehending them when encountered in interactions with others. It is therefore expected that pretense, which is but one symptom of "standing for," by substitution will be increasingly generated during the second year, but that cognizant pretense will only begin to develop toward the middle of the second year.

The second feature is the development of arbitrariness by combinativity. With (a) increasing combination of mappings and/or (b) more numerous and different objects to which mappings are applied, infants' routines become progressively arbitrary while still rule-governed or protosyntactic. It is expected that generating more numerous and varied routines will expand rapidly during infants' second year. Proliferating routines provide the necessary conditions for constructing symbols that are increasingly distanced from, or arbitrarily related to, their referents.

The third essential feature is progressive conventionalization of infants' routines. By reproducing aspects of their everyday interactions infants adapt their routines to their social environment. This adaption enables the "standing for" or mapping of relations embodied in routines to become communicative, because they increasingly share common elements with other persons. It is thus expected that routines not marked by conventionalization will be generated before those that are, and that the latter will develop only gradually during infants' second year.

Proto-operations also begin to be mapped onto each other toward the end of infant's first year (Langer, 1980). Integrating elementary or first-order proto-operations, reviewed in the first section of this chapter, initiates logicomathematical cognition to the second degree. To begin with, infants compose two temporally overlapping collections of a very small number of objects. While still generated very infrequently at age 12 months, as noted on page 8, such contemporaneous collections already constitute potential mappings of compositions upon compositions. Moreover, their products—compositions of compositions— are potential binary elements (i.e., ordered pairs) for all second-order cognition, that is, for physical as well as logicomathematical cognition.

Indeed, infants just begin to map some relational and conditional operations upon the binary elements they have produced. Two operations are central. On the one hand, infants just begin to map adding and subtracting onto two contemporaneous compositions. This action produces minimal ordered nonequivalence between two seriated compositions (e.g., a composition of two objects and a composition of three objects). On the other hand, infants just begin to map one-to-one correspondences onto two contemporaneous compositions. This action produces minimal equivalence between two matched compositions (i.e., 2 two-object compositions).

Only part of the organization of second-order representational operations originates toward the end of infants' first year. This partial organization includes second-order composing and recomposing, one-to-one and one-to-many correspondences, and adding and subtracting. The remaining combinativity, relational and conditional structures, such as substitution and classification, are not yet raised to the second degree. The expectation is that the organization of representational logicomathematical cognition will be filled in or completed during infants' second year.

The prediction is twofold. All extensive structures are expected to be raised to the second degree. This transformation includes, for instance, constructing equivalences upon equivalences by mapping replacement, substitution, and commutativity upon the one-to-one correspondences that infants have mapped upon two compositions, which they have constructed. All intensive structures are also expected to be raised to the second degree. For instance, infants are expected to begin to construct contemporaneous compositions comprising similar objects in each but different objects in both.

Parallel progress is expected in the development of physical cognition. Integrating elementary or first-order protofunctions by mapping them onto each other produces physical cognition to the second degree. To illustrate, the structures of causal means–ends relations are expected to progress from direct ratio-like to more indirect proportional-like dependencies wherein causes and effects covary with each other in circular ways as well as by varying directly. So, for instance, infants construct first-order direct functions defined on small objects that they can roll, such as "Moving is dependent on Pushing" and "Stopping is dependent on Blocking." When they are combined by being mapped onto each other, these means–ends relations form indirect proportional-like functions such as "Moving is dependent on Pushing as Stopping is dependent on Blocking." As with logicomathematical cognition, it is expected that the organization of second-order physical cognition will be completed during infants' second year.

This thesis about the origins of representation is tied to our recursive model of structural development (Langer, in press). This recursive model posits that the organization of cognition is multileveled and multistructural. Different orders and domains of cognition thus coexist. Moreover, the course of its development is multidirectional. Progress is from lower to higher orders of cognition, but higher-order structures also integrate lower-order structures.

First-order cognition originates early in the first year but is incomplete at that stage. The organization of first-order structures is completed during the first year, but its development is not. First-order structures increase in power (e.g., are applied to ever larger single compositions) during the second year and beyond.

Second-order cognition originates toward the end of the first year but is incomplete at that stage. Its organization is completed during the second year, but its development is not. Second-order structures are expected to continue to increase in power after the second year (e.g., they are expected to be applied to ever more numerous compositions).

First-order structures dominate cognitive development during the first year of infancy. While they continue to grow in power during the second year of infancy, they are expected to no longer dominate cognitive development. The major transformation of cognitive development expected during the second year is the origin and progressive development of second-order structures.

Second-order structures are integrative constructions. They evolve out of, or are formed by, infants coordinating part of the first-order structures they have developed during the first year. Infants do this by mapping first-order operations and products onto each other and by mapping first-order functions and products onto each other. These integrations form more powerful structures of operations and functions to the second degree.

First- and second-order structures coexist and develop during the second year of infancy. But the dominance gradually shifts toward second-order logicomathematical and physical cognition. So cognition already forms a bileveled and bidirectional organization of multiple structures during infancy in which second-order cognition begins to integrate first-order cognition. Cognition is becoming representational.

STAGE 5 AT FIFTEEN MO

Phrase-Like Routines

Mappings are our basic unit of analysis and the necessary starting point for this continuing investigation of young children's developing constructive interactions. Constructive interactions occur as a function of infants' actions, whether the acts are mapped onto objects or not. Thus, *mappings* comprise transformational correspondences in the processes and products of subjects' actions and their interactive relations with objects (e.g., displacement when a hand waves a stick) or without objects (e.g., displacement when an empty hand waves). Mappings can therefore be used to measure interaction as directly as possible since they take into account two fundamental functions: (1) relations within subjects' actions (e.g., any ordered series of empty hand waving displacements such as wave empty hand once, then twice); and (2) relations between subjects' actions and environmental objects (e.g., any ordered series of hand waving stick displacements such as hand wave stick once, then twice).

The analyses in this chapter therefore focus on infants' mappings that do not involve objects plus those that do. Infants' mappings are expected to continue developing during their second year. Thus the first chapter of each progressive stage (i.e., Chapters 6, 10, and 14) is devoted to developments in infants' mappings.

Mappings originate during infants' first year. These are first-order mappings that continue to grow during the second year. Most important, we shall see, is that they develop into second-order mappings by infants coordinating their mappings into prgamatic propositions or routines. Thus, we will necessarily begin our investigation of developing cognition during the second year of childhood by examining the parameters of first-order mappings and their elaboration into second-order mappings or routines. Pragmatic propositions or routines are the developing bases for symbolization (i.e., mappings of mappings) and the representational identity of objects (i.e., mappings of object mappings). Among other significant consequences, representational identity expands the pool and power of elements that can be exploited by infants to construct physical and logicomathematical cognitions.

Constructive transformations that entail progressive physical functions, particularly causal and spatial dependencies, are generated by mappings and routines. In this way, infants also generate constructive transformations that entail progressive logicomathematical operations, particularly those that produce equivalence and ordered nonequivalence. These physical functions and logicomathematical operations are considered in this chapter. Infants' physical and logicomathematical constructions with compositions of two or more discrete (nonmalleable) objects, whether they form sets or series, are analyzed in Chapters 3 and 4; those with quasi-continuous (malleable) objects in Chapter 5.

I. From Mappings to Routines

Constructive interactions are progressively differentiated. Mappings are increasingly executed with fine sensorimotor articulation (as will be evident in the 15AE protocol fragment presented below). Mappings also become progressively specialized; they are applied to objects with some constancy, although object constancy is still not predominant (see Section II). To illustrate, mapping "inserting" onto containable objects, such as cylinders and spoons, while mapping "uprighting" onto potential containers, such as cups, is increasingly likely (see 15ST's sequential routine summarized on pages 26 and 27).

Constructive interactions are progressively complex. They combine more than one mapping and more than one object. Two mappings are applied frequently in temporal overlap to one or more objects. Increasingly, these constructions feature logicomathematical properties (e.g., one-to-one correspondences between fine-grained "uprighting" in the 15AE protocol fragment below) and/or properties of physical cognition (e.g., relations between possible, impossible, and uncertain "uprighting" in the same 15AE fragment).

Constructive interactions are progressively integrated. Integration is not yet hierarchical; it is still sequential. Sequential integration is usually marked by linear coordination. Linear coordination is featured by either anticipatory feedforward (e.g., uprighting a cup in anticipation of inserting a spoon) or by retroactive feedback (e.g., modification of mappings to take into account what is possible and not possible). Sequential integration begins to be marked, rarely and at this stage, by circular coordination between anticipatory feedforward and retroactive feedback. Initial circular coordination is manifest most clearly by infants' second-order causal functions that will be considered in the fifth section of this chapter.

While progressively complex, differentiated, and integrated constructive interactions are generated by increasingly fine mappings, this development is certainly not completed by this stage. Furthermore, the advances that are made are not without difficulty. The developing constructions are only partially equilibrated. This partial disequilibrium is a source of progressive development (Langer, 1969b, 1974, 1980; Piaget, 1977). Partial equilibrium coupled with partial disequilibrium is manifest when infants' structuring progresses and, as a consequence, also poses new problems or opens up new possibilities that can not yet be fully exploited:

157.5.	*LH rotates Block 3 to horizontal orientation*
157.5.	*RH index finger touches Block 1*
159.	*LH index finger touches top of front part of B3*
160.3.	*LH index finger presses down on B3*
160.3a.	*B3 rotates to a diagonal upright position*
160.7.	*RH index finger pulls B1 toward self and then exerts pressure down on B1*
160.7a.	*B1 rotates to a horizontal upright position and then falls over flat*
162.	*immediately looks down at B1, as RH index finger touches front of B1, and rests forearm on top of Block 2*
163.	*RH index finger brushes leftward and then rightward against B1, while RH forearm still rests on top of B2*
163a.	*B1 moves to the left and then to the right, coming to rest about 3 inches to back of and to left of Block 4*
164.	*while looking at B2, RH index finger places on top of B2 and slides B2 away and into space that is between B1 and B4*
164a.	*B2 pushes B1 away slightly* (15AE, pages 14 and 15)[1]

Two index fingers only produce this elaborate set of fine interactions. They include mapping uprighting onto two blocks by pressing down on each block with one index finger in partial temporal overlap (Lines 157.5–160.7a). This

---

[1]Protocol fragments are identified by age, subject, and log location. Subjects are indicated by their age in months and their initials. This behavior was produced by a 15-month-old infant whose initials are AE. Log location is given by page number(s) following subject identification, and by line number(s) before each transaction. Consecutive transactions are numbered seriatim from one on (e.g., Lines 162 and 163). Two or more partially overlapping transactions are assigned ordinally averaged numbers in the order in which they are produced (e.g., Lines 160.3 and 160.7). Two or more simultaneous transactions are assigned averaged numbers (e.g., 157.5 followed by another 157.5). A line number followed by the letter "a" appears when it is necessary to present the consequence(s) of transactions that may not be obvious (e.g., Line 160.3a). Hand(s) used by infants is (are) indicated by RH for right hand, LH for left hand, and BH for both hands. Objects used are first identified by their names and number (e.g., Block 3) and then by their initials and number (e.g., B3).

correspondence works successfully with Block 3; but Block 1 falls back flat on the table.

Observing her negative result with Block 1 (Line 162) *15AE* takes into account the negative result due to the resistance of the object. However, the result is not yet positive feedforward; she does not modify her pressing down procedure in order to try to upright the fallen Block 1. Instead, she stops what she is doing and switches to displacing Block 1 with an index finger (Lines 163 and 163a). Then she switches to displacing Block 2 with the same index finger such that it comes to rest between Blocks 1 and 4 and pushes Block 1 slightly (Lines 164 and 164a). She also visually monitors her finely controlled, but different, mappings that produce a three-object composition.

When infants' constructions have developed to this level of regulated control and directedness (i.e., mappings upon objects such as mapping "uprighting" onto dolls and mapping "inserting" onto spoons and cups), then they can begin to be combined into second-order mappings or routines, such as uprighting a cup so as to insert spoons into it (see Langer, 1980, pages 287–289). Newly structured routines coordinate no more than two mappings with each other, for example, uprighting with inserting. Also, they only relate a small number of objects to each other, for example, inserting one spoon at a time in a cup.

Infants' initial routines already include all objects of one class and some of another; but only rarely and by successive one-at-a-time inclusion (see Sinclair *et al.*, 1982). Furthermore, only the most advanced performances are even that inclusive at this initial stage of constructing routines. Still it is worth illustrating an advanced routine by summarizing one generated by subject *15ST*. Sequentially, *15ST*'s unusually advanced construction differentiates and integrates eleven phrase-like mapping forms into one complex and lengthy routine:

1. gathering and holding two forks;
2. uprighting one cup;
3. containing the two held forks, one after the other, in the uprighted cup;
4. containing a third fork in the uprighted cup;
5. almost (or virtual) containing the fourth remaining fork in the uprighted cup;
6. uprighting and holding a second cup;
7. inserting but not containing the held fourth fork in the second uprighted cup held by the other hand;
8. extracting the held fourth fork from the second cup held upright by the other hand;
9. inserting but not containing the held fourth fork in the first uprighted cup (in which the three other forks were contained) while holding the second cup upright with the other hand;

10. extracting the held fourth fork from the first uprighted cup while holding the second cup upright with the other hand; and
11. containing the fourth fork in the second cup held upright by the other hand

Sequential routines of this order are already marked by several criterial features. These features are consistent with the thesis that even initial routines are governed by their own internal regulating rules that generate pragmatic propositions. Several hypotheses about the regulatory rules governing the production of routines are offered in this and the next section.

A first and central hypothesis is that routines are governed by some minimal rules of anticipation. Planning, even if only minor, is actualized several times within 15ST's sequential routine. Two forks are first gathered and then stored in the left hand; the two forks serve as potential prepared objects to be contained. A first cup is uprighted; it serves as a potential prepared container for the forks. The two forks are transferred from one-at-a-time storage in the left hand to the right hand which serves as a potential prepared containing instrument. A third fork is gathered and then stored in the right hand. The fork serves as a potential prepared object to be contained, and the right hand serves as a potential containing instrument. Finally, a second cup is uprighted and held by the right hand; this cup serves as an alternate potential container for the forks.

A second hypothesis is that routines are governed by some minimal rules of reproduction. This hypothesis is manifest several times within 15ST's routine. Preparations, just enumerated, are repeated several times. Each one is followed by containing forks in cups. When combined, these mappings generate phrase-like forms (e.g., pick up and store one or two forks/ upright one cup/ contain fork in cup). The phrase-like routines of 15ST's lengthy production are actual or virtual reproductions of each other.

Reproductive routines repeat combinations of mappings. Both initial mapping combinations and their reproductions are infants' own constructions. The products are rule-governed constructions in which the parts are faithful or virtual copies and variants of each other.

This fact need not imply that infants are already cognizant of their anticipations and reproductions or of the rules governing their pragmatic propositions. For instance, there is no way of knowing whether infants' reproductions are extensions of their anticipations and/or whether infants' anticipations are extensions of their reproductions. In any case, it is not necessary to attribute conscious planning to infants engaged in rule-governed anticipation and reproduction. Infants may or may not have some conscious understanding of all or of some of their routines (for two opposing views on this issue see Epstein, Lanza, & Skinner, 1981, and Lewis & Brooks–Gunn, 1979):

14. *LH raises Red Brush 5 to face*
     level
15. *LH touches RB5 to tip of nose,*
     twice
16. *laughs and looks at experimenter*   (E: *"You're touching your nose."*)

(*15PR*, page 33)

Regardless of the degree of cognizance by the performer, routines already comprise rule-governed anticipations and (actual, variant, or virtual) reproductions of phrase-like forms. So, rules of anticipation and reproduction govern the part–whole and means–ends structures of routines (i.e., if x, then y is possible).

II. Functional Reciprocity

While three contemporaneous mappings on two or more objects remain rare, pairs of mappings (and, of course, single mappings) are generated easily and often. Most pairs include one active and one passive mapping (e.g., Steps 7–11 of *15ST*'s routine presented on pages 26 and 27); some comprise two active mappings (e.g., Steps 5 and 6 of this same routine). The main structural development of paired mappings at this stage consists in coordinating mappings into routines that are split and segregated from each other at the previous stage (Langer, 1980, page 289).

Whether active or passive, the two transformations mapped onto objects are progressively differentiated from each other (e.g., one mapping transforms cups into containers by uprighting them while the other mapping transforms forks into contained objects by inserting them). At the same time the transformations mapped onto the objects are progressively integrated with each other (e.g., uprighting and inserting mappings are coordinated such that container and contained are progressively related spatial trajectories or transforms). Thus, mappings are progressively coregulated with each other into small routines.

Mappings still predominate over objects. Hence, the mappings-to-objects change ratio remains that of more mappings per object than objects per mapping. However, the mode is increasingly shifting to many-to-many mappings-to-objects, as evident in *15ST*'s routine outlined in the previous section.

Mapping constancy, while not yet predominant, is increasing. Infants still change the mappings they apply successively, even to one object or to two identical objects. Yet, routines marked by mapping constancy already constitute a small but substantial body of infants' constructive interactions. For instance, all forks are inserted in two cups and two cups are uprighted by *15ST*. This action furthers the development of mapping predication by both affirmation and negation (compare Langer, 1980, page 290).

In particular, routines extend infants' coordination of objects to the beginnings of functional reciprocity between two types, but no more than two kinds of a very small number of objects. Both the mapping coordinations (e.g., inserting and uprighting) and the object relations (e.g., container and contained or causal agent and patient) are marked by functional reciprocity. A third hypothesis about routines, then, is that they are governed by some minimal rules of reciprocity.

To the extent that it governs the selection of objects being coordinated, reciprocity differeniates and integrates objects as different but related types. Complementarity of this order is purely functional since it is based upon dependency relations that infants construct between objects. Complementary object types are therefore not to be confused with complementary object classes.

This is not to say that the cognition of complementarity between classes is not prepared developmentally by the production of complementary types during infancy and early childhood. This is a traditional hypothesis of functional theories of cognitive development (e.g., Bruner and Vygotsky); and even structural theories (e.g., Piaget and Werner) hypothesize that constructing complementary types is a partial precursor of complementary classes. Rather, the present assertion is that the complementary relations between object types are functional and, as a consequence, are empirical, not logical as they are between object classes.

Since they are contingent and not necessary, functional complementarities change depending upon both the nature of the objects and the uses to which subjects put them. This is always the case, but it is particularly true during infancy when shifts in usage are relatively labile and growing. This phenomenon is reflected in the relative lack of mapping constancy which decreases only gradually during infancy, as we have already seen for the first year (Langer, 1980) and as we are now seeing during the second year. It is also reflected in the addition of new mappings (e.g., insertion) and the at least partial deletion of some old mappings (e.g., dropping).

To the extent, then, that reciprocity contributes to the development of predicating complementary relations between objects, it does so in the guise of functionally dependent types that are limited in comparison with logically necessary classes. Still, this analysis enables us to draw some empirical predictions about the predicate properties of causal agent and patient objects that we will have occasion to test in later chapters. The expectation is that when causal reciprocity is asymmetrical (e.g., when one object is used to hit another), then the objects used by infants are more likely to be different than: (a) when causal reciprocity is symmetrical (e.g., when two objects are used to hit each other), or (b) when a relatively nondependent afunctional relation is constructed (e.g., placing one object next to another).

Mappings remain decidedly compact and perhaps even become more repetitive, as evident in 15ST's routine. Two changes are introduced at this stage. The first change consists of infants elaborating a small set of relatively new mapping forms, such as inserting. Some of these new mapping forms are marked by conventional or semiconventional features (considered in Section III).

The second advance in compactness consists of infants combining elementary mappings into small but coordinated routines, such as "picking-up then transferring and collecting" and "inserting while holding and uprighting." Sequential integration into rule-governed forms begins by coordinating a very small number of elementary mappings into brief but well-designed phrase-like combinations. They are often reproduced many times such that they become fairly well practiced rule-governed routines; they are also applied to several objects, as long as the number is small.

An implication of combining elementary mappings into routines is that the semantic domain constructed by infants can expand exponentially, to the second and sometimes to the third degree. Infants no longer construct the semantic domain as merely representing elementary forms, such as "pushables" and "holdables." The semantic domain is in the process of being expanded exponentially to include combining elementary mappings, usually taken two-at-a-time but sometimes already taken three-at-a-time, into pragmatic propositions.

This is the method by which infants construct pragmatic propositions or routines. These rudimentary phrase-like routines entail minor reconstructive and anticipatory extensions of immediate into mediate representations by infants. Thus, they constitute transitional forms between here-and-now protosymbolization and not-here-and-not-now symbolic systems or languages.

The semantic domain remains protosymbolic insofar as the representations constructed by infants at this stage are not yet fully detached from the objects of their interactions and insofar as they are not yet arbitrary constructions or are not yet fully conventional communicative systems. Yet, the semantic domain is becoming progressively symbolic as a function of infants' developing flexibility in combining mapping forms into small routines or pragmatic propositions marked by rudimentary reproductive and anticipatory features, as well as by elementary functional reciprocity.

III. Rudiments of Symbolization

Conventional and semiconventional features begin to mark routines generated by almost all infants at this stage. Some elaborate on semiconventional constructions which a minority of infants began to generate at stage 4 (see Langer, 1980, pages 291–292). To illustrate, two brushes are used both successively and simultaneously by subject 15PR to brush her hair. Moreover, she interweaves brushing with comparative inspection of the two brushes. Thus, fundamentally, 15PR's routine already comprises aspects of conventional hair brushing.

Brushing is applied to her mouth (or teeth), the table, and her hair by subject

15VL. Mouth brushing is accompanied by the kind of vocalization often generated while brushing teeth. Brushing is applied to his teeth and a doll by subject
15JH, and is accompanied by smiling:

20.	*LH brushes Brush 2 across*	S:	*"Ru, ruh, ruh."*
	mouth		
	(experimenter moves Brush 1		
	closer to subject)		
21.	*LH raises B2 behind head*		
22.	*LH lowers brush-end of B2 to*		
	table and brushes B2 on table		
	top, momentarily		
23.	*LH raises B2 and brushes B2*		
	in her hair		*(15VL, page 17)*

7. *LH grasps and raises Brush by its handle*
8.4. *opens mouth wide*
8.6. *LH inserts brush-end of B into mouth*
10. *LH shakes B up and down, 1 time*
11. *LH removes B from mouth, holds B about 2 inches in front of mouth and looks at*
   B closely
12. *LH touches/taps brush end of B against head of Doll, as smiles broadly*
12a. *D tips, and then remains in same upright position on table*
13. *LH shakes B up and down rapidly, 3–4 times, 1 inch in front of D, as continues*
   smiling   *(15JH, page 1)*

Various features of these "brushing" routines are symptomatic of detaching
mappings from their objects of reference. To begin with, the relations between
actions and objects are no longer restricted to one-to-one correlation. More than
one brush may be used to brush one object (e.g., *15PR*); and one brush may be
used to brush more than one object (e.g., *15VL* and *15JH*). Reference is thereby
extended to nonpresent events.

Moreover, sometimes infants' routines begin to be more gestural pretenses
than actual interactions. Thus, the first of three "brushings" performed by *15VL*
is doubly gestural (Line 20). It is a motor gesture since *15VL* does not actually
brush her teeth but makes a brushing motion across her mouth (while *15JH*
actually brushes his teeth in Lines 7–10). It is also a vocal (probably onomatopoetic) gesture since *15VL* makes teeth-brushing-like sounds to accompany her
brushing motions. Gestural pretense of this order enhances the possibilities for
routines to stand for or symbolize nonpresent events.

Brushing a doll, as performed by *15JH,* is marked by at least three features of
gestural pretense involved in constructing symbolic standing-for relations. First,
the routine substitutes a stand-in, albeit realistic, object of reference (a doll) for
an actual object of brushing. Second, the routine substitutes stand-for actions
(shaking up and down) for actual behavior (brushing up and down). Finally, the

routine is accompanied by some apparent cognizance of the playfulness involved since *15JH* smiles throughout his construction (Lines 12 and 13).

Conventional and semiconventional features also begin to mark some routines not generated until this stage (nonrelevant intervening transactions are omitted in the *15ST* fragment):

29.   *RH grasps rim of Yellow*
      Cup 2 and tilts YC2 toward
      self, as looks inside of YC2
30.   *LH grasps left side of YC2*
      held by RH
31.5 *LH lowers YC2 approximately*
      horizontal flat on table
31.5 *RH releases from rim of YC2*
      and reaches inside of YC2
33.   *RH held inside of YC2 held*
      by LH, for a second, as looks
      at experimenter
34.   *RH removes from YC2 held by*   (E: *"That's empty too."*)
      LH
35.   *RH grasps right side of YC2*
      held by LH
36.   *BH raise YC2 to mouth*
37.   *BH inserts rim of YC2 into*
      mouth and tilts head back,
      tilting YC2 to tilted inverted
      upright position (in a
      drinking gesture)—maintains
      this position a couple of
      seconds   (*E and M chuckle*)

                                                          (*15SG*, page 43)

24.   *RH holding Spoon in proper*
      feeding position, touches S
      gently to head of Doll 1 and
      then removes S from D1
25.   *LH joins RH in holding D1,*   S: *"Mmmmuh, mmmm."*
      while RH continues holding S
31.   *LH picks up Doll 2 and raises*
      D2 to lips of mouth   S: *"Mmmmuh, mmmm."*

                                                          (*15ST*, page 2)

Additional features of detaching mappings from their objects of reference are illustrated in these routines. The fictive nature of the routine is repeatedly pre-established by *15SG* (not all instances of which are reproduced here). Each time *15SG* determines that a cup is empty before pretending to drink from it.

In addition, nonconventional fanciful features begin to be generated in rare instances. At the outset, *15ST*'s routine is entirely conventional; she pretends to be feeding a doll with a spoon and accompanies this action with typical feeding vocalization. But then *15ST* introduces a nonconventional or arbitrary element, so she substitutes the doll for the spoon. The rest of the routine (not reproduced here) remains constant and conventional since she pretends to be feeding herself and accompanies this pretending with typical feeding vocalization.

These constructions, then, begin to develop a syntax of their own. Hence some constructions comprise phrase-like routines. On the one hand, these routines begin to be rule-governed, that is, marked by regularity of reproduction, anticipation, and reciprocity. On the other hand, these routines begin to be marked by flexibility, pretense, and arbitrariness. For instance, two different agents can be substituted for each other (such as a spoon and a doll by *15ST*) within a given routine. Thus, these constructions become progressively detached symbolic forms that begin to stand for nonpresent events or referents.

Another important feature marking symbolic development at this stage is the progressive conventionalization of infants' routines. As always, mappings are generated by infants in accordance with both their own level of understanding and particular sets of interests. At the same time, routines progressively take on properties of conventional usage, for example, pretending to eat with a spoon or pretending to stir a substance in a cup with a spoon:

8. *RH releases Yellow Spoon into Orange Cup*
9. *RH immediately grasps YS again and rotates YS slowly back and forth in OC, 2 times, such that YS touches against edge of OC and jiggles OC slightly*
10. *RH slowly and partially raises and lowers YS up and down in OC, 2 times*

(15NF, page 35)

This routine is instructive because it illuminates how transitional semiconventional forms are generated that will develop into fully conventional forms at the next stage. First *15NF* releases the spoon in the cup. After this he grasps the spoon again; only then does he manipulate the spoon in the cup by first rotating the spoon back and forth twice and then raising and lowering the spoon twice. This is as close as any infant comes at this stage to stirring a spoon in a cup. By the next stage, as we shall see in Chapter 6, this pretense routine has been completely conventionalized.

Syntactic regularity, fictive or playful substitution, conventionalization, and detachment of routines are necessary conditions for developmental transformation of protosymbolization into true symbolization. A subset of mappings are thereby altered into communicative forms which serve as notational substitutes. Notational symbolic substitutes eventually become abstract or detached givens for logical and mathematical cognition.

Development of rudimentary symbolic routines never precedes that of second-order cognition. Early forms of second-order cognition are already manifest at previous stages (Langer, 1980). In this regard it is worth noting that 15ST's routine culminates in rudimentary second-order substitution (discussed more fully in Chapter 4). She constructs two sets by containing forks in two cups and repeatedly substitutes the cup into which the last fork is inserted.

Routines, then, are transitional developments between protosymbolization and symbolization. On the one hand, routines extend beyond protosymbolization since routines combine two or more mappings coordinated with one another. Some of these routines begin to stand for nonpresent events. On the other hand, routines are not yet truly symbolic since the mappings are not yet detached (abstracted) from the consistent aims of their interaction. Only rudiments of detachment are generated at this stage, such as infants not consummating some reproductions and, thereby, producing virtual mappings.

In comparison with their construction of symbolic routines, infants' verbal productions are quite impoverished at this stage. With rare exceptions they are limited to one-word utterances (e.g., Brown, 1973). This limitation, of course, severely hampers any possibility for anything but the most primitive verbal symbolization and provides little, if any, opportunity for syntactic constructions.

Still, infants already try to establish one-to-one symbolic correspondences between individual verbal names and their particular objects of reference. To illustrate, repeated or reiterative naming ("Auto") is first generated by subject 15SG while examining two cars by inversely rotating them while looking at them. The name ("Auto") is repeated once again while 15SG demonstrates its referent to his mother.

He is also one of only two subjects to produce a two-word utterance ("Whaz-zis?"). But in his case, it is done within the context of transacting with quasi-continuous objects as well as discrete objects. It, too, is generated only in the context of examining an object or demonstrating it to his mother. Even though he is always answered, 15SG repeats the question ("Whaz-zis?") over and over. Still, this is already a protosyntactic form of linguistic reference.

The only other two-word utterance generated by another subject is also coupled with demonstrating its object of reference to the mother and saying, "Mommy, here." This is the only verbal denotation generated by any subject at this stage. Of course, many subjects already engage in pragmatic denotation by holding up objects to others. These pragmatic denotations may be accompanied by vocal–gestural denotations, such as "Yah, yah, yah." Some infants also refer others to objects by pointing at them:

31.   *RH touches Blue Brush to top*
      of Red Triangular Column on
      table and moves BB on RTC
      slightly

31a. *RTC moves slightly to right*   S: *"Ehhh, ehh."*

32.   RH *points to RTC and looks*
      at mother   (*15PR*, page 28)

In this instance, pointing is still preceded by straining sounds after the object (see Werner & Kaplan, 1963). It is accompanied by *15PR* looking at her mother. Such behaviors further corroborate the hypothesis that gestural reference emerges from pragmatic behavior (Langer, 1980, page 291).

IV. Representational Object Identity

Comparative inspection within and between objects begins to be coupled with naming, but this coupling is produced by two infants only, as noted in the previous section. For the rest, comparative inspection is still not accompanied by any naming; this is generally also the case when infants comparatively inspect quasi-continuous objects (see pages 90 and 91). Much comparative inspection is still geared toward determining part–whole relations within single objects:

7.   RH *raises Blue Circular Ring 2 off table, rotating BCR2 slowly in air back and*
     forth, 1 time
8.   *looks closely at BCR2, as RH rotates BCR2 even more slowly in air back and forth,*
     1 time   (*15NF, page 7*)

As at the previous stage, differentiated and integrated exploration of internal part–whole relations are coordinated with repeated inverse spatial identity transformations of the object being inspected (see Langer, 1980, pages 292–295).

Sequentially integrating exhaustive part–whole comparative inspection of a few objects before composing them into a set is common. It is also a continuation of exploring objects and small compositions initiated during the first year (Langer, 1980, e.g., pages 292–295). Most comparative inspection is still limited to two objects which is also still the modal size of compositions (see Table 3.4 on page 59); nonrelevant intervening transactions are omitted in the 15VL protocol fragment:

5.   BH *move Plate around and feel all parts of P*
5a.   *P (made of thin plastic) arcs slightly then returns to initial form*
7.   LH *fingers P held by RH*
8.3. RH *lowers P to table, and rests on top of P*
8.7. LH *picks up Brush*
10.5. RH *raises from P*
10.5. LH *holding B, fingers the bristle's of B*
13.   RH *fingers B, both bristles and handle, held by LH*
16.   RH *lowers handle of B so that B touches P*   (*15VL*, pages 1 and 2)

12.   LH *moves Block 1 around in hand (as if inspecting B1), while RH holds Block 2*
12a. *B1 slips out of LH and falls to lap*

13.   *LH picks B1 up from lap, while RH holds B2*
14.   *looks back and forth from B1 in LH to B2 in RH, 2 or 3 times (as if comparing the blocks)*
15.   *LH slides and aligns B1 on top of B2 in RH*   (*15RS*, page 80)

Each object is examined tactually and in detail by *15VL* before it is related to the other so as to construct a two-object composition. Each object is inspected and compared to the other repeatedly before *15RS* composes them into a set in his hands. The objects are coregulated to each other so that they are aligned properly on top of each other in the right hand. This coregulated composition is maintained as a well-organized set while it is transferred to the left hand and placed on the table (not reproduced in the protocol fragment).

A new feature just begins to be added by infants to their structural determination of small numbers of objects. It consists of coordinating comparative part–whole inspection with routines. At first the routines are embedded into part of the comparative inspection such that they are incorporated into it:

187.   *RH grasps head of Doll 1 and lowers D1 to flat position on table*
188.   *immediately raises D1 off table and toward self, inverting D1*
189.5. *RH holds D1 inverted upright about 5 inches above table*
189.5. *LH index finger partially inserts into hole in bottom of D1*
191.5. *looks toward Doll 2, as RH lowers D1 to about 2 inches above table and more horizontal*
191.5. *LH index finger inserts further into D1*
193.   *RH releases from D1 and LH index finger rotates D1 to a tilted upright position*
194.   *LH index finger holds D1 tilted upright for a couple of seconds*
195.5. *RH grasps D1, looks quickly toward VW2*
195.5. *LH index finger lowers D1 to about 3 inches above table*
197.   *RH removes D1 from LH index finger*
198.   *RH holds D1 about 2 inches above table, slightly tilted upright and also rotates D1 laterally about 90° clockwise, as LH grasps D1*
199.   *RH adjusts grasp on D1 (releases and regrasps D1's body at right side again), as LH rotates D1 laterally about 45° clockwise*
200.   *BH rotate D1 counterclockwise (laterally) a little bit, so face of D1 is toward self*
201.   *BH hold D1 still for a second, then hold D1 tilted upright about 4 inches in front of chin*   (*15AE*, pages 140 and 141)

This coordinate sequence interweaves a routine with comparative inspection. It is a close variant and almost perfect reproduction of a coordinate sequence (not presented here) that *15AE* generates a little earlier with the other doll presented in this task. Although not indicated in the protocol fragment (in order to reduce repetitiveness), *15AE* visually monitors his interaction all the time he generates it, except for the two moments when he looks away at two other objects (Line

191.5 and Line 195.5). These visual asides may well be part of 15AE's comparative inspection since he also does this during his first coordinate sequence with the other doll (not reproduced here).

Embedding routines within comparative inspection adds a new exploratory dimension to constructing the identity of objects. It opens up the new possibility of attributing symbolic features to objects. In this way it augments, as does the act of naming, and elaborates upon the identity of objects beyond the confines of determining their actual empirical and here-and-now properties. It creates their possible fictive, or imaginary, and not-here-and-not-now dimensions. This process of constructing the representational, as well as determining the presentational, identity of objects was initiated at the previous stage (see Langer, 1980, pages 373 and 374). It now begins to be enhanced by these additional symbolic and playful means.

A consequent possibility of coordinating comparative with symbolic and playful identity formation is representational, as well as actual, preservation of objects. This possibility was manifest overtly by only one infant at this stage. As expected at its initiation, representational preservation was expressed in a vocal–gestural form only:

11.	LH moves Cylinder 2 toward edge of table	
11a.	C2 falls out of LH to floor	
12.5.	RH reaches down toward floor to look for C2	S: "Oh, uh."
12.5.	LH raises Cylinder 1 from table (experimenter picks up C2 and places on table in front of subject)	(E: "Here it is, here it is.")
		(M: "She got it.")
14.	RH picks up C2	(15HK, pages 35 and 36)

Infants still do not express representational preservation verbally; they only begin to do so at the next stage (see Chapter 6, Section IV).

V. Rudimentary Covariation of Causes and Effects

Much causal experimenting remains semisystematic, as it is at stage 4 (Langer, 1980, pages 295–303). Even when basic causal effects are replicated and monitored, infants' experiments are either not truly controlled or are incomplete. The same object(s) may be used but the actions vary haphazardly (e.g., between dropping and throwing to the floor). So too, actions may be held constant but objects may vary haphazardly (e.g., dropping objects belonging to two different classes in a random order). Alternatively, both actions and objects may be held constant but only objects belonging to one class may be used (e.g., observing the effect of pushing all and only cylinders without pushing any square columns).

Experimentation with discrete objects is becoming progressively controlled and complete, as it is with quasi-continuous objects (see pages 90–92). Causal replications are structured such that altering the independent variable produces ordered differences in the dependent variables. Thus, the functional dependencies are oriented:

   12.   *RH taps Yellow Hexagonal Column seven times on top of Green Cross Ring; as
         LH continues to hold Green Hexagonal Column on table*
   12a. *GCR is progressively displaced to table edge next to self*   (15JH, page 8)

A column is used by *15JH* to displace a ring toward himself; he replicates this displacement effect six times until the ring arrives at the table's edge. Later, in another task, *15JH* uses a doll to knock over and then displace a ring away from himself; this time he replicates the displacement effect three times. Ordered variation is introduced into both causal constructions by *15JH* orienting the direction of the displacement effects, either toward the table's edge near himself or away from himself.

These constructions constitute fairly straightforward first-order causal proto-functions. Ordered variations in the effects (i.e., Targeted Displacements) are dependent upon ordered variations in the causes (i.e., Oriented Tapping). The ordered dependencies of the effects upon the causes are directed one-way functional linkages. Accordingly, both ratio-like functions generated by *15JH* take the form "Targeted Displacements are ordered dependencies of Oriented Tapping."

First-order functions are the most advanced causal constructions generated by infants at the end of their first year (Langer, 1980); they include those categorized tertiary circular reactions by Piaget (1952a). Even then some infants already generate some pragmatic ratio relations, but they remain subordinate structures. To begin with, however, most constructions comprise replicating effects that are directly dependent upon replicating causes without any variation (Langer, 1980); they include those categorized secondary circular reactions by Piaget (1952a). For instance, infants repeatedly bang one object on another in the same way. The direct dependency of effects upon the causes entails one-way reproductive or repetitive functional linkages. Thus the illustrative construction takes the form "Repeated Noise is directly dependent on Repeated Banging."

These initial first-order functions vary neither the independent nor the dependent semivariables. The semivariables are neither ordered nor classified, so they are not oriented. In the illustrative example, Repeated Banging is a particular semivariable, as is Repeated Noise. Particular semivariables are repeatable elements that do not vary. The functional dependency that is thereby constructed is a constant, but not an oriented, direct one-to-one relation.

Two major features, then, mark structural development from initial to more advanced first-order functions. First, their elements progress from particular to oriented semivariables. Second, the relations constructed with these elements progress from direct one-to-one to more indirect ratio-like dependencies. It should not be overlooked that both initial and more advanced first-order functions are one-way relations, since the dependencies are always directed from causes or means to effects or ends only.

Effects may be replicated repeatedly on the same object or they may be replicated on several causal recipients or patients:

10.   *RH pushes Block 3, about 2 inches*
10a.   *B3 pushes Block 2 which pushes Block 1, about 2 inches*
11.5. *RH pushes B3 away, about 4 inches, as looking toward B3, B2, and B1*
115a. *B3 pushes B2 which pushes B1, about 4 inches*   (*15AE*, page 11)
66.3. *RH hits Red Brush on Red Triangular Column on table*
66.7. *LH hits Blue Brush on Blue Triangular Column on table*
68.   *RH pushes RB against RTC about 1 inch*
68a.   *RTC rotates 90°*
69.5. *RH pushes RB against RTC toward experimenter*
69.5. *LH pushes BB against BTC toward experimenter*   (*15PR*, page 31)

Immediate ordered transmission of motion is generated by *15AE* while visually observing her causal construction. Causal chaining is still constructed with pre-existing groupings of objects only (see Langer, 1980, page 301). Two objects are used by *15PR* as corresponding instruments with which to produce equivalent effects upon two patient objects, in partial temporal overlap (Lines 66.3 and 66.7) and simultaneously (Lines 69.5).

The *15AE* construction is still exceptional, but it marks the further development of first-order functions. The advance is featured by progressive detachment of causes from effects. The function is a one-way ratio relation in which "Moving Further is dependent upon Pushing Harder." Introduction of a causal intermediary (Block 2) between the instrument (Block 3) and the patient (Block 1) distances the cause from the effect. Progressive detachment of independent from dependent semivariables makes the pragmatic ratio-like relation increasingly indirect.

More advanced causal constructions just begin to be generated by four infants; their precursors are found at stage 4 at age 12 months (see the *12RD* and *12LL* protocol fragments and analysis in Langer, 1980, pages 302 and 303). They mark the origins of second-order causal protofunctions:

38.   *LH index finger pushes Doll toward.left*
38a.   *D rolls to left about 5 inches*
39.   *LH touches top of D*
39a.   *D stops rolling*

40.   *LH index finger flicks at D again*
40a. *D rolls back and forth without leaving same spot*   (*15VL*, page 3)

Subject *15VL* is the only infant to generate second-order functions twice. In the present instance, *15VL* pushes a doll so that it rolls away. As the doll rolls away *15VL* stops its motion. When the doll stops, *15VL* pushes it again so that it rolls once more.

A general structural–developmental assumption of this research is that sporadic, exceptional production and the most elementary execution possible marks the origins of all new constructions by children. Initiation of second-order functions by only one-third of the subjects is therefore expected, as is the finding that it is generated only once during the entire testing session by all except one of these infants. The latter (*15VL*), as we have seen, generates second-order causal functions twice. The elementary execution of this novel structure is considered a little later in this section.

While first-order causal functions vary independent semivariables only, second-order functions also vary dependent semivariables. Furthermore (and this is the crucial structural development), they covary the independent and dependent semivariables with each other. Infants initiate their second-order structuring by covarying causal means and ends.

Thus, for instance, when the doll is not moving, *15VL*'s hand makes it move; and when the doll is moving, *15VL*'s hand stops it from moving. When the initial effect, then, is that the dependent object rolls away, *15VL* blocks it. In this way she transforms the end or goal from rolling to stopping. As soon as the dependent object stops rolling, she pushes it, thereby transforming the end or goal from stopping back to rolling again. In this way, *15VL* covaries her causal means and ends.

The means infants construct are changed and determined by the ends they produce at the same time as the ends infants produce are changed and determined by the means they construct. The functional dependencies between independent and dependent semivariables begin to be constructed analogically. To illustrate, in *15VL*'s construction stopping is dependent on blocking as rolling is dependent on pushing. In addition, however, pushing is dependent on stopping as blocking is dependent on rolling.

Structural development from first- to second-order functions is fundamental. Ends vary with means or means vary with ends in first-order functions; the dependencies are directed one-way only. The structures of advanced one-way dependencies do not exceed that of a protoratio. With the development of second-order functions, means and ends covary; the dependencies are directed two ways; and the dependencies are analogical. So the structures of second-order dependencies include protoproportions.

This initial stage of structuring second-order functions is constrained by two limiting features. One is a structural constraint upon all second-order functions.

Infants only establish dependencies between independent and dependent variables that are not oriented; their elements are neither ordered nor classified. To illustrate, pushing and blocking are not varied on a continuum by 15VL so they and their products, rolling and stopping, are invariant. Both means and ends are particular elements that do not vary on a continuum.

The second constraint is unique to this initial stage of structuring second-order functions; it begins to be overcome at the next stage (see Chapter 6, Section VII). At the present stage, infants are limited to using their organs, particularly their hands, as the instruments with which to construct second-order functions (as can be readily seen in the 15VL protocol fragment). This limitation is not due to any inability to use objects as instruments when constructing first-order functions (as is readily apparent in the 15AE and 15PR protocol fragments on page 39). Infants are only unable to coordinate two objects in which one serves as an instrumental intermediary when they begin to generate second-order functions.

At their origins, second-order functions do not entail mediate dependencies between causes and effects. The analogical or co-varying dependencies constructed between means and ends are always immediate functions. These do not also require coordinating intermediaries with the causes and the effects.

Only subject 15VL begins to replicate the covarying dependency she constructs. She replicates it once only, and then partially. She makes the doll roll and then stops it. She replicates making the doll roll again but does not continue on to stopping it again. Partial replication indicates only the barest beginning of regulated second-order causality, in which each construction is negated by its successor.

The structure of second-order causal functions (such as that contructed by 15VL) is marked by negation. Each construction is negated by its successor. By reciprocally interweaving causal affirmation followed by causal negation, infants begin to produce second-order functions. The results are controlled causes and effects that covary analogically with each other.

Impossible causal and spatial conditions are also just beginning to be tested at this stage. They meet physical resistance. The results are uncontrolled consequences since the (impossible) effects that infants try to produce are negated by resistances from physical objects (nonrelevant intervening transactions are omitted from the 15ST fragment):

4. *RH stands Doll 2 upright*
   on table between Doll 1
   and Spoon
10. *RH stands D1 upright on*   (E: *"Oh, that's nice."*)
    table next to D2
13. *RH holds S upright on table*
    with handle-end on table,
    next to D2

14. *RH releases S in same position*
     (as in Line 13 and as
     if to stand S upright)
14a. *S falls down flat on table next*
     to D2   (*15ST*, page 6)

33. *LH index finger rolls around Yellow Circular Ring 2 so that YCR2 spins on*
     finger, 2 times, but then YC2 spins off finger to table   (*15EB*, page 13)

186. *RH lowers Rectangular Ring 3 on top of Doll 1, held tilted flat by LH, as*
      looking at this
186a. *rim of RR3 pushes D1 over flat*   (*15AE*, page 163)

Composing a set of elements in which the members are in one-to-one correspondence with each other but without taking into account their differential predicate properties leads *15ST* from constructing possible to impossible physical conditions. She successfully aligns and uprights two dolls but then tries unsuccessfully to do the same with a spoon. Similarly, *15EB* first successfully spins a ring on her finger; but then it spins off her finger. So, too, *15AE* first successfully encircles a rectangular ring around an upright doll (not reproduced in the protocol fragment) before he unsuccessfully attempts to do the same thing to a tilted doll.

Differential results or feedback due to resistances from objects do not yet feedforward to alter infants' subsequent constructions, as they begin to at the next stage (see Chapter 6, Section VII). With a few rare but significant exceptions, infants make no attempts to overcome the resistances of the objects to impossible physical functions or dependencies by modifying their subsequent interactions with these resistant objects. For instance, *15AE* could take into account under what conditions it is and is not possible for him to successfully encircle a doll with a rectangular ring by subsequently uprighting the doll; but he does not. Still, infants at this age generate possible and impossible causal and spatial dependency relations; and they monitor the differential outcomes. In turn, these physical functions provide the necessary preconditions for developing differentiation at the next stage.

Exceptional feedforward or modification by infants of their subsequent interactions as a function of observed object resistance illuminates the interactions and structural disequilibrium necessary to development (nonrelevant intervening transactions are omitted):

37. *RH tries to stand Blue Brush*
     upright on table (bristle
     end up) by carefully touching
     bottom end on table, 2 times
37a. *BB slips and end slides on*
     table so that BB does not

	stand upright but falls	
	flat on table, 2 times	
39.	*LH holds Red Brush upright*	
	and taps end on table, while	
	RH holds BB	
40.	*RH taps BB on table, while*	
	LH holds RB upright on table	
40a.	*BB falls out of RH grasp,*	S: "Ehhh."
	while LH holds RB upright on	(M: "It's hard to make it
	table	stand up, sweetie.")
41.	*RH picks up BB and taps end*	
	of BB on table trying to stand	
	it upright, while LH holds RB	
	upright on table	
42.	*LH raises and holds RB in air,*	
	while RH holds BB upright on	
	table	
43.	*RH releases BB, while LH holds*	
	RB	
43a.	*BB falls flat on table*	S: "Ehhhhhhhh."
48.	*RH touches end of BB on table*	(S begins to cry and kick
	trying to make BB stand upright	under table)
	and releases BB	
48a.	*BB falls flat on table*	S: "Ehhhhhhhh."
	(experimenter makes BB stand	(cries and kicks under
	upright by itself)	table)
49.	*RH touches BB as looks at BB*	
49a.	*BB falls over*	
50.	*RH picks up BB, holds BB by*	S: (laughs)
	bristle end, carefully adjusts	
	BB to make BB stand by itself,	
	and releases BB	
50a.	*BB falls over into subject's*	
	lap	
51.	*RH picks up BB from lap, raises*	
	BB up in air above head, and	
	looks at BB	(15PR, pages 29–30)

Multiple unsuccessful attempts by 15PR to upright a brush produces multiple negative physical feedback. The brush always falls over when 15PR tries to upright it. When the experimenter intervenes and uprights the brush (after Line 48a) 15PR delights in negating it (Lines 49–50). Still, the result may be some feedforward to 15PR's subsequent interactions with the brush since she modifies one aspect of her procedure. She regulates her manipulation of the brush by carefully adjusting its position in relation to the table (Line 50). When this adjustment does not work (Line 50a) she retrieves the brush and examines it visually (Line 51). This kind of extensive testing lays the transitional cognitive groundwork for progressive determination of and differentiation between possible and impossible physical conditions.

VI. Spatial Containing and Its Negation

Containment of objects in a receptacle is still generated one-by-one. Objects are contained consecutively one after the other. Containing two objects at the same time in a receptacle is exceptional. Still, one-by-one containment is progressively regulated, including containment by throwing or dropping objects into a receptacle, as well as placing them in a receptacle. For instance, subject 15VL consecutively throws a brush, a mirror, and another mirror into the same receptacle. The second mirror misses, so she picks it up and throws it into the receptacle successfully.

Directed targeting is progressively precise, whether the aim is containing or hitting, as compared with its initiation at the previous stage (see Langer, 1980, pages 301–303):

172.   *RH throws Block 4 down onto table at Block 3, while looking at this*
172a. *B4 hits B3 and pushes B3 about 1 inch to the left side*   (15AE, page 15)

149.   *as looking toward VW2, RH immediately pushes VW1 rightward and releases VW1 so that VW1 slides rightward on table, fast*
149a. *VW1 hits against VW2, which rotates and moves to the right about 1½ inches, as continues to watch VW2*   (15AE, page 138)

Subject 15AE visually monitors all the targeting she generates, only a small sample of which is presented here. Generally she is already quite accurate as long as the targets are in her near space. This range includes targeting by throwing (first fragment) and by pushing (second fragment).

Targeting affirms spatial placement relations when directed toward containment. Targeting affirms the reciprocal placement relations between container and contained. The container is outside and encompasses the contained, while the contained is inside and encompassed by the container. The aim is spatial envelopment or containment.

Targeting negates spatial placement relations when directed toward hitting. Targeting negates the placement relation of the targeted object. Motion is transmitted transitively from the agent to the patient object. The result is that the initial position of the targeted object is negated and changed to another placement position. The aim is spatial contact and/or displacement.

Emptying just begins to be explored. Emptying negates previously affirmed spatial containing or enveloping. To illustrate, after containing all and only the cars in one receptacle, subject 15HK inverts the receptacle by rotating it so that it turns over and all the cars fall out. A bit later *15HK* repeats this routine of containing all and only the cars followed by emptying them out. One of the cars does not fall out because of the tilted rotation by which *15HK* inverts the receptacle. Thus, she immediately reaches in and takes the remaining car out. This correction by a different mapping completes the repeated affirmation: negation relations between spatial containing and spatial emptying that *15HK* explores.

Unlike containing, which is typically applied one-at-a-time to several objects, emptying is applied simultaneously to several objects. It is just as rare for infants to take out objects from a receptacle one-at-a-time as it is for them to put more than one object at a time into a receptacle. That infants have the capacity to empty objects one-at-a-time is evident from *15HK*'s self-correction. So the mapping procedures are the inverses of each other, as well as the spatial relations of envelopment and emptiness that they produce.

When infants empty receptacles by turning them over, they elaborate their usage into vehicles or instrumental containers for transporting objects. This expansion of the function of receptacles is produced by a few infants only. But it already includes both physical and social recipients that are elaborated from static receptacles into kinetic vehicles. When infants use physical receptacles as vehicles, the transaction usually issues in turning the vehicle over in order to empty it of its contents. When the vehicle is social, the goal is usually to get rid of the object(s). For instance, subject *15NF* places a ring into the experimenter's hand which *15NF* then pushes away from himself.

The functions of receptacles are expanded in one other way at this stage. A few infants begin to use receptacles to cover other receptacles. This includes covering receptacles that do not contain any objects.

The act of covering is initially rudimentary because infants do nothing more than stack one receptacle on top of another. They do not turn over the topmost receptacle even though they are quite able to do so, as is evident from the inverting emptying procedures. Furthermore, they do not align the stacked receptacles so that the cover fits properly on the container. Usually the cover is placed askew across the container and is left that way.

In this way, infants just begin to transform receptacles into both containers and their reciprocals, that is, covers of containers. Thus, both forms of spatial negation are initiated at this stage. Inverse negation is used to empty containers. Reciprocal negation is used to make covers out of receptacles.

VII. Negation of Matched Mappings

Negation only begins to condition mapping correspondences. The introduction of this novel structural element into constructing correspondences results in the origins of reversible equivalence:

30.   *RH rolls Car 3 back and forth, then RH aligns C3 to roll it up and down*
31.   *RH rotates C3 to its side, back to C3's original position, to C3's side, and back to*
       C3's original position   *(15PR, page 53)*

Both displacement (Line 30) and placement (Line 31) correspondences are consecutively negated by *15PR*. Negation of displacement correspondences (Line 30) is not inverted and, therefore, does not issue in reversible equivalence between spatial trajectories. But negation of placement correspondences (Line 31) is inverted and then negated once again. This action produces and re-produces reversible equivalence between spatial positions.

Negating correspondences to form reversible equivalence is a central feature of second-order mapping correlation. Most negation, however, is limited to form-ing nonreversible matchings, such as *15PR*'s displacement correspondences. Reversible negation of correspondences, such as *15PR*'s placement matchings, are still exceptional at this stage.

Much protological activity is invested in generating mapping correspon-dences. Most discrete correspondences still produce single-unit equivalences even though mappings may be repeated precisely and many times:

8.5.   *RH hits head of Doll 1 on table, 8 times*
8.5.   *LH hits head of Doll 2 on table, 8 times*   *(15HK, page 47)*

In actuality *15HK* produces 30-, 7-, 17-, and the above 8-unit equivalence during the same task using cylinders as well as dolls. They are all the products of multiple reproductions of simultaneous mappings that are in one-to-one corre-spondence. This includes precise one-to-one matching between the spatial ori-entations of the objects upon which the correspondences are mapped (e.g., both of the dolls' heads are hit on the table).

Thus, these are well-regulated correspondences. Still, in all likelihood they constitute little more than firmly grounded single-unit equivalences. If they produce anything more it is likely to be nothing but the rudiments of equiv-alences between many units as opposed to equivalences between few units. The quantification involved, if this much, is certainly no more than the basis for such gross ordinal comparisons.

No longer unusual at this stage are matched mappings that produce two-unit equivalences:

44.5.   *LH taps stacked Orange and Yellow Cup on table, 2 times*
44.5.   *RH shakes Yellow Spoon in air, 2 times*
46.3.   *LH slides stacked OC/YC back and forth on the table, 2 times*
46.7   *RH touches cup end of YS to LH held on top of stacked OC/YC*
48.3.   *LH partially raises off stacked OC/YC*
48.7.   *RH touches cup end of YS first to side of OC, then on top of OC (below LH);*
         and then taps YS on top of OC, 2 times

50.5.   *LH taps stacked OC/YC on table, 2 times*
50.5.   *RH shakes YS in air, 2 times*   (*15NF*, page 38)

This performance encompasses producing two-unit equivalences many times
in temporal succession, partial overlap, and simultaneity. They are embodied in
a variety of mapping forms (i.e., tapping, shaking, and sliding). Some are embodied in simultaneous mapping forms, one of which is actual (one hand taps
cups on the table two times), while the other is virtual (the other hand shakes a
spoon two times but does not actually tap it on the table). These, then, provide
occasions for generating mappings of mappings and, thereby, producing the
rudiments of symbolic correspondence operations.

Imprecise but cooperative virtual matching also just begins to be generated by
a few infants. For instance, the experimenter taps the column on the table in
order to draw subject *15EB*'s attention to the task. Instead of reproducing the
experimenter's actual tapping, *15EB* almost taps the same object on the table,
thereby virtually matching the experimenter's behavior.

Three-unit mapping equivalences remain rare (see Langer, 1980, pages 303–
309). Still, one infant (*15HK*) already does so several times. In the first instance,
all the characteristics of the mappings correspond with each other. Three taps
with one brush are followed in partial temporal overlap by three taps with
another brush. In the second instance, numerical equivalence between three
taps is produced consecutively. Furthermore, the mappings producing the three-
unit equivalence differ somewhat. This discrepancy indicates that even three-
unit equivalences begin to be detached from the mappings that produce them.
This is the first step toward abstracting equivalences of this magnitude from their
pragmatic embodiments.

Continuous correspondences, as we have seen many times in this chapter, are
generated with precision and are well regulated as long as they are fairly brief
(e.g., *15NF*'s matched reproductions of tapping, shaking, and sliding objects
presented above). Regulation is marked by coordinated adjustments and self-
correction:

11.   *RH stands Yellow Cylinder 2 upright on table, while LH holds Blue Cylinder 2*
12.   *LH starts to stand BC2 upright on table*
13.   *RH moves to left to help LH stand BC2 upright*
13a. *RH knocks YC2 to its side flat on the table*
14.   *RH helps LH stand BC2 upright on table*
15.   *RH stands YC2 upright on table*   (*15PB*, pages 30–31)

Performances, such as *15NF*'s above, also illustrate the developing coordination of discrete and continuous correspondences. Both actual and virtual continuous correspondences now begin to be integrated with discrete correspondences.
Thus, for instance, at the same time as *15NF* matches tapping with shaking in

many-to-many continuous correspondence she also matches them in two-to-two discrete correspondence.

Continuous correspondences begin to be marked by cooperative as well as virtual enactment:

> *(mother keeps wriggling finger to try to get subject to put Yellow Circular Ring 2 on mother's finger)*
> 31. *RH reaches back up to mother's hand and puts Blue Circular Ring 2 onto mother's finger*
> 32. *LH moves YCR2 to finger of LH like BCR2 is on mother's finger*
>
> (*15EB*, page 13)

Other correspondences begin to be marked by playful pretense (see Section III for illustrative protocol fragments). Together these features of virtual, cooperative, and playful enactment constitute the initial manifestation of symbolic correspondences.

Both one-to-many and many-to-one correspondences are generated with small numbers of objects. Furthermore, these two co-univocal forms begin to be coordinated with each other. Thus, for instance, *15ST* (in the routine presented on pages 26 and 27) begins by generating a many-to-one forks-in-cup relation. She then transforms part of the construction into a one-to-many fork-in-cups relation while simultaneously preserving the other part of the construction as a many-to-one forks-in-cup relation.

Some co-univocals just begin to be marked by protosymbolic features as well. These features are most apparent in the context of playful pretense, as already indicated at the beginning of Section III of this chapter. Thus, for instance, two brushes may be used by subject *15PR* to pretend to brush one object (in a playful routine considered on page 30) and one brush may be used by subjects *15VL* and *15JH* to pretend to brush several objects (in the protocol fragments presented on page 31).

VIII. Precise Two-Step Ordering of Very Small Magnitudes

Continuous ordering by protoaddition to form increasing mapping series (e.g., ⟨ tap, hit ⟩) and by protosubtraction to produce decreasing mapping series (e.g., ⟨ hit, tap ⟩) are already well-established by the previous stage (Langer, 1980, pages 308–312). Most continuous orderings continue to be unidirectional by either adding or subtracting rather than bidirectional by coordinated adding and subtracting (e.g., ⟨ tap, hit, tap ⟩). Continuous mapping ordering (e.g., pushing harder and harder) is central to constructing systematic first-order causal functions with discrete objects, as we have already seen (Section V). It is also a progressively important element in constructing ordered deformations of quasi-continuous PlayDoh objects (see Chapter 5, Section III).

Discrete iterative ordering predominates over continuous ordering, and it extends a developmental trend initiated at earlier stages (Langer, 1980, e.g., pages 309–312). Precision is still usually limited to two-step constructions. Occasional three-step orders are precise when they comprise ⟨ 1, 2, 3 ⟩ series (e.g., of tapping).

Precise two-step ordering just begins to be extended to increasing ⟨ 3, 4 ⟩ series by a few infants:

    7.   *LH taps Blue Cylinder 2 on table, 3 times*
    8.   *LH taps BC2 on table in same position, 4 times*   (*15JH*, page 15)

Similarly, precise two-step ordering just begins to be extended to decreasing ⟨ 4, 3 ⟩ series by a few infants:

  58.   *RH bangs Red Doll 1 on table,*
        4 times
        (experimenter bangs Blue Doll 1
        on table)
  59.   *watches experimenter and smiles*   (*E: "We can both do it."*)
  60.   *RH bangs RD1 on table, 3 times*   (*15PR*, page 50)

This series by *15PR* is particularly noteworthy since she generates a ⟨ 4, 3 ⟩ ordering despite the experimenter's intervention.

Large unit orders continue to be imprecise even when the series does not exceed two steps:

  1.3.   *RH taps top of VW1, 14 times*
  1.7.   *LH taps top of Racer 1, 10 times*   (*15EB*, page 38)

While imprecise, this decreasing ⟨ 14, 10 ⟩ order is generated in partial temporal overlap. As such it provides optimal conditions for comparing the unequal but imprecisely ordered quantities.

Series that exceed three steps are invariably the products of imprecise ordering:

  18.   *LH shakes Blue Cylinder 2 downward, directly above Red Triangular Column 2 but without touching it, 1 time*
  19.   *LH hits BC2 downward onto RTC2, 1 time*
 19a. *RTC2 hits into Red Triangular Column 1 which RTC2 was already touching*
  20.   *LH hits end of BC2 onto RTC2, 2 times*
 20a. *RTC2 displaced to right and pushes RTC1 into BTC1 which hits Blue Cylinder 1 which hits Red Cylinder 1*
 20aa. *smiles as BC1 and RC1 roll to right 1 inch*
  21.   *as looks at objects in array, LH taps BC2 on table top 3 inches to left of RTC2, 3 times*
  22.   *LH taps BC2 on same spot on table, 8 times*   (*15JH*, pages 16 and 17)

The initial mapping by *15JH* is virtual since he shakes Blue Cylinder 2 down but does not actually touch it to anything, whereas all subsequent mappings involve actual hitting or tapping. Virtual mapping provides the possibility of constructing a pragmatic analogue of something like, but not quite, a zero unit. Potentially, this analogue produces a pragmatic ordered ⟨ 0, 1, 2, 3, 8 ⟩ mapping series.

Ordered series are increasingly generated by a mixture of varying mapping forms. Hitting, tapping, and potentially, shaking are used by *15JH*. Ordered series also increasingly comprise a mixture of discrete and continuous magnitudes. The discrete magnitudes increase unidirectionally in *15JH*'s series while they actually decrease unidirectionally from hit to tap in continuous magnitudes. Potentially, the continuous magnitudes in this series are bidirectional from shake to hit to tap.

Dissociation of orders from mappings within the same series and dissociation of discrete from continuous orders within the same series serves to detach the cognitive products from their mode of production and from their particular embodiment, thus permitting progressive abstraction of ordered series as conceptual rather than pragmatic cognitions. It parallels the progress found in abstracting correspondences at this stage, which was considered in the preceding section.

Compositions of Compositions

3

Developing mappings expands the power of infants' cognitive and symbolic constructions, as we began to see in Chapter 2. The power of infants' cognitions progresses to initially structuring second-order operations and functions. These operations and functions include analogical causal dependencies that infants just begin to generate at this stage. It seems reasonable to conclude from this expansion that if infants were limited to routines and individual objects as the elements of their cognitions, then they would still develop at least some second-order cognition.

Infants have another major resource available for generating the elements of second-order structuring. It comprises combinativity operations of composing, decomposing, and deforming that put two or more objects together into configural relations. Together with their derivatives, such as recomposing and reforming, combinativity operations produce sets and series. Sets and series supplement routines and objects as elements of infants' cognitions.

The present chapter inquires into the progress made by infants at this stage in generating such configurations of objects. This inquiry requires determining the basic parameters of the configurations infants construct. This includes determining how many objects infants compose together, the proportion of their compositions that are stable, and the degree to which they compose more than one configuration at a time. This data base establishes the pool of configurational elements available to infants at this stage for logicomathematical structuring. Chapter 4 inquires into the developing first- and second-order operations that infants structure with their constructed sets and series.

I. Predominance of Composing over Recomposing

Composing productivity is uniform. Mean productivity ranges from 4.41 compositions per minute in the four-object additive condition to 7.68 compositions per minute in the eight-object additive condition (Table 3.1, Row 3). The range of mean productivity is a bit narrower in the four-object (4.41–5.09 compositions per minute) than in the eight-object (5.42–7.68 compositions per minute) conditions. Mean productivity is also lower in all class conditions when four objects rather than when eight objects are presented (e.g., Row 3, Columns 2 *vs.* 3). This trend is similar to the differences at age 12 months (Langer, 1980, pages 314–316). Unlike at age 12 months, however, at age 15 months none of the differences between productivity in four- *vs.* eight-object presentations are statistically significant (sign tests).

The average rate of productivity is usually lower at age 15 months than at age 12 months (compare Table 3.1 with Table 13.1 in Langer, 1980, page 315). The only exception is the four-object multiplicative condition; in that condition the rate is slightly higher at age 15 months. Only two of the five decreases in rate from ages 12 to 15 months are statistically significant. They are the four-object additive condition (Mann–Whitney $U = 4$, $p = .01$) and the eight-object disjoint condition (Mann–Whitney $U = 14$, $p = .05$). These occasional decreases from ages 12 to 15 months in producing compositions may be accounted for by the increasing stability (which includes durability) of those compositions that are generated.

Compositions are progressively stable as long as they comprise few objec (irrelevant intervening transactions are omitted):

59. RH holds Doll 4 inverted and
     upright about 4 inches from
     mouth, as looks at D4, while
     LH holds Mirror

60. LH touches handle part of M   S: "Whaz-zis?"
     to bottom part of D4 held by
     RH

61. LH inserts handle part of M   (M: "This is a soldier.")
     into bottom part of D4 held
     by RH

62.3. LH holds handle part of M
       inserted in D4 held by RH,
       for about 5 seconds

62.7. turns and looks toward the
       right

64. looks down at objects held
     in hands, as holds M inserted
     in D in front of self,
     for about 2 seconds

69.	*RH raises D4 off table, as*	
	turns D4 to tilted–inverted	
	upright orientation, while	
	LH holds M in air	*S: "Whaz-zis?"*
70.5	*RH holds D4 horizontal,*	
	about 3 inches in front of D2	
	and about 3 inches above	
	table edge	*(M: "This is a soldier.")*
70.5.	*LH touches mirror part of M*	
	to bottom of D4	
72.	*RH holds the mirror part of*	
	M in contact with the bottom	
	part of D4, moving M	
	around the base of the D4	
	about half-	
	way, for a couple of seconds	*(15SG, page 7)*

Both compositions are durable sets of the same two objects preserved for extended durations. Also, both compositions are monitored visually; both are precisely constructed; both require fairly fine differentiated motor control; and both are accompanied by a verbal demonstrative question. The second composition reproduces the first except that 15SG inverts the mirror in his second construction. All these features of exploring and determining the properties of small sets facilitates fixing them as stable or constant elements for further cognition.

Fine-grained exploration may include transforming one object into an instrument with which to explore another object as a prelude to completing the composition:

75. *RH touches bowl part of Yellow Spoon 1 to front part of Red Cup 1 in a brushing motion (brushing right to left against front of cup)*
76. *RH touches bowl part of YS1 to backside rim of RC1 and then continues to trace rim edge clockwise to the right side of RC1*
77. *RH lowers YS1 bowl down inside of RC1 and releases YS1 there*

(15SG pages 34 and 35)

Tracing a shape feature of one object with another object is the most differentiated and co-regulated exploration generated at this stage.

Composing predominates (Table 3.2). Infants generate two compositions for every recomposition they generate. This ratio is the same as that at age 12 months. In almost all conditions, the proportions of recomposing at age 15 months (Table 3.2) do not change from those at age 12 months (see Langer, 1980, page 327, Table 13.4). Even the conditions under which infants at both ages generate the fewest and the most recomposing remain the same. Fewest recomposing is generated in the four-object disjoint conditions and most recom-

TABLE 3.1
Spontaneous Phase I: Mean Composing Productivity at Age 15 Months

	Class conditions						
	Control	Additive		Multiplicative		Disjoint	
	Four-object 1	Four-object 2	Eight-object 3	Four-object[a] 4	Eight-object[b] 5	Four-object 6	Eight-object 7
1. Mean compositions	13.08	7.33	17.08	9.40	16.73	7.83	11.00
2. Mean duration	2 min 34 sec	1 min 40 sec	2 min 13 sec	1 min 51 sec	2 min 29 sec	1 min 33 sec	2 min 2 sec
3. Productivity per minute	5.09	4.41	7.68	5.07	6.73	5.08	5.42

[a] N = 10 subjects.
[b] N = 11 subjects.

TABLE 3.2
Spontaneous Phase I: Mean Frequency of Composing and Recomposing at Age 15 Months

		Four-object condition			Eight-object condition		
		Thematic 1	*Variant* 2	*% Variant* 3	*Thematic* 4	*Variant* 5	*% Variant* 6
1.	Semicontrol	6.90	7.50	52			
2.	Additive	4.92	2.42	33	11.25	5.83	34
3.	Multiplicative	5.50	3.90	41	9.54	7.18	43
4.	Disjoint	7.75	3.25	26	7.75	3.25	30
5.	All conditions	5.75	3.80	40	9.56	5.44	36

posing is generated in the four-object control conditions. Furthermore, as at age 12 months, there is little difference in rate of recomposing between the four- and eight-object conditions. At age 12 months 6% more recomposing is generated in the eight-object conditions while at age 15 months 4% more recomposing is generated in the four-object conditions.

II. Frequent but Partial Provoked Composing and Recomposing

Variations in composing and recomposing productivity as a function of procedural conditions diminish. The rate is becoming constant from the first to the third test phases within each task, that is, from the procedural conditions of spontaneous transactions to provoked composing to pre-existent compositions (see the Appendix and Langer, 1980, for the experimental details which distinguish the three different testing procedures). This is a decided shift from earlier stages when infants generate most composing in the condition of spontaneous transaction (see, for example, Langer, 1980, pages 317–323).

For the first time procedures designed to provoke composing by containment during the second test phase always result in composing (Table 3.3). All subjects contain at least some objects in both the four-object additive and the eight-object disjoint conditions. Undifferentiated mapping forms (such as dropping and haphazard placing) are usually used to produce global containment (such as heaps of objects and irregular alignments). Exceptions just begin to be generated in which differentiated and coregulated placing is used to contain as many as four objects in one receptacle to form a rough approximation of locating one object in each corner of the container.

Containing in the four-object additive condition is divided almost evenly between containing in two receptacles and containing in one receptacle only. In

TABLE 3.3
Provoked Phase II: Frequency of Containing All or
Some Objects at Age 15 Months

| | Condition | | | |
| | Four-object additive | | Eight-object disjoint | |
Receptacles	All	Some	All	Some
One	4	3	2	7
Two	5	0	2	1

contrast, three-fourths of infants generate single receptacle containing only, while one-fourth contain objects in two receptacles in the eight-object disjoint condition. This difference is not statistically significant ($N = 12$, $x = 3$, $p = .073$, binomial test).

Not only is containing in two receptacles generated by only a minority of infants but the procedure used is minimal and rigid. Infants switch only once between the two receptacles. Their procedure consists of nothing more than containing objects in one receptacle followed by containing some or all of the remaining objects in the other receptacle. Containing does not yet involve flexible switching back and forth between receptacles; flexible containing originates at the next stage (see pages 148–150).

Infants usually contain all objects in a receptacle when dealing with small numbers but not with intermediate numbers. Two-thirds of the subjects contain all objects in the four-object additive condition while two-thirds of the subjects contain only some objects in the eight-object disjoint condition; this difference is statistically significant ($N = 5$, $x = 0$, $p = .031$, sign test).

One-by-one adding objects characterizes almost all containing. This procedure is used by all infants in both conditions. Only three subjects also contain two objects at a time in the four-object additive condition; and they do this once only. Two subjects also contain two objects at a time in the eight-object disjoint condition; and they do this once only. One of these subjects contains two objects at a time in both conditions. No infant contains more than two objects at a time.

Mixed predication typifies composing in receptacles. To illustrate, one subject contains all four circular and all four cross rings, one at a time in one receptacle. The order of containing is Circular Ring 1, Cross Rings 4, Cross Rings 1 and 3, Circular Ring 2, Cross Ring 2, and Circular Rings 4 and 3. Thus this subject contains all the objects in a scrambled fashion in one receptacle only, even though the objects were presented such that they were practically presorted into two classes for the subject. Both order of handling and enclosure (placements) are mixed in their predicate properties. More advanced, unmixed predicating by containing in two receptacles is genrated by infants on rare occasions when (a) the objects are practically presorted in the presentation and (b) the infants are coached verbally.

Self-correcting mixed into unmixed predicate containing just begins to be generated in exceptional instances. To illustrate, during the process of containing two brushes together with a column in one receptacle, subject 15ST switches and contains the brushes in the other receptacle instead. However, after this apparent self-correction she contains another column with the brushes. The final result is that 15ST produces mixed predication after all, even though she contains objects in two receptacles. Infants' classifications of objects in containers are no different when the experimenter intervenes by either correcting their mixed predications or by modeling unmixed predications in two containers. Only three infants were helped in these ways to produce some unmixed predications.

Provoked composing of two sets by spatial sorting on the table during phase II of the testing begins to elicit cooperative sorting by infants. Eleven subjects add objects to the experimenter's sorts in either the eight-object additive or multiplicative condition; but no subject adds objects in both conditions. Thus 7 subjects add cooperatively in the additive condition while 4 subjects do not; and 4 subjects add cooperatively in the multiplicative condition while 5 subjects do not.

Almost all cooperative sorting is limited to infants adding objects to one of the two sorts that the experimenter begins. Nine subjects add objects to one sort while 2 subjects add objects to both sorts; the difference is statistically significant ($N = 11$, $x = 2$, $p = .033$, binomial test). Composing two sets by assisted spatial sorting, then, is generated even less frequently than by containing in two receptacles.

Hence infants' cooperative sorting is limited (a) to participating in only one of two test trials and (b) to adding objects to only one of two provoked sorts. A third important limitation is that even when infants sort cooperatively they do not add all objects. Five subjects add one object; 3 subjects add two objects; 2 subjects add three objects; and 1 subject adds four objects cooperatively.

Finally, infants' cooperative sorting is limited to random predication even though the experimenter always models class consistent sorting for them. Infants' cooperative sorting is split evenly between mixed and unmixed predication. Half the time their addition of objects is class consistent and half the time it is not class consistent. This addition does not vary by class condition since it holds for both the additive and multiplicative conditions. Thus, as we shall see in Chapter 4, Section IV, cooperative sorting by predicate properties that is provoked by social modeling remains more primitive than spontaneous sorting.

Adding to two pre-existing compositions (presented by the experimenter in test phase II) is no longer generated less frequently than subtracting from them (see

Langer, 1980, pages 320–322 for the performances at age 12 months). Eight out of 12 subjects add objects to pre-existing sets in either the four-object control, multiplicative, or disjoint conditions. Two subjects add objects to pre-existing sets in two of these three conditions. No subject adds objects in all three conditions.

Still, adding to pre-existing sets is a decidedly subordinate activity; only 4 out of 12 subjects in the control condition, 4 out of 9 subjects in the multiplicative condition, and 2 out of 8 subjects in the disjoint condition do so. Furthermore, adding objects to pre-existing sets is split evenly between all and some of the test objects. Half the time infants add some test objects to the pre-existing compositions and half the time they add all test objects.

Adding to pre-existent class consistent compositions, like cooperative sorting, produces random predication at this stage. Adding objects to these pre-existing sets is split evenly between mixed and unmixed predication, and this does not vary by class condition. Thus again experimental modeling induces more primitive classification than infants generate spontaneously.

While subtracting objects from pre-existing sets is no longer dominant, deforming them or combining them into one set is still typical. These operations are just becoming well-regulated. For instance, subject 15NF is presented with a matrix-like arrangement of a yellow and orange cup and a yellow and orange spoon plus an alignment of four yellow cups. Subject 15NF combines and recombines all objects into one composition that is totally different from the pre-existing matrix plus alignment. She stacks all five cups on each other and then inserts the two spoons in the topmost cup. After this she decomposes her integrated single composition into two compositions comprising four stacked cups separate from one cup with the two spoons inserted in it. Finally, she reintegrates these two compositions into one by placing the cup with the two spoons back into the stack of four cups. This sequence of composing, decomposing, and recomposing is marked by visual inspection and monitoring, plus careful adjustment of objects to each other. It indicates that infants are more concerned with changing than with building upon models; and, clearly, reorganizing pre-existing compositions is becoming well-controlled and defined.

III. Increasing Size of Compositions

Two-object compositions continue to be infants' dominant constructions (Table 3.4). Two-object compositions are also still more characteristic of infants' productions in four-object (Row 1) than in eight-object conditions (Row 4). The difference in generating two-object compositions in the four- and eight-object additive, multiplicative and disjoint conditions is statistically significant ($N = 12$, $x = 2$, $p = .019$, sign test). It prolongs the differential trend found at age 12

TABLE 3.4
Spontaneous Phase I: Mean Frequency and Percentage of Compositional Extent at Age 15 Months

		Control[a]		Additive		Multiplicative[b]		Disjoint[a]		Total	
		$\bar{X}$	%	$\bar{X}$	%	$\bar{X}$	%	$\bar{X}$	%	$\bar{X}$	%
		1	2	3	4	5	6	7	8	9	10
Four-object condition:											
1.	Two-object	8.60	60	6.25	85	6.90	73	6.00	76	6.86	72
2.	Three-object	3.90	27	0.83	11	1.90	20	1.17	15	1.86	20
3.	Four-object	1.90	13	0.25	3	0.60	6	0.67	8	0.82	8
Eight-object condition:											
4.	Two-object			9.67	56	7.82	47	7.00	64	8.17	55
5.	Three-object			3.92	23	5.00	30	1.75	16	3.51	24
6.	Four-object			2.67	16	2.45	15	1.75	16	2.28	15
7.	Five-object			0.50	3	1.18	7	0.42	4	0.68	5
8.	Six-object			0.17	1	0.27	2	0.00	0	0.14	1
9.	Seven-object			0.00	0	0.00	0	0.08	1	0.03	0
10.	Eight-object			0.17	1	0.00	0	0.00	0	0.06	0

[a]N = 10 subjects in four-object, control and disjoint conditions.
[b]N = 11 subject in the eight-object, multiplicative condition.

months (Langer, 1980, page 324, Table 13.2) which is also statistically significant ($N = 11$, $x = 2$, $p = .033$, sign test). Indeed, the overall differential is almost identical at both ages. The proportion of infants' compositions comprising the minimum of two objects is 15% less in the eight- than the four-object conditions at age 12 months (Langer, 1980, page 324, Table 13.2, Row 1, Column 10 compared with Row 4, Column 10); and it is 17% less at age 15 months (Table 3.4, Row 1, Column 10 compared with Row 4, Column 10).

Two-object compositions comprise a progressively decreasing proportion of infants' combinations even in four-object conditions. They make up 90% of production at age 10 months (Langer, 1980, page 232, Table 10.2, Row 1), decrease to 83% at age 12 months (Langer, 1980, page 324, Table 13.4, Row 1), and decrease further to 72% at age 15 months (Table 3.4, Row 1). This decreasing proportion is a gradual trend. Thus the decrease from ages 10 to 12 months is not statistically significant (Mann–Whitney $U = 44$, $p > .05$), nor is the decrease from ages 12 to 15 months (Mann–Whitney $U = 44$, $p > .05$). However, the decrease from ages 10 to 15 months is statistically significant (Mann–Whitney $U = 15$, $p < .001$).

The proportion of three-object compositions produced in four-object conditions increases from 14% at age 12 months (Langer, 1980, page 324, Table 13.2,

Row 2) to 20% at age 15 months (Table 3.4, Row 2). While a sizable increase in itself (on the order of 43%), it is not the major change found. The major increase is in the production of four-object compositions in the four-object conditions. The proportion increases almost threefold from 3% at age 12 months (Langer, 1980, page 324, Table 13.2, Row 3) to 8% at age 15 months (Table 3.4, Row 3). This increase with age is statistically significant (Mann–Whitney $U = 31$, $p = .01$).

Parallel development marks compositional size in the eight-object conditions. Two-object compositions comprise 68% of production at age 12 months; this is the youngest age tested with these conditions (Langer, 1980, page 324, Table 13.2, Row 4). The proportion decreases by 13% to 55% at age 15 months (Table 3.4, Row 4). This drop is almost exactly the same as the 11% decrease of two-object compositions in the four-object condition from ages 12 months (83%) to 15 months (72%). Also, the decrease in producing two-object compositions in the eight-object conditions from ages 12 to 15 months is not statistically significant (Mann–Whitney $U = 46$, $p > .05$).

Three-object compositions comprise a slightly increasing proportion of production in the eight-object conditions. The increase is from 21% at age 12 months (Langer, 1980, page 324, Table 13.2, Row 5) to 24% at age 15 months (Table 3.4, Row 5). Three-object compositions, then, are the second most frequent set size produced in the eight-object conditions, as they are in the four-object conditions. But, as in the four-object conditions, the increase with age in the production of three-object compositions is not the major change found.

The major increase is in the production of four-object and five-object compositions. Together they comprise 8% at age 12 months (Langer, 1980, page 324, Table 13.2, Rows 6 and 7) and increase to 20% at age 15 months (Table 3.4, Rows 6 and 7). This increase with age is statistically significant (Mann–Whitney $U = 23$, $p = .01$).

Production of six-, seven-, and eight-object compositions remains negligible. They comprise 2% of infants' combinations at age 12 months (Langer, 1980, page 324, Table 13.2, Rows 8–10) and 1% at age 15 months (Table 3.4, Rows 8–10). Moreover, those that are generated by 15-month-olds are no more articulate compositions than those generated by 12-month-olds (see Langer, 1980, pages 325 and 326). With few exceptions they still constitute little more than global heaping together of objects.

Directly manipulating two or more objects to construct compositions first becomes dominant at age 12 months (Langer, 1980, pages 326 and 327); at earlier ages the majority involve direct transaction with one object only (Langer, 1980, pages 57 and 58, 146 and 147, and 233). Directly manipulating two or more objects remains the dominant mode of constructing compositions at age 15 months (Table 3.5).

Direct manipulation of two objects in constructing compositions decreases a

TABLE 3.5
Spontaneous Phase I: Number of Objects Directly Manipulated by 15-Month-Old Subjects to Produce Compositions in All Class Conditions

		Number of objects								
		1	2	3	4	5	6	7	8	Total
Four-object conditions:										
1.	Frequency of compositions	189	187	33	11					420
2.	% Compositions	45	44	8	3					100
Eight-object conditions:										
3.	Frequency of compositions	221	184	58	45	9	1	1	2	521
4.	% Compositions	42	35	11	9	2	0	0	0	99

bit at age 15 months. In the four-object conditions it decreases from 53% at age 12 months to 44% at age 15 months; in the eight-object conditions it decreases from 47% at age 12 months to 34% at age 15 months. In the four-object conditions, most of the decrease with age is compensated by increases in direct manipulation of three and four objects to construct compositions. These constructions increase from 5% at age 12 months to 11% at age 15 months. In the eight-object conditions, most of the decrease with age is compensated by an increase from 35% at age 12 months to 42% at age 15 months in direct manipulation of one object only to construct compositions.

Still, by age 15 months about one in ten compositions are constructed by directly manipulating three or more objects in four-object conditions (Table 3.5, Rows 1 and 2, Columns 3 and 4). Almost one in four compositions are constructed by directly manipulating three or more objects in eight-object conditions (Table 3.5, Rows 3 and 4, Columns 3–8), thus continuing the slow but gradual increase noted at previous stages (Langer, 1980).

IV. Decreasing Mobile Production

Transitional equilibrium characterizes infants' developing combinativity structures at this stage. Significant in this regard, we shall now observe, is a decrease in the proportion of compositions and recompositions that are mobiles without a concomitant increase in the proportion that are stabiles. Instead, infants increasingly generate combined mobiles–stabiles.

Composing is in transition at this stage from parity between mobile and stabile production at the previous stage (Langer, 1980, pages 328–334) to initial predominance of stabiles at the next stage (Chapter 7, Section IV). At age 12 months, 47% of compositions are stabiles and 47% are mobiles in both four- and

TABLE 3.6
Four-Object Conditions, Spontaneous Phase I: Mean Frequency and Percentage of Compositional Features at Age 15 Months

	Class conditions									
	Semicontrol[a]		Additive		Multiplicative[a]		Disjoint		Total	
	$\bar{X}$ 1	% 2	$\bar{X}$ 3	% 4	$\bar{X}$ 5	% 6	$\bar{X}$ 7	% 8	$\bar{X}$ 9	% 10
1. Contact stable	4.20	29	2.50	34	2.60	28	1.58	20	2.66	28
2. Proximity stabile	1.70	12	1.08	15	1.50	16	1.17	15	1.34	14
3. Contact–proximity stable	0.10	1	0.25	3	0.00	0	0.00	0	0.09	1
4. Total stable	6.00	42	3.83	52	4.10	44	2.75	35	4.09	43
5. Contact mobile	4.90	34	2.08	28	2.80	30	2.58	33	3.02	32
6. Proximity mobile	0.70	5	0.33	4	0.80	8	1.00	13	0.70	7
7. Contact–proximity mobile	0.30	2	0.00	0	0.10	1	0.08	1	0.11	1
8. Total mobile	5.90	41	2.42	33	3.70	39	3.67	47	3.84	40
9. Mobile–stabile	2.50	17	1.08	15	1.60	17	1.42	18	1.61	17
10. Causal	3.00	21	1.42	19	2.20	23	1.92	24	2.09	22
11. Noncausal	11.40	79	5.92	81	7.20	76	5.92	76	7.45	78
12. Horizontal[b]	5.40	48	3.08	56	3.00	46	5.08	78	4.14	57
13. Vertical[b]	3.10	28	1.58	29	2.50	38	1.25	19	2.04	28
14. Horizontal–vertical[b]	2.70	24	0.83	15	1.00	15	0.17	3	1.11	15

[a]$N = 10$ subjects in the semicontrol and multiplicative conditions.

[b]Compositions whose spatial dimensions are ambiguous are not scored. Consequently, the dimensional means summate to less than the compositional means.

eight-object conditions. Composing at the present transitional stage is marked by no change in the rate of producing stabiles, but rather by decreasing mobiles production and by increasing production of combined mobiles–stabiles.

The overall proportion of stabiles is similar in the four-object (Table 3.6, Row 4, Column 10) and eight-object (Table 3.7, Row 4, Column 8) conditions. They are also similar to the proportion of stabiles produced in these conditions at age 12 months (Langer, 1980, pages 329 and 330; Table 13.5, Row 4, Column 10; and Table 13.6, Row 4, Column 8). Stabiles constitute somewhat less than half of the compositions constructed at both ages; and this proportion does not vary as a function of the number of presented objects.

The proportion of stabiles is somewhat more variable in the four-object class conditions (Table 3.6, Row 4) than in the eight-object class conditions (Table 3.7, Row 4) but the difference in variability is not statistically significant ($x_r^2 = 8.36$, $df = 5$, $p > .10$, Friedman two-way analysis of variance). In the four-object conditions, the proportion ranges from a low of 35% in the disjoint to a high of 52% in the additive tasks. In the eight-object conditions, the proportion ranges from a low of 42% in the disjoint to a high of 47% in the additive tasks.

TABLE 3.7

Eight-Object Conditions, Spontaneous Phase I: Mean Frequency and Percentage of Compositional Features at Age 15 Months

		\multicolumn{8}{c}{Class conditions}							
		\multicolumn{2}{c}{*Additive*}	\multicolumn{2}{c}{*Multiplicative[a]*}	\multicolumn{2}{c}{*Disjoint*}	\multicolumn{2}{c}{*Total*}
		$\bar{X}$	%	$\bar{X}$	%	$\bar{X}$	%	$\bar{X}$	%
		1	2	3	4	5	6	7	8
1.	Contact stabile	5.08	30	5.27	32	2.58	23	4.28	29
2.	Proximity stabile	2.25	13	1.18	7	1.58	14	1.68	11
3.	Contact–proximity stabile	0.67	4	1.00	6	0.50	4	0.71	5
4.	Total stabile	8.00	47	7.45	44	4.67	42	6.68	45
5.	Contact mobile	5.67	33	5.00	30	3.50	32	4.71	32
6.	Proximity mobile	0.75	4	0.73	4	0.33	3	0.60	4
7.	Contact–proximity mobile	0.25	1	0.45	3	0.67	6	0.46	3
8.	Total mobile	6.67	39	6.18	37	4.50	41	5.77	39
9.	Mobile–stabile	2.42	14	3.09	18	1.83	17	2.43	16
10.	Causal	2.17	13	3.73	22	2.75	25	2.86	19
11.	Noncausal	14.92	87	13.00	78	8.25	75	12.03	81
12.	Horizontal[b]	7.17	57	3.91	50	3.92	52	5.03	54
13.	Vertical[b]	2.67	21	1.91	25	2.33	31	2.31	25
14.	Horizontal–vertical[b]	2.75	22	1.91	25	1.25	17	1.97	21

[a]$N = 11$ subjects in the multiplicative condition.

[b]Compositions whose spatial dimensions are ambiguous are not scored. Consequently, the dimensional means summate to less than the compositional means.

This parallelism between the two ranges further indicates that the differences in variability between the four- and eight-object class conditions is random.

Most stabiles are featured by contact between the objects composed. In the four-object conditions (Table 3.6, Row 1) the proportion is 65% and in the eight-object conditions (Table 3.7, Row 1) the proportion is 64%. The remaining stabiles are almost all featured by proximity in the four-object conditions (Table 3.6, Row 2); the proportion is 33%. Only 2% of stabiles are featured by both contact and proximity (Table 3.6, Row 3). In the eight-object conditions, most of the remaining stabiles are also featured by proximity (Table 3.7, Row 2); the proportion is 25%. However, contact and proximity accounts for 11% of stabiles in the eight-object conditions (Table 3.7, Row 3) which is higher than that in the four-object conditions.

The overall pattern of features marking stabiles is similar to the pattern at the previous stage (Langer, 1980, pages 329 and 330, Tables 13.5 and 13.6, Rows 1–4). Contact is primary while proximity is secondary; contact combined with proximity is negligible. This pattern does not vary by number of objects or class conditions. It is a constant of stabile construction that does not change in the development from stage 4 at age 12 months to the present stage. Indeed, it is a constant of stabile composing as early as stage 1 at 6 months (Langer, 1980, pages 62 and 63, Tables 3.5–3.8, Rows 1–4) which is continuous at stage 2 at 8 months (Langer, 1980, page 149, Table 7.5, Rows 1–4) and at stage 3 at 10 months (Langer, 1980, pages 235, Rows 1–4). The first sign that this constant pattern is subject to developmental change is that 11% of stabiles produced in the eight-object conditions at age 15 months are featured by contact combined with proximity (Table 3.7, Row 3).

Mobiles, like stabiles, are produced in the same proportion in the four-object (Table 3.6, Row 8, Column 10) and eight-object (Table 3.7, Row 8, Column 8) conditions. In this respect, mobile, like stabile, production is also similar to that of the previous stage. Furthermore, mobiles, even more than stabiles, are featured by contact between the objects composed: 79% of mobiles in the four-object conditions (Table 3.6, Row 5) and 82% in the eight-object conditions (Table 3.7, Row 5). Proximity features mobiles even less than stabiles: 18% of mobiles in the four-object conditions (Table 3.6, Row 6) and 10% in the eight-object conditions (Table 3.7, Row 6). As always, mobiles featured by both contact and proximity are least frequent: 3% in the four-object conditions (Table 3.6, Row 7) and 8% in the eight-object conditions (Table 3.7, Row 7). This pattern is like that at previous stages (Langer, 1980). Contact, then, is as much a constant of mobile construction as it is of stabile construction.

Mobile production, however, begins to change importantly in other respects at this stage. This is the earliest age at which mobiles are produced less frequently than stabiles. At ages 6, 8, and 10 months mobiles are produced more frequently than stabiles. At age 12 months mobiles and stabiles are produced in exactly equal proportions. Mobiles begin to be produced less frequently than stabiles at age 15 months in both four- and eight-object conditions.

Still, the differences in producing mobiles and stabiles are not statistically significant in the four-object conditions ($N = 9$, $x = 4$, $p > .05$, sign test), in the eight-object conditions ($N = 10$, $x = 5$, $p > .05$, sign test), and in the four- and eight-object conditions combined ($N = 11$, $x = 5$, $p > .05$, sign test). The decrease in production of mobiles at age 15 months as compared with age 12 months is not statistically significant in both the four-object conditions ($H = 2.17$, $df = 1$, $p > .05$, Kruskal–Wallis one-way analysis of variance) and the eight-object conditions ($H = 1.92$, $df = 1$, $p > .05$, Kruskal–Wallis one-way analysis of variance); but the decrease with age is significant for the four- and eight-object conditions combined ($H = 5.33$, $df = 1$, $p < .05$, Kruskal–Wallis one-way analysis of variance).

Moreover, it is possible to compare the decreasing mobile production with the rate generated at age 10 months for the four-object conditions which are the only conditions tested with subjects under age 12 months (Langer, 1980). Like the decrease from ages 12 to 15 months, the decrease in mobile production from ages 10 to 12 months is not statistically significant ($H = 2.08$, $df = 1$, $p > .05$, Kruskal–Wallis one-way analysis of variance). On the other hand, the decrease in mobile construction from ages 10 to 15 months is statistically significant ($H = 12.00$, $df = 1$, $p < .001$, Kruskal–Wallis one-way analysis of variance).

Mobiles–stabiles constitute 6% of compositions in the four-object conditions and 5% of compositions in the eight-object condition at age 12 months (Langer, 1980, pages 329 and 330). The proportion increases to 17% in the four-object (Table 3.6, Row 9) and 16% in the eight-object (Table 3.7, Row 9) conditions at age 15 months. The increases are statistically significant in the four-object conditions ($H = 6.02$, $df = 1$, $p < .02$, Kruskal–Wallis one-way analysis of variance), in the eight-object conditions ($H = 12.20$, $df = 1$, $p < .001$, Kruskal–Wallis one-way analysis of variance), and when the four- and eight-object conditions are combined ($H = 14.52$, $df = 1$, $p < .001$, Kruskal–Wallis one-way analysis of variance).

The developing pattern, then, is gradual but continuous decrease in proportion of mobile production up to age 15 months. This trend is coupled with gradual but continuous increase in proportion of stabile production up to age 12 months, followed by a leveling off up to age 15 months. Decreasing mobile production from ages 12 to 15 months is not compensated by increasing stabile production. Instead, it is compensated by an increase in the proportion of combined mobiles–stabiles. Mobiles–stabiles are either (a) a transitional form of composing from mobiles to stabiles or (b) a more complex developing form of composing than are mobiles.

Causality continues to decline as a feature of compositions. To begin with, causal relations between the objects composed in the four-object conditions actually increase from 35% at age 8 months (Langer, 1980, page 148) to 47% at age 10 months (Langer, 1980, pages 234–236). Composing marked by causality decreases to 34% at age 12 months (Langer, 1980, page 329, Table 13.5, Row 10) followed by a further decrease to 22% at age 15 months (Table 3.6, Row 10). The overall percentage decrease in causal compositions is 13% from ages 10 to 12 months and 12% from ages 12 to 15 months. Still, the decline is gradual since the decrease from ages 12 to 15 months is not statistically significant ($H = 1.76$, $df = 1$, $p > .05$, Kruskal–Wallis one-way analysis of variance) while the decrease from ages 10 to 12 months is statistically significant ($H = 5.60$, $df = 1$, $p < .02$, Kruskal–Wallis one-way analysis of variance).

Similarly, there is a gradual, but not statistically significant, decrease in generating causal compositions in the eight-object conditions. Eight-object conditions were tested only beginning with subjects at age 12 months. One-fourth of compositions in the eight-object conditions are causal at age 12 months (Langer, 1980, page 330, Table 13.6, Rows 10 and 11) while only one-fifth are causal at age 15 months (Table 3.7, Rows 10 and 11).

It should not be overlooked that causal compositions are a subset of mobiles, since causal relations between objects are kinetic, while not all mobile relations between objects are causal. The development of causal mobiles is partly different from that of mobiles in general. Causal as well as other mobiles gradually decrease in frequency from ages 6 to 15 months. Only causal mobiles diverge from this ontogenetic trend at one age point (i.e., at age 10 months the proportion of causal compositions increases).

Most compositions continue to be constructed in the horizontal dimension. As at age 12 months (Langer, 1980, pages 329 and 330, Tables 13.5 and 13.6, Row 12), at age 15 months the proportion does not vary as a function of the number of objects (Tables 3.6 and 3.7, Row 12). Compositions constructed in the vertical dimension continue to be generated second most frequently (Tables 3.6 and 3.7, Row 13) as they are at age 12 months (Langer, 1980, pages 329 and 330, Tables 13.5 and 13.6, Row 13). Furthermore, compositions constructed in both horizontal and vertical dimensions are still generated least frequently (Tables 3.6 and 3.7); but the proportions are no longer negligible. In the four-object conditions the increase is almost fourfold from ages 12 to 15 months; and in the eight-object conditions the increase is almost twofold. Nevertheless neither increase is statistically significant although the increase in the four-object conditions approaches significance ($H = 3.31$, $df = 1$, $p < .10$, Kruskal–Wallis one-way analysis of variance).

V. Increase in Consecutive and Contemporaneous Compositions

Compositions constructed in temporal isolation from each other continue to decline. The main decrease is in the four-object conditions from their high of about one-third isolated compositions at ages 6 and 8 months (Langer, 1980, pages 75 and 152). Isolated constructions first decrease at age 10 months to about one-sixth of all compositions (Langer, 1980, page 238) but then increase to about one-fourth at age 12 months (Langer, 1980, page 336) before decreasing again to about one-sixth of infants' productions at age 15 months (Table 3.8, Row 1). The decrease of 8% in generating isolated compositions from ages 12 to 15 months is statistically significant (Mann–Whitney $U = 39$, $p = .05$).

Isolated compositions are generated least frequently in the eight-object conditions. They constitute one-tenth of infants' productions (Table 3.8, Row 5). This proportion is almost equal to that of isolated compositions generated at age 12 months (Langer, 1980, page 336). At that age, too, they are generated less frequently in the eight-object than in the four-object conditions, and they constitute about one-tenth of infants' production.

Consecutive compositions continue to be generated most frequently (Table 3.8, Rows 2 and 6) as they are at all previous ages beginning at least at age 6 months (Langer, 1980). Consecutive compositions increase 8% from ages 12 to 15 months in the four-object conditions. This is precisely the proportion that isolate compositions decrease in this age span. Thus, the decrease with age in production of isolate compositions is compensated by an increase in consecutive compositions. On the other hand, consecutive compositions decrease 5% from ages 12 to 15 months in the eight-object conditions.

The upshot is that the proportion of compositions constructed in partial temporal overlap or in simultaneity does not change from ages 12 to 15 months in the four-object conditions. Their total proportion remains only 5% (Table 3.8, Rows 3 and 4). On the other hand, their total proportion increases from 10% at age 12 months (Langer, 1980, page 336, Table 14.1, Rows 7 and 8) to 17% at age 15 months (Table 3.8, Rows 7 and 8) in the eight-object conditions. This increase of 7% with age is statistically significant (Mann–Whitney $U = 29$, $p = .01$). One-sixth of compositions are generated in partial temporal overlap or simultaneously in the eight-object conditions (Table 3.8, Rows 7 and 8). For the first time contemporaneous compositions exceed the production of isolate compositions which only constitute one-tenth of infants' constructions in the eight-object conditions (Table 3.8, Row 5).

These proportions are measures of infants' combinativity operations. That is, they measure the construction of two compositions of objects generated at the same time or in partial temporal overlap. They also measure two compositions of objects not necessarily constructed contemporaneously but which are subsequently transformed in relation to each other and contemporaneously.

These proportions do not simply measure the products of infants' constructions. They do not measure the temporal relations between compositions produced in isolation or consecutively but those that coexist without being transformed in relation to each other. Such measures are not used because they are fundamentally ambiguous. While compositions may coexist objectively in time,

TABLE 3.8
Spontaneous Phase I: Temporal Relations between Compositions at Age 15 Months

	Class conditions									
	Semicontrol[a]		Additive		Multiplicative[a,b]		Disjoint		Total	
	$\bar{X}$ 1	% 2	$\bar{X}$ 3	% 4	$\bar{X}$ 5	% 6	$\bar{X}$ 7	% 8	$\bar{X}$ 9	% 10
Four-object condition:										
1. Isolate	0.90	6	2.08	28	1.40	15	1.83	23	1.59	17
2. Consecutive	13.10	91	4.58	62	7.40	79	5.83	74	7.50	78
3. Partially overlapping	0.40	3	0.67	9	0.40	4	0.00	0	0.36	4
4. Simultaneous	0.00	0	0.00	0	0.20	2	0.17	2	0.09	1
Eight-object condition:										
5. Isolate			0.75	4	1.64	10	2.00	18	1.46	10
6. Consecutive			14.00	82	10.45	62	8.00	73	10.83	73
7. Partially overlapping			1.33	8	3.91	23	0.83	8	1.97	13
8. Simultaneous			1.00	6	0.73	4	0.17	2	0.63	4

[a]N = 10 subjects in the control and multiplicative, four-object conditions.
[b]N = 11 subjects in the multiplicative, eight-object condition.

it is not always possible to determine whether they are also related in infants' transactions. Once constructed, compositions of objects may or may not continue to exist as far as the generating infants are concerned. For instance, infants may consecutively construct a composition on their left and a composition on their right. After that they may never transact with one of the compositions while continuing to transact with the other. Under these conditions there is no way, so far, to determine whether infants are preserving or discarding the composition which they ignore. They are therefore not scored as contemporaneous compositions.

While preferable because of both their objective and subjective precision, the measures used in this investigation are therefore conservative. They underestimate infants' contemporaneous constructions. Hence, they also underestimate the progress made at this stage in forming constant given elements for relational and conditional operations to be analyzed in Chapter 4.

Even if one opts for the more conservative measure of contemporaneous compositions, as we have in our analyses here, one overriding fact emerges. Infants progressively open up more possibilities for constructing new and more powerful cognitive structures. Autogenesis of more numerous contemporaneous compositions of objects produces an enriched source of constant given elements for constructing compositions of compositions. These elements do not simply supplement compositions of objects characteristic of previous stages. Compositions of compositions can also serve as the constant given elements for exchange, correlational, and relational operations. Their rudimentary exploitation by infants at this stage will be the prime focus, though not the only focus, of our analyses in Chapter 4. As we shall see, compositions of compositions are progressively used as the elements for constructing second-order conditional and relational operations such as equivalences upon equivalences.

4

Initial Relations upon Relations within Paired Compositions

Composing two or more objects into a configurational whole or collection is a fundamental combinativity operation that originates in the first year of infancy (Langer, 1980). By the present stage, as we found in Chapter 3, composing is marked by an invariant rate of production that is constant across varying test conditions (i.e., classes, objects, and numbers) and differing procedural conditions (i.e., spontaneous and provoked). Transitional stability (e.g., decreasing mobile without increasing stabile compositions) and determination of the properties of the objects comprising compositions is established by infants as long as their number is minimal (i.e., two or three objects). Still, set size increases a bit, as does contemporaneous composing of two very small sets.

Developments in combinativity structures are the necessary foundation for progress in relational and conditional structures. The present chapter examines infants' extensive constructions. This includes determining whether they are applied to two contemporaneous sets as well as one. It is expected, for instance, that not all three forms of exchange (i.e., replacing, substituting, and commuting) will be applied to two sets when these structures originate. Finally, we will examine infants' intensive constructions. Here, too, we will investigate to what degree consistent classification is applied to single sets and is extended to two contemporaneous sets.

The findings on extensive and intensive constructions are central to the comparative determination of structural development (between as well as within extensive and intensive constructions) and equilibration of logicomathematical cognition at this stage. Questions involved in this determination are taken up in a concluding chapter when we have available the findings on all four stages during the second year of infancy.

I. Initiating Exchange within Paired Compositions

Two structural developments, in particular, make it possible for infants to progress in their construction of exchange operations. One is the increasing set size or number of objects that infants include in their compositions and recompositions. The other is the increasing proportion of compositions and recompositions that infants generate in partial temporal overlap or simultaneously.

Increasing set size permits progress in first-order exchange operations that originate at least as early as age 6 months (Langer, 1980, pages 76–84). First-order exchanges comprise replacing, substituting, and commuting one or more objects within single compositions that are generated consecutively. The resultant products are quantitative equivalence of set sizes notwithstanding the transformations involved by exchanging elements. Thus, by increasing the size of their compositions infants increase the constant givens or elements that are possible to exchange in order to produce quantitative equivalence within single sets. In effect, they provide themselves with the necessary conditions for increasing the size of single sets that they structure as quantitatively equivalent across transformations.

Similarly, by increasing their production of contemporaneous compositions infants increasingly provide themselves with the necessary conditions for structuring exchange operations with two related sets. In this way, infants open up the possibility of also using two sets as the constant givens of or elements for exchange. The two sets may be quantitatively equal or unequal to begin with. Replacing, substituting, and commuting may be applied within two sets, between two sets, or both. The resultant products, as we shall see, are quantitative equivalence, nonequivalence, or indeterminacy between two sets.

Structuring exchanges with two contemporaneous compositions generates two novel cognitive developments that are not possible with first-order exchanges. On the one hand, coordinations upon coordinations become possible. Coordinations or transformations by exchange operations may be imposed upon coordinations or transformations by contemporaneous composing of two sets. On the other hand, necessary quantitative relations may be produced between two contemporaneous sets. Thus, these constructions generate exchange structures to the second power, that is, to second-order operations.

Second-order exchanges originate at this stage; they are not generated during the first year of infancy (Langer, 1980). It is also expected that at their initiation they will not yet be manifest in all three forms of exchange, that their incidence

TABLE 4.1
Number of Subjects Generating Exchange at Age 15 Months

	One composition						Two compositions
	3-object	4-object	5-object	6-object	7-object	8-object	
Replace	6	3	1	0	0	0	0
Substitute	2	0	0	0	0	0	2
Commute	5	2	0	0	0	0	1
Coordinate exchanges	2	1	0	0	0	0	0

will be rare and exceptional, and that their execution will be most rudimentary or primitive.

Replacing is still nothing more than a first-order structure at this stage (Table 4.1). It is always generated with single sets, never with two sets. Still, infants exploit their increased production of compositions that comprise more than two objects (Chapter 2, Section V) in order to generate first-order replacing with ever larger single sets of objects. The result is equivalences within ever larger sets of objects.

This development continues and enlarges the trend begun at age 12 months when 5 of 12 subjects systematically replace elements within three-object sets but not within larger sets (Langer, 1980, pages 337 and 338). Now a third of the subjects replace elements within four- or five-object compositions, as well as a half of the subjects who replace elements in three-object compositions.

No subject replaces elements within compositions comprising six-objects or more. Only 1 subject replaces elements within five-object compositions, and she does so only once. Only 7 of 12 subjects account for all replacing within three- or more object compositions. The remaining 5 subjects generate nothing more than replacement within two-object compositions, the minimum necessary to generate this protological structure.

Replacing within four-object sets is generated once only by two of the three subjects who produce this structure. The third subject, however, does so several times. As expected, the disequilibrium caused by difficulties encountered at this stage in structuring so many elements within a compositions is a generative source of development:

55.5. BH *try to hold Clover Rings 1, 2, 3, and 4 aligned together but CR3 slips out and falls to table*
57.5. RH *picks up CR3 and places CR3 against CR1, CR2, and CR4*
57.5. LH *grasps CR3 while holding CR1, CR2, and CR4*
57.5a. CR4 *flies out of hands onto table*
59.3. *looks at CR4, as RH picks up CR4 and places CR4 against CR1, CR2, and CR3*

59.7.   *LH finger tips grasp CR4 while holding CR1, CR2, and CR3*
61.5.   *RH releases CR4*
61.5a. *CR4 falls onto table*
61.5.   *LH holds CR1, CR2, and CR3*
63.   *RH picks up CR4 and holds CR4 against CR1, CR2, and CR3 held by LH*
                                                    (15SG, pages 95 and 96)

This is one of three replacements with four-object sets generated by 15SG. It is caused, at least in part, by the fragility of 15SG's structuring four-object compositions in his hands. His first two regulatory attempts at self-correction are not successful, but the third is. The result is three consecutive replacements in order to construct and preserve a four-object composition. The replacements are marked by active manipulation of all objects composed and by exchanging two different objects within the four-object composition.

Disequilibrium in structuring larger compositions, then, is the immediate cause of inducing more advanced replacement that applies to increasingly numerous sets. This hypothesis is corroborated by the performances of the two other infants who generate replacements within four-object compositions. Both infants' initial constructions are unstable such that the fourth object falls off or away. They rectify this structural imbalance by replacing the fourth object. This hypothesis is further supported by the finding that the only replacement with a five-object composition generated at this stage is the product of self-regulation directed at overcoming disequilibrium in structuring such a large set:

18.5.   *LH holds Yellow Circular Ring 2, Green Circular Ring 1, Yellow Circular Ring 1, and Yellow Cross Ring 1 aligned*
18.5.   *RH, holding Green Cross Ring 2, moves toward center and grasps YCR2, GCR1, YCR1, and YCrR1 by inserting fingers through the centers of all five rings*
20.5.   *RH holds five rings aligned through their centers*
20.5.   *LH releases five rings but YCrR1 sticks to LH as it pulls away from center and contact with RH*
22.   *LH moves back to center and transfers YCrR1 back to RH which ends up holding all five rings aligned through their centers*   *(15HK, page 18)*

The immediate cause of replacement is disequilibrium in composing a set comprising five elements. This disequilibrium causes self-correction of the "error" of withdrawing an object along with the left hand. The result is the most advanced, and rare, structuring of quantitative equivalence by replacement in a single set generated at this stage.

Symbolic accampaniments to replacements are infrequent and incidental. The most advanced form produced by any infant at this stage consists of asking "Whaz-zis?" about one of the two objects being composed (see the 15SG protocol fragment on page 52). Social play, on the other hand, may begin to have a more integral role in generating replacement. To illustrate, one infant (15EB) holds one ring in each hand and touches them together. After this, *15EB* gives one ring to her mother, playfully (almost teasingly) touches the ring she is holding to the ring held by her mother, and immediately pulls her ring away. Subject *15EB* repeats this playful routine once and thereby produces equivalence within a two-object composition by replacement.

Replacing is the direct product of the game *15EB* plays with her mother. The product, however, is limited to the most elementary replacing possible since it only involves producing equivalence within a two-object set. The same is true of those replacements that are accompanied by symbolization, such as that by *15SG*. This level of construction of protoreplacement has long since been out-stripped in nonplay contexts during the first year of infancy (Langer, 1980).

Neither symbolization nor social play, then, can be constitutive causes of developing replacement. If anything, the obverse may be the case. Replacement may be an ingredient instigating some features of symbol formation and the development of social play. For instance, the by now well-developed ability to replace within two-object sets may be an enabling factor in *15EB*'s playful game with her mother.

Substituting barely begins to become a second-order structure at this stage; it is generated by only one-sixth of the subjects (Table 4.1). One infant generates it only once, while the other infant already generates it three times. First-order substituting with a single set does not exceed compositions that include more than three objects and these, too, are generated by only one-sixth of the subjects. In comparison, one-half of the subjects at age 12 months already substitute objects within single three-object compositions (Langer, 1980, page 339). These data suggest, but are not sufficient to determine, that the origins of second-order substituting is accompanied by diminution or regression in first-order substitut-ing (see Langer, 1982b, for a structural development analysis of the relations between cognitive progress and regress). Whatever the proper interpretation of this apparent decrease in first-order substituting should be, it is only temporary and is fully overcome by age 18 months (page 166, Table 8.1).

Second-order substituting is marked by coordinative part–whole relations be-tween two compositions which produce equivalence, nonequivalence, or inde-terminacy across transformations. Two sets are coordinated with each other and transformed by substitution such that their initial quantitative relations are either preserved or changed by exchanging one or more objects.

While a decided advance over first-order substituting which does not exceed exchanging objects within single sets, second-order substituting is still transi-tional to binary substitution that develops at age 6 years (Piaget, 1952b). In fully-formed binary substitution two or more initial sets are composed. If the initial sets are quantitatively equivalent then: (1) substituting equal numbers of ele-ments between sets necessarily yields quantitatively equivalent sets, while (2) substituting unequal numbers of elements between sets necessarily yields quantitatively nonequivalent sets. If the initial sets are quantitatively nonequivalent then: (3) substituting equal numbers of elements between sets necessarily yields quantitatively nonequivalent sets, while (4) substituting unequal numbers of elements between sets yields quantitatively indeterminate sets unless additional logicomathematical operations are imposed, such as addition and subtraction.

At its origins, second-order substituting only (a) exchanges objects from one composition to another that (b) have unequal numbers of objects:

26. *RH takes Yellow Fork 1 out of Orange Cup 2 which also contains Yellow Fork 2 and Orange Fork 2 as a result of previous insertions*
27. *RH places YF1 on table, picks up YF1 by forkend, and places YF1 (handle-end first) into Yellow Cup 2 which also contains Orange Fork 1 as a result of previous insertions*   (*15ST*, page 40)

After constructing two unequal compositions of four and two objects (not reproduced in the protocol fragment), *15ST* takes one object away from the four-object composition and adds it to the two-object composition. The structure of this incipient second-order substituting takes the form

$$[(OC2 \cdot YF1 \cdot YF2 \cdot OF2) \& (YC2 \cdot OF1)] \approx [(OC2 \cdot YF2 \cdot OF2) \& (YC2 \cdot OF1 \cdot YF1)]$$
$$(4.1)$$

Unlike fully formed binary substitution, objects are not added and subtracted symmetrically (in parallel) and reflexively (by cross-over) between two or more-sets. Binary substitution involves subtracting elements from one set and adding them to a second set while subtracting elements from the second set and adding them to the first such that quantitative equivalence is preserved. Instead, one and only one element is consecutively subtracted from one set and added to another set at this stage. Thus, the exchange is asymmetrical (not parallel) and irreflexive (one-way).

The two compositions are unequal in number (i.e., 4-to-2) to begin with. Then *15ST* substitutes unequal numbers of elements in them (i.e., none to the bigger set and one to the smaller set). By itself, such second-order substituting does not permit determining whether the product preserves the initial inequality between the sets or not. In this particular instance substituting produces two quantitatively equal sets (i.e., 3-to-3).

This transformation of unequal into equal sets can only be calculated by some additional logicomathematical operation (e.g., the function $y = 2x$) or, at a more elementary level, by some precursory logical operation such as second-order correspondence. In this regard it is worth noting that if *15ST*'s initial unequal binary (4-, 2-) element compositions are correlated then they are necessarily in many-to-one correspondence. Following unequal substitution they are transformed into one-to-one correspondence between two (3-, 3-) element compositions. Thus, second-order correspondences are adequate to compute the quantitative transformations brought about by second-order substituting (i.e., whether it results in quantitative inequality or equality).

It should not escape notice that neither the production of first-order substituting with single three-object compositions nor the initial production of second-order substituting with two compositions are accompanied by any symbolic productions, whether gestural or verbal. At its origins, then, second-order substituting evidences independence from symbolic or linguistic development. Indeed, the just developing transformation of first- into second-order substitution is well in advance of any comparable expressive development.

Commuting remains, with one exception, a first-order structure (Table 4.1). As at age 12 months (Langer, 1980, pages 342–344), almost half of the subjects commute single three-object compositions. In addition, a couple of subjects commute four-object compositions at age 15 months while none do at age 12 months. But their constructions are quite limited:

25. *LH places Yellow Circular Ring 2 on Yellow Circular Ring 1 held by RH, next to*
     Blue Circular Rings 1 and 2
26. *LH takes YCR2 off of YCR1 held by RH and LH places YR2 on BCR1 which is*
     next to BCR2.   (15PB, page 31)

While executed precisely, this four-object horizontal–vertical recomposition merely commutes the vertical part of this whole by a single simple transformation.

Relatively complex commuting three-object compositions is progressively coregulated:

56.3. *RH loops Yellow Cross Ring 4 around ends of Yellow Cross Rings 2 and 3 held*
       by LH
57.7. *LH adjusts YCR2 and 3 to YCR4 held by RH by LH pushing YCR2 and 3 into*
       hole of YCR4 held by RH
58.   *LH removes and separates YCR2 and 3 from YCR4 held in RH*
59.   *BH join and clap YCR2 and 3 together, so that the three objects are stacked*
       (YCR4 below YCR2) together in BH
60.   *BH rotate stack of YCR2, 3, and 4 back and forth in hands briefly*
                                                               (15NF, pages 4 and 5)

Tactile exploration of two rings follows their composition into a stack (prior to the fragment), and is in turn followed by tactile exploration of a third ring, YCR4 (just before the fragment). It is added to the two-object composition to form a three-object composition (Lines 56.3 and 56.7). The rings are adjusted to each other in order to encircle and insert the rings in relation to each other. Commuting by recomposing forms a three-object stack (Lines 59 and 60) which requires fairly precise adjustment of the rings to each other and which elaborates upon the initial two-object stack composition.

First-order commuting of three- and four-object compositions is not accompanied by any symbolic or linguistic expression. With the exceptions noted when discussing replacing, this is the consistent pattern marking exchange proto-operations at this stage. The best evidence is that they are autonomous cognitive developments that are independent from symbolic and linguistic developments.

One subject only generates the bare rudiments of second-order commuting and does so only once. Two two-object stabiles are constructed by subject *15JC*. While the left hand places a doll behind a ring in the first composition the right hand holds another doll in preparation. Then the right hand places this doll to the left side of a ring to form the second composition. Upon visually monitoring the second composition, and perhaps to rectify the lack of spatial correspondence between these two numerically corresponding sets, *15JC* recomposes the second set. He moves the doll from the side of the ring to behind the ring.

The product is now in spatial as well as in numerical correspondence, that is, a doll behind a ring matching another doll behind a ring. An object in only one composition is commuted once only in order to maintain the quantitative equivalence between the 2 two-object sets. This is, then, the most primitive form of second-order commuting that can be constructed.

Coordinating exchange operations with more than two-object compositions just begins to be generated by one-fourth of infants at this stage (Table 4.1). Moreover, they are all restricted to first-order constructions with single sets. Their production is not accompanied by any symbolic or linguistic expressions.

II. Correspondence between Two Very Small Compositions

All infants generate minimal one-to-one correspondences between two-object sets or subsets (Table 4.2), and all but two infants do so more than once. Most (89%) of these second-order correspondences match two separate compositions to each other; only 11% comprise two matched parts of a larger singular whole. This development completes the initial structuring of minimal second-order

TABLE 4.2
Frequency of 15-Month-Old Subjects Generating Matched Compositions and Exchanges on these Correspondences

	Objects in each unit			Exchange operations		
Units	2	3	4	Replace	Substitute	Commute
2	12	1	0	0	0	1
3	0					
4	0					

correspondence initiated at age 10 months by 3 of 12 subjects (Langer, 1980, pages 251 and 252) and augmented at age 12 months by 7 of 12 subjects (Langer, 1980, pages 346–349).

The development at this stage is made possible by two prerequisite developments considered in Chapter 3. The first is the significant increase in the frequency with which infants at age 15 months produce four-object compositions. The second is the gradual increase in producing two compositions simultaneously or in partial temporal overlap. This second factor is corroborated by the temporal features of all the corresponding compositions generated at this stage. Eight percent are generated in temporal isolation from each other, 26% in immediate succession, 40% in partial temporal overlap, and 26% in complete simultaneity.

None of the correspondences between two sets are accompanied by expressive symbolic activity. Thus, symbolization is not an indicated third prerequisite development for structuring second-order correspondences—although it obviously does not constitute disproof by itself.

Equilibration of the initial structure of second-order correspondences is marked by two important features, decreasing lability and increasing class consistency. Ten infants generate second-order correspondences by matching stabiles, as well as any others they produce by matching mobiles and/or mobiles–stabiles. Only 38% of all second-order correspondences comprise mobiles and 5% comprise mobiles–stabiles; the majority (57%) comprise stabiles.

Furthermore, most second-order correspondences are now class consistent. Fifty-eight percent match two compositions or two parts of one composition that are unmixed in thier predicate properties, and 9% are partly unmixed. Only 33% are mixed in their predicate properties.

Second-order correspondences are necessary prerequisites for exchange operations to produce quantitative equivalences between two sets. Corresponding sets or subsets constitute potential constant given elements for generating second-order (exchange) equivalences upon (correspondence) equivalences. However, this potential is still not actualized at this stage, with one rudimentary exception (Table 4.2) which is presented and analyzed on page 78; it will begin to be actualized at the next stage (Chapter 8, Section I).

Constructive processes and products may (15JH) or may not (15SG) be identical when infants generate two-to-two correspondences;

   38.   *looks at Green Cross Ring*
  39.5. *RH places/holds Yellow Hexagonal Column flat on GCR*
  39.5. *LH places/holds Green Hexagonal Column flat on Yellow Cross Ring (both YHC and GHC are held ½ inch apart)*
  41.5. *RH raises YHC and touches YHC in mid-air to GHC, 1 time*
  41.5. *LH raises GHC and touches GHC in mid-air to YHC, 1 time*
   43.   *looks up at experimenter as beams broadly*   (15JH, page 10)

52.5.   *RH uprights stack of Red Cup 2 in Red Cup 1 on table about 1-½ inches forward*
from where they had been so that they are very near table edge

52.5.   *LH lowers Yellow Cup 2 tilted upright onto table*   (15SG, page 32)

These fragments reflect the range of second-order correspondences generated. That by *15JH* corresponds in all respects. The mappings (place and hold on) are the same, the outcomes (two-object stabile stacks) are the same, and the matchings are precise (parallel spatial placements as well as numerical equivalence between the two stacks). Spatial proximity between the two stacks suggests that they may be two matched parts of one larger composition.

The matched parts are constructed simultaneously (Lines 39.5). They are transformed simultaneously into one-to-one correspondence between the two held objects (Lines 41.5) which may or may not now be in two-to-two correspondence with the two objects remaining in close proximity on the table. In any case, both the matched parts (Lines 39.5) and their transform (Lines 41.5) are well-regulated constructions with which the creator is satisfied (Line 43). The predicate properties of the initial matched parts (Line 39.5) are unmixed in order (process) of construction but mixed in enclosure (product). The transform (Lines 41.5) is unmixed in both predicate order and enclosure.

In contrast, both constructive process and product differ in the two compositions generated by *15SG*. One composition (a two-cup stack) was prepared by *15SG* (but not reproduced in the protocol fragment) before it becomes part of the correspondence with the other composition which is generated in the course of constructing the matching. The mappings differ in form (uprighting *vs.* lowering). The outcomes have different spatial properties (a stack *vs.* an alignment): They are not two parts of a larger whole but are separate compositions, and they vary in predicate enclosure properties (the stack is unmixed and the alignment is partially unmixed). Still the result is two-to-two numerical equivalence.

Quantitative correspondence between two minimal sets, then, can begin to be detached from both its constructive processes and products (i.e., *15SG*'s construction), even though this is still not usually the case (i.e., *15JH*'s construction). Dual detachment of the constructive processes and products in second-order structuring of quantitative equivalence promotes abstracting the cognitive form from its embodiment or content. Equivalence can then become a representational as well as a presentational cognition.

Only one infant generates even rudimentary correspondence between 2 three-object compositions:

47.5.   *RH touches Red Cylinder 2 to ends of Blue Cylinder 1 and Blue Triangular*
Column 1

47.5.   *LH pushes Red Cylinder 1 into Blue Triangular Column 2 and Red Tri-*
angular Column 2

47.5a. *BTC 2 and RTC 2 move left, 1 inch*   (15JH, page 19)

One composition is a noncausal stabile while the other is a causal mobile. Both are mixed in their predicate enclosure properties. Still, they are simultaneous constructions; and they each involve one-to-two object relations. Thus, this construction also coordinates one-to-one (bi-univocal) with one-to-many (co-univocal) matchings. The result is initial integration of both forms of second-order correspondences. Such second-order co-univocal correspondences are rare at this stage since they require 2 one-to-many correlations which are also matched with each other.

Most co-univocal constructions still form first-order structural relations. But they involve increasingly numerous member elements, are progressively regulated, and may include a social dimension. For instance, an extended one-to-four correspondence relation between consecutively encircling one doll in all four rings is produced by subject 15VL together with the experimenter. All three possible and reciprocal forms of encircling are attempted by 15VL: (1) she tries to insert Doll 3 in Ring 1 at the same time as she tries to encircle Ring 1 around Doll 3, (2) she encircles Ring 1 around Doll 3, and (3) she consecutively inserts Doll 3 in Ring 3, Ring 2, and Ring 4.

This co-univocal construction is associative. All three spatial transforms produce equivalent results (i.e., doll in ring and ring around doll, ring around doll, and doll in ring) and are consecutively performed by 15VL. These three transforms exhaust the different ways it is possible to relate a ring and a solid object to form this spatial enclosure relation. Therefore, there is closure to the associative structure of this one-to-many correspondence.

III. Ordering Two Very Small Compositions

The development of ordered nonequivalence by protoaddition and protosubtraction lags behind the progress in structuring equivalence by correspondence, as it does during most of the first year of infancy. Structuring first-order series with single compositions approaches that of first-order correspondences by age 12 months (Langer, 1980, pages 357–364). There is, as we shall see, parallel development between first-order series and correspondences at the present stage. Structuring second-order series with two contemporaneous compositions, on the other hand, continues to lag developmentally at this stage. At each new level of structural complexity, ordered nonequivalence is a more difficult developmental attainment than is equivalence.

Composing single sets continues to provide the given elements for developing a wide range of ordered mappings. For instance, a fairly precise bidirectional (adding following by subtracting) continuous ⟨hit, hit harder, hit⟩ series is generated by subject 15RS banging on a stack of four rings he has just composed. A precise decreasing (subtracting) discrete ⟨5, 4⟩ series is generated by subject 15VL:

36.5.   RH *moves Spoon 1 toward midline and hits S1 against Spoon 2, 5 times*
36.5.   moves S2 toward midline and hits S2 against S1, 5 times
38.5.   RH *hits S1 on table, 4 times*
38.5.   LH *hits S2 on table, 4 times*   (*15VL*, page 60)

Both orders are as advanced as any mapping series generated by protoaddition and protosubtraction at this stage.

Single set composing also continues to constitute the elements for developing a wide range of orderings within the compositions themselves. To illustrate, in one sequence subject 15PB gathers two green rectangular rings and two red cross rings in her left hand and stacks them on the table as a four-object set, gathers up three of these rings in her left hand as a three-object set, picks up the fourth ring and places them in the experimenter's hand as a four-object composition, and finally takes back three of these rings as a three-object set. Thus, 15PB generates a bidirectional ordered series of ⟨4-, 3-, 4-, 3-⟩ element compositions and recompositions. Single element are added and subtracted systematically to generate this well-regulated, and partially social, ordered series within a single set.

The development of second-order nonequivalence between two compositions parallels that of second-order correlational equivalence (described in Section II). First, all second-order series comprise two separate compositions; none comprise two ordered parts of a larger single whole. Second, none are accompanied by expressive symbolic activity. Third, only 30% involve mobiles and 10% involve mobiles–stabiles, while 60% involve stabiles. Fourth, most (60%) comprise compositions that are class consistent in their predicate enclosure properties; 15% are partly unmixed, while only 25% are mixed.

One difference remains in their respective developments at this stage. While all infants generate second-order correspondences, and all but two do so repeatedly (see Section II); only seven (of twelve) infants generate second-order series and all but one infant does so only once. This difference implies that initiating second-order series is more difficult than second-order correspondences.

Still, constructing second-order series does progress at this stage. At age 12 months only 4 (of 12) infants generate second-order series and they all comprise two contemporaneous sets of ⟨two-, three-⟩ elements (Langer, 1980, pages 358–360). By age 15 months, most still comprise ⟨two-, three-⟩ element sets (e.g., 15JH); but rudiments of two sets comprising ⟨three-, four-⟩ elements are also generated by two infants (e.g., 15JC from whose protocol fragment nonrelevant intervening transactions are omitted):

12.5.   RH *holds side of Red Cylinder 2 on Blue Triangular Column 1 and Red Triangular Column 1*
12.5.   LH *holds end of Blue Cylinder 2 on Red Triangular Column 2, looks up at E and smiles*   (*15JH*, page 15)

78. LH *places Circular Ring 2 over experimenter's LH index finger such that all 4 rings are on experimenter's LH index finger, looking first at experimenter's finger, then experimenter's face, then experimenter's index again*

79. LH *places Block 3 on table diagonal flat between Block 2 and Block 1*

83. RH *places B3 into experimenter's RH*

84. RH *picks up Block 4 and places B4 on B3 held by experimenter's RH*

84a. *B4 falls off B3 onto table (experimenter collects B4 and replaces it on top of B3 in her RH)*

85. *looks toward B1*

86. LH *picks up B1 and places B1 on top of B4 which is on top of B3 in experiment-er's RH) experimenter holds B1 on top of B4 with fingertips and thumb)*

87. *turns to the left and looks toward B2, looks at experimenter's RH for a couple of seconds, looks at B2, looks at experimenter and then toward wall space in back of experimenter for about 6 seconds*   (*15JC*, pages 60 and 61)

The ⟨2-, 3-⟩ element ordering by *15JH* is definitive in comparison to the ⟨3-, 4-⟩ element ordering by *15JC*. Subject *15JH*'s performance is featured by (a) parallel but not quite identical constructions, that is, place side on and place end on, which produce two (b) simultaneous and (c) stabile compositions that are (d) mixed in predicate enclosure properties. Furthermore, *15JH*'s smiling may indi-cate some cognizance of his construction.

Different placements are first used by *15JC* to produce two apparently unrelat-ed compositions comprising four and three elements, respectively (Lines 78 and 79). But then a three-element composition is stacked in the experimenter's right hand (Lines 83–87). The final product is a four-object composition on the index finger of the experimenter's left hand and a three-object composition in the experimenter's right hand. While different in form, both compositions are sta-biles constructed on the experimenter's hands and both are unmixed in predicate class properties. Moreover, *15JC* looks at both the three-object stack of blocks and the remaining unstacked block but does not do anything with it (Line 87).

Adding two compositions together to produce one larger whole, subtracting a part from a larger whole to produce two smaller compositions, or both, is gener-ated by seven infants. This is no change from the rate at age 12 months (Langer, 1980, pages 362–364).

Adding and subtracting sets are each generated by essentially equal numbers of infants (Table 4.3, Columns 1 and 2). With few exceptions the sets added and subtracted are equal in number of member elements (e.g., subtracting two objects from a four-object composition to yield 2 two-object compositions). With one exception in which an infant decomposes one six-object composition into 2 three-object compositions, the two sets always comprise two objects each. This is the minimum required to generate these structures. Coordinating adding and subtracting two sets into reversible structures is unusual (Columns 3–5).

Integrating two compositions into one and disintegrating one into two com-positions are marked by both articulate and labile features. Together with the

TABLE 4.3
Number of 15-Month-Old Subjects Adding and Subtracting Units

Units	Integrate	Decompose	Integrate & decompose	Decompose & integrate	Total coordinated
Equal	3	4	1	1	2
Unequal	1	1	1	0	1
Total	4	5	2	1	3

lack of increase in frequency of production from age 12 months, this combination of features supports the hypothesis that this is a transitional stage in integrating and disintegrating sets:

36.   RH *uprights Red Triangular Column 1 on table, as LH holds Red Brushes 1 and 2*
37.   LH *transfers RB1 and RB2 to RH*
38.   LH *picks up Red Triangular Column 2 and uprights RTC2 on table parallel to RTC1, as RH holds RB1 and RB2*
39.   RH *touches handles of RB1 and RB2 to top of RTC2*
39a. *RTC2 is knocked to side*
40.   RH, *holding RB1 and RB2, lowers to grasp RTC2*
40a. *RB1 hits RTC1 and knocks RTC1 to side*   (*15ST*, pages 9 and 10)

On the one hand, *15ST*'s preparation of the two compositions she is about to integrate is relatively articulate (i.e., she composes two columns by parallel uprighting and she interrupts this procedure by transferring the other composition from one hand to the other). On the other hand, the integration becomes labile (i.e., she accidently knocks over both columns). The resultant product is therefore still quite impermanent.

IV. Expanding Classification by Similarities

The shift from predication by differences and random predication to predication by similarities is partially initiated at age 12 months, but only with very small sets of additive classes and not at all with multiplicative and disjoint classes (Langer, 1980, pages 364–367). The trend toward predication by similarities is extended to most class conditions during this stage. Still, the shift toward class consistent composing of very small sets is far from complete as we shall now detail.

Most classifying remains restricted to single sets as infants still construct about 90% of their compositions consecutively or in temporal isolation (Table 3.8). Thus, the production of compositions constructed simultaneously or in partial temporal overlap is still not large enough to be evaluated statistically for class consistency. Nevertheless, one portend of the developmental trend should be recalled when infants construct two compositions in quantitative correspondence (see page 79). Only one-third of their second-order correspondences comprise compositions that are not at all class consistent.

Predication in the additive condition, as it began at age 12 months, tends to be by single compositions comprising identical objects. In the four-object condition, the random probability ratio is two-to-one favoring composing complementary rather than identical objects. The observed order of handling (as defined in Langer, 1980, page 95) two or more objects in order to compose them into a set is in the opposite direction, that is, almost entirely by objects with identical properties (Table 4.4, Row 1, Columns 1–3); this difference is statistically significant ($N = 12$, $x = 2$, $p = .019$, sign test). The enclosure properties (as defined in Langer, 1980, page 95) of the objects composed are in the same direction but the ratio is not as strong (Row 1, Columns 4–6), and therefore only approaches statistical significance ($N = 12$, $x = 3$, $p = .073$, sign test).

In the eight-object additive condition, the random probability ratio favors composing complementary over identical objects by four-to-three. For order, the observed ratio favors identities by more than four-to-one (Table 4.4, Row 4, Columns 1–3); this approaches but is not statistically significant ($N = 12$, $x = 3$, $p = .073$, sign test). For enclosure, the ratio is in the same direction but much weaker (Row 4, Columns 4–6), and is therefore not statistically significant ($N = 10$, $x = 4$, $p = .377$, sign test).

Predication begins to be class consistent in the multiplicative conditions, but

TABLE 4.4
Spontaneous Phase I: Mean Frequency of Class Consistent Composing at Age 15 Months

	Order			Enclosure		
	Unmixed 1	Partly unmixed 2	Mixed 3	Unmixed 4	Partly unmixed 5	Mixed 6
Four-object condition:						
1. Additive	3.33	0.08	0.58	4.33	0.00	3.00
2. Multiplicative[a]	3.60	0.10	0.20	5.00	0.40	4.00
3. Disjoint	2.83	0.67	1.08	4.17	0.33	3.33
Eight-object condition:						
4. Additive	8.25	0.67	1.75	10.08	0.67	6.33
5. Multiplicative[b]	2.82	5.73	0.82	4.09	8.73	3.91
6. Disjoint[b]	4.75	0.25	0.92	5.92	0.42	4.67

[a]$N = 10$ subjects.
[b]$N = 11$ subjects.

only in the order and not yet in the enclosure properties of the compositions. In the four-object condition, the random probability ratio is two-to-one favoring composing complementary over disjoint objects. For order, the observed ratio is almost entirely by complementary objects (Table 4.4, Row 2, Columns 1–3), and is statistically significant ($N = 8$, $x = 1$, $p = .035$, sign test). However, for enclosure the observed ratio is only five-to-four favoring complementary objects (Row 2, Columns 4–6) and is not statistically significant ($N = 9$, $x = 5$, $p = .746$, sign test).

In the eight-object multiplicative condition, the random probability ratio is five-to-two favoring composing identical and complementary objects (mixed and partly unmixed) over disjoint objects (mixed). For order, the observed ratio is almost entirely by identical and complementary objects (Table 4.4, Row 5, Columns 1–3) and is statistically significant ($N = 11$, $x = 2$, $p = .033$, sign test). For enclosure, the observed ratio favors identical and complementary objects by more than three-to-one (Row 5, Columns 4–6), but is not statistically significant ($N = 11$, $x = 4$, $p = .274$, sign test).

Predication also begins to be class consistent in the disjoint conditions, but not fully. In the four-object condition, the random probability ratio favors composing disjoint over identical objects by two-to-one. For order, the observed ratio favors identical objects by almost three-to-one (Table 4.4, Row 3, Columns 1–3), and is statistically significant ($N = 11$, $x = 2$, $p = .033$, sign test). For enclosure, the observed ratio differential in favor of identical objects is much smaller (Row 3, Columns 4–6); yet it is still statistically significant ($N = 11$, $x = 2$, $p = .033$, sign test).

In the eight-object disjoint condition, the random probability ratio favors composing disjoint objects four-to-three over identical objects. For order, the observed ratio favors composing identical objects by more than five-to-one (Table 4.4, Row 6, Columns 1–3), and is statistically significant ($N = 10$, $x = 1$, $p = .011$, sign test). For enclosure, the observed ratio slightly favors composing identical objects (Row 6, Columns 4–6), but is not statistically significant ($N = 10$, $x = 4$, $p = .377$, sign test).

The overall developmental trend across class conditions is, with the specific exceptions just analyzed, toward increasing predication by similarities of individual very small sets or couples composed in temporal isolation or consecutively (cf., Inhelder & Piaget, 1964; Roberts & Fischer, 1979; Nelson, 1973; Riccuiti, 1965; Starkey, 1981; and Sugarman, 1983). Specific factors begin to emerge within this general developmental trend.

Order of combining objects into sets is more likely to involve similarities than is enclosure of the compositions. The ratios of unmixed to mixed predication are higher for order (Table 4.4, Columns 1–3) than for enclosure (Columns 4–6) in all class conditions (Rows 1–6). These ratio differences between order and enclosure are corroborated by the statistical results (i.e., as we have just seen, order is always as or more significant than enclosure).

Still, as they have been since at least age 6 months (Langer, 1980), order and enclosure are hardly differentiated properties; in the main they remain syncretically fused with each other. They correspond in 91% of the compositions where order applies in the four-object conditions (i.e., where two or more objects are directly contacted by infants in order to construct compositions), 86% in the eight object conditions, and 88% overall. These correspondences are only slight decreases from those at age 12 months (Langer, 1980, page 365).

A second factor in developing predication by similarities is the number of objects. Class consistent order and enclosure are as or more likely to be generated in small number (four) than intermediate number (eight) object conditions.

A third factor is causality. Only one-fifth of infants' compositions are causal (Chapter 3, Tables 3.6 and 3.7). Only 28% of infants causal compositions are unmixed in enclosure[1]; 12% are partly unmixed; while 60% are mixed. Thus, for instance, infants are more likely to use a square column to push a cylinder and a cylinder to push a square column than to use a square column to push another square column or a cylinder to push another cylinder. The reverse predicate features mark noncausal compositions (which comprise 80% of infants' constructions). Only 25% of infants' noncausal compositions are mixed in enclosure; 17% are partly unmixed; while 58% are unmixed.

These findings are consistent with the structural developmental hypothesis that predication tends in opposite directions in noncausal and causal combinativity. Class relations are progressively predicated upon combining elements with similar or identical properties. Class relations are progressively differentiated from causal relations. Causal relations are progressively designed to determine differences and efficient relations between causal agents and affected patients.

These analyses have considered spontaneous predication by infants. With specific exceptions already detailed, the overall trend is toward expanding spontaneous predication by similarities. This level of predication by similarities is not matched by infants' provoked predication in phases II and III of the testing procedure. The basic findings on containing in receptacles, imitating experimental modeling of sorting, matching additional objects to sets presorted by class properties, and reorganizing mismatched compositions have already been presented (Chapter 3, Section II).

The overall thrust of the results on predication generated by these evocative

---

[1]Enclosure is the optimum measure for these purposes since most causal compositions are generated by infants directly contacting one object only. Thus order does not apply as a measure of most causal compositions.

procedures is that they do not provoke predication by similarities to the degree spontaneously generated by infants at this stage. If anything, the provoked testing procedures evoke extensive operations, such as constructing two sets that are quantitatively equivalent by applying correspondence operations to the presentations, rather than intensive (predicate) operations. The manifest effect upon predication is that some compositions and recompositions just begin to unmix in class properties, but more are random or mixed. Intensive operations as much as extensive operations are autogenic interactions with the environment.

5

Elaborating Reversible Transformations of Malleable Objects

Transforming quasi-continuous (malleable PlayDoh or clay) objects includes unique constructions not possible with discrete (nonmalleable) objects, as well as constructions possible with both types of objects. Transforming combined (malleable and nonmalleable) objects includes constructions not possible with either discrete or quasi-continuous objects alone, as well as constructions possible with all three types of objects. It is possible, for instance, to compose two objects into a configuration or collection of two objects, whether the two objects are discrete, quasi-continuous, or both. Two quasi-continuous objects can also be composed into one object that unites the two into a larger whole. Only a discrete and a quasi-continuous object can also be composed into one combined object, which creates a larger whole conserving the differentiation between the different types of parts.

So far we have examined infants' developing constructions with discrete objects at this stage. Since these are equally applicable to quasi-continuous and combined objects it is not necessary to explore them in any detail. It should not be overlooked, however, that much, perhaps most, of infants' constructions with quasi-continuous and combined objects explore their unique transformational properties. Also, the main but not exclusive focus of our analyses will now be on infants' developing constructive interactions that are unique to quasi-continuous and combined objects.

I. Examining One's Own Transformations of Objects

Comparative inspection marks infants' interactions with quasi-continuous objects, as it does their interactions with discrete objects. Infants examine objects carefully before, during, and after transforming them. Furthermore, they carefully compare the transformed objects as long as the resultant set is very small:

24.   *LH swings Large Strand back
      and forth, 3 times, as watches
      LS closely*

24a. *LH lowers LS so that 2 inches
      of LS are on table and swings
      LS back and forth, as watches
      LS*

25a. *LS swings back and forth with
      the lower part of LS brushing
      against table*   (15NF, page 26)

25.   *BH swing Large Ring back and
      forth about 3 inches above
      table, as watches lower part of
      LR*

25a. *bottom part of LR swings back
      and forth, a few times*

26.   *BH pull LR apart into a large*   (M: *"I always thought it*
      strand (LS)   *was for later, I*

27.   *BH continue to move apart,*   *just never even thought—")*
      opening out LS into long strand

28.   *BH continue to move LS apart;
      LS splits into two parts
      (small piece s1 about 3 inches
      long in LH and large piece LS
      about 16 inches long in RH)*

29.5. *LH moves s1 in air to left*

29.5. *RH holds LS such that
      approximately 6 inches of LS
      lowers onto table, as looking at
      LS*

31.   *turns head and looks at s1*   (M: *"Yeah . . ."*)
      held by LH, while RH holds LS

32.   *LH fingers s1 a couple of*   (M: *"You call it clay."*)
      *seconds as looks at s1, while
      RH holds LS*

33.   *LH releases s1 on table about*   (M: *"Clay?"*)
      5 inches to left of left end   (E: *"Uh-huh."*)
      of LS held by RH

34. *LH grasps left end of LS*   (M: *"Clay."*)
35. *LH raises left end of LS about*
    3 inches above table while RH
    holds right end of LS
35a. *all of LS raises off table and*
    stretches out
36. *BH hold elongated LS for*   (E: *"Yeah, this would be*
    split second, as looking   *clay and some other*
    at middle part of LS   *stuff we'll have is*
37.5. *LH immediatedly splits off*   *PlayDoh."*)
    about a 2-inch piece (s2) from
    left end of LS
37.5. *RH holds right end of LS about*
    5 inches above table edge (as
    in Line 29.5), while new left
    end of LS lowers immediately
    onto table and then falls over
    table edge to right and dangles
    in air in front of table edge,
    as looking at LS
39. *looks at s2 held in LH as fingers*
    it a second, while RH holds LS
40. *LH releases s2 onto table about*
    3 inches to left of s1 and a
    little to back of s1, while RH
    holds LS
41. *LH grasps LS at its middle*
    while RH holds right end of LS
42. *BH break LS into two new*   (M: *"PlayDoh."*)
    pieces (RH piece LS1 is about 5
    inches long; LH piece LS2 is
    about 9 inches long)
43. *LH immediately places LS2 on*
    table in back of and perhaps
    partially overlapping s1,
    while looking at LS1 held by
    RH   (15SG, pages 50 and 51)

Before experimenting with the large strand, 15NF produces the strand by
breaking open a large ring (not presented in the fragment). She varies the way in
which she swings the strand and observes the resultant variations in deforming it.
All deformations are transient, rhythmic, and kinetic; some are also contingent
because they are partially dependent upon another object (here, the table) against
which the strand is moved. Though not reproduced here, 15NF's experiment
continues for seven more variants of swinging the strand back and forth. Each
transformation produces multiple transient and variant deformations in the

strand. Thus, while the effects are transient, their very numerous reproductions facilitate their cognition by their producer.

As with 15NF, only a small, but representative portion of 15SG's performance is presented. The fragment presented here begins with 15SG watching what happens (i.e., rhythmic deformations) to the bottom part of the large ring when he swings it by its top part. This observed multiple deformation is the end of a six-step series of experimenting with swinging and shaking the large ring in variant ways. Throughout, the resulting effects are transient rhythmic, kinetic deformations in the large ring which 15SG visually observes.

Repeated decomposing of the large ring by 15SG is also consistently followed by comparatively inspecting the resultant transformations (i.e., construction of couples out of a single object). Observation includes tactile as well as visual inspection of the products. They are composed into a stabile comprising small, medium, and large pieces, that is, an ordered series of objects (discussed in Section III).

While 15NF's and 15SG's experimenting produces deformations in the objects, much experimenting with quasi-continuous objects does not transform them any more than it does discrete objects:

6.   *RH moves Ball 3 closer to LH so that LH finger can touch B3, while LH holds Ball 1 and rolls Ball 2 out of hand*
6a. *B2 rolls across table*
7.   *RH rolls B3 out of hand*
7a. *B3 falls to table, but doesn't roll very far*
8.   *LH rolls B1 out of hand*
8a. *B1 rolls across table close to B2*
9.   *LH picks up B1 and rolls B1 to table*
9a. *B1 rolls to left near B2 again*   (15RS, page 65)

Two infants also just begin to demonstrate the transformations they have made. After deforming the large ball, subject 15HK shows it to the tester, then she visually and tactually examines it herself. While 15HK does this only once, the only other infant (15SG) who demonstrates his transformations does so several times. Subject 15SG also refers verbally to the objects he demonstrates. He repeatedly shows an object and asks "Whaz-zis?." However, he is the only subject who does this.

II. Instrumental Deforming

Deforming is the most frequent transformation generated under all test conditions (Table 5.1, Row 1). It extends infants' predominant tendency to deform quasi-continuous objects beginning at least as early as age 6 months (Langer, 1980, page 103). Furthermore, many deformations, unlike other transforma-

TABLE 5.1
Mean Frequency of Combinativity Proto-operations Generated by 15-Month-Old Subjects in Quasi-Continuous and Discrete—Quasi-Continuous Conditions

	One object			Three objects			Discrete quasi-continuous	
	Phase I 1	Phase II 2	Phase III 3	Phase I 4	Phase II 5	Phase III 6	Phase I 7	Phase II 8
1. Deform	6.75(3.58)[a]	2.60(1.40)	4.91(1.82)	4.00(0.90)	2.80(0.80)	7.64(2.00)	8.45(1.64)	4.36(0.82)
2. Reform	0.08	0.00	0.00	0.20	0.00	0.00	0.00	0.00
3. Break	0.17	0.20	0.27	0.30	0.20	0.64	0.36	0.45
4. Reconstruct	0.00	0.00	0.00	0.00	0.00	0.00	0.09	0.18
5. Decompose[b]	1.92	2.30	4.82	1.20	2.30	3.00	0.73	1.82
6. Recompose	0.17	0.00	0.00	0.00	0.00	0.00	0.00	0.00
7. Compose		0.30	0.54	0.50	0.10[0.10][c]	0.45[0.09]	0.00	0.00
8. Redecompose		0.20	0.27	0.30	0.10	0.18	0.00	0.00
9. Attach							1.80[0.64]	1.18[1.54]
10. Redetach							1.36	0.91
11. Detach							1.00[0.27]	1.54
12. Reattach							0.00	0.36[0.36]
13. Number of subjects	12	10	11	10	10	11	11	11
14. Mean duration	1 min 40 sec	1 min 5 sec	1 min 40 sec	54 sec	56 sec	1 min 50 sec	2 min 8 sec	2 min 7 sec

[a]Mean frequency of proto-operations involving multiple transformations are given in parentheses.
[b]The frequencies are necessarily underestimated because, when possible, subjects were not allowed to decompose by biting.
[c]Mean frequency of attempted but not sucessfully executed transformations are given in square brackets.

tions, continue to involve multiple mappings, such as extended squishing together of a ring-shaped object with a hole into a solid object with no hole.[1]

Infants' rate of deforming varies little as a function of the test conditions. The
range is from a mean of 2.40 to 4.05 deformations per minute in the three test
phases of the one object condition (Table 5.1, Row 1, Columns 1–3). The range
is from a mean of 3.00 to 4.44 in the three test phases of the three object
conditions (Row 1, Columns 4–6). In the combined discrete–quasi-continuous
condition, the range is from a mean of 2.06 in the provoked phase (Row 1,
Column 8) to 3.96 in the spontaneous phase (Row 1, Column 7).

Thus, deforming rates do not vary as a function of the number of objects with
which infants are interacting; the rate of productivity tends to be higher in the
spontaneous- than in the provoked-testing procedures. This pattern is substantially similar to that at age 12 months (Langer, 1980, pages 371–373).

Deforming is well-regulated and directed in most instances, as it is already
becoming during stage 4 (Langer, 1980, pages 369–371). These developing
features of deforming are amply illustrated in the protocol fragments presented in
Section I. They also illustrate how deforming is becoming a progressively self-
controlled and self-observed combinativity proto-operation. Much deforming, as
we have seen, is executed with precision and directed variation. Precise and
varied deforming requires that infants at least partly anticipate, reproduce, and
monitor their transformations of quasi-continuous objects. Otherwise these deformations and their varied reproductions would remain imprecise and haphazard.

Occasionally, infants' anticipations are expressed overtly:

1. *BH simultaneously touch edges of Large Rectangular Ring*
2. *looks up at experimenter, smiling*
3. *BH make simultaneous pinching motions over edges of LRR but without touching*
   LRR   (15NF, page 25)

Corresponding virtual or potential deformations are the first "transformations"
generated by 15NF, that is, before she generates any actual deformations. These
symbolic (i.e., gestural pretense) mappings are accompanied by symptoms (smiling and looking at the experimenter) of some cognizance by 15NF of what she is
doing.

Together with the gestural and verbal demonstrative behavior (considered in
Section I) that originates at this stage, these developments point to progressive
practical reflection by infants upon their deformations. Infants also increasingly
draw others into participating in their deformations (e.g., by extending a long

---

[1]For measurement purposes, multiple deformations are treated as single determinations since it is
not possible to determine how many actual deformations make up multiple deformations. Thus,
deformations are always measured conservatively.

strand toward the experimenter and then draping the strand over the experimenter's hand). A social dimension is thereby added by infants to their cognizance of their constructions.

Reforming remains as rudimentary as at age 12 months (Langer, 1980, pages 373 and 374). Reforming is generated by two infants only: once by one infant and twice by the other (Table 5.1, Row 2), and it is applied to single objects only. The internal part–whole relation of the object is deformed; then it is reconstructed by an inverse deformation producing a representational identity operation. Reforming is applied to malleable ring objects only; it is still never generated with malleable solid objects.

Contingent deforming is generated by all infants (e.g., by smearing or banging a PlayDoh object on the table top). The major advance is in instrumental deforming. All but one infant generate contingent deforming in the combined discrete–quasi-continuous condition by using a tongue depressor as an instrument for deforming PlayDoh balls. Deforming is generated frequently in this condition (Table 5.1, Row 1, Columns 7 and 8). Most are products of contingent transformations (i.e., $\bar{X} = 6.09$ in phase I and $\bar{X} = 3.64$ in phase II).

Tongue depressors are usually used to press on PlayDoh balls. This type of instrumental deforming involves asymmetrical mappings (i.e., pressing nonmalleable objects onto malleable objects). But it is also sometimes the product of symmetrical mappings (e.g., one hand pushes a PlayDoh ball down against the tip of a tongue depressor that is being pushed into the ball by the other hand). Here contingent transforming is generated simultaneously and reciprocally with both the ball and the tongue depressor being used as instruments to deform the ball only.

Contingent deforming just begins to include a social dimension. For instance, subject 15JC presses a PlayDoh ball down on the ball part of a combined tongue depressor and ball that the experimenter holds by the tongue depressor and extends to 15JC. The experimenter is used here as an intermediary in order to contingently deform the ball attached to the tongue depressor. This act requires 15JC to coregulate her transformation with the behavior of the experimenter in a precise fashion.

Clearly, contingent deforming is becoming regulated, controlled and directed. This hypothesis is corroborated by the other types generated at this stage. For instance, tongue depressors are used as handles with which to press or hit attached PlayDoh balls on the table, thereby deforming the balls.

III. Matching Deformations to Construct Congruence

Contingent deforming is increasingly used to produce corresponding transformations in single objects. Most contingent deforming involves repeatedly hitting an object on the table top. The mappings are consecutive but equivalent. The resultant deformations are equivalent but progressive. On the one hand, the deformations are reproductive because they are alike; on the other hand, the deformations are ordered because the cumulative effect is to progressively flatten the object. In this way infants consecutively generate and coordinate corresponding and ordered deformations of single quasi-continuous objects.

Mapping correspondence marks repeated contingent deforming. Each deformation reproduces the preceding, with the exception of the first contingent deformation. The entire sequence produces seriated contingent deformation of the ball since it constructs an order structure by increasingly flattening the PlayDoh ball. Equivalent units of deformation by correspondence are thereby coordinated with ordering these units into a series of increasing deformations.

Matched deforming of single malleable objects by infants is standard by now:

1. *RH carefully picks up Large Ball*
2.3. *looks at LB closely*
2.7. *RH rotates LB around slowly*
4. *LH grasps LB held by RH, as looks at LB*
5. *BH thumbs dig into LB making two indentions*　　　　　　(15JH, page 23)

Careful visiomotor examination plus identity transformations (rotations) of the large ball precedes 15JH generating one pair of corresponding deformations in the ball. Many other corresponding deformations are generated repeatedly and consecutively on the same part of the object and, thereby, also produce coordinate orderings. Others are generated simultaneously on different parts of the object:

10. *RH thumb and forefinger dig slowly into Ball 3, as looks at B3 closely*
10a. *two deep indentation marks in B3*　　　　　(15NF, pages 30 and 31)

3. *BH hold Large Ball as BH thumbs press into LB, indenting LB*
4. *BH lower LB to tabl. without release*
5. *BH thumbs press into LB again, indenting LB further*　　　(15EB, page 20)

Carefully matched indentations are generated by 15NF. She does the same with several different objects (not reproduced here). They are preceded, accompanied, and followed by close visual monitoring. Like 15EB's corresponding deformations, some of 15NF's matched deformations are also reproduced on the same two parts of the object.

Both infants also generate ordered increasing deformations (though this is only presented here in the 15EB protocol fragment). The corresponding deformations are simultaneous while the ordered deformations are consecutive. Thus, equivalent units are coordinated with ordered units of deforming. In addition, both infants generate coseriated ordered deformations. Hence, equivalent units of deforming are also coordinated with coseriated units of deforming. This coordination enhances structuring the relations between equivalence and ordered nonequivalence.

Corresponding deformation of two objects has become standard. This includes nine infants who do so by simultaneously transforming both objects. This act enhances comparative determination of the equivalent (intensive) part–whole changes produced in the form of two objects:

2. *LH dangles Circular Rings 1 and 2 together so that bottoms of CR1 and CR2 touch table*

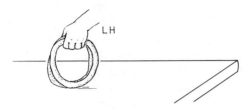

3. *LH lowers CR1 and CR2 to table*
3a. *CR1 and CR2 squash into oval shapes*

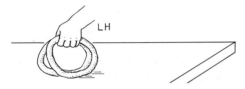

4. *LH releases CR1 to table but holds on to CR2*
5. *LH places CR2 on table next to CR1*

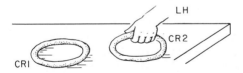

6. *LH picks up CR2 and places CR2 on top of CR1*

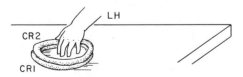

7. *LH picks up CR2 which raises CR1 since CR1 is slightly stuck to CR2*
7a. *CR1 falls back to table from CR2 held in air by LH*
8. *LH places CR2 on table next to CR1*

9. *LH picks up CR2 and replaces CR2 on talbe*
10. *LH touches CR1, LH picks up CR1 and places CR1 on top of CR2*

(*15PR*, pages 19 and 20)

One organ is used to deform two circular rings into two oval rings (Lines 2–3a). The deformations are progressively constructed by lowering the rings to the table. Having transformed both objects into oval rings, *15PR* proceeds to compare them by repeatedly placing them in spatial one-to-one correspondence with each other. Comparison of the corresponding deformations is checked by two spatial matching procedures. The oval rings are aligned next to each other, and they are superimposed on top of each other. Thus, spatial placement correspondences coordinated with protoreversible commuting are applied by *15PR* to her corresponding deformations of two rings. This type of proto-operational comparison between the form (intensity) of two objects marks the origins of measurement. Protomeasurement enables pragmatic yet systematic investigation and determination by *15PR* of the equivalence deformations she has constructed.

Protomeasurement is fundamentally imprecise and incomplete; furthermore, it is rarely generated. These deficiencies are to be expected at its initial stage, of course. Still, protomeasurement initiates structuring geometric congruence (i.e., spatial equivalence) by infants applying spatial correspondence transformations (i.e., aligning and superimposing) to their corresponding object transformations (i.e., matched part–whole deforming of two objects). The underlying and general structural hypothesis is that (spatial) transformations applied to (object) transformations construct equivalence—or here, congruent part–whole deformations (see Beilin & Klein, 1982, for further developments in spatial congruency during early childhood, and Piaget & Inhelder, 1967, for middle and late childhood). On this analysis, measurement is a derivative, second-order operation.

A variety of mappings generated by infants at this stage construct simultaneous deformations in two objects that are in one-to-one correspondence with each other (e.g., squeezing two balls together and simultaneously twisting a small piece in each hand between a finger and thumb). The most unusual mappings that construct corresponding simultaneous deformations employ tongue depressors instrumentally. Only two infants do this.

Constructing corresponding deformations in three objects is still rare. They are generated clearly by only three infants. Furthermore, only one infant correspondingly deforms three objects at the same time, while the other two infants produce them seriatim.

Ordered mappings systematically produce seriated deformations. Usually they are produced by protoaddition and, thereby, result in series of increasing deformations:

12. *RH hits Large Piece 1 progressively harder on table, 10 times*

(*15HK*, page 27)

11. *RH raises Circular Ring 1 about 1 inch off table, holding CR1 tilted upright, looking at CR1*

12. *RH holds CR1 about 1 inch above the table for a couple of seconds, as squeezes one part of CR1's rim between thumb and index*

12a. *CR1 flattens in that spot*

13. *RH extends CR1 away from self about 3 inches as opens fingers (CR1 still about 1 inch above table)*

13a. *CR1 stays stuck to index finger for a second and then falls onto table in space about ½ inch in back of and slightly to left of Circular Ring 3 with flattened part of CR1 visible*

14. *RH index finger presses down on top of flattened portion of CR1 and then raises about 1½ inches*

14a. *CR1 partially raises off table and immediately relowers*

14aa. *CR1 flattened further in already flattened spot*   (15AE, pages 119 and 120)

Ordered deforming may be contingent (15HK) or not (15AE). Both are now well-regulated and monitored.

Instruments also begin to be used to generate contingent protoaddition:

9. *RH touches Tongue Depressor 1 to side of Ball 1*

9a. *B1 rotates a little on table*

10. *RH pushes TD1 slightly down on top of B1*

10a. *TD1 only makes slight indentation in B1 and B1 rotates (so experimenter holds B1 in place for subject)*

11. *RH presses TD1 into B1 about ½ inch and RH pulls TD1 out of B1*

12. *RH presses TD1 hard into same hole in B1 and RH immediately pulls TD1 out of B1*

13. *RH presses TD1 ¼ inch into B1 but in a different place on B1*

14. *RH pulls TD1 out of B1*   (15NF, pages 77 and 78)

A bidirectional mapping series ⟨ touch, push, press, press hard, press ⟩ is generated by 15NF (Lines 9, 10, 11, 13, and 15, respectively). Additive and subtractive deformations are coordinated by 15NF. The additive mappings yield increasing transformations that are ordered from no deformation (Lines 9 and 9a) to a deep indentation (Line 11). The coordinate subtractive mapping produces a smaller indentation in a different part of the same whole (Lines 13 and 14). The final product of this bidirectional ordered mapping series is a big and a small indentation in the ball. Since these final two deformations are contemporaneous with each other they form a decreasing ⟨big, small⟩ ordered series that is readily susceptible to comparative determination by the infant who has constructed it.

Using instruments to contingently generate unidirectional ordered deforming is no longer unusual. However, each progressive deformation obscures the preceding deformation of unidirectional orderings. Thus, too, in the additive portion of 15NF's series, every time 15NF increases the size of her indentation she obscures its previous size. However, her construction is uncommon for this stage since she continues on to form a bidirectionally ordered series by deforming another part of the whole.

By this procedure, *15NF* partially detaches the transformational product (ordered ⟨ big, small ⟩ deformations) from the transformational process (addition and subtraction) by which she constructs it. At base, protological products are always functions of the mappings or routines generated by subjects. Detaching and preserving the products facilitates comparative determination; in this instance, the results are manifested by *15NF* comparing the ordered inequality of the part–whole deformations that she constructed.

In another sequence, *15NF* does not use an instrument and begins by generating corresponding deformations that produce equivalent indentations (see the *15NF* protocol fragment presented on page 96). She continues by increasing the size of one indentation:

13.   *RH thumb digs into indentation (produced in Line 10) in Ball 3*
13a.   *deeper indentation in B3 which sticks to RH thumb*
14.   *RH thumb slowly rises with B3 on it, as looks closely at B3*
15.   *RH forefinger flicks against B3 knocking B3 off RH thumb*
15a.   *B3 rolls across table about 3 inches to left*
16.3.   *RH thumb digs into hole in B3*   (*15NF*, page 31)

Here *15NF* starts out with equivalent and contemporaneous indentations. Twice she adds to the size of one indentation while leaving the other constant. By (a) beginning with contemporaneous equalities, (b) following up with repeated contemporaneous inequalities, (c) detaching the inequalities from the processes of their construction, and (d) preserving the inequalities, *15NF* generates close to optimum conditions for comparing (1) equivalent part–whole transformations, (2) increasingly nonequivalent part–whole transformations, and (3) the difference between equivalent and ordered nonequivalent part–whole transformations. This comparative activity is clearly illustrated by yet another sequence of deformations generated by *15NF*:

6.   *LH thumb digs into Large Ball, and LH thumb removes immediately*
6a.   *deep indentation in LB*
7.   *LH thumb digs into same indentation in LB as forefinger and LH middle finger squeeze into LB making two additional small indentations*   (*15NF*, page 34)

Ordered increasing deformations are generated by *15NF*. In partial temporal overlap she also generates two smaller deformations that are in one-to-one correspondence with each other. Thus, the final product comprises ⟨ big, (small: small) ⟩ part–whole transformations. Nonequivalences and equivalences are thereby preserved side by side and, as in the previously considered constructions by *15NF*, optimize comparing equivalences, nonequivalences, and their interrelations.

IV. Coordinating Decomposing with Breaking and Deforming

Breaking ring objects into strands or breaking solid objects into rings or strands is not yet generated frequently (Table 5.1, Row 3). Still, breaking is generated by most subjects (83%), with 50% generating breaking two or more times. Furthermore, breaking is now generated in all test conditions by some subjects. Most breaking continues to be applied to rings, as it is at previous stages. Now, 50% of subjects break rings only, 17% break solids only, and 17% break both rings and solids.

Breaking, as we have already discussed, may be preparatory to contingent transforming (e.g., 15NF's experimental deforming considered on pages 90–92). Contingent breaking also originates at this stage. As expected at its origins, contingent breaking is not yet generated by most infants; it is generated by one-third of the subjects only. Three subjects used an instrument (a tongue depressor) to break malleable objects contingently. Only one subject generates contingent breaking without an instrument. After placing circular rings on the experimenter's upright index finger, the subject's:

55.   *RH grasps and pulls Rings 4 and 5 against and off experimenter's finger*
55a. *R4 and R5 break in one place against experimenter's finger*   (15JC, page 37)

These transformations are unusual in at least two other ways. First, they correspondingly break two objects at the same time; this action produces two equivalent strands. Second, they involve another person in the breaking procedure. Instrumental breaking is applied to solid PlayDoh objects:

21.3. *LH rotates Ball 2 around*
21.7. *RH inserts Tongue Depressor 2 into B2*
  23. *RH pushes TD2 further into B2 held by LH*
23a. *TD2 goes through B2 and partly comes out other side*
  24. *RH raises TD2/B2 by TD2 and looks closely at TD2/B2*
  25. *RH lowers TD2/B2 such that B2 touches table*
  26. *LH grasps and pulls B2 off TD2 held by RH*
26a. *B2 is broken open into a curved slab.*   (15NF, page 84)

Two consecutive instrumental breaks are generated by 15NF. The first transforms the solid into a ring. The second transforms the ring into a slab. Both transform the object's intensive part–whole structure and are carefully monitored by the infant generating them. Neither affect the object's extensive part–whole structure; the object is not changed in either amount or number.

Reconstructing broken into unified objects remains rare (Table 5.1, Row 4). Reconstructing is generated by two subjects only, and only one does so twice:

100. *BH grasp and pull Ball 1 in opposite directions (to either side) such that B1 starts to separate in the middle, revealing the part of Tongue Depressor 1 inserted through B1; TD1 is positioned vertical flat during this action*

100a. *B1 is "opened up," revealing TD1*

101. *BH holds B1 "opened up" for a second*

102. *BH move extremities of B1 toward center again, closing B1 around TD1*

102a. *TD1 is once again concealed from view at its middle in B1 (15JC, page 104)*

After this, subject *15JC* repeats breaking and reconstructing the ball-around-the-tongue depressor in precisely the same way.

Initially *15JC* negates the intensive (form), but not extensive, part–whole structure of the object by breaking the ball open. She immediately inverts her negation by reconstructing the ball. Thus she affirms the intensive part–whole structure of the object and preserves its initial form as well as its solidity. Moreover, she generates this reversible structural relation between negation and affirmation twice in a row. In effect, *15JC* initiates a pragmatic yet regulated intensive identity operation between breaking and reconstructing.

Decomposing is progressively coordinated with breaking and deforming, thereby forming articulate and reproducible routines:

3. *BH break Ring 1 open at one place*

4. *BH open R1 out into an approximately horizontal and extended strand*

5. *BH split R1 into two strands (LH holds larger of two strands)*

6. *RH extends smaller strand (s1) to experimenter*   (15JC, page 31)

5. *BH break Ring 2 open at one place, as looking at R2*

6. *BH open R2 out into a strand (meanwhile experimenter is holding up two strands in front of subject)*

7. *as looking at R2, BH split R2 into two strands (LH holds smaller of two strands)*
(15JC, page 33)

Breaking leads to deforming which leads to decomposing, in precisely the same way in both instances. All her transformations are also visually monitored by *15JC*. Three transformations, then, are well-differentiated and integrated with each other to form sequential routines coordinating breaking with deforming with decomposing.

Decomposing continues to be the second most frequent transformation applied to quasi-continuous objects (Table 5.1, Row 5). The range is from a low of 0.34 decompositions per minute (in the discrete–quasi-continuous, phase I, condition) to a high of 2.89 decompositions per minute (in the one object quasi-continuous, phase III, condition). This range is not different in any significant way from that generated at age 12 months (Langer, 1980, page 372, Table 15.1, Row 5). Decomposing productivity, then, remains constant. Decomposing productivity during the test phase designed to provoke it lies well within the overall range (Table 5.1, Row 5, Column 2). Thus decomposing continues to be neither stimulated nor inhibited by experimental modeling.

Contingent decomposing remains unusual. It is generated by two subjects once only:

38. *RH pushes Tongue Depressor 2 into Ball 2*
39. *RH pulls TD2 out of B2*
39a. *a piece of B2 is pulled off and sticks to TD2* (*15ST*, page 60)

This is not the first time that *15ST* tries to use an instrument to decompose a PlayDoh object; but it is the only time she is successful.

Corresponding decomposing of single objects into equivalent parts is generated by four subjects; three of the four do so more than once. Invariably, the decompositions produce a small number of matched elements only:

20. *RH pulls Piece 1 (about ½ inch in diameter) up off tip protruding (i.e., part just tugged out) from Ball 1 held by LH*
21. *RH places P1 about 1 inch to right and front of Tongue Depressor 1*
22. *RH pulls Piece 2 (about same size as P1) off tip protruding from Ball 1 held by LH*
23. *RH drops P2 about 1 inch in front of P1* (*15JC*, page 99)

The decomposed parts grouped together are matched in size. Hence, the equivalence produced between the elements is in their extensity. There is no evidence of any attempt to also match the shape or form of the elements, that is, to also produce intensive equivalence between the decomposed parts.

Ordered nonequivalence by decomposing objects into smaller and smaller parts is generated by half of the subjects; all but one of these subjects do so more than once. Asymmetrical geneological series are usually still limited to producing small numbers of descendant elements from a single object; though intermediate numbers (ranging from about 7 to 11 elements) are sometimes generated:

42. *BH split Large Strand into Large Strand 1 (about 5 inches long) held by RH and Large Strand 2 (about 9 inches long) held by LH* (M: *"PlayDoh."*)
43. *LH places LS2 in back of and partially overlapping Strand 1 on table, while looking at LS1 held by RH*
44.5. *LH grasps LS1 at opposite end from RH, as looking at LS1*
44.5. *RH raises LS1 about 2 inches in air* (M: *"Clay."*)
46. *BH split LS1 into S2 and S3 (about 3 inches long)*
47. *LH drops S3 about 1 inch in back and right of LS2 as looks at S3, while RH holds S2* (*15SG*, page 52)

The asymmetrical geneology of descendant elements is visually monitored by 15SG, as is their preservation as a stabile composition. This infant is also the only subject who generates two asymmetrical geneologies and preserves them as compositions.

V. Negating Composing and Attaching

Recomposing decomposed parts remains rare (Table 5.1, Row 6) as it has been in all previous stages (Langer, 1980). In its precursory form recomposing reconstitutes the extensity but not the intensity of the initial whole:

44. *LH sticks Piece 1 back to Large Piece (originally a large ring) by using fingers and then thumb pushing P1 into LP held by RH*
45. *LH picks up Piece 2, while RH holds LP*
46. *LH thumb and fingers manipulate P2 into LP such that P2 becomes a part of LP held by RH*   (15RS, page 60)

Recomposing is still a decidedly precursory reversible structure. It barely begins to reconstitute the quantitative properties of the initial whole, and it ignores the predicate properties of the whole.

Composing objects not previously decomposed is generated by a bare majority of infants (7 subjects); and only one-third of the subjects do so more than once. Furthermore, composing is not yet generated in all conditions (Table 5.1, Row 7). The rate of composing is equivalent to that of the previous stage (Langer, 1980, page 372, Table 15.1, Row 7). In comparison with deforming and decomposing, then, composing quasi-continuous objects remains a decidedly subordinate combinativity structure, as it is throughout infancy.

Composing is not induced by experimental modeling (Table 15.1, Row 7, Column 5). Indeed, almost no composing is induced in the subjects by this experimental procedure designed to provoke it. Composing, like decomposing, is an autogenetic construction.

Contingent composing begins at this stage but, as is expected at its origins, is rarely generated:

12. *LH slams Rings 1 and 2 down on table*
12a. *R1 and R2 are stuck together in a clump R1/R2*
13. *LH picks up R1/R2*
14. *RH pulls R2 off R1 held by LH*
14a. *R1 is broken into a strand*   (15RS, page 61)

Negating composing by redecomposing is a reversible structure initiated at the previous stage (Langer, 1980, page 389). As was found at the previous stage, this reversible structure is generated more frequently than its reciprocal, negating decomposing by recomposing. Both forms of negation, however, produce nothing more than extensive identity. No attempt is made to produce intensive (predicate) identity, as is apparent in *15RS*'s performance.

There is a small increase in generating redecomposing at this stage. While still infrequent, five subjects generate redecomposing and three of these subjects do so more than once (Table 5.1, Row 8). The development is gradual since one-fourth of subjects at age 12 months begin to redecompose (Langer, 1980, page 389) and one-half of subjects redecompose at age 18 months (this volume, page 205).

Negation dominates infants' structuring of conglomerate discrete–quasi-continuous objects just, as we have seen, it does infants' interactions with quasi-continuous objects alone. Seven subjects attach (Table 5.1, Row 9) while eleven subjects detach (Row 11) conglomerate objects. Furthermore, six subjects re-detach conglomerate objects they have attached (Row 10), while three subjects reattach (Row 12) conglomerate objects they have detached. Sometimes these reversible structures are generated repeatedly (e.g., the *15NF* protocol fragment on page 99).

Both forms of negation are reversible but reciprocal structures. Still, the form that ends up negating the conglomerate structure of the objects dominates. Attachment negated by redetachment is more likely to be generated than detachment negated by reattachment.

Ordered attachment by protoaddition (*15JC*; see also *15NF* on page 101) begins to be structured at this stage, as does ordered detachment by protosubtraction (*15EB*). Nonrelevant intervening transactions are omitted in the *15EB* protocol fragment:

34. *LH raises Tongue Depressor 1 while looking at TD1, as RH holds Ball 1 in air*
35. *LH rotates TD1 around so that ungrasped end of TD1 touches against B1 held by RH*
36. *LH immediately inserts end of TD1 about ½ inch into B1 held by RH*
37. *LH manipulates TD1 side-to-side a little bit into B1 held by RH*
37a. *TD1 inserts about ½ inch further into B1*   (*15JC*, page 100)

6. *LH pulls Tongue Depressor 1 left several times but does not pull TD1 completely out of Ball 1 held by RH*
12. *RH pulls B1 while LH holds TD1*
12a. *B1 almost comes off TD1*
15. *LH holding TD1 raises B1 to chin*
15a. *B1 falls off TD1 and rolls onto table*   (*15EB*, page 46)

An ordered increasing series of deeper penetrations is generated by *15JC*. An ordered decreasing series is generated by *15EB*. The effort involved in generating seriated attachment and detachment plus the readily observable resulting part–whole transformations of conglomerate objects provide optimal conditions for infants to link attachment with protoaddition and detachment with protosubtraction.

STAGE 6 AT EIGHTEEN MONTHS

II

Sentence-Like Routines

6

Constructing routines or pragmatic propositions (e.g., using one thing as a subject with which to do something to another thing) characterized by anticipation, reproduction, and reciprocity just begins to progress to the next level or degree of semantic differentiation and integration at this stage. Infants begin to combine mappings (e.g., uprighting cups, inserting spoons, etc.) into phrase-like routines (e.g., uprighting a cup and inserting spoons into the cup) at the previous stage. Combining mappings into phrase-like routines begins to be generalized into combining phrase-like routines into simple sentence-like routines at the present stage (e.g., uprighting a cup then inserting and stirring a spoon in the cup followed by licking the spoon). As expected, in the beginning simple sentence-like routines are produced infrequently. Furthermore, they are limited to linear and minor forms only; they are not marked by any features of hierarchization.

Progress in combining routines includes substantial development in symbolization, whether linguistic (two and sometimes three word utterances such as "I have it") or not (e.g., pretending to pour liquid from an empty cup onto a doll). In general, symbolization in action still outstrips (e.g., is more complex than) symbolization in words at this stage. This continues the trend found throughout infancy so far.

Symbolic development has important consequences for constructing representational identity of objects. These representational developments plus developments in structuring physical (causal and spatial) and logicomathematical (correspondence and ordering) phenomena by mappings and routines are the foundations for cognitive progress at this stage. This includes progress in constructing more powerful first- and second-order cognitions.

09

I. Transition to Planned Routines

Infants generate planned constructions using all objects within brief time spans and small spatial frameworks. Planned constructions are applied to all objects only when they are limited to a small number. They usually involve two and sometimes three contemporaneous mappings that are well differentiated and integrated with each other. The results are relatively well-designed (a) coordinations between mappings and (b) relations between small numbers of objects. They have therefore been designated rule-governed routines (see Chapter 2).

This characteristic is illustrated by one sequence of well-organized routines that represent but a small portion of subject 18MK's systematic transactions. They are preceded and followed by many repetitions and variations on a basic theme. It consists of successively setting up two cups with one hand such that the other hand can then insert (i.e., place, move, hit, or press) one spoon into one cup at a time while simultaneously holding another spoon outside of the cup.

Integrated constructions, in 18MK's sequence, are prepared by pairs of mappings. A cup is uprighted with one hand while two spoons are held by the other hand. Then one spoon is inserted and moved up and down or pressed into the cup. All the while the other spoon is held by the same hand. The insertions are marked by semiconventional features to which we return in Section III. They are followed by gestures that analogize the actual "insertion" mappings, to which we also return in Section III. The sequence culminates in three contemporaneous mappings applied to all four objects. The same hand continues inserting (and removing) one spoon into (from) one cup while holding the other spoon outside the cup. At the same time the other hand uprights and touches the remaining cup.

From the beginning of the sequence, the mappings are all coordinated as well as differentiated. Uprighting, inserting, moving up–down, and holding are coordinated to each other in a planful way such that the three objects are pragmatically related to each other, even though uprighting precedes inserting and holding. At the end of the sequence uprighting and touching are generated at the same time as inserting and holding. The mappings and three objects involved in inserting and holding continue to be well differentiated and integrated. During their enactment inserting and holding are split from the other interactions of uprighting and touching the remaining cup. At the time of construction the only apparent link is that the interactions are generated simultaneously. Shortly thereafter it becomes evident that the subject has prepared the conditions for successive protological constructions:

34. *LH inserts Red Spoon into Yellow Cup, not looking, while LH holds Yellow Spoon outside of YC*
35. *LH moves RS up and down inside of YC, not looking, while LH holds YS outside of YC*
35a. *YC is knocked over* (18MK, page 7)

The results are successive and reproductive insertions of the same spoon into the two different cups, thereby forming reversible correspondences coordinated with reversible substitutions to be analyzed in Chapter 8.

Anticipation is becoming a well-established feature of two and three contemporaneous mappings with a small number of objects. Its initial source may well be the constructive extension of reproduction applied to new elements by infants. For instance, subject *18JHe*'s right hand picks up and transfers to the left hand all and only the four circular rings out of a randomly organized display of eight objects.

Both *18MK*'s and *18JHe*'s interactions are marked by anticipation. In both instances, as in those generated by all the other subjects at this age, it is still not possible to determine definitively whether anticipations are initially nothing more than extensions of reproductions. In most instances anticipations produced at this stage involve reproduction. Subject *18MK* is typical in this regard. The sequence presented above follows upon *18MK* first inserting a spoon into a cup which eventually causes the cup to tip over. This accident is rectified by *18MK*; she uprights the cup so as to reinsert a spoon. Thus, the causes of anticipatory behavior may include accidental, correcting, and reproductive components.

The possibilities of other, alternative or complementary, causes of anticipatory interactions should not be underestimated. Anticipations may be by-products of second-order protological constructions. Recall in this regard that *18MK*'s anticipations are generated in the context of coordinated and reversible correspondences and substitutions. Also note that *18JHe*'s anticipations are generated in the context of selectively grouping all the elements belonging to one of the two classes of objects presented.

Three contemporaneous mappings are generated with ease, as is evident in *18MK*'s routine. While still not generated as frequently as single and paired mappings, three contemporaneous mappings are produced with some frequency. Eighteen-month-old infants are able to generate three transformative actions (a) at the same time, (b) which are split from each other, (c) and yet are sufficiently interwoven with each other (d) to produce anticipatory protological constructions across small temporal durations.

Mappings continue to predominate over objects since mappings continue to be generated in rapid succession. The mappings-to-objects change ratio remains fundamentally unaltered. One-to-one ratios remain in the minority; mappings are changed much more frequently than objects. However, as is also illustrated in the above protocol fragment, the mode is many-to-many mappings-to-objects.

Mapping constancy is no longer unusual. The same transformations are applied successively to a small number of objects. Mapping constancy is becoming as frequent in nonexperimental as in experimental constructions. For instance, it marks *18JHe*'s groupings of all the elements belonging to one class in his left hand. Moreover, mapping constancy is no longer restricted to successive transformations. It is extended precisely to brief routines (e.g., *18JHe's* repeated "pick-up then transfer and collect" sequences). It is extended less precisely to somewhat longer routines (e.g., *18MK's* repeated "inserting while holding and uprighting" sequences).

II. Conventionalization of Symbols

Mapping combinations or routines still do not exhibit many features that mark fully syntactic constructions; for instance, they lack hierarchic organization. Yet routines are already marked by other features of syntax, such as interruption that is clearly and repeatedly evident in *18MK's* routines (see Goodson & Greenfield, 1975). Although rule-governed, routines are only protosyntactic because they are constructed by the individual and may (e.g., insert spoon into cup) or may not (e.g., pick up, transfer, and collect all objects) also conform to conventional or semiconventional rules of behavior (cf., Greenfield, 1978; Reifel & Greenfield, 1982). Moreover, their enactments are less permanent and probably much less constrained (or have many more degrees of freedom) than fully syntactic forms. In this way routines are more idiosyncratic constructions and less efficient as potential communicative systems than are fully syntactic linguistic forms. Consequently, routines are less amenable to the social feedback necessary if they are to be elaborated into fully communicative symbolic systems.

Conventional and semiconventional features progressively mark routines that are already generated at previous stages as well as at this stage. To illustrate, subject *18BB* repeatedly brushes her hair, front to back and left to right, with the front (bristle side) and the back of a brush, with the front and back of a mirror while observing this in a mirror, with a spoon, and with her right hand. Thus *18BB* interchanges conventional (a brush) and semiconventional (a mirror, a spoon, and her right hand) objects to brush her hair in a variety of conventional and semiconventional (e.g., back of the brush) ways. Another subject (*18PC*) tries to use a conventional object (a circular ring) as a bracelet in both conventional (around his left hand wrist) and semiconventional (around his left hand thumb) ways. At one point he marks his pleasure at and cognizance of his playful routine by squealing with joy. These interactions may comprise fairly long, varied, and elaborate routines (e.g., hair brushing).

Conventional and semiconventional features also mark routines that are new but may have been prepared for at previous stages (e.g., by nonconventional ways of stirring of spoons in cups). For instance, spoons are now used to pretend to scoop out of receptacles and to scoop off the table. They are also used to stir in and eat from a cup. Thus, subject *18PC* generates a routine that he prepares by inserting a spoon in a cup that he adjusts to facilitate the insertion. This action leads into stirring the spoon in the cup, taking the spoon out and licking its cup end, followed by retroactive appreciation (i.e., vocalizing "Mmmm."). After a momentary pause most of the routine is reproduced; the routine is repeated several times a little later in the task with added expressive features (i.e., vocal appreciation, laughing, blinking, and making a face).

Finally, conventional and semiconventional features mark routines that are, at least in part, new to this stage:

19. *RH takes out Green Doll in upside-down position from Orange Cup 2 which is the top cup in previously constructed stack of OC2/Yellow Cup 2/Yellow Cup 1/Orange Cup 1*

20. *BH turn GD right-side up in air and place GD down on table right-side up to the right of the stack of four cups*

21. *RH grasps edge of OC2, extracts OC2 from stack of four cups, brings OC2 close to self, and tilts OC2*

22. *looks in OC2 as BH hold OC2 tilted close to self*

23. *mouth makes drinking motion on OC2 held tilted by BH*

24. *BH withdraw OC2 from face and hold OC2 over table*

25.5. *RH tilts OC2 over GD as if pouring on GD, as smiles*

25.7. *LH picks up GD (one-half way through RH's pouring action with OC2)*

25.8. *LH holds GD closer to lip of "pouring" OC2 held tilted by RH*

28. *RH places OC2 upright on table, while LH holds GD*

29. *LH places GD inside of OC2*

30. *RH picks up OC2 with GD inside, RH tilts OC2 with GD inside toward face and looks inside*   (18BB, pages 33 and 34)

The routine generated by *18BB* is as complex and well-designed as any at this stage. It includes preparatory adjustment and observation, pretend drinking from a cup, pretend pouring from the same cup onto a doll and/or pretend giving a doll a drink from the cup, containing the doll in the cup, and a final observation of the doll in the cup.

Both *18PC*'s and *18BB*'s routines include large elements of pretense, as do many of the other routines sketched on page 112. While *18PC*'s pretense is more expressive, *18BB*'s pretense is more flexible. It includes transforming pretending to drink liquid from an empty cup into pretending to pour liquid from the same cup onto a doll (and/or giving it a drink) to possibly some pretense about a doll in a cup.

These routines are transitional between protosymbolization and true symbolization as previously defined (Langer, 1980, pages 5 and 6). Some, as we have just seen, involve playful pretense; this is one feature of constructing mappings of mappings. Playful routines (such as pretending to pour liquid from an empty cup onto a doll) begin to stand for or to represent real mappings (such as actually pouring liquid from a container onto an object). They are marked by transformational substitutions (e.g., an empty cup for a full cup).

Some playful routines just begin to include substituting objects with abstract features for objects with prototypical features (see Rubin, Fein, & Vanderberg, 1983, for a recent review of pretend play). For instance, subject *18BB*'s right hand brushes his hair, front to back, with one triangular column for 10 seconds while his left hand does the same with another triangular column. Playful routines even begin, on rare occasions and in rudimentary ways, to transform organs into substitutes for instruments (cf., Kaplan, 1968; Overton & Jackson, 1973). Recall, for instance, that *18BB* (on page 112) uses her hand as a substitute for a brush.

The development of rudimentary conventional verbalization is facilitated, at least in important aspects, by transposing semisymbolic achievements onto a new medium: language. According to this hypothesis, transposition of this elementary order requires little more as its mechanism than correspondence coordinated with substitution. The requisite level of protological coordination is already generated by stage 4 at age 12 months (Langer, 1980, Chapter 14); it is further consolidated during the preceding (Chapter 4) and present (Chapter 8) stages.

It has been hypothesized (particularly by Werner, 1948) that transitional rudiments of semisymbolic linguistic usage can be partially traced to analogical gestures that are vocal and onomatopoetic in form (e.g., Whaaaaaaaa" while tossing a racer onto the table, "Heyyy . . . eyyaaaaey" while hitting a racer, "Boom, boom" in conjunction with tapping one cylinder on another two times, and "Poo . . . poo" while rubbing the face of one spoon on another). Corroborating evidence may come from infants' practical reflection upon their symbolic analogizing:

31. *LH pushes Car*   S: "Vroummmm. . ."
                                                            (*18PC, page 12*)

6. *RH pulls Cylinder 2 toward self*
     on table in upright position
7. *turns to mother as RH holds C2*   S: "Vroum, vroum?"
                                                            (*18PC, page 79*)

In the second fragment, *18PC* couples (a) substituting a cylinder for a vehicle with (b) onomatopoetic representation of the event marked by a questioning tone. The obvious interpretation, that remains untested however, is that *18PC* questions the adequacy of substituting cylinder-in-motion for car-in-motion as a referent for the onomatopoeic symbol "vroum." If correct, this interpretation implies that infants at this stage begin to reflect upon their own linguistic activity (cf., Franklin, 1979; and Karmillof–Smith, 1979). The implication is that infants are beginning to be cognizant of their own symbolic functioning. As a consequence they may themselves now find questionable the adequacy or appropriateness of some of the symbolic forms that they are generating.

Still, at this stage, infants are hardly scrupulous in adhering to conventional appropriateness and usage. Linguistic convetion is subordinated to establishing correspondences between symbols and referents (irrelevant intervening transactions are omitted from the *18JHo* fragment):

33. RH *places Car 4 on her head and leans head forward with C4 on it*
33a. *C4 stays stuck in her hair*
34. *head leans forward further and nods,*   S: *"Dow, dow,"*
     2 times, with C stuck in hair
35. *RH pushes C off her head*   S: *"Cars."* (*18SO*, page 58)

49. *RH transfers Red Brush 1 to LH as*
     RH continues to hold Red Brush 2   S: *"Bruysh . . . bruysh."*
55. *RH drops Blue Square Column 4*   S: *"Bluy."*
     while holding RB2 (mother catches
     BSC4 and tosses BSC4 onto table
     behind Red Square Column 3)
56. *RH lifts BSC4 while still holding RB2*   S: *"Block."*
                                                     (*18JHo*, pages 72 and 73)

On the one hand, *18SO* generates precise two-to-two mapping correspondence between his symbolic productions ("Dow, dow") and his action referents (nodding twice). On the other hand, his vocalizations are only in imprecise correspondence with conventional usage. His symbolic production ("Cars") is also only in imprecise correspondence with his object referent (Car 4) since the name is marked plural while the referent is singular.

The transitional process by which infants transform imprecise into precise symbolic correspondence is captured, in part, by *18JHo*'s constructions. The symbols and referents are in precise correspondence. "Bruysh, bruysh" is in two-to-two correspondence with Brushes 1 and 2; and "Bluy" is followed by its corrected form "Block" in one-to-one correspondence with Blue Square Column 4. As far as conventional usage is concerned, "Bruysh" corresponds imprecisely to "Brush"; so does "Bluy" which corresponds imprecisely to "Block." "Bluy" is both (a) an apparent articulatory extension of "Bruysh" and (b) is immediately elaborated into the conventional form, "Block."

Protological correspondences involved in generating general representational relations continue to precede and outstrip conventional linguistic correspondences. On the present hypothesis, protological constructions (particularly correspondences and substitutions) are structural developmental sources of the significance that representational relations have for infants at this stage. Infants' protological constructions of representational relations provide the meaning to their symbolization and, as such, the basis upon which infants elaborate symbolic correspondences with conventional linguistic forms.

In many instances infants' individual verbal symbols already correspond precisely with conventional forms at this stage. Even then the representational range of their symbolization is more primitive than their protological capacities. Usually their syntax is still limited to one-word utterances, as previously reported (e.g., Brown, 1973) and as also found in this research. At most infants generate two-word, and rarely three-word or four-word, utterances that reiteratively or repetitively symbolize two, and rarely three or four, identical objects or events in one-to-one symbols-to-referents correspondences (see Sugarman, 1983). As we have seen, symbolic correspondence, to this limited degree, is not dependent upon conventional usage (e.g., *18JHo* and *18SO* presented on page 115). But it does begin to characterize infants' conventional speech (irrelevant intervening transactions are omitted from the second *18SO* fragment and from the *18KM* fragment):

20.	*RH tries to put Car 1 in LH but C1 falls*	S: *"Drop."*
21.	*RH picks up C1 and tries to place C1 in LH but C1 falls*	S: *"Drop."* (18SO, page 58)
34.	*LH picks up Blue Brushes 1 and 2 that are stuck together*	S: *"Brush."*
3.5.	*LH brushes bristles of Blue Brush held by RH with bristles of Red Brush, 3 strokes*	S: *"Brush, brush, brush."* (18SO, pages 40 and 43)
3.5.	*RH touches Spoon 2 to nose*	S: *"Nose."* (18JHo, page 47)
43.	*RH picks up VW4 while continuing to hold Racer*	S: *"Car, car, car, car."*
7.	*RH picks up VW4 and puts it in experimenter's LH*	S: *"Car-car-car-car."*
10.	*RH places Racers 3 and 4 on table*	S: *"Car-car-car."* (18KM, pages 23 and 27)

Even when coordinated within the same context, infant's precise symbolizations are invariably more primitive than their protologic (e.g.; *18KM*). Occasionally, their symbolizations are on a par with their concomitant protological constructions (e.g., *18SO*, page 58). The level of their symbolic activity never outstrips the protologic with which they are coordinated.

Most precise symbolic correspondences generated by infants at this stage, as we have just seen, still do not exceed reiterations. At most they are precursors of "pluralization" (Werner, 1948, following Stern & Stern, 1927). Reiterations precede pluralizations, if we follow the Sterns' characterization of pluralizations, since pluralizations are applied consistently to "different exemplars" of the same class while reiterations are not. Reiterations only name identical object properties. Reiterative naming is consistent with the level at which infants classify objects at this stage (see Chapter 8, Section IV). Moreover, the referents of reiterations include actions as well as objects. For instance, subject *18KM* repeatedly pounds the end of a racer on the table and says "Car-car-car" timed with the first three bangs. Taken together, then, the data are most consistent with the hypothesis that reiterations holophrastically represent event features rather than well-differentiated and integrated object and action features.

Symbolic correspondences negate, as well as affirm, referents (i.e., objects and events). They may be generated in response to a social request, both when someone tries to give things to the infant (e.g., *18JC* says "No, na") and when someone tries to take things away (e.g., *18SO* says "No . . . no . . . no . . .mine"). Verbal negations are also generated by infants in correspondence with self-initiated virtual (e.g., *18KM* says "NO,NO," as she touches an object to the experimenter's hand and then immediately withdraws it) and actual (e.g., *18JC* says "Take," as she takes back a ring she previously placed over her mother's finger) giving of objects to another and then taking them back. Finally, negation begins to be used by infants in planful, directive, and anticipatory ways when they decide to terminate their interactions and/or to undo some or all of previous interactions whether by themselves or by another (e.g., *18BB* says "No," as she pushes all the objects to the experimenter while looking at the experimenter).

Symbolic negation includes correspondences not only between symbols and referents, but between different symbolic forms of expressing negation. The most frequent manifestations are generated by corresponding gestures (e.g., shaking head side to side) and words (e.g., "No"). Occasionally, verbal negation ("No") begins to be coordinated successively with a possessive form of affirmation ("Mine") that serves, at the same time, to reiterate in inverse form the initial negation.

The most advanced possessive forms of verbal affirmation found at this stage are expressed by subject *18SO*. He begins by repeatedly generating two-word utterances ("Have it") that affirm his possessing some rings (by holding them close to himself). The experimenter expands these two-word utterances into a grammatical three-word utterance ("I have it"), which is immediately imitated twice by *18SO*. These verbal affirmations are generated while *18SO* is constructing continuous spatial correspondences between seven of the eight presented rings by pulling them all closer to himself. In this way his possessive affirmations may be direct but imprecise notations of the placement equivalences that he is constructing between these seven rings.

Symbolic negation begins by establishing empirical correspondences between symbols and their referents (irrelevant intervening transactions are omitted):

39.   *RH takes out all four spoons by their handles from*
      Orange Cup 2 (after having inserted all four spoons in
      OC2)

40. *looks in bottom of OC2 (quite closely—head bends,
     nose all the way to rim of cup) while RH holds all
     four spoons*   S: "No-mor."
41. *RH transfers all four spoons to LH which places all
     four spoons down to the right of the array*   S: "There."
                                                               (18BB, page 24)

The symbolic correspondences generated by 18BB are limited to empirical constructions. As yet, protosubtraction is not marked by logical necessity. Taking all the spoons out of the cup (in which 18BB had previously placed the spoons) is not logically determinative by itself. That is, subtracting four spoons from a cup containing four spoons does not necessarily equal zero spoons in a cup in 18BB's constructions. That result requires redundant empirical determination or verification by looking into the cup. Then the negation correspondence between a cup empty of spoons and its verbal symbolization ("No-mor") is generated.

This interpretation is corroborated by 18BB's productions a little further on (not reproduced here). Again 18BB checks to see if anything remains in the cup from which she and the experimenter have removed all the objects. Collateral corroboration is also provided by previous findings of redundant empirical verification activity by infants as young as 10 months old (Langer, 1980, pages 216 and 217). It is further provided by other symptoms that empirical verification without logical necessity is generated by infants at this stage.

This construction by 18BB is also marked by partial cooperative correspondence coupled with negation of both the experimenter's and her own moves. This behavior indicates developing flexibility and reversibility of correspondences and substitutions (analyzed in Section VI, this chapter, and Sections I and II, Chapter 8). Of importance here is to note that 18BB monitors and regulates the cooperative correspondence. These procedures are expressed in both gestural (smiling) and vocal–intonational ("Der?") symbolic forms.

At this stage all infants make reference to objects. Infants continue to generate personalized and pragmatic forms of reference to objects. The prime form consists of giving objects to another person and, sometimes, taking them back. Occasionally, giving still involves virtual rather than actual transfer of objects, or it involves sequential combinations of virtual and actual transfer of objects.

There is a decided shift, however, to conventional forms of referring to objects. Ten out of 12 subjects use conventional forms of making reference. Nine subjects generate gestural or vocal, that is, nonverbal forms of referring another person to objects. Two different gestural forms of reference are generated. One is a demonstrative form while the other is an indicative form of gestural reference.

The demonstrative form is the simplest because it is fundamentally pragmatic. Pragmatic demonstrations constitute simple preverbal reference by actually showing objects to another person. This pragmatic demonstrative is hardly detached from its objects of reference. It requires physical contact with and manipulation of the objects of reference. In this way, it necessarily conforms, in part, to the structure of the objects being demonstrated. For instance, showing requires molding of infants' hands in accord with the size of the objects shown and does not permit reference to distant objects.

Nevertheless, pragmatic demonstratives already constitute interpersonal communication. They involve taking into account the social context, the persons with whom infants are communicating. Pragmatic demonstratives certainly exceed self-reference to objects; they extend protosymbolization to include demonstrating to others the objects of infants' reference.

Gestural indications may constitute more complex forms of reference. At their most advanced level, gestural indications consist of pointing to objects or places while looking at them. Infants comprehend, as well as produce, gestural indications by pointing. As compared with pragmatic demonstratives, pointing is a detached form of reference. Pointing coordinated with looking need have no similarity to the structure of the objects of reference and no longer requires actual physical contact with them. This behavior makes it possible to begin to refer others to distant objects (e.g., Werner & Kaplan, 1963; Bates, 1979).

It should not be overlooked, however, that even the most advanced forms of gestural reference remain fundamentally protosymbolic. The reason is structural, that is, an endemic property of the gestural medium. Even pointing can never be fully detached from its objects of reference. This fact is made most evident by the lack of temporal detachment that marks all gestural indication. Pointing cannot be used as a socially communicative form of making reference to nonpresent, past or future, objects or events.

Vocal forms of denotative reference are also generated (see Werner & Kaplan, 1963). Some accompany gestural demonstratives (e.g., showing something while saying "Da."). Most accompany gestural indication (i.e., pointing at objects) and are more or less intelligible to others (e.g., "Boila Mama," "Ba," "Da," and "Thas thus"). Yet others (e.g., "Dey") are generated independent of gestural reference, although they usually accompany transformative constructions (e.g., pushing one object with another).

Vocal denotations, particularly when yoked with gestural reference, may be precurosry to verbal denotations:

120.	*RH replaces Red Spoon in Red Cup*	S: *"Dat dere."*
121.	*RH points toward experimenter*	*(18HS,* page 33)

Thus, in other contexts this same infant generates articulate verbal denotations that are the expected developmental derivatives:

22.	*Rh points toward the cabinet, while looking at experimenter*	S: *"That there."*
		(18HS, page 15)

Further evidence for the hypothesis that vocal denotations prefigure verbal denotations is provided when they are coupled to form two-word utterances (e.g., "Da brush."). Corroboration is particularly strong when the two-word utterances are also yoked with gestural demonstratives (e.g., saying "Da brush," while offering an object to the tester).

Nine of the 12 subjects generate verbal denotations. They take demonstrative forms (e.g., "See," "Here," "Look," and "Look it"). Most of these verbal demonstratives are coupled with gestural demonstratives (e.g., holding up and showing an object). Others, however, are coordinated with gestural indicatives (i.e., pointing). Some verbal demonstratives are already generated independently of any gestural reference (e.g., subject 18BB says "Look," while placing a spoon in a cup). Even though they are typically coupled with transformative constructions they constitute relatively detached communicative reference since they presume understanding on the part of another person without literally indicating the object of reference.

The most detached verbal references, generated by 5 of the 12 subjects, begin to take on protosyntactic form (i.e., "Whas zat?," "What's this?," "There," "That," and "Ooh, Mamma"). Almost all verbal indicatives are coordinated with gestural reference in order to draw another person's attention to the speakers' referents. The potential exceptions are either locatives symbolizing infants' spatial constructions (e.g., saying "There," while grouping four spoons together) or are questions about objects that they are inspecting comparatively (see Section VI) and to which infants are referring (e.g., "What's this?" while tactually examining an object). Still, the exceptional verbal indicatives are always coordinated with infants' transformative constructions of the referential object(s) when not accompanied by gestural reference.

References to and denotations of objects just begin to be coordinated with each other. Vocal and verbal forms are coordinated semisyntactically by some infants (e.g., "Da brush."). Other infants coordinate verbal forms semisyntactically (e.g., "Look it."). Both types never exceed the minimum of two-unit utterances necessary to coordinate semisyntactically reference with denotation. Moreover, the former type is limited to semiconventional reference (e.g., "Da"); and the latter type is limited to global, undifferentiated forms of denoting objects (e.g., "it"). Yet, even these most rudimentary syntactic forms are generated rarely by only a few 18-month-old infants.

Gestural reference also begins to be coordinated with verbal denotation. The most advanced form, which may involve the rudiments of a comparative, was generated by only one infant who pointed twice at a red cylinder and said "Red" each time. Reiterative pointing to one object is combined with reiterative naming of that object. This action results in the minimal level of coordinate pluralization possible—namely, once-repeated pointing to one object coordinated with once-repeated naming of the same object.

III. Expanding Representational Object Identity

Comparative inspection of and familiarization with the internal part–whole relations characteristic of single objects by individual and by coordinated perceptual modalities, such as touch and vision, is well regulated (nonrelevant intervening transactions are omitted):

21. *looks at one end of Triangular Column 2, as RH fingers the rougher grain on the unfinished surface of that end*
22. *RH slides fingers down smooth body of TC2*
23. *RH fingers surface of other end (apparently the subject notices texture differences between ends and body of column)*
26. *BH hold TC2 up toward one-way mirror, as smiles*
27. *BH hold TC2 to one-way mirror about 7 seconds, as looks at TC2 in mirror*

(18BB, page 73)

To begin with *18BB* carefully inspects, in succession, three main parts of one triangular column, that is, both of its rough ends and of its smooth body. Comparative inspection of these three parts is carried out by two perceptual systems, tactual and visual, in coordination with each other. It is followed by visual inspection of the whole object, which includes extensive comparative inspection of the mirror image of the object, only some of which is presented here; he then proceeds to do the same thing with two other objects.

Regulated comparative inspection of objects and their mirror images is generated frequently by *18BB*. This new feature of comparative inspection makes it possible for infants to begin to relate and distinguish real and virtual objects, that is, things and their representations, in another medium. Most subjects, however, still do not spontaneously compare objects with their mirror images. (But, then, the present research was not designed to elicit such representational comparative inspection. It is therefore not possible to make any definitive determination on this point from the present research.) Nevertheless, it is clear that infants are adding a new dimension to their constructive conceptions of objects. They are beginning to compare and coordinate objects with their representations.

Infants interweave regulated inverse spatial transformations of parts of single objects with regulated inversions of the whole object. Inverting parts (e.g., repeatedly spinning car wheels 360°) are coordinated with inverting the whole (e.g., repeatedly rotating a car 360°) via correspondence. The resultant is the construction of well-differentiated and integrated identity of single objects (irrelevant intervening transactions are omitted):

152. *BH rotate Car, as looks at C*
153. *LH grasps C as RH spins wheel of C*
153a. *C slips and drops to floor*
154. *looks down, then looks up at experimenter (experimenter returns C)*

155.3. *RH touches C*
155.7. *LH touches C*
  157. *RH picks up C*
  158. *LH spins wheels of C held by RH*
  162. *BH rotate C*   (18PC, page 9)

Interpolated within this sequence, *18PC* preserves in practical memory his construction of the object's identity. First, he searches after the car when it slips out of his hand. Then he reproduces his initial corresponding inversion of the parts (Line 158) and the whole (Line 162). Thus, all the conditions hypothesized as necessary to forming pragmatic object identity are coordinated within the same sequence of transactions (see Langer, 1980, pages 38–40).

The conditions necessary to representational identity of single discrete objects, at least reproductive representation, are thereby also beginning to be generated by infants (see Piaget, 1954). They are augmented by other self-generated conditions analyzed later in this section. Antecedents are generated as early as the fourth stage at 12 months when infants begin to construct reproductive representational identity of single quasi-continuous objects (Langer, 1970, pages 373 and 374).

Representational preservation extends object identity over increasing temporal durations and more numerous intervening transactions. For instance, between losing and getting back a block he just knocked to the floor, subject *18TT* transacts with three other blocks. This includes the construction of three minimal compositions. In between *18TT* alternates between looking for the block on the floor and looking toward the experimenter. He smiles in apparent appreciation when the experimenter gives him the block he was looking for.

Representational preservation is frequently expressed and communicated vocally (e.g., "Oh, oh," while looking after a cylinder that has rolled off the table to the floor). On the other hand, verbal expression and communication of representational preservation is still generated only once by one infant (*18SO*). Both the action and object of loss ("Dropped it.") and of retrieval ("Get it.") are represented by *18SO* in two related two-word utterances.

Representational preservation is also marked by planned loss, searching, and retrieval by another infant (nonrelevant transactions are omitted from the fragment):

23. *LH throws Brush 2 to left of chair (to floor), looking*   S: *"Ah."*
24. *searches (looks at) floor to left of chair until mother*
     picks up and replaces B2 to left of array   (18KM, page 62)

This routine is reproduced repeatedly by *18KM*. The result plus its observation is replicated three times by *18KM* keeping her manipulation constant. After this, *18KM* varies the manipulation a bit (i.e., from throwing Brush 2 to the left to flinging it to the left but behind her). She observes the spatial variation in the result and searches after the object. These protoexperimental features are combined with rudimentary aspects of social games. The routine involves planned hiding (if only momentarily) and seeking after an object. It requires participation of another to retrieve the object for the infant. This is a game-like interaction many infants already generate by stage 3 at 10 months (Langer, 1980, pages 212 and 213).

Comparative observation coordinated with identity transformations are extended to very small sets. A few infants simultaneously invert two objects while visually inspecting them. For instance, one infant (*18ML*) compares three different objects while another infant (*18JC*) compares two identical objects. Both infants begin by repeatedly and simultaneously applying inverse spatial transformations to a set of two objects while visually observing the set. Subject *18ML* continues on to visually observing a third object while applying the same inverse spatial transformations to it. Subject *18JC* continues on to replicating his comparative observations on one of the two objects making up his initial set.

Comparative observation of coordinate with identity transformations of as many as four objects are generated by some infants:

1. *LH lifts Blue Brush 1 and holds BB1 in air very briefly, as looks at BB1*
2. *LH lowers BB1 to table about 3 inches in front of where it was*
3. *RH lifts Blue Brush 2, holds BB2 horizontally flat in air in front of self, bristles down, as looking at BB2*
4. *RH rotates BB2 so that bristles are up and holds BB2 a little more, as looks at BB2*
5. *RH lowers BB2 onto table about 2 inches in front of Blue Triangular Column 1, as looks at triangular columns*
6.5. *RH releases BB2, as looking toward red brushes*
6.5. *LH releases BB1*
8. *RH rotates Red Brush 2 to horizontal position*
9.5. *RH raises RB2*
9.5. *LH grasps Red Brush 1*
11. *LH raises RB1 off table*
12. *holds both red brushes horizontally flat in air with bristles up, about 3 inches apart, with RB1 held a little lower than RB2, as looks at them very briefly*
13. *RH lowers RB2 onto table about 2 inches to right of BB2, as looks toward BTC1*
(*18TT*, page 20)

This sequence is particularly instructive because *18TT* selects all and only the brushes for comparative inspection. He selects them out of a random array of eight objects, where the other four objects are divided into two blue and two red triangular columns. This level of selection by predicate properties is typical at this stage (Chapter 8, Section IV). Relatively unusual still is the way in which *18TT* couples predicate selection with consecutive comparative inspection of all the objects selected. This includes inverse spatial transformations of one of the objects selected (Lines 3 and 4). Moreover, the sequence is interspersed with comparative visual observation of three of the triangular columns not selected (Lines 5 and 13).

IV. Progressive Covariation of Causes and Effects

Causal transformations are progressively differentiated and coordinated (non-relevant intervening transactions are omitted):

1.   *RH index finger touches Car 2 on its right side*
1a.   *RC2 moves a bit toward self*
2.   *RH index finger placed on top of RC2 and thumb helping at the back of RC2, pushes RC2 about 2 cm*
3.   *RH index finger pushes RC2 toward self about 5 cm, while thumb gets raised, and immediately pushes RC2 away from self about 5 cm with more force while looking at rest of array*
3a.   *RC2 rolls forward and turns 90°*
10.3.   *LH pushes Doll 2's head lightly*
10.7.   *RH reaches toward D2*
12.3.   *LH withdraws from D2*
12.7.   *RH pushes D2*
14.   *RH index finger pushes D2, then LH index finger pushes D2, then RH index finger pushes D2, and then LH thrusts D2 (all in rapid succession)*
14a.   *D2 rolls a bit away from self*
15.   *BH extend wiggling following D2 after D2 rolls away*   ′ (*18TT*, page 43)

Differential causal mappings (Lines 1–3a) are elaborated by *18TT* into coordinated causal sequences (Lines 10.3–15). The latter include simple sequential coordinations of differentiated and reciprocal causal transformations (Line 14). They culminate in apparent gestural reproduction of the causal effect (Line 15). Progressive control over simple causal sequences is thereby being established. Sometimes control includes symbolizing the causal event.

Progressive causal control is also manifest by advances in instrumentation:

14.   *LH pushes Cross Ring 2 away and against the other cross rings*
14a.   *CR2 pushes the line of the three cross rings closer to experimenter*
                                                         (*18JHe*, page 18)

37.   *taps Blue Cylinder 1 on top of Red Cylinder 1, 12 times*
37a.   *RC1 moves progressively further to the left until, on eighth tap, RC1 touches Blue Triangular Column 1*
37aa.   *on taps 9–12, RC1 pushes BTC1 to the left about 1 to 2 inches*
37aaa.   *immediately after twelfth tap, RC1 falls flat in front of BTC1 and rolls close to table edge*
38.   *LH grasps RC1 as laughs and looks up at experimenter*   (*18JC*, page 52)

Prior to the event described in the *18JHe* protocol fragment, *18JHe* constructed an alignment of four yellow cross rings. Then he removed one of them, Yellow Cross Ring 2, and used it as an instrument to push the alignment of the remaining three rings, thereby constructing an extended causal chain reaction. In addition to setting up the component parts of a causal chain, *18JC* controlled the effect of the dependent variable (Line 38). We will return to this latter feature of causal control later in this section.

Transitive transmission of motion resulting in causal chains are generated as early as stage 4 at 12 months (Langer, 1980, pages 296 and 301). At that age, however, infants only transmit motion to pre-established groupings of objects. Now, as we have just seen, infants also begin to set up all the component parts necessary to a causal chain that they then set in motion. Here one object is transformed by infants into an instrument, and one or more objects are transformed by infants into intermediaries. The result is immediate transmission of infants' causal actions, that is, transitive transmission where all the component objects in the causal chain move in an observable fashion.

A few infants coordinate immediate transmission within single sets (a feature of first-order functions) into two simultaneous and corresponding causal chains (a feature of second-order functions). When initially constructed, second-order transitive transmission is only applied to two pregrouped sets of objects. This advance, then, parallels that of the initiation of causal chains applied to single sets at stage 4 at 12 months:

3.5.	LH pushes Yellow Rectangular Ring 1 away and against Yellow Cross Ring
3.4a.	YRR1 pushes YCR away
3.5aa.	YCR pushes Green Cross Ring 2 away
3.5.	RH pushes Green Cross Ring 1 away and against Yellow Rectangular Ring 2 and then pushes it to the right
3.5a.	GCR1 pushes YRR2 away and to right
3.5aa.	YRR2 pushes Green Rectangular Ring to right (18JHe, page 18)

Subject *18JHe* works from the two alignments presented to him in the countercondition. Each hand grasps one of the two rings closest to him. With these two rings as causal instruments he constructs two simultaneous and corresponding causal chain reactions.

Such constructions are necessary prerequisites for infants to compare phenomena of immediate transitive transmissions with each other. They are essential in order to evaluate and, eventually, to determine which causal phenomena are physically equivalent and which are nonequivalent. In turn, such determinations of immediate transitive transmissions are structural developmental prerequisites to the eventual determination of mediate transitive transmissions. In the latter, mediate phenomena, the intermediary components do not move, but the instrumental and final objects in the causal chain are displaced in observable

ways. Understanding mediate causal transitivity does not develop until late childhood and preadolescence (Piaget, 1974).

Advances in controlled instrumentation are manifest in another important
way at this stage. Infants form progressively regulated, extended, and monitored
experiments:

2.	*RH picks Circular Ring 4 up, as looks at*	
	CR4	S: *"Look."*
3.	*as looking at Doll 3, RH moves CR4*	
	to the right quickly	
3a.	CR4 knocks Doll 4 flat such that D4	
	lands on Circular Ring 3	
4.	*RH hits CR2 leftward against D3*	
4a.	*D3 falls flat and rolls closer to subject*	
5.	*looks at D4 and then at D3, as holds CR4*	
6.	*RH hits CR4 leftward against Doll 2*	
6a.	*D2 falls flat and slides to the left*	
7.	*RH hits CR4 leftward against Doll 1*	
7a.	*D1 wiggles but does not fall flat*	
	(simultaneously with Line 7, experimenter	
	slides D2 flat into its approximately original	
	place)	
8.	*RH moves CR4 in air to the right and*	
	then immediately hits it leftward against D1	
8a.	*D1 falls flat this time and slides to left*	(18JC, pages 27 and 28)

It should not be overlooked that the protological groundwork for such controlled protoexperimental constructions is prepared no later than stage 4 at 12
months (Langer, 1980). By then all infants construct repeated substitutions within 2-element sets and one-to-many correspondences. The substitutions and correspondences characterizing *18JC's* performance certainly do not exceed this
protological structure. And, as we shall see in Chapter 8, substitutions and
correspondences are constructed at a more advanced level during the present
stage.

Progress in experimenting, such as that of *18JC*, inheres in infants applying
their previously prepared protological cognitions to the relations they generate
between independent and dependent variables at this stage. Infants now use one
object as a controlled instrument with which to replicate a causal effect on all
objects of a certain kind, as long as the set is small. These experiments are
marked by three general features. First, they are well-regulated. They are replicated several times in a row. They also correct or insure the intended results
when attempts are not successful (e.g., *18JC*, Lines 7–8a). Second, the causal
constructions are well-monitored. Infants observe the components of their causal
constructions before, during, and after their executions. Third, the major com-

ponents of the causal constructions are differentiated by their predicate properties (Chapter 8, Section IV). Typically, the instrumental object or agent is different in kind from the target objects or patients (e.g., 18JC uses a circular ring to knock over all the dolls). Thus, causal control is progressively imposed by infants upon both the independent (agent) and dependent (patient) variables of their causal constructions.

Instrumental control extends to reciprocal covariation between independent and dependent variables (for a more elaborate second-order causal construction see the 18JC protocol fragments on pages 179–181):

64.   RH *pushes Green Triangular Column 1 into side of Yellow Cylinder 1*
64a.   YC1 *rolls to the left (experimenter hits Yellow Triangular Column 1 into YC1,* YC1 *rolls toward subject)*
65.   RH *touches edge of YC1 with edge of GTC1 preventing YC1 from rolling further*
65a.   YC1 *is displaced slightly in opposite direction*
66.   RH *pushes GTC1 into side of YC1*
66a.   YC1 *rolls to left (experimenter returns YC1 using Yellow Triangular Column 1)*
67.   RH *touches GTC1 against YC1 to stop YC1 from rolling*
68.   RH *pushes end of GTC1 into YC1*
68a.   YC1 *rolls toward experimenter*   (18JHo, page 14)

Covariation, then, is expanded to instrumental differentiation. When the dependent variable (Yellow Cylinder 1) is stationary 18JHo uses the independent variable (Green Triangular Column 1) as an instrument with which to set the dependent variable in motion (Lines 64–64a, 65, and 68–68a). Reciprocally, when the dependent variable is in motion 18JHo uses the independent variable as an instrument with which to stop the motion of the dependent variable (Lines 65 and 67). Thereby, one of the factors limiting infants' structuring second-order functions at the previous stage (page 41) begins to be overcome.

Instrumental differentiation does not merely consist of segregated use of an object as a different causal instrument in different circumstances without relating the uses to each other. Reciprocal interweaving of the dual instrumental usages of an object applied to the same patient object marks the beginnings of true differentiation and coordination. In this way, infants begin to generate the necessary conditions for integrating their causal instrumental differentiations of independent variables. Correlatively, infants begin to generate the necessary conditions for integrating their causal differentiations of dependent variables, that is, they generate movement with nonmovement (or stopping) of patient objects. It follows that reciprocal covariation between independent and dependent variables can begin to be differentiated and integrated.

Reciprocal covariation marks the origins of protoproportions at the previous stage (page 40). The functions constructed are entirely pragmatic. Yet they are sufficiently detached from both particular mappings and objects to form precursory proportions, such as "Pushing is to Moving as Blocking is to Stopping." In this way, protoproportions are precursory to preproportions.

Protoproportions are functional dependencies established between as few as two objects. At a minimum, preproportions require the prior formation of two distinct functional equivalence classes, such as "pushing" instruments and "touching" instruments (Grize, 1968/1977). For purposes of making the distinction clear, then, we might call the protoproportion formed "instrument" and the preproportion formed "instruments."

Reciprocal interweaving (of "setting a patient object into motion" with "stopping its motion") is replicated by *18JHo*. This replication indicates that it is becoming a regulated causal construction. That is, *18JHo* successively negates each causal construction by a subsequent causal construction. Negation progressively marks causality as a general feature of experimenting at this stage.

Negating causal transformations is used by *18JHo* to construct successively inverse movement relations. Negations are used by other infants in order to construct successively inverse spatial relations (e.g., to knock over objects they have uprighted). Negation, then, begins to be generalized as an operation with which to structure various forms of experimenting.

While the conceptual structures generated include relatively complex constructions, such as causal negation of spatial relations, any accompanying symbolic expressions are most limited, for instance, to onomatopoesis. This limitation is quite typical; infants construct more complex cognitive than expressive structures. These findings serve to further support the hypothesis that cognitive development during this stage is not dependent upon symbolization. If anything, cognition greatly outstrips symbolization and serves to provide symbolization with some initial causal significance. The result is the formation of primitive causatives, such as an onomatopoetic form.

Causal affirmation is necessary to confirm the effect of an independent variable. Causal negation, on the other hand, is necessary to disconfirm the effect of an independent variable. Causal affirmation, then, must be coordinated with causal negation in order to make experimental determinations.

We have just seen how infants generate protoproportions by reciprocally interweaving causal affirmation with causal negation to produce controlled effects. At the same time, infants continue to generate impossible causal conditions which, as a consequence, meet physical resistance. The result is the negation of effects that they are trying to produce:

19. *RH places Green Cylinder 1 in horizontal*
     orientation on Yellow Cylinder 1 lying on table
19a. *GC1 rolls across table into subject's lap*   (18JHo, page 10)

55. *RH puts Red Car on top of Yellow Car and then*
     tries for about 15 seconds to pile RC and YC
     using BH holding them together

55a.   *RC and YC keep falling*
 56.   *RH picks up RC and*
       bangs RC on YC, about 10 times
 57.   *RH tries to place RC on top of YC*
57a.   *RC falls to lap*   (*18BB*, page 16)

 10.   *LH places Red Rectangular Ring 1 vertically on the*
       head of Doll 1 (as if to see if it could remain there
       balanced)
10a.   *RRR1 falls off*
 11.   *LH picks up and*
       places RRR1 on RRR2   (*18ML*, page 44)

 25.   *RH sets Doll 1 on its head*
25a.   *D1 falls over*   (*18ML*, page 45)

 43.   *RH tries to balance Doll 2 on top of Doll 1*
       for about 10 seconds (it does not work)
 44.   *RH lets D2 go on the head of D1*
44a.   *D2 falls over*   (*18ML*, page 46)

Resistance by the objects negates *18JHo*'s placing one cylinder on top of another. Object resistance also negates *18BB*'s balancing of one car on another. Subject *18ML* experiments with stacking (page 44 fragment), balancing (page 45 fragment), and combined stacking and balancing (page 46 fragment). Differential results are generated in the stacking experiment. Negative results are generated when *18ML* stacks vertically a rectangular ring on a doll's head (page 44, Lines 10 and 10a). Immediately afterward *18ML* generates a positive result by stacking horizontally the same ring upon an identical ring (page 44, Line 11). All *18ML*'s subsequent experimenting with balancing and combined stacking–balancing generates negative results.

Differentiation between possible and impossible dependency relations is barely initiated at the previous stage (pages 41–44). Striking progress is made at this stage but only when the objects stand in simple relations to each other (irrelevant intervening transactions are omitted):

 20.   *RH uprights Cylinder 1*
 21.   *LH picks up Cylinder 2 and stacks C2 on C1 (experimenter assists with balance)*
 22.   *LH picks up Rectangular Ring 1 and tries to lay RR1 horizontally on the stack—*
       RR1 dangles off the top at half-mast
 23.   *LH removes RR1 and places RR1 on table*
 24.   *LH picks up Rectangular Ring 2 and tries same maneuver with it but this time*
       holding on firmly to the frame of RB
 25.   *LH tries to lay RR2 horizontally on the stack and does not remove his hand this*
       time so RR2 does not dangle
 26.   *LH removes RR2 and places RR2 on table*
 33.   *LH tries same maneuver with RR2 on stack which does not work again*

34.   *LH removes RR2 and places RR2 on the table*
35.   *RH tries same maneuver with RR2 for about 15 seconds but it does not work—the most subject achieves is that RR2 dangles off the top of C2 at half-mast*
36.   *RH removes RR2 and places RR2 on table*   (18ML, page 34)

This is only a small part of a long sequence of coregulative transformations by 18ML devoted to constructing a balanced stack. Resistance by the objects begins to be taken into account (e.g., Lines 22–25). It feeds forward to 18ML's subsequent mappings; they are adjusted so as to try to overcome the objects' resistance. Most particularly, 18ML grips the stack of two cylinders so that they will not tumble; he does not let go of the ring when trying to place it on top of the stack, and he painstakingly tries to coregulate the ring with the stack for extended periods of time. At times (not reproduced here), 18ML also solicits the experimenter's help when he is unsuccessful. Nevertheless, and notably, he never tries to copy the experimenter's successful procedure.

This behavior, then, extends the constructive process whereby possible and impossible contingent causal and spatial relations of equilibrium between objects are gradually determined by infants' experimenting (see Piaget, 1954). Some results are entirely negative; others are distinguishably positive or negative depending upon the conditions. Resistance of the objects' structures influences which constructions by infants are possible and which are impossible. Thus, infants' experimenting generates conditions for differentially determining physical possibility from physical impossibility.

Most experimenting, as we have been seeing, is extended to unordered sets which include an intermediate number of objects. Some experimenting involves keeping the causal transformations constant; but then the objects comprising the set are mixed by predicate properties. For instance, the same result (displacing rings to the floor on the subject's right) is replicated repeatedly and monitored intermittently by subject 18SB. It is replicated with all the eight objects without regard to their predicate properties. The replication is achieved by 18SB keeping the causal mapping and the spatial direction constant for the entire unordered set of objects.

Conversely, some experimenting by infants holds the object set constant while semisystematically varying the causal transformations. For instance, all and only the dolls are selected for experimenting by subject 18TT. Moreover, causal transformations are applied to each doll at least two times within the experimental sequence. The ordered variation ⟨ hit slightly and hit slightly, push slightly, throw, touch, hit, throw, throw ⟩ in causal transformations are semisystematic. The results are combinations of differential and replicated results.

Experimenting remains rare in which both the causal transformations and the object set are held constant. To illustrate, corresponding causal transformations (hitting) are applied by one infant (18JHe) to all and only the triangular columns and not the brushes with which they are interspersed on the table. He successfully hits three columns and misses one. Corresponding spatial transformations (uprighting) are negated by corresponding causal transformations (hitting) by another infant (*18KM*). While not applied to all the columns presented, they are applied to columns only.

Thus, classification barely begins to influence a primary new element in experimenting which, as we have seen, develops at this stage, namely, reciprocal interweaving of affirmation with negation. Classification begins to regulate experimenting in accordance with the level of intensive and extensive protologic constructed at this stage (Chapters 7 and 8). With rare exceptions, intensive protologic only applies to single classes of objects when predicate properties enter at all into infants' experimenting. In parallel fashion, extensive protologic is almost always limited to structuring single sets for experimenting, albeit single sets that are sometimes extended to intermediate numbers of objects.

V. Progressive Spatial Coregulation

Exceptional containing of two classes of objects into two receptacles just begins to be generated at this stage. But it happens only when the presented array is almost completely prestructured for the subjects into two separate groups of objects (e.g., a group of dolls separate from a group of rings placed on the table between two receptacles).

Containing is progressively marked by reciprocal covariation. To illustrate, one infant (*18TT*) adjusts Receptacle 2 with her right hand in partial temporal overlap with targeting Doll 1 into it with her left hand. The rest of the dolls are then thrown into the same receptacle. Subsequent separate containing of the other class of objects (rectangular rings) in Receptacle 1 is marked by anticipatory reciprocal covariation. Subject *18TT* adjusts Receptacle 1 several times before throwing all the rings into it. Anticipation is further manifest by *18TT* looking beforehand at the objects he is about to contain, particularly when prevision of the to-be-contained objects is concomitant with adjustment of the container.

Containing by reciprocal covariation, then, is progressively regulated. It is featured by concomitant and anticipatory adjustment of the target container and the projectiles (contained). It is also featured by anticipatory observation of the projectiles. Finally, progressive regulation is featured by ever more precise targeting. While errors are still made, most infants now approach precision in their containing when the receptacles are close at hand, such as that produced by *18TT*. This level of precise targeting is not limited to containing. For instance, *18TT* also throws one ring onto another.

Covariation of reciprocal containing progressively manifests two additional features. The first is negation of containing by inverting the receptacle and emptying it out (see Hetzer, 1931). The second is negation of containing by transforming receptacles into their reciprocals, namely, covers with which to

close other receptacles. This action is accompanied by the more typical limitation of (a) extensive operations to single sets and (b) intensive operations to mixed
predication when applied to two classes of objects.

All objects from both presented classes are typically contained in mixed order
and enclosed in one receptacle. When it occurs, imprecise targeting into a
container can be corrected immediately. Containing all or most objects may be
negated by turning the receptacle over and dumping the objects out onto the
table. On rare occasions, negation begins to be coordinated with affirmation;
some subjects try to empty all the objects from one container into another.

Alternatively, reciprocal containing of all objects in mixed order and enclosure may be coordinated with imprecise reciprocal closing of the container
with another receptacle. Imprecise closure of this pragmatic form is generated
fairly frequently at this stage. Precise closure requires taking the relative spatial
dimensions of the objects being matched into account. Precise closure still
exceeds the power of spatial protoreciprocity at the present level. Still, some
infants are satisfied with their imprecise closures. These infants proceed as if they
have taken care of everything and as if their self-determined task has been
completed.

Other infants are not satisfied. They continuously rotate the covering receptacle. Consequently, they sometimes construct precisely coregulated reciprocal
closure. Yet, they are not satisfied; they continue to manipulate the covering
receptacle and, consequently, disrupt the precise spatial alignment which they
have just constructed.

Sometimes infants construct closures when both receptacles are empty. Other
times they empty the covering receptacle of all its contents and fill the container
with all the objects. The latter constructions indicate that infants already begin to
distinguish between containers and covers. On the other hand, covers and contained objects are not yet fully differentiated. Contained objects are removed
from receptacles before receptacles are transformed into covers. But then, transformations fluctuate between trying to use receptacles as covers and as contained
objects by pushing one receptacle into another. This conceptual lability about
spatial relations may also account for why infants continue to manipulate the
covering receptacle even when they have just successfully constructed precisely
coregulated closures.

Indeed, embedding or containing receptacles within each other is often generated successfully (irrelevant intervening transactions are omitted):

2. *RH places Clover Ring 1 in Receptacle 2*
3. *RH grasps Receptacle 2 (experimenter releases from receptacles)*
4. *BH lift Receptacle 2 and place it on/in Receptacle 1*
5. *BH push Receptacle 2 flush inside of Receptacle 1 (as far down as it will go)—
    receptacles lift up partially from table and immediately lower, due to pressure
    exerted*

 6.   *BH lift Receptacles 2/1 off table and hold them in air in an almost perpendicular
      position to table, as looks inside*
 7.   *BH replace Receptacles 2/1 on table*
 8.5. *LH pulls Receptacle 2 out of Receptacle 1*
15.   *LH holds Receptacle 2 on top of Receptacle 1, as looks at experimenter*
16.   *BH push Receptacle 2 down inside Receptacle 1—it is not flush inside of Recep-
      tacle 1 (end further from subject sits up in Receptacle 1)*
17.   *BH release nearer end and try to push further end of Receptacle 2 down inside
      Receptacle 1*
24.   *BH turn receptacles to horizontal position*
25.   *BH lift and replace Receptacle 2 in Receptacle 1—it lowers flush inside Recepta-
      cle 1*   (18HS, pages 9 and 10)

Receptacles are transformed into both containers and contained objects by
18HS. In addition, receptacles begin to be transformed into containers of containers (Lines 2–7). First, *18HS* embeds a ring in one receptacle. Then she
embeds that receptacle with the ring inside it in another receptacle (see Greenfield, Nelson, & Saltzman, 1972). Embedding is marked by much regulated self-
correction when the fit is not achieved precisely.

VI. Progressive Negation of Matched Mappings

Discrete mapping correspondences continue to construct small number equivalences in immediate succession. As at previous stages they do not exceed the
formation of three-unit equivalences, but they are progressively regulated:

 3.   *RH taps Yellow Cylinder upright on table in front of array, 3 times*
 4.   *RH holds YC tilted upright on table briefly as rotates it clockwise and then
      counterclockwise*
 5.   *RH taps YC upright on table, 3 times*   (18JHe, page 27)

Regulation is marked by two important features in *18JHe's* three-to-three
successive correspondence. First, it is marked by inverse spatial comparison
(rotations) of the object used to construct the correspondence (Line 4). Second, it
is marked by precise spatial orientation of the instrumental object. Before (Line
3) and after (Line 5) rotating it, the instrumental object is held in an upright
position in order to tap it three times on the table. Indeed, *18JHe* coordinatively
constructs a precise continuous correspondence between his precise discrete
correspondences. As will be discussed more fully later in this section, simultaneous coordination of discrete with continuous matchings originates at this
stage.

Discrete mapping correspondences are progressively conditioned by negation;
such constructions have already been presented in Section V. They all include

single-unit correspondences between one mapping form applied to a few objects (e.g., pushing over four dolls in a row). These are followed immediately by single-unit correspondence between a second mapping form applied to the same object (e.g., uprighting all four dolls in a row), where the second negates the first mapping form. The compositional results of these same constructions are equivalences within sets; these results are considered in Chapter 8, Section II.

The results of negating correspondences are both precise single-unit (one-to-one) and multiple-unit (many-to-many) equivalences of up to four-to-four matchings. A routine produced by subject *18ML* is clearly indicative of the role negation begins to play in discrete mapping correspondences. Since the protocol fragment would become inordinately lengthy, we will summarize *18ML*'s initial single-unit matchings. He begins by turning all and only the four brushes (out of an eight object display) upside-down, one after the other, such that they are placed with their bristle side on the table surface. He immediately follows up with:

27. *RH picks up Red Brush 3 and turns RB3 right side up (bristles up)*
28. *LH picks up Red Brush 1, puts RB1 on its side, and pauses*
29. *LH turns RB1 over (upside down) and pauses*
30. *LH turns RB1 right side up*
31. *LH grasps Blue Brush which is bristle side down and turns BB right side up*
32. *LH turns Red Brush 4 right side up (always does this by clasping the brush's handle)*
33. *LH turns Red Brush 2 right side up, so all brushes are bristle side up*
                                                                                        (18ML, page 8)

Two sets of single-unit mapping correspondences are generated by *18ML*: (1) A one-to-one upside down placement function applied consecutively to four brushes, but such that the first equivalence class is constructed in temporal overlap and the product is preserved momentarily. (2) A one-to-one right-side-up placement function applied consecutively to the same four brushes, but such that the second equivalence class is constructed in temporal overlap and the product is preserved momentarily. By negation, the first (upside-down) mapping function is converted into the second (right-side-up) mapping function. The transformational product is equivalence between consecutive four-unit discrete mappings (see Forman, 1982).

The objects involved are all and only the brushes. This is consistent with the single-class predication by similarities typically generated at this stage. Correspondence has developed into a second-order operation conditioned by negation.

Since both operations are elements of the same construction, it is possible to draw two hypotheses. The first hypothesis is that at least some extensive structures (here, correspondences) are more advanced in their development than some intensive structures (here, classificatory predication). The second hypothesis is that the coordinative disequilibrium (as defined in Langer, 1982b) engendered by this structural developmental disparity is an initial cause of transforming first- into second-order classificatory predication.

One-to-many and many-to-one correspondences are expanded in extent and they are elaborated into second-order structures. Increasingly, co-univocals are marked by protosymbolic features as well. But then their range of application does not exceed the power of multiplicative matchings generated at stage 4 by 12-month-olds (Langer, 1980, pages 305 and 306). They are neither expanded in extent nor do they entail second-order structures:

3.5.	*LH partially lifts Spoon 1 to upright position*	
3.5.	*RH touches Spoon 2 to nose*	S: *"Nose."*
5.5.	*RH touches S2 to mother's mouth*	
5.5.	*LH holds S1 on table*	
7.	*RH inserts cup part of S2 into mouth, licks, and removes S2*	*(18JHo, page 37)*

57.	*RH strokes Square Column 4 through mother's hair*	
58.	*RH strokes SC4 through own hair*	
59.	*RH extends SC4 to experimenter (experimenter takes SC4 and strokes it through hair)*	
60.	*RH strokes Brush 2 through hair*	*(18JHo, page 73)*

Pretense, in the first co-univocal, includes substituting the infant's own noses for her mouth and "feeding" her mother as well as herself (see page 112). In the second co-univocal, pretense includes substituting a square column (an abstract object) for a brush (a prototypical object) and "brushing" her mother's hair as well as her own. These protosymbolic co-univocals multiplicatively match small numbers within single sets only.

Symbolic correlations, then, begin by being more primitive than correlations that are not marked by symbolic features but already match two sets at the previous stage (Chapter 4, Section 2). On this hypothesis, infants can only begin to impose correlational relations onto a gestural medium by restricting their range of application. Nevertheless, such impositions or transpositions begin to provide the significance necessary to transform symbolization into a notational system for correlational constructions. This is part of the ongoing process whereby symbols are detached eventually into powerful representational systems of constant givens of operational structures. As we have seen, this ongoing process is picking up momentum and becoming both intensive and extensive at this stage.

Continuous mapping correspondences are progressively well-regulated:

40.	*RH pushes Car on table away from self*
40a.	*Spoon displaced at an angle*
41.	*RH lifts C up to right side*
42.	*LH moves S back almost to its exact original angle of placement*

(18PC, page 3)

8.3.   *RH places Doll 3 on table (almost exactly at its original place)*

(18TT, page 49)

Two features mark regulated continuous correspondences at this stage. The first is deferring correspondences while infants interpolate intervening transactions. While 18PC interpolates only one transaction, 18TT interpolates several transactions (not reproduced in the protocol fragment). The second feature is precision in reconstructing the initial state of affairs, thereby producing spatial congruence between the first and second placement relations. Both subjects displace the objects such that the replacements match exactly the objects' initial placements before the intervening transactions. Relative precision is extended to matching fairly large numbers of continuous mappings. For instance, subject 18SO reproduces moving objects toward himself six times in a row.

Constructing regulated continuous correspondences, marked by both delay and precision, makes it possible to also generate protosymbolic matchings. This is precisely what develops at this stage. Two manifestations were found most frequently. Regulated continuous mapping correspondences (coordinated with substituting) are generated: (a) between pretending to brush hair, and (b) between pretending to stir food in an empty cup. The latter form of protosymbolic correlation is sometimes even elaborated into including corresponding pretending to feed and eat the stirred food from the empty spoon which was stirred in the cup.

These same regulatory features mark the constructions of continuous (e.g., roll back and forth) coordinated with discrete (e.g., roll two times) mapping correspondences (irrelevant intervening transactions are omitted):

2.	*RH touches VW4, then rolls VW4 back and forth (vertically), 2 times*	S: "Car."
3.	*RH displaces over Racers 2 and 3, touches VW3, then rolls VW3 back and forth (vertically), 2 times*	S: "Car."
4.	*RH touches Racer 1, then rolls R1 back and forth in small arc (R1 was already facing at an angle)*	
8.5.	*RH rolls VW2 forward and back vertically, such that VW2 faces in at VW1*	
8.5.	*LH rolls VW1 forward and back vertically, such that VW1 faces in at VW2*	
10.5.	*RH picks up VW2*	
10.5.	*LH picks up VW1*	S: *(sounds like)* "Look." or "Book."
12.	*RH and LH hold VW2 and VW1 together in air with bottoms facing each other*	

14. *RH and LH rotate VW2 and VW1 such*
     that wheels of each VW face down
15. *RH and LH place VW2 and VW1 down*
     on table in upright position
16.5. *RH rolls VW2 back and forth, 2 times*
16.5. *LH rolls VW1 back and forth, 2 times*   (*18KM*, page 22)

Subject *18KM* continues constructing many more identical or variant coordinate mapping correspondences beyond those reproduced here. The initial portion of the sequence reproduced here is accompanied by minimal verbal reiteration ("Car") which holophrastically represents event features of the correspondences. It is not possible to determine definitively whether some of the correspondences also involve pretense (e.g., whether *18KM* is symbolically representing the movements of real cars). Other constructions, however, are more clearly marked by pretense which further indicates that infants can construct protosymbolic correspondences. These are embodied, for instance, in infants' pretending to stir food in an empty cup and then feeding and eating from the empty spoon used to stir the cup.

Progress in coregulative control of correspondences is striking:

16. *RH picks up Yellow Spoon 1 and LH picks up Orange Spoon 2*
17. *BH simultaneously turn bowl ends in and toward self so bowl-ends hit against*
     each other:

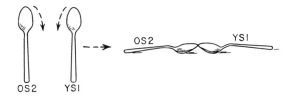

18. *BH hit bowl-ends together a couple more times, then hit bowl ends on table,*
     alternately, fast (experimenter taps Orange Cup 2 and Yellow Cup 1 alternately
     on table)
19. *BH alternate tapping of bowl-ends becomes simultaneous tapping (experimenter*
     imitates, hitting cups simultaneously on table)
20. *BH stop tapping and hold spoons up in air*   (*18PC*, pages 67 and 68)

Co-regulative control is marked by precision of matching the bowl-ends of the spoons against each other, by rapid alternating tapping, and by switching from alternating to simultaneous tapping.

This protocol fragment also highlights some central features in the development of cooperative correspondences. Infants are now very adept at such interactions within the constraints of their cognitive level and intentions. They selectively engage in cooperative correspondences. Here, for instance, *18PC* is not engaged even though the experimenter is imitating him. Instead, *18PC* first constructs mapping correspondences that are reciprocal to his initial matchings. He transforms tapping the spoons against each other into tapping the spoons alternately on the table. Then he constructs mapping correspondences that are inverse to his second correlations and to the experimenter's imitations. He transforms alternate into simultaneous tapping of the spoons on the table. When the experimenter persists in imitating him, *18PC* stops tapping all together.

The element of negation, then, is entering into and conditioning cooperative correspondences, as it does all other mapping correlations at this stage. The structural developmental constraint upon negating cooperative correspondences is that it is an autogenetic construction at its origins. Infants begin to negate their own and cooperative correspondences, as already observed in *18PC*'s constructions. Thus too, another infant (*18SB*) replaces flat all objects that the experimenter places upright. What the experimenter uprights, yet another subject (*18JHe*) partially knocks flat, then partially uprights, and finally knocks flat. Successive alternating productive negation of cooperative correspondences, such as that generated by *18JHe*, is still rare at this stage. Yet, it indicates that reversible correspondences are becoming regulated.

On the other hand, none of the subjects imitate negations of correspondences initiated by the experimenter. These contrastive performances support the hypothesis that productive negation is autogenetic and that it precedes, ontogenetically, reproductive negation. Productive negation begins to condition all correlation relations, including cooperative constructions. Reproductive negation does not yet enter into infants' mapping correspondences, whether or not they are cooperative.

Cooperative correspondences begin to be constructed in routines. To illustrate, although his procedure differs from that of the experimenter, subject *18HS* watches the experimenter's pretending to stir and eat routine and then performs a similar routine. Prior to this performance, *18HS* spontaneously used a spoon and a cup to pretend to stir and eat many times. Here *18HS* engages in a cooperative correspondence that is conventional in its pretense.

No more than half of the infants at this stage embodied cooperative correspondences in routines. Still, the initiation of symbolic cooperative correspondences is significant since it is both conventional and communicative. As such it initiates symbolic notation of correspondence that is interpersonal in its expressive properties. This quality is a prerequisite to consensual cognitive communication between children and others. It is also prerequisite to children's use of symbolization as an instrument with which to expand their cognitive constructions in two important ways. The first is to use symbolic embodiments as constant elements or givens of cognition. The second is to use symbols as a medium for the cultural transmission of knowledge.

VII. Precise Two-Step Ordering of Small Magnitudes

Both discrete and continuous mapping orders are expanded greatly; but the progressive predominance of discrete over continuous ordering continues:

50. *looks at Car, as RH taps Brush on table, 2 times (experimenter replaces C on table)*
51. *(as experimenter acts) RH holds B about 3 inches above table*
52. *RH taps B on C, 5 times, such that C moves about 1 inch to left (experimenter meanwhile lifts Doll and places it upright directly behind C)*
53. *RH taps B on C, 4 times, such that C moves about another $\frac{3}{4}$ inch to left*
54. *RH taps B onto Plate, 1 time*
54a. *P wiggles*
55. *looks at P, as RH withdraws B toward self*
56. *RH taps B on table near edge on right, 3 times, watching*
70. *RH taps P upright on table, 2 times, as moves P to left about 2 inches*
71. *RH taps P upright on top of C, 3 times*
71a. *C moves to left slightly on first two taps and then about 4 inches to left on third tap*
6.3. *RH taps Doll 5 in its approximately original space, 7 times*
6.7. *LH taps Doll 2, about 2 times, on table in about its original space, starting on about fifth tap of D5 (not tapping as hard as D5)*
(10.3.–10.7. *tapping is a little syncopated:*)
10.3. *RH taps D5 upright and hard on table in about its original space, 13 times*
10.3a. *on eleventh tap, D5 knocks Doll 4 flat*
10.7. *beginning on fourth tap of D5, LH taps D2 upright behind C and then moves it slowly to left for a total of 5 inches as taps it, 11 times, laughing*
(14.3–14.7. *tapping is mostly simultaneous:*)
14.3. *RH taps D5 upright on table near edge and 2 inches to right of flat D4, 22 times*
14.3a. *on last tap, D5 lightly hits D4, displacing it to left slightly so it touches P*
14.7. *beginning on ninth tap of D5, LH starts tapping D2 on table in space 5 inches to left of C, about 10 times all together, smiling*   (18SB, pages 3–6)

These protoadditive and protosubtractive relations are constructed within the first two procedural phases of the first task administered to 18SB. Even though irrelevant intervening transactions have been omitted for the sake of brevity, it should still be apparent that several discrete and continuous orderings are generated by 18SB within a brief time span, in fact, within a period of less than a minute and a half. Obviously infants do not proliferate orderings at this rate throughout their transactions. Nevertheless, these orderings provide some measure of their current potential generative capacities.

The first series is an extended but imprecise bi-directional discrete ⟨ 2, 5, 4, 1, 3 ⟩ ordering (Lines 50–56). The second series is a precisely increasing discrete ⟨ 2, 3 ⟩ ordering (70–71a.). The third series is a partially overlapping imprecise discrete ⟨ 7, 2 ⟩ ordering coordinate with a precise continuous ⟨ tap hard, tap ⟩ ordering (Lines 6.3–6.7.). The coordination is between homogeneous orderings because both are orders, that is, both are produced by protosubtraction. Similarly, the fourth series is a homogeneous coordination of an imprecise discrete ⟨ 13, 11 ⟩ decreasing order and a precise continuous ⟨ tap hard, tap ⟩ decreasing order (Lines 10.3.–10.7.). The fifth is an imprecise discrete ⟨ 22, ≈ 10 ⟩ decreasing order (Lines 14.3.–14.7.)

    Most uni-directional mapping orderings, as we have just seen, still consist of two-step series. Discrete two-step orderings are not precise when the units entail large numbers of mappings (e.g., *18SB's* ⟨ 7, 2 ⟩, ⟨ 13, 11 ⟩, and ⟨ 22, ≈10 ⟩ orderings). They are most likely to be precise when the largest unit does not exceed three mappings(e.g., *18SB's* ⟨ 2, 3 ⟩ ordering). Rare precise two-step orderings begin to be generated in which the largest unit is five mappings:

     26.   *RH taps Column 2 on table, 4 times*
     27.   *LH picks up Column 1, while RH holds C2*
     28.   *RH holds C2 to C1 and LH holds C1 to C2*
     29.   *RH raises C2 and LH raises C1*
     30.   *BH hit C1 and C2 at each other, 5 times, symmetrically*   (*18BB*, page 46)

     28.   *RH moves Yellow Spoon up and down in Yellow Cup, about 5 times*
   28a. *YC moves slightly closer to Red Cup*
     29.   *LH grasps YC*
  30.5. *LH tips YC toward self*
  30.5. *RH grasps YS*
  32.5. *RH dips YS up and down in YC, about 4 times*
  32.5. *LH slowly raises YC off table*   (*18HS*, page 30)

    These precursory constructions, then, may produce either increasing (*18BB*) or decreasing (*18HS*) precise two-step ⟨ 4, 5 ⟩ or ⟨ 5, 4 ⟩ mapping orders. It is obvious that they are more likely to be more precise the more the mappings are discrete and homogeneous in form. For example, tapping and hitting are more discrete and homogeneous mapping forms than stirring, which is more continuous and irregular. This is why *18BB's* protoaddition is likely to be more precise than *18HS's* protosubtraction. The difficulty in measuring mapping forms as they become more continuous and irregular limits their utility to infants as instruments of practical intelligence. Indeed, the same difficulty affects this research endeavor to measure precisely infants' constructions. This is the reason why the figures given in Lines 28 and 32.5. of the *18HS* protocol fragment are qualified with "about," so as to indicate the uncertainty in measurement.

    The same measurement difficulties underlie the construction by infants (and experimental measurement) of precise continuous orderings. Nevertheless, fairly precise two-step continuous orderings continue to be generated frequently. For instance, *18BB* constructs an increasing ⟨ tap, hit ⟩ order while *18SB* constructs decreasing ⟨ tap hard, tap ⟩ orders.

These precise continuous orderings are coordinate with precise discrete orderings. Coordinations of this type and precision are increasingly generated at this stage. The probability of constructing precisely coordinated orderings is increased when they are minimal (i.e., two-step series) and when the same relational proto-operation (i.e., addition or subtraction) is generated to produce orderings whose directions are homogeneous (i.e., increasing or decreasing). This structural hypothesis is confirmed by the precise coordinate orderings generated by infants at this stage. Most are two-step and homogeneous.

Constructing two-step orderings such that the two units are produced simultaneously or in partial temporal overlap originates by stage three at 10 months (Langer, 1980, pages 226–227). It increases in frequency and regulation at this stage. As argued previously, such constructions enhance infants' comparative determination (a) of the protological properties of the addition and subtraction used to produce orderings and (b) of the extensive magnitudes of the resultant nonequivalences. Increasing frequency and regulation of series featured by temporal overlap is apparent in *18BB*'s constructions. The last three orderings are featured by partial temporal overlap. Moreover, two of these orderings are coordinate and therefore permit comparative determination of both discrete and continuous relational proto-operations and ordered nonequivalences.

Temporal overlap just begins, but rarely, to enter into the construction of three-step orderings:

29.5.   *RH hits down on Block 1, one time*
31.5.   *LH hits down on table where Block 6 had been, 2 times*
31.5.   *RH hits down on B1, 3 times*   (*18TT*, page 10)

The discrete ⟨ 1, 2, 3 ⟩ order generated by *18TT* is precise. Most unidirectional three-step orderings are still imprecise. Rare four- and five-step unidirectional series begin to be generated at this stage; but they are invariably imprecise. Bidirectional orderings also rarely exceed three-step series. When they do exceed three steps they are invariably imprecise (e.g., *18SB*, Lines 50–56, presented on page 139).

More than two-step unidirectional continuous orders that are precise also begin to be generated:

31.   *RH pounds the end of Racer 4 on table*   S: *"Car-car-car."*
                                                          (timed with first
                                                          three bangs)

32.   *RH pounds harder and faster, near the other racers*
      (these were close to begin with)   (18KM, page 26)

As is apparent, it is not possible to determine the number of steps in such continuous series. Multi-step bidirectional orderings are always partially imprecise. For instance, one infant (18SB) generates a nine-step continuous bidirectional 〈 place, drop, throw, throw, place, throw, place, drop, place 〉 ordering. While this ordering is unusual in its extent for this stage, its partial precision is not.

Stabilizing Compositions
of Compositions

Beginning to combine phrase-like routines into sentence-like routines augments the elements with which infants structure their cognitions. It establishes a more complex and powerful set of constant givens as well as an enlarged set. These factors make possible developments in second-order cognitions, such as in protoproportional causal functions. These findings further support the hypothesis that infants would develop relatively advanced second-order cognitions even if routines and individual objects were their only source of cognitive elements.

Parallel progress, as we shall now see, is made by infants in structuring configurations or collections of objects. This progress enhances the sets and series of objects that infants also use as elements for their cognitive structuring. More advanced sets and series complement more advanced routines and progressively representational objects as necessary elements of infants' developing cognition. An important manifestation is a shift in the proportion of spontaneously producing two basic combinativity operations. Composing predominates up to and including the previous stage. Recomposing begins to predominate at this stage. Other important, but newly occuring manifestations are the origins of producing flexible containing in two receptacles by recursion.

I. Predominance of Recomposing over Composing

Composing productivity at age 18 months ranges between 5.34 and 9.60 compositions per minute (Table 7.1, Row 3). While the range is a bit wider at

TABLE 7.1
Spontaneous Phase I: Mean Composing Productivity at Age 18 Months

| | Control[a] | Additive | | Multiplicative | | Disjoint | |
	Four-object 1	Four-object 2	Eight-object 3	Four-object 4	Eight-object 5	Four-object 6	Eight-object 7
1. Compositions	16.00	10.58	12.91[c]	18.55[c]	18.00	13.91[c]	8.36[c]
2. Time	2 min 36 sec	1 min 36 sec[b]	1 min 42 sec[d]	2 min 17 sec[b]	2 min 14 sec[b]	1 min 29 sec[b]	1 min 32 sec[b]
3. Productivity per minute	6.17	6.89[b]	8.72[d]	8.15[b]	9.30[b]	9.60[b]	5.34[b]

Class conditions

[a]N = 6 subjects.
[b]N = 10 subjects.
[c]N = 11 subjects.
[d]N = 9 subjects.

age 18 months, it remains comparable to that at age 15 months which is 4.41–7.68 (Table 3.1, Row 3, page 53).

The range of compositional productivity, then, remains quite uniform. The means do not differ much by class conditions. The range is comparable for the four-object and eight-object conditions. It is 6.17–9.60 compositions per minute in the four-object conditions and 5.34–9.30 compositions per minute in the eight-object conditions. Even the biggest difference in mean rate, that between the four-object and the eight-object disjoint conditions, is not statistically significant ($N = 10$, $x = 4$, $p = .377$, sign test).

Mean composing rate is higher in all but the eight-object disjoint condition at age 18 months than at age 15 months (compare Table 7.1 with Table 3.1). Nevertheless, none of the differences are statistically significant. Even the largest difference in rate of productivity between ages 15 and 18 months, which occurs in the four-object disjoint condition, is not significant (Mann–Whitney $U = 67$, $p = .34$).

While the overall rate of composing does not change until age 18 months, the duration of individual compositions continues to increase. For instance, one infant constructs and preserves a three-object composition on the table while interacting with several other objects. These interactions are preparatory to constructing a second composition which comprises four objects. In addition, the second composition is varied by follow-up transactions. The first composition, then, is preserved for a longer duration than the second composition. The first composition in particular is preserved beyond the time of the interactions used to construct it. In this way, the first composition still does not represent the mode at this stage. Nevertheless, an increasing fraction of compositions are preserved by 18-month-olds beyond the duration of their constructions.

Increasing durability and stability of compositions is manifest in one other way at this stage. Infants generate compositions featured by protosymbolization of a conventional and pretense nature with some frequency (see Chapter 6). For instance, they insert a spoon in a cup and repeatedly stir the spoon in the cup; then they reproduce the same composition several times. Repeated stirring of a spoon in a cup requires some duration and indicates compositional durability. Reproductive composing is a form of preservation by correspondence over a period of time. It indicates that protosymbolization is beginning to facilitate stability and transformation of compositions into constant givens for constructions such as representational equivalence over time.

Recomposing predominates for the first time (Table 7.2). Compositions constitute about 60% and recompositions only about 40% of the collections constructed by 15-month-olds for both four- and eight-object conditions (see Table 3.2 on page 55). The proportions are reversed at age 18 months. Recompositions constitute about 60% of the sets and compositions only about 40% in both four- and eight-object conditions. This ratio shift with age from a predominance of

TABLE 7.2
Spontaneous Phase I: Mean Frequency of Composing and Recomposing at Age 18 Months

		Four-object condition			Eight-object condition		
		Thematic 1	Variant 2	% Variant 3	Thematic 4	Variant 5	% Variant 6
1.	Semicontrol[a]	4.00	11.83	75			
2.	Additive[b]	4.92	5.67	54	6.91	6.00	46
3.	Multiplicative[b]	7.45	11.09	60	6.25	11.75	65
4.	Disjoint[b]	5.91	8.00	58	3.82	4.55	54
5.	All conditions	5.75	8.73	60	5.68	7.56	57

[a]N = 6 subjects.
[b]N = 11 subjects in the multiplicative and disjoint four-object conditions, and in the additive and disjoint eight-object conditions.

compositions to recompositions is significant in both the four-object (Mann–Whitney $U = 22$, $p = .01$) and eight-object (Mann–Whitney $U = 25$, $p = .01$) conditions.

The proportions are uniform across class conditions as well, with two possible exceptions. At the upper end of the range, recompositions constitute three-quarters of the collections constructed in the semicontrol, four-object condition (Table 7.2, Row 1, Columns 1–3). At the lower end of the range, a little less than one-half of the sets generated in the additive, eight-object conditions are recompositions (Table 7.2, Row 2, Columns 4–6). This is the only condition in which less than a majority of the collections are generated by recomposing. Recomposing is the predominant mode of set construction in all the other six conditions tested.

This dramatic shift to combinativity by recomposing has many potential implications. One is overriding and may be mentioned here, although its full significance will not become apparent until Chapter 8. Increased recomposing provides progressively stable structural conditions for constructing protological cognitions. That is, it provides an enlarged pool of collections as constant givens for structuring exchanges, correlations and orderings.

II. Initial Flexibility in Provoked Composing and Recomposing

Composing and recomposing become progressively robust in the provoked, phase II, procedural conditions that provide receptacles, modeling sorting, and pre-existing model compositions. Moreover, infants' constructive procedures under these provoked conditions just begin to be flexible. For instance, some infants switch back and forth or recursively between two contemporaneous compositions in order to construct them.

All 18-month-old subjects use receptacles to compose sets in the second procedural phase of testing the four-object additive and the eight-object disjoint class conditions. While containing single compositions is still the preferred mode, most subjects also contain two temporally overlapping compositions. Subjects now construct one composition in each receptacle, but such that the first set is preserved while the second is composed. There are no differences by conditions (Table 7.3). In the four-object additive condition, four subjects contain single sets in single receptacles only while eight subjects also contain two contemporaneous sets in two receptacles. In the eight-object disjoint conditions, three subjects contain single sets in single receptacles only while seven subjects also contain two contemporaneous sets in two receptacles. From age 15 to 18 months, the increase in containing two contemporaneous collections in the four-object additive condition is not statistically significant ($x^2 = 0.67$, $df = 1$, $p > .05$); but in the eight-object disjoint condition it is statistically significant ($x^2 = 2.82$, $df = 1$, $p < .05$).

There is a gradual increase at age 18 months in containing all rather than only some objects from the rate generated at age 15 months (see Table 3.2 on page 55). Most composing by containment, whether into one or two sets, is still generated by adding objects one-by-one at this stage. However, the necessity of adding elements one-by-one in order to contain them is waning; it is used exclusively by only four subjects. The other eight subjects also add objects two-at-a-time; however, it should be stressed that one-by-one addition is still used most frequently even by these eight subjects. Two subjects even contain objects four-at-a-time, but once only. Both instances, however, are rudimentary and global. Both hands are used by one infant to grasp the heap of four objects presented by the experimenter; then both hands dump all four objects into one container. The result is an undifferentiated heap of objects. Four-at-a-time containing generated by the other infant is a bit more differentiated since each

TABLE 7.3
Provoked Phase II: Frequency of Containing All or Some Objects at Age 18 Months

| | Condition | | | |
| | Four-object additive | | Eight-object disjoint | |
Receptacles	All	Some	All	Some
One	4	0	1	2
Two	8	0	5	2

hand grasps two objects. But, then, both hands simultaneously toss the four objects at the receptacles.

Mapping forms used to contain objects are often undifferentiated; dumping and tossing are typical in this regard. The most frequent mapping forms used to contain objects, dropping and placing, are a bit more differentiated. Yet, these too are executed without regard to differentiated placement. The resultant compositions are global and undifferentiated constructions, such as contained heaps.

Composing by containing begins to be generated flexibly. Much composing by containing, as already noted, results in forming two contemporaneous collections. Less and less are infants constrained to single composing within one container only. Binary composing requires switching from containing some objects in one receptacle to containing other objects in a second receptacle. Since there are no differences in this regard between the four-object additive and eight-object disjoint conditions we may analyze the data together.

Infants generate fifteen binary compositions by containing (Table 7.3, Row 2). Ten of these constructions do not exceed the minimum of one switch between receptacles required to construct two contemporaneous collections. The procedure consists of nothing more than containing all the members of the first set in one receptacle and then switching once only to the second receptacle in order to contain all the members of the second set. This minimal procedure is the one generated by all infants at age 15 months when they compose two collections in two receptacles (page 56).

Five binary compositions, generated by four infants, are constructed by a more flexible and extensive, recursive procedure. Recursion requires switching two or more times between receptacles. In the most flexible construction, for instance, subject 18HS first places three objects in Receptacle 2, then one object in Receptacle 1, then one object in Receptacle 2, then one object in Receptacle 1, then one object in Receptacle 2, and finally one object in Receptacle 1. Thus, 18HS recursively switches five times from one receptacle to the other in order to contain eight objects into two contemporaneous compositions.

Various features of composing by containing which develop at this stage, then, indicate that binary collections are beginning to be stabilized or preserved. Potentially, the most advanced preservation, as we have just seen, is still generated by only one-third of infants at this stage. It occurs when infants contain two collections by recursion. This level of recursive set construction is marked by the following sequence of transformations: beginning to contain a first set, suspending structuring this first collection, switching to beginning to contain a second set, suspending structuring this second collection, reinitiating structuring the first set in order to expand it, and so on.

Potentially, recursive switching back-and-forth between receptacles entails repeatedly preserving two sets, at least, during the flexible process of construction. An implication of progressive preservation of two contemporaneous collections by containing is constituting binary sets as constant givens. These given elements may then be treated as the content upon which to progressively operate protologically. The potential products are more powerful protoinferential constructions (see Chapter 8).

One expectation is that 18-month-old infants exhaustively contain objects as member elements of sets when the number of objects presented is small, as in the four-object additive condition. The hypothesis is that all four objects will be contained into one or two sets such that no objects will remain ungrouped. The findings confirm the hypothesis (Table 7.3, Columns 1 and 2). All 12 subjects compose all rather than some of the four objects by containment such that all objects are included as members of a set.

A second hypothesis is that 18-month-olds tend to exhaustively contain objects as member elements of sets when an intermediate number of objects is presented. The expectation is that most but not all subjects will contain all objects into one or two sets such that no objects will remain ungrouped in the eight-object disjoint condition. Six out of 10 subjects compose eight objects by containment such that all objects are included as members of a set (Table 7.3, Columns 3 and 4). The remaining four subjects contain most but not all objects. These four subjects contain 5–7 objects; 1–3 objects are left as remainders that are not included in any set.

One infant constructs two contained sets but expresses her unwillingness to include all the objects, that is, her exclusion of some objects by repeated verbal negation, saying "No." She also gives objects back to the tester, including objects already contained. Another infant (18SO) expresses his complete inclusion of all eight objects into two sets by verbal affirmation, saying "All done." as he contains the eighth object. These are the only instances in which composing by containing is marked symbolically at this stage. While rare, such symbolic expressions lend support to the claim that two contemporaneous compositions are progressively preserved as constant given elements.

These rare symbolic productions lend additional credence to the claim that protological affirmation (here inclusion of elements into binary sets) and negation (here exclusion of elements by recursive switching) are more advanced cognitive activities than linguistic affirmation and negation. Most strikingly, logical affirmation and negation by recursive inclusion of all eight objects into binary sets is never matched by equivalently complex symbolic affirmation and negation. Indeed, as we have seen, only one symbolic affirmation and only one symbolic negation (and these of the simplest form possible), are generated by infants at this stage, in conjunction with logical affirmation that is generated by all infants, and logical negation that is generated by several infants.

A third hypothesis is that quantification of binary sets is facilitated by their progressive stabilization as given elements. Eight infants generate binary sets in the four-object additive condition. Five of the eight binary sets comprise two

TABLE 7.4
Provoked Phase II: Extensive by Intensive Properties of Objects Contained in Two Receptacles at Age 18 Months

| | Predicate properties | | | | | |
| | Order | | | Enclosure | | |
Quantitative properties	Unmixed 1	Partly unmixed 2	Mixed 3	Unmixed 4	Partly unmixed 5	Mixed 6
Four-object additive:[a]						
1. Equal sets	1		4	1		4
2. Unequal sets	1		2	0		3
Eight-object disjoint:[b]						
3. Equal sets	1	1	2	1	1	2
4. Unequal sets	2	0	1	2	0	1

[a]N = 12 subjects.
[b]N = 10 subjects.

numerically equivalent sets (Table 7.4, Rows 1 and 2). Each of the binary sets comprise two objects. Most of these (four out of five) are mixed by predicate properties; only one binary set is unmixed. These equivalence sets, then, are not biproducts of infants grouping identical objects. Constructing equivalence sets are not a function of infants' matching identical objects. Moreover, almost all the binary sets are mixed by predicate properties, whether or not the sets are quantitatively equivalent. Extensive equivalence (quantitative affirmation), then, is linked with intensive nonequivalence (predicate negation).

In the eight-object disjoint condition, only four of the seven binary sets comprise two numerically equivalent sets (Table 7.4, Rows 3 and 4). Each of these equal sets comprises four objects such that all eight objects are included. Only one of these three numerically equivalent binary sets is fully unmixed by predicate properties. Again, then, producing quantitative equivalence between binary sets cannot be attributed to matching identical objects.

Most contained composing is still generated by adding objects only. But subtracting contained objects is generated ever more frequently such that objects are taken away from contained collections as well as added to them. In 8 of the 22 compositions by containment generated by the subjects, subtracting is coordinated with adding objects to reconstruct the initial sets into variant sets. Retroactive reconstruction may be used to construct quantitative equivalence between two contemporaneous collections. For instance, after subject 18MK places all four objects presented (two cross and two circular rings) into one receptacle, she consecutively takes out and places one cross and one circular ring in the other receptacle. Retroactive reconstruction results in transforming an initial single set into two contained sets marked by extensive equivalence. The mixed predication marking the initial single collection is not, however, changed into two unmixed classes.

The most extended retroactive reconstruction generated at this stage interweaves constructing two contained sets with union of the two sets into a single larger set. The sequence begins when subject *18KM* constructs two collections by first placing two spoons in Receptacle 2 and two rings in Receptacle 1 such that all the presented objects are included. Thus, her initial binary sets are marked by both extensive equivalence (two-to-two) and unmixed predication (spoons and rings). She reconstructs the two sets by uniting them into a single set. She reconstructs the single set (by replacement) into a reproduction of her initial two sets. She reconstructs (by replacement) the two sets into a reproduction of her initial single set. She reconstructs (by replacement) the single set into a reproduction of her initial two sets. Finally, she reconstructs (by replacement) the two sets into a reproduction of her initial single set.

Flexible reconstruction of this extended order is marked by an important structural feature. Reversible replacements consecutively interweave simultaneous binary identity sets with successive single identity sets. Moreover, reversible replacements consecutively and repeatedly (a) compose binary into single identity sets and (b) decompose single into binary identity sets.

The products therefore also include regulated reproductions of binary and single identity sets as they are transformed into each other. This construction has potentially significant implications for symbolizing identity sets. Reproducing binary and single identity sets despite their transformations provides the structural foundations for detaching representation of sets from their instantiation in presentational configurations. Thus, reversible replacements serve as a structural source of protosymbolic identity sets.

Regulated self-correction of containing two collections is still unusual at this stage. It marks the constructions by three infants only. After containing four triangular columns and two circular rings in Receptacle 1, subject *18BB*'s

16.5.   *RH drops Circular Ring 4 in Receptacle 1*
16.5.   *LH drops Circular Ring 3 in Receptacle 2*
18.   *LH quickly takes CR3 (sole object) out of Receptacle 2 and places CR3 in Receptacle 1 (all objects are in Receptacle 1)*   (*18BB*, page 69)

Self-correction by *18BB* follows rapidly after what she apparently considers to be a mistaken containment. Self-generated feedback results in retroactive modification by *18BB* of dual into single containment.

Self-correction by the other two infants is manifest by vacillating between containers. For instance, after containing all four brushes in Receptacle 2, subject *18KM*'s

10. *RH holds Square Column 3 over Receptacle 2, looks to Receptacle 1, looks to Receptacle 2*
11. *RH holds SC3 up, as moves to left, glancing quickly at Receptacle 2 S: "No"*
12. *RH puts SC3 in Receptacle 1, looking*   (18KM, page 64)

Visiomotor vacillation between containers is resolved by *18KM* containing the square column in a separate container from that in which she has contained the brushes. It is accompanied by the simplest form of verbal negation ("No"). This is the only instance in which infants in any way mark symbolically their self-correction.

With rare exceptions, experimental procedures designed to induce containment by predicate properties are ineffective. When subjects mix objects from different classes in the same receptacle, the experimenter corrects them by transferring the misplaced objects. Typically, infants do not take the experimenter's corrections into account in their subsequent containing. They continue to contain by mixed predicate properties. Only two infants evidence any positive effect. One infant continues containing in accordance with the experimenter's corrections in both the four-object additive and the eight-object disjoint conditions, while the other infant does so only in the simpler four-object additive condition.

Both self-directed and other-directed corrective regulations remain minimal at this stage, and no priority of one over the other is detectable. Only one of the three self-corrective infants cooperates with the experimenter's directed corrections; that is, only one infant overlaps both groups. We may therefore hypothesize that at first self-directed and other-directed corrections or adjustments are independent factors regulating infants' structuring of contained collections.

While containing objects in receptacles results in binary composing by two-thirds of the subjects, experimental modeling (during procedural phase II) of composing two sets by spatial sorting does not. Infants continue to sometimes add cooperatively individual objects to one of the experimenter's two groupings. With the exception of one child, infants do not add cooperatively to both sets the experimenter is constructing. Moreover, infants do not include all the objects presented, again with the possible exception of the same one child.

As they do at previous stages, infants sometimes add cooperatively individual objects to one of the two groupings modeled by the experimenter. Most frequently, however, they unite the two modeled sets together with individual objects. Essentially, they collapse the two modeled sets into a single larger whole configuration. When the experimenter follows up by regrouping infants' reconstructions into two sets, infants repeatedly undo the experimenter's two sets by combining them into ever larger single compositions. Often infants continue to include additional objects in the single configuration into which they repeatedly transform the experimenter's attempts to model two sets.

The only potential behavioral exception to this pattern of collapsing together modeled sets marks the origins of flexible recursive switching between two compositions in order to sort objects. This exceptional construction parallels the previously analyzed initiation of contained composing of two sets by recursion. While formally parallel, there may also be some differences between the two. First, recursion is generated by one subject only when the experimenter models two sets. At its origins, then, this is even rarer than recursion to contain two sets, which is generated by four subjects. Second, as we shall see, the one instance of recursive sorting at this stage is primarily a product of negation or self-correction while all recursive containing is directed and does not involve self-correction.

Even this exceptional recursive sorting by one infant (18BB) is directed primarily to constructing a single set of all the cups. She stacks three cups into the first cup placed by the experimenter. She ignores the first spoon which the experimenter has placed separately from the first cup. She never adds objects to the first spoon. Instead she discards the spoons handed to her. Thus, by negation, 18BB ends up with a residual heap of three spoons separate from both the first spoon placed by the experimenter and from the stack of four cups that 18BB constructs.

Twice 18BB corrects her own misplacement of spoons in the stack of cups in the process of constructing a stacked set of all four cups. Self-regulations by retroactive correction permit the formation of two contemporaneous sets by a flexible recursive switching procedure, even if the second set is not much more than a residual heap of three discarded spoons. Self-corrective regulations are also further indications that 18BB is directed toward her own constructive structuring of the objects and, basically, ignores the experimenter's model of two sets.

A variety of gestural (extending hand to experimenter and opening and shutting it), vocal ("Eh, eh"), and verbal ("Want dat") symbols are used by 18BB to communicate to the experimenter which objects she wants (affirmation) and which she does not want (negation). When given cups she stacks them with the other cups. When given spoons she discards them into a heap, either immediately or after self-correction. Her symbolic expressions, then, tend to corroborate the interpretation that even 18BB is not so much cooperating with the experimenter's model of sorting two sets as she is trying to complete her own design of stacking all and only the cups. One important consequence, nevertheless, is the initiation of recursively composing two sets.

Most adding to two pre-existing compositions presented by the tester to the subjects in phase II are limited to augmenting one of the two pre-existing sets. Though infrequent, adding to two pre-existing compositions just begins to be generated with some systematicity. To illustrate, not only does one infant (18JHo) simultaneously add one element to each pre-existing composition; but a bit later he replaces them in partial temporal overlap (see Chapter 8, Section I for analyses of replacing in two sets at this stage). Thereby, 18JHo generates extensive equivalence by coordinate correspondence and replacement between two sets of three elements each (see Chapter 8, Section II for analyses of correspondences between two sets at this stage). The extensive equivalence classes *18JHo* constructs are not dependent upon predicate identity or classification since he repeatedly mismatches the objects. He puts a green rectangular ring together with the set of red cross rings and a red cross ring together with the set of green rectangular rings.

In most instances, reforming pre-existent compositions remains relatively undifferentiated and global (see Langer, 1980, pages 322 and 323). Systematic reorganization is generated by only a minority of infants. Even these systematic reorganizations are restricted to forming single sets. Yet, these deformations are no longer nonarticulate recompositions such as pushing all objects together to form a heap. Infants' deformations become articulate and produce well-formed recompositions, such as stacks. While they are all still restricted to producing single sets, articulate recompositions may already include all or nearly all objects. So, for instance, subject *18MK* recomposes two pre-existing alignments of cups and spoons plus extra spoons into a stack comprising the cups which she embeds in each other and the spoons which she inserts in the topmost cup. The stack includes all the objects presented. Thus, articulate recomposition, while restricted to forming single sets, may already include all or nearly all objects.

III. Continuing Increase in Size of Compositions

Two-object compositions continue to lose their dominant position in infants' combinations. For the first time, less than half of infants' compositions comprise two objects only in the eight-object conditions. The main compensating increase is in the production of the largest sets possible in these conditions, namely, five- to eight-object compositions, which, however, still constitute only the smallest fraction (17%) of infants' compositions. While most of infants' compositions still comprise two objects only in the four-object conditions they, too, are decreasing in frequency. They, too, are also compensated by an increase in the largest compositions possible in these conditions. These four-object sets now constitute the second largest fraction (27%) of infants compositions.

Two-object compositions are generated more frequently in the four-object (Table 7.5, Row 1, Columns 3–8) than in the comparable eight-object conditions (Table 7.5, Row 4, Columns 3–8). The overall difference of 14% approaches statistical significance ($N = 12$, $x = 3$, $p = .073$, sign test). This is similar to the 15% difference found at age 12 months (Langer, 1980, page 324) and the 17% difference found at age 15 months (page 59).

Even in the four-object conditions, two-object compositions comprise an ever decreasing proportion of infants' combinations. This continuous developmental trend begins at age 12 months and is augmented by a drop from 72% at age 15

TABLE 7.5
Spontaneous Phase I: Mean Frequency and Percentage of Compositional Extent at Age 18 Months

| | Class conditions | | | | | | | | Total | |
| | Semicontrol[a] | | Additive[b] | | Multiplicative[b] | | Disjoint[b] | | | |
	X̄ 1	% 2	X̄ 3	% 4	X̄ 5	% 6	X̄ 7	% 8	X̄ 9	% 10
Four-object condition:										
1. Two-object	7.33	46	8.25	78	11.45	62	7.18	52	8.70	60
2. Three-object	2.00	13	0.83	8	2.82	15	2.09	15	1.90	13
3. Four-object	6.67	42	1.50	14	4.27	23	4.64	33	3.90	27
Eight-object condition:										
4. Two-object			5.64	44	8.42	47	4.18	50	6.15	46
5. Three-object			2.82	22	2.67	15	1.45	17	2.32	18
6. Four-object			1.82	14	3.92	22	1.36	16	2.41	18
7. Five-object			1.18	9	1.67	9	0.45	5	1.12	8
8. Six-object			0.36	3	0.33	2	0.27	3	0.32	2
9. Seven-object			0.27	2	0.17	1	0.27	3	0.24	2
10. Eight-object			0.82	6	0.83	5	0.36	4	0.68	5

[a] $N = 6$ subjects in the semicontrol, four-object condition.
[b] $N = 11$ subjects in the additive eight-object condition, in the multiplicative four-object condition, and in both disjoint conditions.

months (Table 3.4, Row 1, page 59) to 60% at age 18 months (Table 7.5, Row 1). The 12% drop with age is not statistically significant (Mann–Whitney $U =$ 45, $p > .05$). Three-object sets are also generated less frequently in the four-object conditions. The drop is from 20% at age 15 months (Table 3.4, Row 2, page 59) to 13% at age 18 months (Table 7.5, Row 2).

Together, then, there is a 19% drop in generating two- and three-object sets from ages 15 to 18 months in the four-object conditions. This decrease is compensated by a 19% increase in four-object compositions from ages 15 months (Table 3.4, Row 3, page 59) to 18 months (Table 7.5, Row 3). This increase with age is significant (Mann–Whitney $U = 39$, $p < .05$).

The proportion of two- and three-object compositions also decreases in the eight-object conditions. Two-object compositions decrease by 9% and three-object compositions decrease by 6% from ages 15 months (Table 3.3, Rows 4 and 5, page 56) to 18 months (Table 7.5, Rows 4 and 5). However, neither of these decreases with age are statistically significant.

The 15% decrease in generating the smallest compositions is compensated by increases in generating intermediate size compositions. There is a negligible 3% increase in producing four-object sets from ages 15 months (Table 3.3, Row 6, page 56) to 18 months (Table 7.5, Row 6). There is an 11% increase in producing five- to eight-object sets from ages 15 months (Table 3.3, Rows 7–10, page 56) to 18 months (Table 7.5, Rows 7–10). This increase with age in generating five- to eight-object sets is not statistically significant (Mann–Whitney $U = 45$, $p > .05$).

Even two-object compositions, as we will see in Chapter 8, continue to be progressively elaborated. The main advance is in constructing 2 two-element sets. In some instances, these sets entail a variety of binary relations, such as correspondences between the two sets. In other instances, as we have already remarked in Chapter 6, single two-object sets entail progressively elaborate conventional and symbolic features, for instance, when infants pretend to pour liquid from an empty cup onto a doll.

Three-or-more-object sets constitute the majority of compositions generated in the eight-object conditions for the first time. While still in the minority in the four-object conditions, they now comprise 40% of the productions. The main increase is in the production of four-object compositions. While rarely generated at age 15 months, four-object compositions comprise a substantial proportion of set production at age 18 months. Twenty-seven percent of the compositions generated in the four-object conditions comprise all four objects. The proportion of four-object compositions increases in all class conditions from age 15 months. The increase is most striking in the semicontrol condition where four-object compositions are now generated almost as frequently as two-object compositions.

No appreciable change occurs in the production of four-object compositions from ages 15 to 18 months in the eight-object conditions. The frequency of five-

TABLE 7.6
Spontaneous Phase I: Number of Objects Directly Manipulated by 18-Month-Old Subjects to Produce Compositions in All Class Conditions

		Number of objects								
		1	*2*	*3*	*4*	*5*	*6*	*7*	*8*	*Total*
Four-object conditions:										
1.	*Frequency of compositions*	201	323	20	35					579
2.	*% Compositions*	35	56	3	6					100
Eight-object conditions:										
3.	*Frequency of compositions*	204	161	38	26	5	6	1	6	447
4.	*% Compositions*	46	36	9	6	1	1	0	1	100

to eight-object compositions almost triples from a total of 6% at age 15 months to 17% at age 18 months. Thus, almost one-fifth of infants' combinations now consist of sets that comprise an intermediate number of objects.

Many of the intermediate sized compositions are still inarticulate labile compositions, such as heaps. This is particularly so in the case of eight-object compositions which tend to be global. Still, an increasing number are progressively stable, differentiated, and articulate compositions. They constitute progressively equilibriated and enlarged sets of constant givens. As such, they provide the elements necessary for progressive operational constructions to be analyzed in Chapter 8.

With two possible exceptions, little change occurs in the proportion of compositions generated by direct transactions with one to eight objects from ages 15 months (Table 3.5, page 61) to 18 months (Table 7.6). The two potential exceptions are a 10% decrease with age in the proportion of compositions infants construct by directly manipulating one object only and a concomitant 12% increase in compositions constructed by directly manipulating two objects in the four-object conditions. The 10% decrease in single object manipulation in order to construct compositions is not, however, statistically significant (Mann–Whitney, $U = 55$, $p > .05$).

IV. Increasing Stabile Production

Progressive development of combinativity structures is marked by several significant trends at this stage. They include increases in the proportion of stabiles with reciprocal decreases in the proportion of mobiles and combined mobiles–stabiles. The proportion of compositions and recompositions featured by causality and the proportion of two-dimensional, horizontal–vertical constructions do not change.

Most significant is the continuing and progressively inverse associations between age and rate of generating mobiles. Older infants generate proportionately
fewer mobiles. The first shift occurs by stage 4 at age 12 months when infants'
constructions split evenly between 47% mobiles and 47% stabiles, with a small
remainder of combined mobiles–stabiles (Langer, 1980, pages 329 and 330,
Tables 13.5 and 13.6). The second shift occurs by stage 5 at age 15 months when
the frequency of constructing mobiles continues to decrease while stabile production does not change but combined mobiles–stabiles increases (pages 61–
65). The third shift occurs at the present stage when mobile production continues to decrease while stabile production increases.

Stabiles outnumber mobiles 52% to 37% in the four-object conditions (Table
7.7, Rows 4 and 8). This difference approaches significance ($N = 12$, $x = 3$,
$p = .073$, sign test). Stabiles outnumber mobiles even more strongly in the
eight-object conditions where the ratio is more than two to one favoring stabiles
(Table 7.8, Rows 4 and 8). The difference is significant ($N = 12$, $x = 2$, $p
= .019$, sign test).

Stabile compositions constitute the majority for the first time in the four- and
the eight-object conditions (Tables 7.7 and 7.8, Row 4). Producing stabiles
increases 9% in the four object conditions from age 15 months (Table 3.6, Row
4) but is not significant (Mann–Whitney $U = 55$, $p > .05$). Producing stabiles
increases 15% in the eight-object conditions from age 15 months (Table 3.7,
Row 4). This increase is significant (Mann–Whitney $U = 22$, $p < .01$).

The proportion of stabiles ranges from a low of 39% in the four-object disjoint
condition to a high of 66% in the four-object additive condition. Indeed, the
four-object disjoint condition is the only task that results in a minority of stabiles,
such that infants produce more mobiles than stabiles in this condition. Overall,
and in all five other test conditions, infants generate more stabiles than mobiles,
with stabiles always constituting the majority.

The rate of producing stabiles is uniform in the eight-object conditions. The
range extends only from a low of 57% in the additive condition to a high of 62%
in the multiplicative condition (Table 7.8, Row 4). The rate is more variable in
the four-object condition, ranging from 39% to 66% (Table 7.7, Row 4).

Parallel distributions, we will see, characterize the ranges of producing
mobiles and stabiles. For both, the rates of productivity are highly uniform in the
eight-object conditions. They are more variable in the four-object conditions.

The proportion of stabiles featured by contact, proximity, and combined contact–proximity, does not change from ages 12 to 18 months in the eight-object
conditions (Table 7.8, Rows 1–3, Columns 1–8). About two-thirds of stabiles
are featured by contact at ages 12, 15, and 18 months. This proportion does not
vary as a function of class conditions at age 18 months.

More stabiles than mobiles are featured by proximity or combined contact–
proximity in the eight-object conditions (compare Rows 1–3 with Rows 5–7 in

TABLE 7.7
Four-Object Conditions, Spontaneous Phase I: Mean Frequency and Percentage of Compositional Features at Age 18 Months

| | Class conditions | | | | | | | | | |
| | Semicontrol[a] | | Additive | | Multiplicative[b] | | Disjoint[b] | | Total | |
	X̄ 1	% 2	X̄ 3	% 4	X̄ 5	% 6	X̄ 7	% 8	X̄ 9	% 10
1. Contact stabile	1.33	8	3.83	36	4.18	23	2.73	20	3.25	22
2. Proximity stabile	4.50	28	2.67	25	3.09	17	1.64	12	2.78	19
3. Contact–proximity stabile	3.50	22	0.50	5	2.18	12	1.09	8	1.58	11
4. Total stabile	9.33	58	7.00	66	9.36	51	5.45	39	7.58	52
5. Contact mobile	4.00	25	2.08	20	4.73	26	3.82	27	3.58	25
6. Proximity mobile	0.17	1	0.83	8	1.18	6	1.73	12	1.08	7
7. Contact–proximity mobile	0.33	2	0.08	1	0.91	5	1.18	8	0.65	4
8. Total mobile	4.50	28	3.00	28	6.82	37	6.73	48	5.30	37
9. Mobile–stabile	2.17	14	0.58	6	2.27	12	1.73	12	1.60	11
10. Causal	3.83	24	1.25	12	4.36	24	4.18	30	3.30	23
11. Noncausal	12.17	76	9.33	88	14.18	76	9.73	70	11.20	77
12. Horizontal[c]	8.00	55	7.00	73	8.27	66	8.55	76	7.95	69
13. Vertical[c]	2.67	18	2.27	24	3.18	26	1.73	15	2.44	21
14. Horizontal–vertical[c]	3.83	26	0.27	3	1.00	8	0.91	8	1.21	10

[a]N = 6 subjects.
[b]N = 11 subjects.
[c]Compositions whose spatial dimensions are ambiguous are not scored. Consequently, the dimensional means summate to less than the compositional means.

TABLE 7.8

Eight-Object Conditions, Spontaneous Phase I: Mean Frequency and Percentage
of Compositional Features at Age 18 Months

		Class conditions							
		Additive[a]		Multiplicative		Disjoint[a]		Total	
		$\bar{X}$	%	$\bar{X}$	%	$\bar{X}$	%	$\bar{X}$	%
		1	2	3	4	5	6	7	8
1.	Contact stabile	5.36	42	6.25	35	3.55	42	5.09	38
2.	Proximity stabile	1.09	8	3.00	17	0.73	9	1.65	12
3.	Contact–proximity stabile	0.91	7	1.92	11	0.64	8	1.18	9
4.	Total stabile	7.36	57	11.17	62	4.91	59	7.91	60
5.	Contact mobile	2.36	18	3.75	21	2.09	25	2.76	21
6.	Proximity mobile	0.82	6	0.25	1	0.18	2	0.41	3
7.	Contact–proximity mobile	0.27	2	0.50	3	0.36	4	0.38	3
8.	Total mobile	3.45	27	4.50	25	2.64	32	3.56	27
9.	Mobile–stabile	2.09	16	2.33	13	0.82	10	1.76	13
10.	Causal	2.73	21	3.25	18	1.64	20	2.56	19
11.	Noncausal	10.18	79	14.75	82	6.73	80	10.68	81
12.	Horizontal[b]	5.18	52	6.83	58	1.70	29	4.73	50
13.	Vertical[b]	2.73	27	2.33	20	2.60	44	2.55	27
14.	Horizontal–vertical[b]	2.09	21	2.67	23	1.60	27	2.15	23

[a]$N = 11$ subjects in the additive and disjoint conditions.

[b]Compositions whose spatial dimensions are ambiguous are not scored. Consequently, the dimensional means summate to less than the total compositional means.

Table 7.8). These features mark one-third of stabiles and only one-fifth of mobiles. These features are particularly prominent characteristics of stabiles generated in the eight-object multiplicative condition, where they are almost as frequent as contact features of stabiles.

The proportions of these features changes from ages 12 to 18 months in the four-object conditions (Table 7.7, Rows 1–3, Columns 1–10). At age 12 months, more than three-quarters of stabiles are featured by contact. This decreases to about two-thirds of stabiles featured by contact at age 15 months. By age 18 months only a little more than two-fifths are featured by contact. This change with age is most marked in the semicontrol condition where almost all stabiles are featured by either proximity or combined contact–proximity.

Mobile constructions are in the decided minority by age 18 months. Mobiles do not constitute a majority of the constructions generated in any of the test conditions. In the four-object conditions, a little more than one-third of the constructions are mobiles (Table 7.7, Row 8). The proportion is even less in the eight-object conditions where mobiles constitute a little more than one-fourth of the constructions (Table 7.8, Row 8).

Mobile production decreases a negligible 3% from age 15 months (Table 3.6, Row 8, page 62) in the four-object conditions. But it drops 12% from age 15 months (Table 3.7, Row 8, page 63) in the eight-object condition. This decrease with age is compensated by a significant increase in stabiles (see page 158). Rate of producing mobiles varies somewhat as an intersective function of class by number of objects conditions. The range is from a low of 25% mobiles in the eight-object multiplicative condition to a high of 48% in the four-object disjoint condition. Rate of producing mobiles is almost perfectly uniform in the eight-object conditions, ranging between 25% and 32%. Rate of producing mobiles is more variable in the four-object conditions, ranging between 28% and 48%.

The proportion of mobiles featured by contact, proximity, and combined contact–proximity does not change from ages 12 to 18 months in the eight-object conditions (Table 7.8, Rows 5–7, Columns 1–8). About three-fourths of mobiles are featured by contact at ages 12, 15, and 18 months. This proportion does not vary as a function of class condition at age 18 months.

The proportions of these features marking mobiles generated in the four-object conditions decreases at age 18 months (Table 7.7, Rows 5–7, Columns 1–10). More than four-fifths of mobiles are featured by contact at ages 12 and 15 months. It decreases to two-thirds at age 18 months with a reciprocal increase in the proportion of mobiles featured by proximity and combined contact–proximity. This shift is most pronounced in the four-object disjoint condition where 43% of mobiles are featured by either proximity or combined contact–proximity.

Mobile–stabile constructions are generated a little less frequently at age 18 months than at age 15 months. They comprise a little more than one-tenth of infants' compositions in both the four object (Table 7.7, Row 9) and eight-object conditions (Table 7.8, Row 9). Thus, the proportions do not vary substantially across class and number of objects conditions. The range is only from a low of 6% of all constructions in the four-object additive condition to a high of 16% in the eight-object additive condition.

Causal compositions comprise about one-fifth of infants' constructions in both the four-object (Table 7.7, Rows 10 and 11) and eight-object conditions (Table 7.8, Rows 10 and 11). The proportions do not change from age 15 months (Tables 3.6 and 3.7, Rows 10 and 11, pages 62 and 63). As with the other features analyzed so far, the rate at which causality marks composing is uniform in the eight-object conditions; the rate is more variable in the four-object conditions. In the eight-object conditions the range is only between 18% and 21%, while in the four-object conditions the range is between 12% and 30%.

The dimensional features of compositions do not change from ages 15 months to 18 months (Tables 7.7 and 7.8, Rows 12–14). Most are constructed in a single horizontal dimension. Construction in a single vertical dimension is second most frequent. Construction in two dimensions, horizontal and vertical is least frequent, although substantial in the eight-object conditions.

The trend is again toward greater uniformity in the eight-object conditions. The range of producing horizontal–vertical constructions is only between 21% and 27% in the eight-object conditions. In the four-object conditions, the range is between a low of 3% in the additive and a high of 26% in the semicontrol conditions.

V. Continuing Increase in Consecutive and Contemporaneous Compositions

Isolated compositions not preceded or followed by another composition become ever more rare. In the four-object conditions, generating isolate sets decreases from 17% at age 15 months to 7% at age 18 months (Table 7.9, Row 1). This decrease with age is significant (Mann–Whitney $U = 32$, $p = .025$). In the eight-object conditions, producing isolate sets decreases from 10% at age 15 months to 5% at age 18 months (Table 7.9, Row 5). These proportions do not vary as a function of class or number of object conditions at age 18 months since isolate sets never exceed 10% of infants' combinativity productions.

Consecutively combining objects into sets continues to predominate (Table 7.9). The proportion increases in the four-object conditions from 78% at age 15 months to 88% at age 18 months (Table 7.9, Row 2). This increase with age is significant (Mann–Whitney $U = 25$, $p = .01$). The proportion does not change in the eight-object conditions; it is 73% at age 15 months and 71% at age 18 months (Table 7.9, Row 6). Most consecutively constructed sets are the products of variations upon initial thematic compositions; at this stage more recompositions are generated than compositions (see Table 7.2).

The increase in consecutively constructed sets accounts for the decrease in isolate sets in the four-object conditions. Partially overlapping and simultaneous composing remain infrequent (Table 7.9, Rows 3 and 4). Still, their total proportion (6%) is now equivalent to that of isolate composing (7%).

Sets generated in partial temporal overlap and in simultaneity now constitute one-fourth of all infants' constructions in the eight-object conditions. They exceed the generation of isolate sets, and by a factor of five. Partially overlapping composing increases from 13% at age 15 months to 21% at age 18 months (Table 7.9, Row 7). This increase is not statistically significant (Mann–Whitney $U = 60$, $p > .05$) although it accounts for both decreases in generating isolate and consecutive sets. As in the four-object conditions, the proportion of simultaneously combining objects into two sets remains constant and very small (Table 7.9, Row 8). While more than one-fourth of the sets are constructed in partial temporal overlap or simultaneously in additive and multiplicative conditions, they are never generated in the disjoint condition.

TABLE 7.9
Spontaneous Phase I: Temporal Relations between Compositions at Age 18 Months

					Class conditions					
	Semicontrol[a]		Additive[b]		Multiplicative[b]		Disjoint[b]		Total	
	X̄ 1	% 2	X̄ 3	% 4	X̄ 5	% 6	X̄ 7	% 8	X̄ 9	% 10
Four-object condition:										
1. Isolate	0.83	5	1.00	9	0.64	3	1.27	9	0.95	7
2. Consecutive	14.50	91	9.58	91	15.91	86	12.18	88	12.78	88
3. Partially overlapping	0.67	4	0.00	0	1.82	10	0.27	2	0.68	5
4. Simultaneous	0.00	0	0.00	0	0.18	1	0.18	1	0.10	1
Eight-object condition:										
5. Isolate			0.73	6	0.58	3	0.82	10	0.71	5
6. Consecutive			8.45	65	11.83	66	7.55	90	9.35	71
7. Partially overlapping			3.36	26	4.92	27	0.00	0	2.82	21
8. Simultaneous			0.36	3	0.67	4	0.00	0	0.35	3

[a]N = 6 subjects.
[b]N = 11 subjects in the multiplicative and disjoint four-object conditions, and in the additive and disjoint eight-object conditions.

Elaborating Relations upon Relations within Paired Compositions 8

Progressively stable, flexible, and durable composition is combined with increasing production of recompositions and of contemporaneous compositions. Set size also increases, although this features individual compositions and recompositions more than it does two contemporaneous compositions and recompositions. These structural developments mark both infants' spontaneous and their provoked combinativity.

Progressive combinativity foundations are thereby constructed by infants for structuring coordinated second-order representational cognitions. Second-order constructions are at the heart of progress in relational and conditional structures at this stage. Correspondences increasingly produce two quantitatively equivalent compositions. Adding and subtracting objects increasingly produce two ordered nonequivalent compositions. All exchange operations transform these matched compositions and series to produce equivalences upon equivalences and orders upon orders. Thus equivalences are mapped onto equivalences, and orders are mapped onto orders. By these mappings upon mappings infants progressively construct representations of equivalences and orders.

Progress in intensive structuring parallels these developments in extensive structuring. Infants begin to structure second-order or representational classification. They generate pairs of coordinate compositions that are unmixed in their predicate properties such that they are featured by both similarities and differences. As expected, at its origins this development is limited to only one of the simplest class conditions—an additive class structure.

I. Expanding Exchange within Paired Compositions

All forms of exchange are now applied to two contemporaneous compositions or subcompositions. They are, however, constrained by many limitations. The most striking constraint is that exchanges between two collections are limited to single operations. With one rudimentary exception, coordinated exchange (e.g., substituting and commuting) between two compositions or subcompositions is not generated. Moreover, most exchanges are still applied to single compositions. But now, and this is a second major advance at this stage, these exchanges include coordinating, replacing, substituting, and commuting.

Replacing is still mainly applied to single compositions (Table 8.1). Replacing elements within single three-or-more-object compositions is generated by all 12 subjects (Table 8.1). Most are limited to three- and four-object compositions.

Infants replace as many as two elements in their four-object compositions. But they do not replace more than a single element in five- to seven-object compositions. Yet the equivalence relations they produce by replacing only one element may be quite precise. For instance, after removing a car and rotating it, subject 18PC replaces the same car in its initial position in a five-object alignment she previously constructed. This precision is accompanied by symbolic rudiments (18PC vocalizes onomatopoetically, "Vroum, vroum.")

All the objects composed are sometimes replaced when compositions are constructed that contain no more than three elements. For instance, subject 18BB generates five successive replacements within a three-object composition she has constructed. The first two are exact reproductions of each other by precise replacement of a brush. After this, 18BB switches to replacing a spoon, switches back to replacing the brush, and finally switches to replacing a mirror. In this way 18BB replaces all three objects comprising her composition. In between, 18BB brushes her hair with each object.

Progressively reversible replacement is marked by flexibility and pragmatic associativity. Infants begin to switch between objects replaced within the same compositions; and they return to replacing an initial object after replacing other

TABLE 8.1
Number of Subjects Generating Exchange at Age 18 Months

	One composition						Two compositions
	3-object	4-object	5-object	6-object	7-object	8-object	
Replace	6	5	4	2	1	0	1
Substitute	6	4	1	0	1	0	5
Commute	6	7	4	2	1	1	3
Coordinate exchanges	3	6	1	3	0	0	1

objects. Thus, for instance, the sequence of compositions and five recompositions by *18BB* form a flexibly reversible equivalence structure marked by associativity:

$$[(B, M, S) \pm B] \sim [(B, M, S) \pm B] \sim [(B, M, S) \pm S] \sim [(B, M, S) \pm B] \sim$$
$$[(B, M, S) \pm M] \sim (B, M, S) \qquad (8.1)$$

Increasingly the relations between objects combined into compositions are stabile static relations and not mobile kinetic relations (see pages 157–161). Therefore, the compositions in Eq. (8.1) are marked by commas between the initials of the objects instead of > (for definitions of the notation see Langer, 1980, pages 81–84, 157, and 342–344). Minus and plus signs before the objects replaced represent subtracting and adding the same object from the three-object compositions. Quantitative equivalence is preserved in Eq. (8.1) regardless of which object is replaced. Neither the object nor the order of replacement affects equivalence. Thus, replacing is also becoming pragmatically associative.

Replacement exchanges of this order reflect both progressive regulation and reversibility. Progressive regulation is marked by three features. The first is not new to this stage. Infants repeatedly reproduce the same replacement with the same object. A second regulatory feature, while not new to this stage, increases in frequency and efficiency. Infants progressively correct mistakes and try to overcome difficulties in their constructions.

A third regulatory feature originates at this stage. Infants begin to conserve replacements even when they interpolate two types of transformations. In one type, infants interpolate routines with objects before replacing them. For instance, *18BB* consistently interpolates a (sometimes conventionally appropriate) brushing routine with each object before replacing it; replacement is repeated five times across such interpolated routines by *18BB*.

In the other type of interpolated interaction, infants compose an unrelated second collection of objects while or between replacing objects in an initial composition that they have constructed:

33–45. *LH holds Doll 1*
  33. *RH picks up Doll 3 and places D3 upright in Circular Ring 4*
  34. *RH picks up Doll 4 and places D4 upright in Circular Ring 3*
  35. *RH picks up Doll 2, holds D2 in air above the objects briefly as looks at them, and places D2 upright in Circular Ring 2*
 35a. *D2 displaces CR2 slightly*
  36. *RH thumb pushes over D2 which falls flat just outside of CR2*
  37. *RH picks up D2 and holds D2 upright in CR2; in process right arm pushes D4 out of CR3 (experimenter grasps D4)*
  38. *RH releases D2 which falls flat inside CR2*
  39. *RH uprights D2 inside CR2 (experimenter simultaneously re-uprights D4 inside CR3)*
  40. *RH pushes D4 over*

41. RH *immediately picks up D4 and places D4 upright inside Circular Ring 1*
42. RH *picks up D4 and places D4 upright inside CR3*
43. RH *pushes over D3 which rolls toward experimenter*
44. RH *reaches for D3 (experimenter places D3 upright behind CR4)*
45. RH *picks up D3 and replaces D3 upright in CR4*
46. LH *transfers D1 to RH which places D1 upright in CR1*

(18SB, pages 46 and 47)

Several collections (Lines 35–42) are composed by *18SB* inbetween replacing objects in one collection (Lines 33 and 43–45). Together with another composition (Line 46), *18SB* also potentially generates four corresponding two-object subcompositions, and/or two corresponding four-object subcompositions (see Section II). Furthermore, replacing is coordinated with substituting (Lines 38–41), which will be considered at the end of this section.

Replacing is progressively coregulated, as well as regulated. Elements comprising the equivalence sets are reciprocally adjusted to each other in order to conserve replacement. To illustrate, first subject *18JC* uprights a red cylinder to serve as a causal patient. Then she uses a blue cylinder as an instrumental object with which to tap precisely and repeatedly on the uppermost end of the red cylinder. When, as a consequence, the red cylinder falls over, the result is observed and transformed by *18JC* so as to reconstruct the initial upright state of the patient object (i.e., she uprights the red cylinder again). Once again she uses the instrumental object precisely and repeatedly to tap on the uppermost end of the patient object. The products are manifold reproductions of quantitative equivalence by coregulated replacement. These are accompanied by careful visual observation and some onomatopoeic ("Boom") encoding.

Other analogous forms of coregulated replacement are also generated at this stage. One, whose general form we have come across previously, involves inserting and stirring two or more spoons in a cup. If, as a consequence, the cup falls over or is tilted, infants upright the cup and reproduce equivalences by replacing; that is, after uprighting the cup they reinsert the spoons and continue stirring. Another related form is a by-product of infants' correcting their own constructive transformations. To illustrate, in apparent anticipation of his later maneuvers, subject *18JHe* composes three of the four rings he subsequently uses as recipients for dolls. Then, in succession, he places three dolls upright in three recipient rings. The last insertion is not successfully executed and is marked by some symbolic cognizance (a slight chuckle, "Heh"). The error is immediately rectified. The product is equivalence by coregulated replacement.

One infant generates either (a) replacing two elements in one four-element composition, or (b) replacing single elements in 2 two-element subcompositions, or (c) both:

7.5. RH *lowers Block 4 on top of Block 3, unaligned*
7.5. Lh *lowers Block 1 on top of Block 2, unaligned*

7.5a. *B4 and B1 touch*
  9. *BH raise B1 and B4*
  10. *BH lower B1 and B4 on top of B2 and B3 again*
 10a. *B1 and B4 barely make contact*
  11. *BH hold B1 and B4 on B2 and B3, as smiles at experimenter*
  12. *BH release B1 and B4 on top of B2 and B3, then looks at blocks*

(18TT, page 1)

This is the most advanced form of replacing generated at this stage; even though the status of this construction is somewhat ambiguous as to whether it involves replacing in only 1 four-object composition or in 2 two-object compositions. This same infant also generates potential replacing in two compositions in another context.

To the limited extent to which symbolic expressions are produced by infants when replacing objects, the relevance of the symbolization to the ongoing exchange is indirect at most. In this regard, *18PC's* onomatopoetic representations (given on page 166) are typical in two ways. The first way is general to all subjects at this stage. The symbolic expressions do not refer to the subjects' replacements. Rather, they refer to or denote an event (action) aspect or an object involved in the subjects' construction of the initial composition. The second way is that most of the symbolic behavior still consists of vocal or bodily gestures rather than speech.

The most advanced symbolic expression, generated by one subject only, (*18BB*), occurs after the infant stacks three cups together. It takes dual, redundant forms. At the same time, *18BB* communicates to the experimenter that she wants the fourth cup by both gestural (open–close hand movements toward the desired object) and by verbal ("Want that") reference. Again, then, the symbolic activity is generated in order to facilitate construction of the original composition, not replacement within it.

Substituting elements within single compositions of three or more objects is generated by 10 (of 12) subjects. Most substitutions are still limited to three-object compositions. But as many subjects substitute in four-or-more as in three-object compositions (Table 8.1). One restriction characteristic of earlier stages still holds. Most substitutions are irreversible exchanges; inverse substituting is still rarely applied to single compositions that include three or more objects.

As many as two elements are substituted in three-object compositions. Typically, infants directly manipulate only one object in these exchanges. They take away one element from a three-object composition and substitute another single element in its place. Infants rarely manipulate two objects in these exchanges. It is unusual for infants to take away two elements from a three-object composition and substitute two other objects in their place to reform a three-object composition. As may therefore be expected, only single elements are substituted within four-or-more-object compositions.

Regulative attempts to overcome physical resistances by objects are one source of infants extending substituting to four-or-more-object compositions:

9.   RH places Circular Ring 3 on Circular Ring 1 and, in process, RH knocks Doll 2 flat and either RH or CR3 moves CR1 and Circular Ring 2 such that the three circular rings overlap each other (i.e., not in a neat stack) (experimenter places Doll 4 upright ½ inch to left)

10. RH picks up D2 and places D2 flat on CR3 but D2 rolls off onto table and over edge to chair seat

11. RH picks up D4 and places D4 tilted flat on and within CR3, CR1, and CR2 stack   (18SB, page 44)

Doll 4 is successfully balanced on the stack by 18SB in place of Doll 2 when it rolls off.

The major development in substituting at this stage consists of exchanges involving two contemporaneous compositions (Table 8.1). All but one of the five subjects generating second-order substitution do so once only. The exceptional subject, 18SB, does so three separate times.

Three forms are generated at this stage. One form already involves exchanging objects between two compositions or subcompositions:

14. RH holds Circular Ring 2 on Blocks 1 and 2, briefly

15. RH touches CR2 on Circular Ring 3 and Block 4, briefly

16. RH places CR2 on B1 and B2   (18JHe, page 9)

After composing two collections (not reproduced in the protocol fragment), 18JHe adds a third element to one collection; then he takes the third element away from the first collection and adds it to the second collection; finally he takes the third element away from the second collection and adds it back to the first collection. Several features of this construction are noteworthy. Most significant is the element of reversibility. Almost all infants who generate second-order substitution also invert the exchange.

Initially 18JHe composes two quantitatively equivalent collections; each collection comprises the minimum of two objects. Objects are not exchanged between these two compositions. Rather, a third object is first added to one collection, then it is added to the other collection, and then it is returned to the first collection. This form of substitution has two consequences. After their initial equivalence, the two compositions are never again equal to each other. One collection always comprises two elements when the other comprises three elements. Consecutively, however, the two collections are equal; in turn they each comprise three objects. This includes the precursory reversible identity element of returning the additional object to the first composition.

It is the general case that the form of reversibility that conditions second-order substitution at this stage is always consecutive. The exchanges are always from one composition of objects to a second, and then from the second composition to the first. Infants never generated simultaneous exchanges of elements between two compositions.

The structure of *18JHe*'s constructions, then, forms second-order substitution in which

$$<(CR2 > RC1, RC2) \& (CR3, RC4)> \approx <(RC1, RC2) \& (CR2 > CR3, CR4)> \approx <(CR2 > RC1, RC2) \& (CR3, RC4)>. \qquad (8.2)$$

Together the two contemporaneous ordered sets remain symmetrically unequal over both the first, direct transformation and the second, inverse transformation. The ampersand indicates that the two compositions are contemporaneous. Consecutive substitution inverts the two ordered compositions even though the quality of the member sets varies.

In fact, infants need make no effort to construct simultaneous equivalence between the member sets in order to generate substitution within two compositions:

30. *RH place Yellow Spoon 1 in Orange Cup 2 (all four spoons are now together in OC2)*
31. *LH picks up Orange Cup 1 and then immediately sets OC1 down*
32. *RH picks up Yellow Cup 2, transports YC2 across array, and places YC2 down in front of OC1*
33. *RH takes Orange Spoon 1 out of OC2 and inserts OS1 in YC2*
34. *RH beats OS1 in bottom of YC2, about 6 times*
35. *RH replaces OS1 in OC2*   (*18BB*, page 24)

In *18BB*'s initial construction of two compositions and throughout her transformations of the two compositions, they are always quantitatively nonequivalent to each other. Nevertheless, *18BB* conserves quantitative equivalence within the whole comprising the two compositions by inverse substitution, that is,

$$[(OS1, OS2, YS1, YS2 > OC2) \& (OC1, YC2)] \approx [(OS2, YS1, YS2 > OC2) \& (OC1, OS1 > YC2)] \approx [(OS1, OS2, YS1, YS2 > OC2) \& (OC2, YC2)]. \qquad (8.3)$$

Consecutively, the two sets comprise (5, 2), (4, 3), and (5, 2) elements, while the whole of 7 elements remains invariant.

Infants just begin in rare instances to generate quantitative equivalence between two compositions. For example, subject *18SB* first constructs two stacks, one comprising four columns and the other comprising two columns (with the tester helping *18SB* to make the stacks steady so that they do not topple). The four-object stack is topped off by Red Cylinder 2 and the two-object stack is topped off by Yellow Triangular Column 1. Then *18SB* takes Red Cylinder 2 off the four-object stack and stacks it on Yellow Triangular Column 1. Consecutively, then, *18SB* forms two stacks comprising (4, 2) and (3, 3) elements. A product is simultaneous quantitative equivalence (3, 3) between the two stacks.

The second form of second-order substitution does not include any interchange of objects between two compositions. It only includes exchanging objects within two compositions or subcompositions. For instance, in another task subject *18SB* first constructs two ordered subcompositions of 〈 3-, 2- 〉 objects, respectively (see *18SB* protocol fragment and analysis on pages 167 and 168). The first subcomposition comprises a stack of Circular Rings 1 and 2 with Doll 2 placed upright inside the stack, and the second subcomposition comprises Doll 1 placed upright inside Circular Ring 3. After this she substitutes Doll 3 for Doll 2 in the three-object subcomposition and then inverts this by substituting Doll 2 for Doll 3 to form a three-object identity set. Finally, she substitutes Doll 4 for Doll 1 in the two-object subcomposition and then substitutes Doll 3 for Doll 4 to form a two-object equivalence (but not identity) set.

Throughout *18SB* conserves the quantitative relation between the 〈 3-, 2- 〉 object ordered subcompositions by exchanging single elements within but not between the two subcompositions. Thereby, she structures extended second-order substituting:

<(CR1, CR2, D2) & (CR3, D1)> ≈ <(CR1, CR2, D3) & (CR3, D1)>
≈ <(CR1, CR2, D2) & (CR3, D1)> ≈ <(CR1, CR2, D2) & (CR3, D4)>
≈ <(CR1, CR2, D2) & (CR3, D3)>   (8.4)

This structure is featured by inverse substituting within the three-object subcollection but not the two-object subcollection. Significantly, this structure conserves the ordered 〈 3-, 2- 〉 object series, as does *18JHe*'s substitution (pages 170 and 171).

The third form of second-order substitution just begins to be generated. It requires exchanging objects between and within two compositions or subcompositions. For instance, first subject *18SB* places a Yellow Spoon flat on upright Yellow Cylinder 3 and then Red Spoon 3 flat on upright Yellow Cylinder 2 (with the experimenter helping to make the spoons balance on the cylinders). After constructing these two quantitatively equivalent and spatially corresponding two-object subcompositions, *18SB* substitutes Red Spoon 2 for Red Spoon 3 within the second subcomposition. Then she exchanges elements between the two subcompositions by substituting Red Spoon 3 for the Yellow Spoon in the first subcomposition. Thus, *18SB* conserves quantitative equivalence and spatial correspondence within and between the two subcompositions.

It should not be overlooked that the mappings and routines that are used to generate second-order substitution become progressively differentiated, coordinated, and regulated. Consider *18SB*'s constructions. Red Spoon 2 is transferred from the left to the right hand in anticipation of the left hand taking Red Spoon 3 off Yellow Cylinder 2 and the right hand substituting Red Spoon 2 on Yellow Cylinder 2. An accidental by-product of substituting Red Spoon 2 for Red Spoon 3 is that Red Spoon 2 knocks the Yellow Spoon off Yellow Cylinder 3 and knocks

Yellow Cylinder 3 over. This act decomposes the first subcomposition. The disruption leads *18SB* to generate a coregulative sequence of interactions that entail substitution in the second subcomposition as well. Her right hand uprights Yellow Cylinder 3 in anticipation of transferring Red Spoon 3 from her left to her right hand which then places Red Spoon 3 on Yellow Cylinder 3.

Commuting elements within single compositions is generated by all subjects (Table 8.1). Most are no longer limited to three-object collections; rather, commuting is now usually applied to four-object compositions. Even commuting of five-object compositions is generated as frequently as commuting of three-object compositions; and commuting of six-object compositions is already generated by four subjects. Commuting of seven- and eight-object compositions is rare. As at age 15 months, inverse commuting of three-or-more object compositions is also rare.

Unlike substituting and replacing, it is not at all unusual for infants to commute two and even all three elements comprising three-object compositions:

21.   *RH places Green Circular Ring 2 and Yellow Cross Ring 2 on top of Yellow Circular Ring 1, very carefully to form a stack of three objects*
22.   *RH picks up GCR2/YCR2/YCR1 by holding onto the outer edges*
23.   *RH turns GCR2/YCR2/YCR1 stack over in the air so YCR1 is on the bottom and places stack on table*   (18ML, page 18)

What is still unusual for this stage is that the transformation is so carefully regulated; *18ML* holds the stack together by picking up all the rings by their edges. This method enables him to commute precisely all three objects at the same time while keeping the other features of the composition constant. The sole difference between the initial composition and its recomposition is the order of objects. The order in the recomposition is the reciprocal of the order in the composition.

Commuting four-or-more-object compositions rarely involves interchanging more than one or two objects. Moreover, it is usually not as well-regulated as commuting three-object compositions. Sometimes, it is precipitated by attempts to overcome physical resistances from objects. In most instances, however, commuting four-object compositions is no longer the extension of accidental beginnings but is already partially systematic.

Even commuting five-object compositions is sometimes marked by initial systematicity. For instance, first subject *18JHo* constructs a two-dimensional (horizontal–vertical) composition by placing two objects so that they bridge three other objects. He commutes this five-object set by recomposing it into a one-dimensional (horizontal) structure.

Rudimentary attempts are made by two infants to commute six-object compositions with some systematicity. The most advanced construction, generated by subject *18BB*, is even marked by some self-correction of objects which she drops in the process of displacement. Commutativity is generated by *18BB* shifting four elements of a six-object composition to the right, indicating some systematicity to the process of transformation. But the product is nonsystematic; the alignment is transformed into a partial help. In comparison, the few instances of commuting seven- and eight-object compositions are entirely nonsystematic, in both process and product of construction.

Commuting two contemporaneous compositions is generated by one-fourth of the subjects (Table 8.1). Unlike commuting single compositions, commuting two compositions is not generated frequently by these infants: it is generated once only by each infant. This indicates that second-order commuting is only in its initial stage of development.

A structural indicator is that at its origin second-order commuting is limited to exchanging the order relations between objects within each of the two compositions or subcompositions. Unlike true (formal) binary commuting, elementary second-order commuting never exchanges the order relations between compositions or subcompositions. The most advanced form includes commuting all the objects within each composition:

12. *LH picks up Yellow Cross Ring 2 and places YCR2 on stack of Red Rectangular Ring/Green Cross Ring 2/Green Cross Ring 1*
13. *LH picks up Yellow Cross Ring 1 and brings YCR1 up toward face, holding YCR1 by its edge, looking at it for a few seconds*
14. *LH places YCR1 on Green Circular Ring 1*
15. *LH picks up YCR1 and GCircR1 as a unit and rotates them 180° in the air*
16. *LH slides fingers through YCR1 and GCircR1 and places YCR1 and GCircR1 down on the table with GCircR1 on top*
17. *RH picks up stack of YCR2/RRR/GCR2/GCR1 as a unit, holding onto frame by pinching out and inside*
18. *RH turns stack over in air and places stack of YCR2/RRR/GCR2/GCR1 back down on table in reverse stacked manner*   (18ML, page 19)

First *18ML* composes two contemporaneous collections of four and two objects respectively (Lines 12–14); only the last move in constructing the four-object stack is reproduced in the protocol fragment (Line 12). In succession he inverts the order of object placement within each set (Lines 15 and 16 and 17 and 18, respectively) such that

$$[<YCR2 > RRR > GCR2 > GCR1> \ \& \ <YCR1 > GCircR1>] \leadsto$$
$$[<GCR1 > GCR2 > RRR > YCR2> \ \& \ < GCircR1 > YCR1>]. \qquad (8.5)$$

The transformations are executed with precision and care; they are well-regulated. Moreover, *18ML* commutes the two compositions by corresponding transformations. Both compositions start off as stacks; in turn, each is inverted, such that both compositions end up as stacks again. The ampersands indicate that commuting conserves the relation within the two contemporaneous compositions, that is, of preserving equivalence ($\leadsto$) within each composition.

The two compositions are not quantitatively equivalent and they are mixed by predicate properties. This is the form of two of the three second-order commuting structures generated at this age. Infants only produce quantitative equivalence between the members comprising each composition and in the whole comprising both compositions.

Another structural indicator that second-order commuting is in its initial stage of development is that only one infant conditions it by inverse reversibility. Moreover, this infant (*18TT*) only generates it once between two subcollections of two blocks each. Two corresponding stacks of two blocks each are initially constructed by *18TT*. These two stacks are transformed by *18TT* into two corresponding alignments of two objects each. Inverse transformations reconstitute the initial two corresponding stacks of two objects each:

$$[\langle\, B1\,\rangle\, B2\,\rangle : \langle\, B4\,\rangle\, B3\,\rangle] \leadsto [\langle\, B1,\, B2\,\rangle : \langle\, B4,\, B3\,\rangle] \leadsto$$
$$[\langle\, B1\,\rangle\, B2\,\rangle : \langle\, B4\,\rangle\, B3\,\rangle] \tag{8.6}$$

This is the only reversible structure of second-order commuting generated at this stage. The colons indicate that the two sets are in one-to-one correspondence throughout, that is, invariant and equal across commuting.

The coordination of two exchange operations is generated by 11 subjects (Table 8.1). These coordinations are all still limited to sequential interweaving; at this stage infants never generate two exchange operations at the same time. With one minor exception, the prerequisite condition of even two sequentially coordinate exchanges of two sets is not yet generated.

Coordinating exchanges usually involves single four-object compositions; but some already apply to somewhat larger compositions. Most interweave replacing with commuting. Coordinating replacing with substituting (e.g., the *18SB* protocol fragment on pages 167 and 168) and substituting with commuting is generated less frequently. Still some of these are already quite elaborate and extensive. For instance, subject *18ML* interweaves repeated substituting, replacing, substituting, and replacing in a three-object stack of cylinders and rings. The sequence is marked by many regulative attempts to overcome physical resistances by the objects to *18ML*'s limited abilities to stack them. (As we have seen many times, possible and impossible vertical balancing is a difficult problem of some interest to infants at this stage.)

Coordinating three exchange operations is generated by three subjects. They, too, consist of sequentially interweaving. They are applied to single sets only. To illustrate, after inserting all four spoons in an orange cup, subject *18BB* transfers all four spoons to a yellow cup. This initial substitution is inverted by a second substitution to produce a reversible equivalence structure. All four spoons are reinserted in the orange cup. The order in which the four spoons are placed in the orange cup are then repeatedly commuted. Finally, two spoons are consecutively taken out and replaced in the orange cup. Thus, *18BB* constructs an extensive equivalence set of five objects by sequentially coordinating reversible substituting, commuting, and replacing of objects within the set.

II. Articulation of Correspondences between Two Very Small Compositions

Second-order correspondences continue to develop. They are marked by progressive detachment, flexibility, and regulation. Thus they are increasingly exploited as cognitive givens. They are increasingly used as elements for exchange operations that produce equivalences upon equivalences. They are also increasingly used as elements for experimentation that produces covarying dependencies.

All infants but one generate one-to-one correspondences between two minimal compositions or subcompositions in which the matched units include no more than two objects each (Table 8.2). Most of these 11 infants generate such constructions several times. No infant generates correspondences between three or more compositions or subcompositions (Table 8.2). For instance, infants insert one spoon in one cup and then another spoon in another cup or construct two stacks of two objects each. These same infants never generate three pairs of spoons-in-cups or three stacks of two objects; but we will consider this behavior further on pages 177–179.

Only two infants generate one-to-one correspondences between two compositions or subcompositions of three objects each (Table 8.2). One infant, *18SB*, produces it only once; his construction of two matched stacks of three objects, and its analysis, has already been presented on pages 172 and 173. Two corresponding compositions of three objects each are generated twice by the other infant. After several transformations, including substitution, subject *18JHe* builds two matched stacks of three objects in the first construction. Not only are

TABLE 8.2
Number of 18-Month-Old Subjects Generating Matched Compositions and Exchanges on these Correspondences

	Objects in each unit			Exchange operations		
Units	2	3	4	Replace	Substitute	Commute
2	11	2	1	2	3	4
3	0					
4	0					

the two stacks quantitatively equivalent to each other, but they differ consistently by predicate properties (i.e., three cross rings and three rectangular rings). Each stack is then given separately to the experimenter. In the second construction, 18JHe generates one composition with two imprecisely parallel alignments. Again, the two subcompositions are quantitatively equivalent and differ by class properties (i.e., three brushes and three triangular columns).

Only one infant generates true one-to-one correspondences between two compositions of four objects each (Table 8.2). To begin with, this subject 18HS constructs two corresponding compositions of two objects next to himself (i.e., a doll and a column by his right hand and two dolls by his left hand). The two corresponding compositions are immediately expanded by 18HS simultaneously and then alternately placing objects in the tester's two hands. The procedure includes changing the order of alternation plus regulated correcting of unsuccessful placement. Prime consideration is given by 18HS to achieving extensive (numerical) equivalence between the two compositions rather than intensive (predicate) equivalence within each composition. Both compositions end up containing four-member elements while each composition is only partly unmixed by class membership.

Four infants produce compositional prerequisites for correspondences between 2 four-object configurations that do not yet meet the requirements of quantitative equivalence structures. Furthermore, each infant does so only once. Since these compositional prerequisites constitute transitional constructions, they are worth reviewing.

A composition of all four triangular columns is constructed by subject 18TT haphazardly placing them next to each other. Then a separate composition of all four brushes is constructed by 18TT haphazardly placing them next to each other. Both units include four member elements, both units differ consistently by predicate properties, and both units are stabile compositions preserved contemporaneously after they are constructed. Missing is any overt indication that the elements of the two unarticulated compositions are matched in one-to-one correspondence by 18TT, since they form very different configurations.

A composition of all four rectangular rings is first constructed by subject 18PC. He labors to construct continuous correspondence within the first composition by establishing one-to-one matchings between the spatial orientations of the four rectangular rings. This construction involves repeated regulatory attempts to balance all the rectangular rings in equivalent upright positions by setting them on one of their long edges. This is still too difficult a sensorimotor feat for 18PC and requires the experimenter's assistance to be executed successfully. Yet, 18PC persists: he does not give up. After all rectangular rings are uprighted in close proximity to each other, 18PC tries unsuccessfully to upright a clover ring. This act is a possible indication that 18PC attempts to extend the correspondence to two matched compositions of four objects. After his inability to upright the clover ring, *18PC* loosely collects all four clover rings together. Thus, he constructs two stabile compositions of four objects each that consistently differ by class properties and that are preserved beyond the constructive process. These constitute necessary conditions for, but not overt manifestations of, one-to-one matching between two compositions of four objects.

One composition comprising two subcompositions is constructed by subject *18BB*. First she nests all four cups in each other; then she inserts all four spoons in the uppermost cup. After observing her construction, *18BB* takes out all four spoons and forms them into a separate unarticulated heap. Thereby she too generates the necessary conditions for, but not overt manifestations of, both one-to-one matching between 2 four-object subcompositions and between 2 four-object compositions.

Part of the construction by the fourth infant, *18SB*, has already been reproduced on pages 167 and 168. She completes it by pushing the rings together so that they all touch, but so that none overlaps another anymore. Then she takes out each doll from the ring in which she had inserted it and gives all four dolls to her mother. In this way, she creates the necessary conditions for, but not the overt manifestations of, one-to-one matching between (a) two subcompositions of four dolls and four rings when all the dolls are inserted in all the rings, and (b) two compositions when she gives the four dolls to her mother and leaves the four rings together on the table. Moreover, it should be noted that the process of construction consists of uprighting a doll in a ring four times. The procedure, then, also produces the potential conditions for constructing four matching subcompositions of two objects each. However, this is the only instance of its kind generated at this stage.

The measures of correspondences between compositions used here are strict. They require one-to-one spatial and numerical matching between contemporaneous configurations that are marked by both proximity and separation (e.g., two parallel stacks of three objects that are near each other but not touching). Consequently, these developmental data are conservative measures of infants' correspondence construction. Thus for instance, the construction by *18SB* is not scored as either 4 corresponding two-object subcompositions or 2 corresponding four-object subcompositions. The reason is that the construction is ambiguous since it is not marked by proximity and separation. These strict measurement criteria may account for the slightly less advanced correspondence development found here than that reported in other studies (i.e., Sinclair, *et al.*, 1982; Sugarman, 1983). By less stringent criteria, constructions such as that by *18SB*, might well be scored as correspondences between 4 two-object units and 2 four-object units.

Most quantitatively matched compositions or subcompositions are class consistent in their enclosure properties. Of the total production, 60% are unmixed by predicate properties, 6% are partly unmixed, and 34% are mixed. Class consistency means that each unit includes similar objects only and that all these objects are different from the objects included in the unit with which it is matched in one-to-one quantitative correspondences. Thus two-thirds of the quantitatively equivalent compositions constructed at this stage differ in their predicate properties so that they are class consistent.

Correspondences between two compositions or subcompositions are progressively stable constructions. Nine of the 11 subjects who generate two corresponding units do so by matching two stabiles, as well as any they produce by matching two mobiles or two mobiles–stabiles. Of the total production of two corresponding units at this stage, 69% match two stabiles, only 28% match two mobiles, and 3% match two mobiles–stabiles.

Stabiles facilitate temporally detaching the products (quantitative equivalence between two compositions or subcompositions) from the processes of their constructions (one-to-one matching). The most important consequence for cognitive development is that infants transform equivalence compositions into constant given elements. These elements serve as more powerful "knowns" or content for operations that construct more advanced forms of cognition.

We have already considered in Section I how this is accomplished by infants who apply exchange operations to two compositions or subcompositions. Some of these involve constructing correspondences between two stabiles that include equal numbers of objects. Infants preserve and use some of the resultant equivalence compositions as given elements for subsequent and coordinated exchanges. Thus, 11 subjects generate corresponding compositions or subcompositions of two objects each. In turn, these equivalent compositions are used as the elements for replacement by two subjects, for substitution by three subjects, and for commutativity by four subjects (Table 8.2). Exchange operations are still never applied to corresponding compositions that comprise more than two objects each. Thus, as expected, using two equivalent compositions as the knowns for constructing equivalences upon equivalences takes the simplest form possible early in its development.

Corresponding mobiles are more difficult to exploit as elements for cognitive elaboration since most lack constancy and last only as long as the construction. Hence, the quantitative equivalences produced are usually labile in comparison to those produced with corresponding stabiles. In this way, the equivalences (products) are not as easy to detach as elements from the correspondences (their processes of construction). Still, it is not completely impossible to separate them, especially when the matched mobiles are reproduced or varied repeatedly:

42.5.   *RH hits Spoon 2 leftward against Cup 2*

42.5a. *C2 slides to the left a bit so there is a 2 inch separation between C2 and Cup 1*

42.5.   *LH strokes Spoon 1 to the right, starting from about 5 inches to the left of C1, and then very lightly hits bowl end of S1 to back of C1 and table space behind it*

44.5.   RH hits S2 against right side of C2
44.5a.   C2 slides next to and touching C1
44.5.   LH very lightly hits S1 against back of C1 which does not move
46.5.   RH hits S2 against right backside of C2
46.5a.   C2 wiggles and moves slightly closer to subject
46.5.   LH hits S1 against left backside of C1
46.5a.   C1 moves slightly closer to subject (C1 and C2 stay in contact)
48.5.   RH hits S2 against right backside of C2
48.5a.   C2 falls over toward subject pushing C1 very slightly to the left as it falls
48.5.   LH hits S1 lightly against left backside of C1 (which does not move)

(18JC, page 60)

Corresponding mobiles are the elements that 18JC varies to produce second-order causal functions.

Matched causal mobiles are invariably mixed by predicate properties. The class of objects used as the causal agent in each set are different from the class of objects treated as the causal patients (as illustrated by the 18JC fragment). Still, this does not account for all the mixed matchings since only 13% of all corresponding sets or subsets involve causal relations.

Co-univocal correspondences, both one-to-many and many-to-one matchings, are progressively systematized, monitored, and coordinated. They are also progressively coordinated with one-to-one (bi-univocal) correspondences. This coordination may be made apparent by considering 18JC's transactions preceding those in the preceding protocol fragment (irrelevant intervening transactions are omitted):

11.   BH separate spoons in air while holding them by their handles, as looks toward cylinders
12.   RH hits bowl end of Spoon 2 against Cylinder 1 and Cylinder 2, while LH holds Spoon 1
12a.   C1 and C2 move away from subject as they simultaneously separate a few inches
13.5.   LH hits bowl end of Spoon 1 to right and then to left against C1
13.5a. C1 displaces slightly .
13.5.   RH hits bowl end of S2 leftward against C2
13.5a. C2 rotates from approximately vertical to horizontal position
15.5.   LH hits S1 against C1
15.5a. C1 moves to right about 2 inches
15.5.   RH hits S2 leftward against C2 and then hits S2 leftward against C1 and simultaneously toward self
15.5aa. C2 moves about 2 inches to the left behind C1
15.5aaa. C1 moves about 4 inches to the left and toward subject so that C1 is between C2 and subject
17.3.   LH pushes bowl end of S1 against left end of C1
17.3a. C1 moves about 2 inches to the right

17.7.   RH *pushes bowl end of S2 against right side of C1*
17.7a. C1 *rotates from horizontal to vertical position and then rolls toward subject*
20.   BH *quickly brings S1 and S2 together again as simultaneously push them against the back side of C1 toward self*
20a.   C1 *rolls a little toward subject*
21.   RH *hits bowl end of S2 against back side of C1 and toward self, while LH holds S1*
21a.   C1 *rolls all the way over table edge to floor*
28.   BH *move spoons in air to either side of C2, as looking at upright C2*
29.3.   LH *hits S1 rightward against C2*
29.3a. C2 *tumbles over toward the right and hits S2 in process of falling*
29.7.   RH *hits S2 leftward against C2 (just a split second after S1 hits it) (meanwhile mother places C1 upright on table about 4 inches behind C2)*
30.   RH *hits bowl end of S2 against backside of C2, as looking at C2, while LH holds S1*
30a.   C2 *rolls close to table edge*
31.   *looks at C1, while BH hold spoons*
32.   RH *moves S2 in air to the right of C1 and hits S2 leftward against C1*
32a.   C1 *slides upright about 3 inches in an arc to left and toward subject*
33.   BH *hit S1 and S2 together and against backside of C1*
33a.   C1 *falls flat and rolls closer to subject and about 3 inches behind C2 which is between C1 and subject*
34.   RH *immediately hits S2 to left in air about 1 inch above C1 and then hits S2 back to the right, as looking at C1 which rocks in place slightly, while LH holds S1*
35.   *looks at C1, as BH hold S1 and S2 in air above C1 very briefly*
36.5.   RH *hits S2 leftward against right end of C1*
36.5.   LH *hits S1 against backside of C1, hitting C1 toward self, keeping S1 in contact with C1*   (18JC, pages 58 and 59)

The sequence includes one-to-two causal relations generated in simultaneity and in succession. It is interwoven with its reciprocal, two-to-one correspondences. These causal co-univocals are generated in partial temporal overlap and in simultaneity. Both co-univocal forms are also interwoven with repeated one-to-one causal relations between two sets generated simultaneously.

This level of sequential coordination expands infants' means of transforming different correlation operations into each other. In this way, it facilitates practical cognition of the pragmatic relations between one-to-one, one-to-many, and many-to-one matchings. When consolidated, this practical knowledge provides solid structures upon which to develop abstract knowledge about the operational relations between one-to-many, many-to-one, and one-to-one correspondences.

This coordination has important consequences for infants' experimentation. Applied, as such coordinations repeatedly are, to causal phenomena, by *18JC* and other infants at this stage, they augment the continuing elaboration of infants' logic of experimentation. In particular, they elaborate very small equivalence classes of independent semivariables and of dependent semivariables, plus second-order functional relations between dependent and independent semivariables. Such coordinations allow progressive structuring of a very small class of patient objects that are affected systematically by a very small class of instrumental objects.

Expanding the scope of co-univocal matchings is facilitated when infants begin to embody them in functional and conventional playful routines. For instance, infants generate one-to-many relations by stirring one spoon in several cups and they generate many-to-one relations by placing several spoons in one cup. These matchings are already regulated since infants correct misplacements.

III. Conserving Two Very Small Ordered Compositions

Ordered compositions upon compositions are at the heart of the developments in relational structures at this stage. Two partially ordered compositions or subcompositions are constructed such that they form seriated nonequivalence. Additionally, two compositions are integrated to form a larger whole and one larger whole is decomposed into two smaller parts.

Seven subjects generate two contemporaneous units forming $\langle 2\text{-}, 3\text{-}\rangle$ element orders. Some take the form of two related parts:

1. *RH takes Circular Ring 2 from experimenter and places CR2 flat on Circular Ring 1 (experimenter extends Doll 2)*
2. *RH squeezes rims of CR2 and CR1 together quickly, so CR2 and CR1 are aligned*
3. *RH picks Doll 1 up*
4. *LH takes D2 from experimenter and places D2 upright in CR2/CR1 stack, while RH holds D1 (experimenter extends Circular Ring 3)*
5. *RH quickly extends D1 toward CR2/CR1 stack and then withdraws D1*
6. *LH takes CR3 from experimenter and immediately places CR3 on table approximately 2 inches to right of CR2/CR1 stack, while RH holds D1*
7. *RH places D1 upright in CR3* (18SB, page 49)

Two parts comprise this stabile composition. The first part is carefully coregulated so that the two rings are matched precisely and a doll can be inserted into both rings at once. The second part is constructed in partial temporal overlap with the first part. The generative procedure includes self-regulatory modification of the movement to compose the second doll with the first part before using that doll as an element to construct the second part of the composition. The product is a two-part composition. The parts are similar in form (intensity); they differ only in quantity (extensity). Without imputing any hierarchic properties to the two parts, they nevertheless constitute an ordered series of $\langle 2\text{-}, 3\text{-}\rangle$ element parts of a larger whole.

The ordered series of ⟨ 2-, 3- ⟩ element subcompositions are extended in time and preserved over four operational transformations (see pages 171 and 172 for a summary of the rest of *18SB*'s elaborate production and its analysis). After finishing the two-part composition *18SB* consecutively substitutes elements in the two parts. This substitution results in objects being repeatedly exchanged within the parts while the ordered series of ⟨ 2-, 3- ⟩ element subcompositions is preserved.

In this way, a few infants just begin to conserve ordered nonequivalences in very small series at the same time as they transform the elements comprising the series. This is one means by which infants begin to detach ordinal quantification from the particular elements comprising their very small series constructions. The difference between two- and three-element subcompositions is held constant regardless of what elements are substituted for each other within the subcompositions. Conservation also furthers developments in coordinating structures of partially ordered nonequivalence relations (by addition and subtraction) with unordered quantitative equivalences (by exchange operations).

Most ordered series of ⟨ 2-, 3- ⟩ elements involve two compositions rather than subcompositions:

46.   *RH picks up Yellow Racer 2 and Yellow Rectangular Ring 2*
47.5. *RH picks up Yellow Rectangular Ring 1 under YRR2*
47.5. *LH picks up Red Rectangular Ring 1 and Yellow Racer 1*   (*18HS*, page 43)

11.   *RH places Orange Spoon 2 in Orange Cup 2*
12.   *RH picks up Yellow Spoon 2 and places YS2 in OC2*
13.   *LH picks up Yellow Spoon 1 and places YS1 in Orange Cup 1*
(*18BB*, page 23)

While both subjects generate two compositions of ⟨ 2-, 3- ⟩ elements, their constructions represent the range generated at this stage. The ordered series constructed by *18HS* is relatively labile and nonpermanent because both compositions are mobiles. In contrast, *18BB*'s ordered series is comparatively permanent. Both compositions constructed by *18BB* are stabiles, and she preserves them for a short duration during which she interacts with another object (not included in the protocol fragment excerpted here).

Five subjects generate two contemporaneous units that form ordered series of ⟨ 3-, 4- ⟩ elements. Two of these 5 subjects are among the 7 subjects who also generate ordered series of ⟨ 2-, 3- ⟩ element units; 3 are not. All together, then, 10 subjects generate series of 2 ⟨ 2-, 3- ⟩ and/or ⟨ 3-, 4- ⟩ element compositions or subcompositions.

As with ⟨ 2-, 3- ⟩ element series, few ⟨ 3-, 4- ⟩ element series involve two parts of a larger whole. To illustrate, subject *18SB* constructs one large composition, with two parts next to each other. The first part comprises four objects, three circular rings with a doll uprighted in one of the rings. Its construction includes encircling a ring around the doll and self-correction when the doll falls over. The second part comprises three objects, one circular ring with two dolls uprighted in the ring.

The procedure *18SB* uses to construct the second part is the reciprocal of that used to construct the first part. Construction of the second part begins with lifting a ring from around a doll and ends with trying unsuccessfully to insert two dolls upright in one ring. Consequently, the parts as well as the procedures used to construct them are reciprocal to each other. The first part matches one doll to three circular rings while the second part matches two dolls to one circular ring. Thus, the first part constitutes a one-to-many correlation while the second part constitutes a reciprocal many-to-one correlation. The product is an ordered series of ⟨3-, 4-⟩ element parts of a larger whole.

While *18SB* clearly constructs an ordered series of ⟨3-, 4-⟩ element subcompositions, the construction of another subject, *18JHe*, is more ambiguous in this regard. He collects all four rectangular rings out of the presented array and uprights one doll in each rectangular ring except one, by leaving the remaining fourth doll alone. This includes self-correction of one error in placing a doll upright in a rectangular ring. Thus, *18SB* matches three upright dolls to four flatly lying rectangular rings to form one stabile composition; and, in this way, may well have constructed an ordered series of two ⟨3-, 4-⟩ element parts of a larger whole. This interpretation requires assuming that the three upright dolls constitute one part and the four lying down rectangular rings constitute another part of the composition. Since *18JHe* provides no further evidence on this score in his subsequent transactions with the objects, the interpretation necessarily remains equivocal.

Most series of ⟨3-, 4-⟩ elements involve two compositions rather than two parts of one composition and, in this way, are unambiguous orderings. Thus, in another instance, subject *18JHe* clearly constructs an ordered series of ⟨ 3-, 4 ⟩ element units. He begins by constructing an unaligned stack of four circular rings to his right. In partial temporal overlap he also constructs an unaligned stack of three blocks to his right. The product is two parallel but separate unaligned stacks of three and four objects, respectively.

Six subjects generate two contemporaneous compositions or subcompositions that form imprecise ordered series of ⟨ 2-, many- ⟩ elements. Invariably these series order a two object unit with a four- to six-object unit. Infants do not pair a three-object unit with a five- or more object unit.

Integrating two compositions or part compositions into one larger whole, or disintegrating one composition into two smaller compositions or part compositions, is generated by almost all subjects (Table 8.3). Integrating two sets or subsets into one larger whole (Column 1, Rows 1–3) predominates over decomposing one whole into two sets or subsets (Column 2, Rows 1–3).

Integration is almost always applied to two compositions or part compositions

TABLE 8.3
Number of 18-Month-Old Subjects Adding and Subtracting Units

	Integrate	Decompose	Integrate & decompose	Decompose & integrate	Total coordinated
Equal	7	2	5	3	8
Unequal	3	0	2	0	2
Total	8	2	6	3	9

that are quantitatively equivalent, whether adding is all that takes place (Column 1, Rows 1–3) or whether adding is followed by subtracting (Column 3, Rows 1–3). Adding equivalent compositions or subcompositions is almost always limited to integrating two units of no more than two objects each. Only two subjects also integrate two sets or subsets of three objects each. Integrating two unequal compositions or subcompositions ranges from adding two-object with three-object configurations, to adding two-object with six-object configurations.

Disintegrating one composition always results in two equal compositions or part compositions, whether it is followed by integration (Column 4, Rows 1–3) or not (Column 2, Rows 1–3); decomposing never produces quantitative nonequivalence between the resultant units. Disintegrating is always limited to decomposing single four-object compositions into two units of two objects each. Subjects never decompose their five-or-more-object compositions into two units.

Coordinate addition and subtraction is generated as frequently as either one of them (compare Columns 1 and 2 with Column 5 in Table 8.3). Inverse coordination is limited to integrating two compositions or subcompositions of two objects each and disintegrating one composition of four objects. This minimal limit is never exceeded at this stage.

One half of the subjects initiate inverse coordinations by integrating two units into one larger whole. They follow up by disintegrating the larger whole back into two identity sets or subsets. Often this involves little more than simply holding two objects in the right hand and two objects in the left hand, bringing both hands together to form a single four-object composition, and then separating both hands to reconstruct the initial compositions.

Other inverse coordinations are more complex and extensive. These include adding and subtracting two contemporaneous collections contained in two receptacles. Consider, for instance, subject 18KM's sequence of constructions and reconstructions that she begins by placing two spoons in Receptacle 1 and two cross rings in Receptacle 2. She then unites the 2 two-object units into one larger four-object whole, decomposes this into two identity sets of two objects each, reunites them into one larger identity set of four objects, decomposes this into two identity sets of two objects each, and reunites them into one larger identity set of four objects. All this is done by containing the objects in the two receptacles.

Throughout *18KM* visually monitors her constructive procedures where the objects are contained and whether or not the receptacles are empty. She also always uses Receptacle 1 as the vehicle for transporting and transferring the two cross ring set into Receptacle 2 which she always uses as the container to integrate the two sets into a larger but global whole. This integration requires reciprocal consecutive usage of Receptacle 1 as a container and as a vehicle–dispenser. It also requires reciprocal simultaneous usage of Receptacle 1 as a vehicle–dispenser and Receptacle 2 as a container.

Integration is usually still global and undifferentiated in procedure and product; *18KM*'s constructions are typical in this regard. Both the unifying process and the parts unified are relatively unarticulated (e.g., the objects are always dumped together into a heap by *18KM*). Decomposition is usually more articulate and differentiated in procedure and product; *18KM*'s constructions are typical in this regard as well. The two smaller sets are always constructed by *18KM* selecting the two cross rings from the heap in one receptacle; the two rings are then placed together in the other receptacle. The product is always reproduced, namely, two smaller sets equivalent in quantity and distinct in predicate properties.

Inverse integration (of two sets into one) and decomposition (of one set into two) is generated three times in sequence by *18KM*. This is the most advanced reversibility between adding and subtracting units within one sequence generated at this stage. More typical at this stage is negating integration by disintegration only once within any given sequence of constructing sets by reversibility.

Initiating inverse coordination by disintegrating one larger whole into two units is generated by half as many infants as generate coordination beginning with integration (compare Column 3 with Column 4, Table 8.3). The few infants who initiate inverse coordination with disintegration also do so much less frequently than infants who begin with integration. Furthermore, they do not repeat their inverse coordinations within any sequence.

Progress in generating ordered series of single compositions is minor as compared with the just outlined major developments in generating order relations between two contemporaneous compositions. Yet most ordered series generated by infants at this stage still involve single compositions only. When precise, most of these ordered series involve adding and subtracting single objects which transform two- and three-element compositions into each other. Still, 10 infants extend these precise ordered series to transforming three- and four-element compositions into each other (i.e., ⟨ 2-, 3-, 4- ⟩ and ⟨ 4-, 3-, 2- ⟩ as well as ⟨ 3-, 4- ⟩ and ⟨ 4-, 3- ⟩ element sets). Six infants extend their ordered series to include transforming four- and five-element compositions into each other; and 3 infants extend them to include transforming five- and six-element compositions into each other.

Protoassociativity of adding and subtracting is still basically limited to ordered series that do not extend beyond three-element compositions (see Langer, 1980, pages 359–361). Extension of protoassociative adding and subtracting to ordered series involving four-element compositions just begins to be manifest by a few infants. This phenomenon indicates continuing progressive detachment of adding and subtracting from their particular mapping processes and, thereby, their transformation into second-order operations.

Bidirectional reciprocal iteration is extended to four-element compositions by almost all infants. Seven infants do so precisely. Most are still only partially symmetrical (e.g., ⟨ 2-, 3-, 4-, 3- ⟩ and ⟨ 4-, 3-, 4- ⟩ element consecutive sets). Fully symmetrical and percise reciprocal iteration is generated by three infants (i.e., ⟨ 2-, 3-, 4-, 3-, 2- ⟩ and ⟨ 4-, 3-, 2-, 3-, 4- ⟩ element consecutive sets). Precise bidirectional reciprocal iteration is extended to five- and six-element sets by one infant, respectively. In all instances, the reciprocal iteration is only partially symmetrical (subject 18JC generates ⟨ 5-, 4-, 5-, 4-, 5-, 4- ⟩ and ⟨ 4-, 5-, 4-, 5-, 4- ⟩ element consecutive compositions and subject 18SB generates ⟨ 5-, 6-, 5- ⟩ element consecutive compositions).

IV. Class Consistency within Paired Compositions

Classification continues to be primarily a property of single compositions, since most are still generated consecutively (Table 7.9). Generation of contemporaneous compositions is increasing rapidly in the eight-object conditions (Table 7.9, Rows 7 and 8). However, the rate is still not sufficient to permit statistical evaluation of their predicate properties, except in two tasks. Predication in contemporaneous compositions appears to be a random mixture of unmixed and mixed classification in those tasks where infants still generate insufficient data for statistical evaluation.

Predication is unmixed in one task, the eight-object additive condition, where five subjects generate contemporaneous compositions. Both order ($N = 5$, $x = 0$, $p = .031$, sign test) and enclosure ($N = 5$, $x = 0$, $p = .031$, sign test) properties of these compositions are unmixed. Thus, about half of the subjects construct temporally overlapping sets in the eight-object additive condition by both (a) manipulating each class of objects consecutively and (b) including each class of objects in separate and distinct compositions. Predication is random in the other task, the eight-object multiplicative condition, where seven subjects generate contemporaneous compositions. Both order ($N = 5$, $x = 1$, $p = .188$, sign test) and enclosure ($N = 6$, $x = 3$, $p = .656$, sign test) properties of the compositions are random.

Overall, predication in the additive conditions continues to be by identical properties of objects comprising individual compositions. In the four-object condition, the random probability ratio is two-to-one favoring composing objects with complementary rather than identical properties. The order of handling two or more objects to compose them is almost entirely by identical properties (Table 8.4, Row 1, Columns 1–3), and is statistically significant ($N = 11$, $x = 1$, $p = .006$, sign test). The results on enclosure of compositions are almost as strong (Table 8.4, Row 1, Columns 4–5) and are also statistically significant ($N = 12$, $x = 2$, $p = .019$, sign test).

In the eight-object additive condition, the random probability ratio is four-to-three, favoring composition by complementary over identical properties. The mean frequencies for order of composition are three-to-one in favor of identical properties (Table 8.4, Row 4, Columns 1–3), which is statistically significant ($N = 10$, $x = 2$, $p = .055$, sign test). The ratio difference is three-to-two in favor of enclosure by identical properties (Table 8.4, Row 4, Columns 4–6). While these results are not statistically significant, they are in the same direction as that for order ($N = 11$, $x = 3$, $p = .113$, sign test).

In the multiplicative conditions, predication varies as a function of the number of objects presented. In the four-object condition, the random probability ration is two-to-one favoring complementary over disjoint properties. The ratio difference found approaches eight-to-one in favor of order by complementary properties (Table 8.4, Row 2, Columns 1–3), which is statistacally significant ($N = 11$, $x = 1$, $p = .006$, sign test). While the ratio difference for enclosure is in the same direction, that is, almost three-to-one in favor of complementary properties (Table 8.4, Row 2, Columns 4–6), the differences are not statistically significant ($N = 10$, $x = 4$, $p = .344$, sign test).

In the eight-object multiplicative condition, the random probability ratio is five-to-two favoring unmixed and partly mixed (identical and complementary) over mixed (disjoint) predication. The mean frequencies for order are two-to-one

TABLE 8.4
Spontaneous Phase I: Mean Frequency of Class Consistent Composing at Age 18 Months

	Order			Enclosure		
	Unmixed	*Partly unmixed*	*Mixed*	*Unmixed*	*Partly unmixed*	*Mixed*
Four-object condition:						
1. Additive	8.00	0.08	0.36	8.25	0.92	1.25
2. Multiplicative[a]	10.55	0.09	1.36	12.45	0.64	4.36
3. Disjoint[a]	6.36	0.09	2.82	6.55	1.18	6.18
Eight-object condition:						
4. Additive[a]	4.00	0.09	1.36	6.45	2.18	4.27
5. Multiplicative	3.75	3.08	3.42	5.83	5.67	7.92
6. Disjoint[a]	4.18	0.00	1.00	6.09	0.27	2.60

[a]$N = 11$ subjects.

in favor of identical and complementary properties (Table 8.4, Row 5, Columns 1–3) and are not statistically significant ($N = 12$, $x = 4$, $p = .194$, sign test). The mean frequencies for enclosure are less than three-to-one in favor of identical and complementary properties (Table 8.4, Row 5, Columns 4–6) and are also not statistically significant ($N = 12$, $x = 7$, $p = .806$, sign test). Overall, predication is random in the eight-object multiplicative condition.

Predication tends to be by identical properties in the disjoint conditions, but more so in the eight- than in the four-object condition. In the four-object condition, the random probability ratio is two-to-one favoring disjoint over identical properties. The mean frequencies for order are over two-to-one in favor of identical properties (Table 8.4, Row 3, Columns 1–3), which is not statistically significant ($N = 11$, $x = 3$, $p = .113$, sign test). The mean frequencies for enclosure are about even (Table 8.4, Row 3, Columns 4–6), which is not statistically significant ($N = 11$, $x = 3$, $p = .113$, sign test).

In the eight-object disjoint condition, the random probability ratio is four-to-three favoring disjoint over identical properties. The mean frequencies for order are four-to-one in favor of identical properties (Table 8.4, Row 6, Columns 1–3), which is statistically significant ($N = 10$, $x = 1$, $p = .011$, sign test). The mean frequencies for enclosure are over two-to-one in favor of identical properties (Table 8.4, Row 6, Columns 4–6) which is also statistically significant ($N = 11$, $x = 1$, $p = .006$, sign test).

By and large these results indicate that the trend toward composing similar or identical objects into individual configurations begun at age 12 months and augmented at age 15 months continues at age 18 months. Moreover, order of handling similar or identical objects is as likely or more likely than is enclosure of similar or identical objects in order to construct individual compositions (Table 8.4, Columns 1–3 vs. 4–6).

At the same time the association between order and enclosure is very high where order applies (i.e., where two or more objects are directly contacted in order to construct compositions). They correspond in 88% of the compositions in the four-object conditions, 85% in the eight-object conditions, and 87% overall. Thus there is little decoupling of order and enclosure after age 15 months (Chapter 4).

The number of objects presented only partially serves to modulate predication by similarities. Both order and enclosure are more likely to comprise similar or identical objects in the four-object than the eight-object additive conditions (Table 8.4, Rows 1 and 3 vs. 4 and 5). However, in the disjoint conditions, the ratio favoring unmixed predication is higher in the eight-object than in the four-object condition (Row 3 vs. Row 6); this difference is reflected in the statistical analyses presented above.

Infants are more likely to combine different objects in their causal compositions than in those that are not causal. When infants construct causal compositions, they tend to use different classes of objects as agents and as patients (e.g., they are more likely to use a cylinder to push a square column than to use a cylinder to push another cylinder). The result is a lower proportion of enclosure involving similar or identical objects in causal compositions (43% unmixed, 15% partly unmixed, and 41% mixed) than in noncausal compositions (58% unmixed, 13% partly unmixed, and 29% mixed).

The differential between the rate of mixed causal and noncausal compositions is lower than at age 15 months (Chapter 4). The decreasing differential may be accounted for, at least in part, by increasing production of symmetrical causality at age 18 months. Symmetrical causal compositions (e.g., banging two objects against each other) are more likely to comprise similar or identical objects than are asymmetrical causal compositions (e.g., banging one object against another).

Relations within Paired Compositions of Malleable Objects

While some of the forms are necessarily and naturally unique, development in infants' transactions with quasi-continuous objects and with combined discrete and quasi-continuous objects parallels their development with discrete objects. Structuring coordinate second-order operations progresses such that infants' cognition becomes increasingly representational. This development continues to build upon the main trend in cognitive development initiated toward the end of the first year of infancy.

Two general features highlight this development. The first entails progressive coordination of operations with two sets or series, such as constructing two geneological orders by decomposing two objects into two series of objects. The second comprises advances in reversibly coordinating two operations that negate each other. This negation generates a third, identity operation which may represent the initial extensive and/or intensive part–whole condition. For instance, all infants now invert attaching and detaching of combined objects such that they reproduce at least their initial extensity.

I. Fine Examination of Object Transformations

Detailed examination still marks infants' transformations of quasi-continuous objects. As always, examining objects may precede and/or accompany and/or follow upon their transformation. Comparative inspection is extended to all objects when the set presented is small in number, and may involve a variety of visiomotor coordinated with fine-grained tactilomotor exploration:

1. *LH touches Ball 1, then looks at LH fingers and makes a face*
2. *LH touches B1, picks up B1, and turns B1 around in hand quite slowly*
3. *LH puts B1 back down on the table where it was*
4. *RH bunches B1, Ball 2, and Ball 3 together*
4a. *B1 rolls away*
5. *RH touches B2 and B3*
6. *LH picks up B1 and holds B1 in air for about 13 seconds while fingers make tiny movements on B1 exploring its stickiness*   (18ML, page 26)

The information obtained may not always be pleasing. Yet, similar forms of inspection are extended to all the objects presented. This includes quite extensive tactilomotor exploration of the PlayDoh substance. Examination may be followed up by extensive and semisystematic experimenting with all the objects coupled with close observation (irrelevant transactions are omitted):

7. *LH drops Ball 1 from about 4 inch height*
7a. *B1 rolls away on table*
9. *LH drops B1 from about 4 inch height*
11. *RH drops Ball 3 from about 4 inch height*
11a. *B3 rolls away*
13. *RH drops B3 from about 4 inch height*
13a. *B3 falls on Ball 2, causing B3 to roll far*
29. *cupped LH rocks B2 gently so that B2 rolls around*
31. *LH drops B2 from about 4 inch height*
31a. *B2 rolls out of LH*
38. *LH holds B2 in open palm and rocks gently*
38a. *B2 falls down on subject's lap*
40. *LH holds B2 and overturns from about 2 inch height*
40a. *B2 drops on table and rolls a little*
41. *LH drops B2 on the table in a different way*
41a. *B2 rolls and falls to the floor*
47. *RH splays fingers so B2 falls through fingers, as watches this intently*
47a. *B2 rolls away*
54. *RH cups B3 in palm and overturns, as looks closely at this*
54a. *B3 rolls away*
58. *RH rocks B1, B2, and B3 in cupped hand, then overturns hand*
58a. *B1, B2, and B3 roll away*   (18ML, pages 26–29)

To begin with, *18ML* follows inspection of each object by replicative dropping of one object at a time while holding the height from which the object is dropped constant. After this, he varies the height from which he drops the balls. He also varies the way in which he drops the balls. His final variation consists of dropping all three balls together.

Routines begin to tinge experimenting at this stage (e.g., rocking objects in 18ML's hand before overturning them). Routines also begin to enter into infants' visiomotor and tactilomotor exploration of small numbers of objects. For instance, the same 18ML couples examining rings with twirling them around on his left hand index finger.

Linguistic denotation of objects barely begins to be generated. Two infants only name the material out of which the objects are made. One infant calls it "Clay?" As soon as the other infant is presented with an object, he names it "PlayDoh" twice, once with a questioning intonation as he looks at his mother. Two other infants name the shapes of the objects. One (18JC) names the circular form only of some ring-shaped objects repeatedly as follows: "Circo," "A circa," "Circa," "Circo," "Circle," "Circa," and "Circle." Naming is accompanied by close visual inspection of the rings plus some looking and smiling at the tester. The other infant (18SO) names the form of some ball shaped objects only, repeatedly calling them "Ball."

Subjects 18JHe and 18JHo are the only infants who verbally express any prior knowledge about PlayDoh or clay. In all other respects, however, their transactions with quasi-continuous objects do not differ in any marked way from that of other infants at this stage. The same is true for 18JC and 18SO, who are the only infants to verbally name the shape of objects.

II. Expanding Reforming to Construct Form Identity

Deforming continues to dominate infants' transformations of quasi-continuous objects. It is the most frequently generated transformation (Table 9.1.). Not only are deformations generated frequently, but they also often involve multiple transformations such as mushing a ring shaped object into a blob (Row 1).

Infants are progressively cognizant of their deformations. They anticipate their transactions by gestural mappings; they also reflect expressively upon their deformations of objects. For instance, before deforming an object, subject 18ML manually gestures requesting and/or deforming them. During and after increasingly deforming an object, subject 18JHe giggles and laughs at what he is doing. Sometimes his expressive behavior may be self-directed while at other times it is probably directed toward communication with another person (by looking at his mother while giggling). In either case, the expressive behaviors represent early overt manifestations of practical reflection by infants upon their own transformations.

Practical reflection by infants upon their own constructions manifests itself in causal as well as expressive behaviors. Causal practical reflection originates at this stage. Infants just begin, in rare and most rudimentary instances, to elaborate upon their deformations for second-order purposes. To illustrate, subject

TABLE 9.1

Mean Frequency of Combinativity Proto-Operations Generated by 18-Month-Old Subjects in Quasi-Continuous and Discrete–Quasi-Continuous Conditions

	One object			Three objects			Discrete–quasi-continuous	
	Phase I 1	Phase II 2	Phase III 3	Phase I 4	Phase II 5	Phase III 6	Phase I 7	Phase II 8
1. Deform	11.75 (4.00)[a]	10.22 (2.78)	7.17 (3.17)	8.75 (3.08)	3.58 (0.50)	9.75 (2.83)	17.43 (2.00)	11.71 (1.14)
2. Reform	0.50	0.11 (0.11)	0.08	0.08	0.00	0.33	0.00	0.00
3. Break	0.67	0.00	0.42	0.33	0.33	0.83	1.29	0.71
4. Reconstruct	0.08	0.00	0.00	0.00	0.17	0.25	0.29	0.00
5. Decompose[b]	7.42 (0.17)	1.44	3.67	4.50	1.25	3.67	2.29	0.57
6. Recompose	0.42 (0.08)	0.78	0.00	0.00	0.08	0.67	0.00	0.00
7. Compose		0.78 (0.11)	1.17 (0.08)	2.33	0.25 (0.08)	0.92	0.29	0.14
8. Redecompose		0.44	0.50	1.08	0.00	0.58	0.00	0.00
9. Attach							1.14 [0.43][c]	2.00 [0.57]
10. Redetach							0.71 [0.14]	1.86
11. Detach							1.43	1.29
12. Reattach							0.43	0.57
13. Number of subjects	12	9	12	12	12	12	7	7
14. Mean duration	2 min, 10 sec[d]	1 min, 26 sec	1 min, 36 sec[e]	1 min, 46 sec[e]	0 min, 55 sec[e]	1 min, 59 sec[e]	1 min, 52 sec	1 min, 15 sec

[a]Mean frequency of proto-operations involving multiple transformations are given in parentheses.

[b]The frequencies are necessarily underestimates because, when possible, subjects were not allowed to decompose by biting.

[c]Mean frequency of attempted but not successfully completed transformations are given in square brackets.

[d]Based on duration for 10 subjects.

[e]Based on duration for 11 subjects.

18ML makes large indentations in a PlayDoh ball. Then he uses these indentations as holes in which to fit his thumb, so as to pick the ball up and playfully project it back to the table. His expressive behavior (giggling) indicates that *18ML* is cognizant of this causal elaboration upon his transformation of the object. This is still an unusual achievement for infants at this stage, and is precursory to the coordinate experimenting-and-transforming that develops at the next stage (see pages 262 and 263).

Reforming the intensive (form) identity of objects by inverse deformations that negate initial direct deformations progresses in several ways. Reforming increases in frequency and is generated by one half of the subjects (Table 9.1, Row 2). Moreover, it is no longer entirely limited to transforming ring shapes. Reforming begins to be applied to solid shapes (i.e., balls and cubes of PlayDoh).

At its origin, reforming solid objects is not as prevalent as reforming ring objects. Also, reforming solid objects is not as well regulated as reforming ring objects is becoming. Reforming solid objects is imprecise, undifferentiated, and limited as compared with reforming ring objects. For instance, both the procedure (pressing and squeezing) used by subject *18JHe* and the product are global in character: the reformed object (a lump) only roughly approximates its initial ball shape. Reforming is also not repeated in any way. In contrast, subject *18JHo* reproduces inverse deforming of a ring three times in a row. Carefully he adjusts his grasp of the ring to generate inverse deformations. He generates them while holding the ring in the air and observing his constructions, and he produces relatively exact replicas of the ring's initial form.

Contingent deforming is generated frequently. The major advance is in instrumental deforming. This advance is particularly evident in the task which combines discrete with quasi-continuous objects. All infants use a tongue depressor as an instrument with which to deform the PlayDoh ball(s). Deforming is generated frequently in this task (Table 9.1., Row 1, Columns 7 and 8). Most are the product of contingent transformation.

The usual form of contingent instrumental deforming at this stage uses detached tongue depressors to press on detached PlayDoh balls. Subject *18JC* is most prolific in this regard since he does this 38 times in the first test phase and 10 times in the second. Two other forms are less frequent. Tongue depressors are used to beat or press attached PlayDoh balls on the table. For instance, subject *18JHe* does this with two combined objects at the same time. Tongue depressors are used to beat or press attached PlayDoh balls on other PlayDoh balls (e.g., subject *18SB* does this repeatedly). Corresponding deformations in two PlayDoh balls, analyzed in Section III of this chapter, are generated by *18JHe's* and *18SB's* instrumental transformations. But while *18JHe's* equivalence constructions are the products of symmetrical and nonreciprocal transformations, *18SB's* equivalence constructions are the products of reciprocal and asymmetrical transformations.

Instrumental deforming is progressively regulated as well as multiformed. Moreover, it is becoming planful: infants deliberately prepare their instrumental deforming. For instance, just before executing his simultaneous contingent deforming of two PlayDoh balls, *18JHe* sets-up the material:

13.5.   *RH raises Tongue Depressor 1/Ball 1 off table, rotating it so B1 is up*
13.5.   *LH raises Tongue Depressor/ Ball off table, rotating it so B is up*
  15.   *LH holds TD/B and RH holds TD1/B up in air near to each other but not touching, as laughs*
  16.   *turns around toward mother, holding the two sets before mother*

(*18JHe*, page 49)

Corresponding mappings simultaneously set up the two combined discrete–quasi-continuous objects in equivalent positions for contingent deforming. This act is accompanied by pragmatic reflection upon or cognizance of his construction by *18JHe*; he laughs and shows the preparation to his mother. Then *18JHe* deforms both objects equivalently (not included in protocol fragment). Thus, matched spatial mappings prepare matched contingent deforming of two objects.

III. Expanding Matched and Ordered Sets of Deformations

Matched deforming of the part–whole structure of one or two objects at the same time is progressively regulated, whether the procedures are contingent, noncontingent, or a combination of contingent and noncontingent mappings. Coseriated deforming of two objects is also not unusual and is progressively regulated. Matched deformation of three or four objects is rare and is the upper limit, while coseriated deformation never exceeds transforming two objects. There is, then, an apparent developmental delay in ordered deformation as compared with corresponding deformation. Ordered deformation of more than two objects is more difficult to generate than corresponding deformation.

Matched deformation of the part–whole structure of single objects is becoming semisystematic:

  6.   *BH lift Ball about 1 inch off table and squeeze B a little*
  6a.   *slight indentations in and flattening of B*
  7.   *BH squeeze B between thumbs and forefingers*
  7a.   *further indentations in and flattening of B*
  8.   *BH place B on table and push index fingers down into B*
  8a.   *deep indentations in and flattening of B*   (*18JHe*, page 28)

25.5.   *RH grasps right side of Ball S:*   "Baw, baw . . . baw . . ." *(fades)*
25.5.   *LH fingers (especially thumb and index) lightly squeezes and rubs on left side of B*

25.5a.   *slight flattening of B and small protrusion on B*
27.   *LH index finger rubs at B held by RH*
27a.   *very shallow depression in B*
28.   *LH thumb and index finger pinch up a tiny part on left side of B, 2 times*
28a.   *two small protrusions on B*   (*18JC, page 31*)

Both infants generate multiple and varied corresponding transformations of single objects in a fairly controlled fashion. Subject *18JHe* varies his corresponding deformations from slight to medium to deep indentations. In this way, he constructs an ordered increasing series of matched deformations, and he preserves equivalent deformations at the same time as he increases their magnitude. Subject *18JC* also preserves corresponding deformations, but they are small protrusions rather than deep indentations. Thus, the orderings by these two subjects are constructed in opposite directions (i.e., increasing indentation *vs.* protrusion); but the products are isomorphic, (i.e., coseriated deformations).

Infants use discrete objects to consecutively generate corresponding ordered deforming of single quasi-continuous objects in the combined discrete and quasi-continuous objects conditions. Usually they use a tongue depressor as an instrument with which to contingently deform a PlayDoh ball. A tongue depressor is repeatedly pressed into or upon a PlayDoh ball which produces both matched and ordered deformations. Infants also grasp a combined discrete and quasi-continuous object by the tongue depressor and use it as a handle with which to repeatedly bang the PlayDoh ball on the table top. This action also produces both matched and ordered deformations in the quasi-continuous object.

Corresponding deformations of two objects begin to be differentiated and coordinated, contingent and noncontingent procedures:

3.5.   *RH presses down on Piece 2, flattening it*
3.5.   *LH presses down on Piece 1, flattening it*
5.5.   *RH picks P2 up and squeezes P2, indenting it*
5.5.   *LH picks P1 up and squeezes P1, indenting it*   (*18JHe, page 30*)

Observation and anticipation precede *18JHe*'s matched transformations. Both objects are simultaneously deformed in identical and differentiated two-part sequences. First, both objects are contingently deformed by pressing them into the table which flattens them. Then they are both deformed noncontingently by squeezing them in the air which makes indentations in them.

Four is the maximum number of objects that are correspondingly deformed at this stage; but it is still generated by one infant (*18JHo*) only. The transformations include the range of contingent coseriated deformations generated at this stage. These are repeated equivalent deformations of two objects, imprecisely equivalent deformations of four objects at the same time, and repeated equivalent deformations of the initial two objects. The maximum correspondence consists of simultaneous but imprecisely equivalent deformations of four objects. The ordered increasing deformations are extensive. They are applied simultaneously or alternately to two objects forming extended coseriated deformations.

One other form of ordered deformations is becoming autonomous. It involves stretching or twisting PlayDoh in order to elongate it. One-half of the subjects elongate objects without it leading to either breaking or decomposing them. At previous stages, this form of additive deformation invariably results in breaking and decomposing. Transitional forms are also generated. Two-part constructions are generated that manifest partial autonomy. First the objects are elongated. But the infants do not stop at this point; rather they stretch the objects until they are eventually decomposed into two.

IV. Decomposing Objects into Two Ordered and Two Matched Sets

Breaking objects is generated by all infants. The rate at which infants break objects increases as well; all infants but one break objects at least two times (Table 9.1., Row 3). All infants break ring objects. Breaking is increasingly extended to solid objects. Five infants break solid objects, but only two infants break them more than once.

Instrumental breaking is generated by two of the three subjects in the combined discrete and quasi-continuous conditions where this form of contingent transformation is possible. Both subjects generate instrumental breaking repeatedly. They also monitor their transformations visually and tactually.

The tongue depressor is used by subject 18JHe as an instrument with which to successively break two objects. As soon as he has made a hole in a PlayDoh piece, 18JHe detaches the instrumental object and attaches it to a PlayDoh ball he is going to break next. He is, then, beginning to use the tongue depressor as a flexible instrument for breaking different objects. Flexible instrumentality is further indicated by his subsequent usage of the tongue depressor. He makes a hole in the PlayDoh piece by increasingly pushing the tongue depressor into it, while he makes a hole in the PlayDoh ball by inversely twisting it (clockwise and counterclockwise) around the tongue depressor. In these different ways he transforms solid objects into rings. After this, he exhibits overt cognizance of his construction by showing the resultant ring to the tester while smiling at her.

Corresponding instrumental breaking marks subject 18JC's transformations. In succession he makes two holes in a ball. Shortly afterwards he successively makes two slits in the ball. A bit later he reverts to making holes in the ball. The transformational procedures used to make holes are equivalent and the procedures used to make slits are also equivalent. In each case the transformational products are ordered nonequivalences between big holes and small slits in the ball.

Reconstruction progresses at this stage. Five of 8 subjects negate breaking objects by sealing some, but not all, of their breaks (Table 9.1., Row 4). Reconstruction negates breaking objects which transforms their intensive part–whole (predicate) properties while not affecting their extensity (quantitative part–whole properties). Reconstruction, then, is a new form of producing intensive identity.

Reconstruction begins by being global and nonregulated. It may be generated several times by a given infant; but these generations are always imprecise or incomplete. For instance, holes and slits are made in PlayDoh balls and then negated by roughly kneading the broken balls. The resultant reconstructions are irregular globs of PlayDoh which only roughly resemble the initial balls. Nevertheless, even global and nonregulated reconstructions negate breaking solid into ring objects and breaking ring into solid objects. These reconstructions are primitive, yet they begin to conserve the identities of both solid and ring properties of objects.

Primitive reconstruction may already be contingent when the initial form is solid. After breaking solid objects, infants often reconstruct their global identities by kneading the objects into the table top. Even instrumental reconstruction is generated by two infants who use tongue depressors flexibly to break PlayDoh balls. That is, after some of the breaks made by *18JHe* and *18JC*, they use the same tongue depressors to globally press the broken objects together again.

Reconstructions that are transitional to regulated negation of breaking are generated by four infants. Transitional reconstruction is generated only when the initial forms of the objects are rings (irrelevant transactions are omitted from the *18JHo* fragment):

5. *BH immediately pull Large Ring apart in one place, forming one long strand (BH hold either end of LR)*
6. *BH bring ends back together again such that the original circular shape is approximated; holds LR like this briefly with ends touching*　　　(18JC, page 41)

61. *BH break Large Ring*
62. *BH push the two broken ends together again,*
   but cannot get ends to stick　　　　　　　　　*S:　"Ria."*
67. *BH hold LR with ends touching and then crossed*
68. *BH place LR on table with ends crossed*　　　(18JHo, pages 45 and 46)

16. *RH thumb and index finger squeeze Large Ring*
16a. *LR breaks at that point*
17. *RH picks up one end of LR so that LR uncoils into a strand in the air*
18. *RH puts strand of LR back down on table*
19. *BH start folding strand of LR into itself*

20. *BH press ends of LR to another part of strand of LR*
21. *BH open LR up into an arc shaped strand*   (*18ML, pages 12–22*)

Transitional reconstructions are only somewhat articulated and regulated. Nevertheless, they more precisely and fully conserve the intensive features or the identity of ring objects. For instance, first 18ML breaks the ring and transforms it into a strand. He immediately attempts to reconstruct its curvilinear form and press the strand back into a circular ring, but ends up with a pretzel-like ring. Moreover, he negates his reconstruction by once more opening up the pretzel-like ring into a strand. Thus, two reversible transformations are successively, if only partially precisely, applied to the object. The result is the bare beginnings of a second-order identity operation, and 18ML is the only infant who generates this advanced construction.

Decomposing is progressively controlled and regulated. It can be precisely coordinated with deforming (as in the following decomposition which is a continuation of a sequence of deforming by *18JHe* not presented here):

17.5. *LH index finger pushes into center of Ball (previously deformed such that it resembles a "dumbbell"), making indentation and then splitting off a small piece*   (*18JHe, page 28*)

Decomposing can also be precisely coordinated with breaking:

10. *BH break previously squished Ring apart into long piece*
11. *BH pulls R into two parts*   (*18KM, page 38*)

Decomposing can also now be precisely targeted at a part of a whole object in order to overcome resistance by the object's substance to subjects' efforts at decomposing:

20.5. *RH fingers push into Ball (deformation and partial decomposition)*
20.5. *LH fingers push into B (deformation)*
22. *BH remove from B (when raises RH, part of B where RH was exerting pressure tears and comes up with RH; this portion still remains attached to main slab though)*
23. *RH pulls away from B stuck to fingers and B lowers back to main body*
24. *BH split off that part of B that almost came off in Line 22* (*18JHe, page 29*)

On the other hand, the resistance of the object's substance can also be used to advantage in decomposing it. For instance, subject 18JC leaves a PlayDoh object that is attached to his right hand thumb in place so that his left hand can split a part off it.

Contingent instrumental decomposing is a further indication that decomposing is progressively controlled and regulated. It is generated repeatedly by two of the three subjects tested in the combined discrete and quasi-continuous task.

While the subjects visually monitor their transformations, the procedures are still unarticulated pushing and rubbing of the tongue depressors against the PlayDoh balls in order to decompose them.

Producing single two-element sets by decomposing a larger whole into two parts no longer dominates infants' decompositions. Infants often decompose a large object into numerous smaller objects with which they construct a set comprising numerous elements. For instance, the well-regulated features of subject 18JC's transformations are manifest from the outset. He breaks a ring into a strand before decomposing it in two. Throughout, he visually monitors his own decompositions. The decompositions are geneological, that is, they produce an ordered series of parts decreasing in size. Throughout, he gathers the consecutive parts in his right hand and, in this way, preserves them as a single set of numerous elements. Finally, he places almost all the parts together on the table in a clump. Thereby, most elements are preserved as a discrete stabile composition and as a continuous semicomposition. The final set, then, constitutes a relatively stable if unarticulated single set that includes numerous, but not all, ordered elements constructed by decomposing one larger whole.

Multiple decomposing of a larger whole into a set of smaller parts by 18JC does not stop here. He immediately proceeds to another ring. Regulative adjustment of 18JC's grip on the second ring precedes decomposing it. Decomposing the larger whole ring produces a small geneological series of three parts decreasing in size. The parts are preserved as a second stable set of three elements separate from but contiguous to the first, more numerous set. While including fewer members than the first set, the second set is conserved as a more articulate configuration of three ordered elements.

All together then, 18JC constructs two sets that include more than two members each. The sets are stable and preserved together but as differentiated collections of elements. Differentiation is marked by both spatial separation and configurational dissimilarity. While not generated as frequently as single sets with multiple membership, constructing two sets comprising more than two elements is no longer exceptional (irrelevant transactions are omitted):

40. *RH picks up Ring (previously crumpled up) which breaks in half such that RH holds half of R in air*
41. *RH swings R all about so the bulk of R falls to table (a little Piece remains in his hand)*
42. *RH places P in mother's already open hand*
43–47. *RH continues to break off little pieces and deposits them in mother's hand (subject does this in the same manner of holding onto one end of a bigger piece, shaking it in the air until it falls); a small piece remains clamped between his fingers which subject deposits in mother's hand; repeats this 6 times over the course of 1 minute; mother ends up with six pieces in her hand*

52–56.   *RH picks up end of Larger Piece on table, swings LP around until larger*
         portion falls off, and deposits the smaller portion in mother's hand; repeats this
         3 times

57.   *the last time, the Fourth Piece was larger than the others in mother's hand so*
      RH removes FP and breaks FP in half by pinching its center

58.   *RH puts both equal pieces simultaneously in mother's hand*

                                                              (18ML, page 23)

Like *18JC*, the procedure used by *18ML* to decompose objects is constant. Subject *18JC* decomposes by repeatedly splitting objects in two. The procedure used by *18ML* is more unusual; he always decomposes by swinging objects such that the major portion falls off.

Both infants construct two stable sets, one after the other. But *18ML* preserves the two sets by depositing the elements in his mother's hands. Thus, he adds a social dimension to his constructions not present in *18JC*'s performance, but not at all unusual at this stage. Infants often show or give their creations to their mothers or the tester at this age.

While both infants use corresponding decomposing routines, the elements they construct differ. The elements produced by *18JC* are progressively smaller and they form two geneologically ordered series. The elements produced by *18ML* correspond to each other, that is, are roughly equivalent in size to each other. Indeed, *18ML* even corrects his constructions when one part turns out bigger; he takes it back from his mother's hand and decomposes it into two equal parts. Moreover, *18ML* constructs two sets of imprecisely equivalent number; they comprise elements of similar sizes. The two sets constructed by *18JC* are nonequivalent in both number and size of elements.

Decomposing objects into two sets is generated by 75% of the subjects. Two subjects construct two corresponding sets, each of which includes exactly the same number of elements. Three subjects construct two geneological series of ordered elements that progressively decrease in size. Overall, however, decomposing two larger whole objects into two sets does not usually result in either corresponding equivalence between sets or ordered geneological nonequivalence within sets. Constructing two equivalence or geneological sets by decomposition is still exceptional at this stage.

Constructing single geneological sets by decomposition is a common achievement. All subjects but one decompose one larger whole object into an ordered series of parts progressively decreasing in size. Most subjects do so several times. A few subjects generate geneological decomposition as many as six times within one testing phase of one task. Usually they do not preserve the ordered series they construct so that there is no overt indication that they are producing more than single geneological series.

Almost all subjects also construct single corresponding sets by decomposing numerous parts of about equal size from one larger whole object. Often they do this repeatedly, although not necessarily consecutively, within one test phase of one task. Since they tend not to preserve the sets of equal sized elements, there is no overt indication that they are producing more than correspondence within single sets.

Most infants do not accompany decomposing with any expressive behavior. When they do, they are usually unarticulated vocalizations that are perhaps onomatopoeic, such as "Pah," "Hoh," and "Toe." One infant accompanies two of his many decompositions by uttering "Car." Only one infant (18SO) is descriptively articulate. Her verbal productions are sprinkled throughout her performance that comprises repeated pulling pieces off rings and balls. These decompositions are accompanied by three types of verbal expression. The first comprises "I broke it," "Broke it," and "I broke." The second comprises "Peel," "Peeling," and "Peel; Pee-ile." The third comprises "Doo!," "Ball," and "Doo; Ball!"

That is the most sophisticated linguistic behavior generated by any infant at this stage. Subject 18SO verbally describes her decompositions by three basic phrases (i.e., "I broke it," "Peeling," and "Doo; Ball!"). Yet, she is the only infant who verbally symbolizes any transformations of quasi-continuous objects. Moreover, neither 18SO nor any other subject manifests any comparable linguistic behavior when transacting with discrete or combined discrete and quasi-continuous objects.

V. Number Permanence

Recomposing previously decomposed parts is generated by half of the subjects, all but one of whom do so two or more times (Table 9.1, Row 6). Recomposing is becoming well-regulated. It is featured by repeated recompositions or multiple inverse transformations of previous decompositions:

31.   BH pull Large Ball apart (RH holds major portion; LH holds smaller portion)
32.   BH put pieces of LB back together, as simultaneously squeezes and digs fingers into the PlayDoh (composition and deformation)
33.   BH stretch out LB (deformation into a flatter shape)
34.   RH pulls a piece off LB held by LH, 3 times
35.5. RH squeezes 3 pieces together with major portion of LB (composition)
35.5. LH squeezes LB (deformation)   (18HS, page 27)

Recomposing continues to be a pragmatic extensity operation. It is used by infants, including 18HS, to reconstitute the initial extent of the larger whole object which is decomposed into smaller parts. Reversibility between decomposing and recomposing is becoming relatively well-regulated. It may even be coordinated with relatively well-regulated deformation. But it is still not featured by pragmatic intensity operations.

The closest that any subject comes to recomposing the intensity as well as the extensity of objects is subject *18JHe*'s recomposing that follows upon his decomposing presented on page 200. The decomposed part is replaced by *18JHe* in its original location. He pushes it into the original whole. Replacing the decomposed part in its original location on the larger whole is prerequisite but insufficient for intensive reversibility.

Composing is generated by 75% of subjects; these subjects compose repeatedly (Table 9.1, Row 7). Composing is beginning to be regulated. For instance, subject *18HS* transfers five small PlayDoh pieces to her right hand which composes them into one larger whole by squeezing them together. Then she composes the resultant clump with another ball to form an even larger whole. Thus subject *18HS* constructs a still small and imprecise but ordered series of increasing quasi-continuous magnitudes.

While beginning to construct rudimentary ordered increasing series by composition and more advanced ordered decreasing series by decomposition, infants' cognizance of these operations and their transformational consequence remain strictly pragmatic. This fact becomes apparent in infants' reactions to invisible compositions by the experimenter during phase II testing. Up to age 18 months infants continue to transact with the transformed set as if nothing changed in the number and magnitude of objects (Langer, 1983). At this stage, a few infants begin to be cognizant but perplexed by the transformational consequences:

(experimenter removes Balls 2 and 3 and brings back a Large Ball)

1. *RH picks up the remaining Ball 1 and sets B1 down in front of self*
2. *RH begins to point (closed palm with extended index finger) toward the experimenter who has taken the other two balls (experimenter places LB on the table)*
3. *RH immediately picks up LB and places LB near self and B1*
4. *RH again begins to point (requesting) to the experimenter repeatedly, and finally vocally, "eh, eh" (high pitch) (experimenter extends her empty hands to show that she has nothing that she is hiding)*
5. *looks around the room (suspiciously), then looks at LB*
6. *RH picks up LB, holds LB near eyes, and looks at LB*

(18ML, pages 29 and 30)

The number transformation by the tester from three to two objects was not visible to *18ML*. Nevertheless, he searches for the third object when the experimenter puts back one instead of two objects. His search behavior reflects his equilibriated structure of numerical permanence. While analyses of single object permanence since Piaget (1954) have been numerous (e.g., Bower, 1977; Gratch, 1979), they do not reach the quantitative issue of number permanence.

Number permanence is yet to be compensated by logical composition of quasi-continuous quantity. When one malleable object is added quasi-continuously to another, two complementary results are produced. First, the number of objects does not increase: it decreases. One quasi-continuous object added quasi-continuously to another equals one quasi-continuous object, not two. Second, the magnitude of the resultant is larger than each of the objects added together. Subject 18ML does not infer these two complementary transformations. Searching for a third object, then, reflects both (a) an equilibriated structure of number permanence, and (b) a disequilibriated structure of logical composition.

Infants just begin to reconstruct all the basic features constituting object identity. At its origins, object identity is the product of reversibility between composing and decomposing. It is not yet the product of reversible decomposing and recomposing which, at this stage, is still limited to negating extensity but not intensity.

Redecomposing, like recomposing, is generated by half of the subjects (Table 9.1, Row 8). Some subjects redecompose repeatedly. For instance, a little while after 18JC semicomposes seven objects into one larger whole, he redecomposes it back into the original seven objects. Almost all redecomposing negates the extensive but not the intensive properties of quasi-continuous objects, thereby producing quantitative but not predicate identity. Subject 18JC is unusual in this regard; only a minority of infants redecompose the original intensity as well as extensity of the objects they have composed. Not only does 18JC redecompose the intensive as well as the extensive identity of objects in this instance, but he does so in two other instances as well. He is able to do this because his compositions consist of nothing more than sticking objects together without squeezing them. Hence, he can just pluck them off again. Indeed, 18JC goes on to composing some of these objects again.

The longest reversible sequence, generated by subject 18JHo, consists of seven negations between composing and redecomposing. The sequence begins with composing. It is followed by redecomposing, composing, redecomposing, composing, redecomposing and composing, and ends with redecomposing. Interspersed in this reversible sequences is spatial inversion of the objects and showing the objects by the infant to his mother. Together with the repeated negations, these activities mark progressive regulation of reversibility between composing and redecomposing.

Attaching and detaching discrete and quasi-continuous objects is generated repeatedly by all infants (Table 9.1., Rows 9 and 11, Columns 7 and 8). Detaching is becoming well-regulated. Infants rotate and monitor the combined objects so that they are in good working positions. Anticipatory preparation of the arrangement of the whole combined objects puts them into optimum states for easy and immediate detachment of the discrete and quasi-continuous parts from each other.

Attaching is also becoming well-regulated. For instance, subject 18JHe begins by composing two quasi-continuous balls into a larger flatter whole. This act prepares it for reproductive attachment with two tongue depressors by sticking two tongue depressors in approximately perpendicular to the relatively flat Play-Doh. He then lifts and shows his construction to his mother.

This construction also marks the origins of corresponding attachment. Rudimentary equivalence relations are thereby produced in the part–whole structure of combined discrete and quasi-continuous objects. However, these equivalence relations are generated rarely. Only 33% of the subjects construct them, and they never do so more than once.

Reversibility between attachment and detachment also originates at this stage and is already becoming well-regulated (e.g., rotating PlayDoh balls to prepare attaching). It is constructed in both the order of attachment undone by detachment and of detachment undone by attachment. Both forms are generated repeatedly by all infants; often the reproductions are consecutive. They are sometimes accompanied by nonverbal expressive behavior such as laughing. The overall results are the reproductions of extensive and intensive identity. These reversible identity operations conserve the structure of conglomerate discrete–quasi-continuous objects and of separate discrete and quasi-continuous objects.

STAGE 7 AT TWENTY-ONE MONTHS

III

10

Planned Routines

Substantial progress marks infants' structuring of routines or pragmatic propositions and linguistic symbolization. The pace of linguistic development accelerates such that it is rapidly catching up with nonlinguistic symbolic development. The first sign of language beginning to outstrip symbolization in routines is generated by this stage. It occurs when infants refer to immediately nonpresent events that have just taken place a moment ago. Temporal extension of transactions from the nonpresent into the present by symbolic notation is simple with language; but it begins to stretch and often exceed the structural limits of symbolization in routines.

No facet of this development, including that of linguistic notation, is comparable yet to the structural development in infants' logicomathematical and physical constructions at this stage. This lag in linguistic development is most apparent when compared to infants' developing construction of causal and spatial functions. Not only do infants progressively form consolidated second-order structures but they progressively determine the boundaries between physically possible and impossible dependencies in space and causality. This discovery necessarily includes experimenting with actual physical phenomena in order to explore their relations to potential physical phenomena.

I. Consolidation of Planned Routines

Planned routines are generated with ease using all types of objects, whether realistic or not, to form sentence-like structures. Infants tend to repeat their routines one or more times. Thus, routines continue to be governed by the rule of reproduction, as they also are by anticipation. To illustrate, subject 21AF's left hand picks up Doll 1 in anticipation of the right hand uprighting it. But first the right hand has to upright Doll 4 which it is holding. This act permits the left hand to transfer Doll 1 to the right hand for uprighting next to the other two dolls which the right hand has just uprighted. Reciprocity, as always, also governs routines; it is most clearly evident in infants many and varied spoon-in-cup feeding routines.

Combining a small set of two and three temporally overlapping mappings with a small set of objects to form protosyntactic sentence-like routines is consolidated into a stable form at this stage. Consolidated routines are marked by several key features. Routines are marked by coregulating part processes with each other. For instance, subject 21EN collects all and only the rings by transferring them from one hand to the other. This part process is then combined with another part process, that of using the transferring hand to adjust the rings so that they will be matched in one-to-one spatial placement correspondence in the collecting hand.

Consolidated routines are often marked by protological features, as they are at previous stages. We have just noted the correspondence constructed by 21EN. We could just as well point to 21AF's construction of an alignment by uprighting four dolls. Moreover, the objects of these routines include all and only the members of one of the two classes of objects presented to these infants.

Consolidated routines are increasingly impervious to disruptions by minor interruptions; these may include self-correction. Thus, for instance, 21EN interrupts his ring collecting routine by picking up a doll. This "mistake" does not derail 21EN's routine as it would have at a younger age. Instead, 21EN simply corrects his error by placing the doll back on the table and proceeds to complete his routine using rings only.

Consolidated routines are also increasingly flexible. Variants and extensions that directly derive from the theme of the routines are generated with increasing frequency. To illustrate, the theme of one of subject 21SS's routines is dipping a spoon in a cup followed by pretending to eat from the spoon. After repeating this routine many times, 21SS extends the routine by pretending to drink from the cup. Later in her production 21SS flexibly varies her theme by (a) pretending to feed her mother, (b) substituting another spoon, and (c) substituting another cup.

Finally, consolidated routines are often marked by symbolic features, as is evident in 21SS's pretenses. These symbolic features include arbitrary elements (e.g., 21SS chooses whether to eat, drink or pour from a cup), and figurative elements in which acts and objects are substituted for each other so that they serve to symbolically stand for one another. They also include conventional elements that foster communication with others.

Mappings still predominate over objects. They remain compact in form and are increasingly constant. Three overlapping mappings are, as always, unusual, while two overlapping mappings are commonplace. Differentiated, as well as coordinated, overlapping mappings are progressively well-formed, controlled, and finely articulated:

44.5.   *RH places on table palm up with Mirror lying and balancing on index finger*
44.5.   *LH raises Doll 1 to mouth*
46.5.   *RH index finger balances M*
46.5a. *M falls off RH index finger*
46.5.   *LH holds D1 to mouth*
48.   *LH lowers D1 away from mouth*   (21PG, page 4)

Routines, as just noted and illustrated, are progressively marked by conventionalization coupled with arbitrariness; these qualities foster detaching routines from their usual settings. Such decontextualization enhances transforming protosymbolic routines into symbolic forms. This enhancement applies to both the mappings and the objects that infants combine to produce protosyntactic routines.

Detaching objects of routines from their prototypical constructive contexts begins at the previous stage (see Chapter 6). A few infants begin to substitute nonrealistic objects (e.g., a block) for a realistic object (e.g., a brush) or a realistic object (e.g., a spoon) for a realistic object (e.g., a brush) by age 18 months. The frequency of such substitutions, which couple conventional with arbitrary elements, is augmented rapidly at this stage. For instance, subject 21RR pretends that a clover ring is a cookie to eat after which she names it "Cookie."

More significant for detaching the objects of routines, and the main structural advance in abstracting routines at this stage, are infants' substitutions when they combine objects by reciprocity. In the prototypical detachment generated at this stage, infants combine a realistic with a nonrealistic object. To illustrate, at first subject 21AL merely touches a brush to the top of a cylinder. This act leads 21AL to brush the top of the cylinder as if it might be a doll. Once started, 21AL substitutes a second nonrealistic object (another cylinder) into this routine. Both brushes and square columns are substituted in the routine of another subject, 21KM. Two brushes are used by 21KM to brush all four columns. This substitution extends the routine to include brushing the side of one of the columns. Arbitrary nonrealistic objects, then, are beginning to be substituted for the objects of play routines as well as the subject of the play. At previous stages, as we have seen, they could only be substitutes for the subject of the play.

Thus, 21AL's routine comprises one-to-many (agent-to-patient) relations while 21KM's routine takes a more robust many-to-many (agent-to-patient) form. Both involve substitutions that foster detaching the objects of routines from their initial self-generated and, perhaps, ordinary socioconventional contexts. Detachment, it may be hypothesized, is particularly enhanced when infants make substitutions in both the agent and patient objects comprising routines governed by reciprocity (e.g., 21KM's routine). In addition, detachment is fostered when infants substitute nonrealistic patients in the place of the realistic patients of their reciprocal routines. Effectively, these substitutions make one patient form stand for or symbolize another patient form within infants' routines and, thereby, foster their abstraction into progressively nonfigural forms of symbolization.

The most advanced form of detaching objects of routines governed by reciprocity at this stage is generated by one infant only:

1. *RH picks up Red Cylinder 1
   and stands RC1 upright on and
   middle of Blue Square Column
   2*

2. *RH picks up Red Cylinder 2
   and stands RC2 upright on and
   middle of Blue Square Column
   1*

3.5. *RH points to RC2/BSC1*   S: *"Boats. Boats."*
3.5. *LH points to RC1/BSC2
     (experimenter places Red
     Cylinder 3 and Blue Square
     Column 3 on table)*

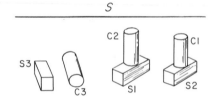

5. *RH picks up RC3 and stands
   RC3 upright on BSC3
   (experimenter moves RC1/BSC2
   around making boat noises,*   S: *"Boat."*
   "Toot, toot, toot, toot.")
                                            (M: *"How many boats?"*)
                                            S: *"Free, free, free."*
6. *RH moves RC3/BSC3 to left
   and then jerks it suddenly up
   toward experimenter*
6a. *RC3 falls off BSC3 and rolls*   (M: *"Can you make the boat go?"*)
    *away
    (experimenter rolls RC3 back
    toward subject)*
7. *RH picks up RC3 and stands
   RC3 upright on BSC3*

8.	*RH slides RC3/BSC3 to left*	S:	*"Twee, wee, wee, twee."*
9.	*RH releases from RC3/BSC3 and swings to left hitting RC3 and RC2*	S:	*"Ohhh, ha, ha, ha."*
9a.	*RC3 falls off BSC3 and C2 falls off BSC1*		
10.	RH picks up RC2 and stands RC2 upright on BSC1		
11.	*RH slides RC2/BSC1 between RC1/BSC2 and BSC3*		
12.	BH tap on table, 3 times (subject seems excited)		
13.	*RH slides RC1/BSC2 to left toward mother*	S:	*"Ha, ha. Beep, beep."*
13a.	*RC1 falls off BSC2 close to mother*	S:	*"Oh, oh."*

(21RR, pages 33 and 34)

Nonrealistic objects are combined by 21RR into three identical pairs to stand for realistic objects, which 21RR calls "Boats." Also, 21RR knows that whole objects are made up of combined parts. Accordingly, she combines two nonrealistic objects to stand for one realistic object. Thus, two objects are substituted for one object. She makes this substitution three times (Lines 1–5) and coordinates it with replacement two times (Lines 5 and 7 and Lines 9 and 10).

Multiple detachment of objects, then, is generated by 21RR applying two complementary forms of substitution. Nonrealistic objects are substituted for realistic objects, and two combined objects are substituted for single objects. The result is that 21RR constructs her own playful symbolic routine that is becoming conventionalized.

It may therefore be hypothesized that creating such routines is rooted in substitution and correspondence compositions plus spatial dependency functions between the objects comprising the compositions. These foundational operations and functions will be considered more fully at a later point. It may equally be hypothesized that creating such routines is directed toward and fosters infants' cognition of the arbitrary yet conventional rule-governed properties of symbolic systems, particularly that of language. In this regard it should not be overlooked that the routine is coupled with verbal symbolization which will be analyzed at a later point.

It is more difficult to determine when mapping combinations that are parts of routines are detached from their initial self-generated and sociocultural contexts than it is to determine when objects are detached. Still, mapping detachment begins to be revealed when infants flexibly vary the themes of their routines. The detachment is most evident in infants' pretend play:

37. *BH move Car 4 left to right in*
     air (as if C4 were flying)
38. *BH lower C4 and hold C4 on*   S: *"Mmmh, mmm."*
     table   *(car noises)*
                                               (21CP, page 40)

3.   *RH slides Orange VW to the*   S: *"Sshhooooooh—."*
     left about 6 inches and then
     back to the right about 5
     inches, while LH holds VW1,
     VW2, VW3 and VW4 against chest
4.   *RH raises OVW high above table*
     as looking up at OVW, while LH
     holds VW1, VW2, VW3 and VW4   S: *"Oooooh—."*
     against chest
5.   *RH lowers OVW to table and releases it while*
     LH holds VW1, VW2, VW3 and VW4 against
     chest
6.   *RH takes VW1 from LH which now holds*   S: *"Ssshhhhhhhh."*
     VW2, VW3 and VW4 against chest   *(21CL, page 139)*

Subject 21CP pretends to drive or fly a car in the air. Whichever interpretation is correct, the mapping is detached from its ordinary context before being transformed into a more usual form accompanied by onomatopoesis. Flying a VW is intermingled with driving it by 21CL. Both flying and driving are accompanied by continuous onomatopoesis.

Occasional playful routines begin to be constructed in which the symbolic pretense applies to more than a single set of two objects. The three boat routine by 21RR (presented on pages 212 and 213) is as extended as any generated at this stage. More typical playful routines at this stage apply to two objects only (irrelevant intervening transactions are omitted):

4.5.   *RH holds and moves Doll 1 next to Yellow*   S: *"Ech, ddoo, doo,*
       Doll (as if they are having an interaction)   *eh, dooda."*
4.5.   *LH holds and moves YD next to D1*
12.5. *RH index finger with D1 inserted on it*
       wriggles D1 around in air so that D1 and YD
       hit each other and "interact" together
12.5. *LH index finger with YD inserted on it*
       wriggles YD around in air so that YD and
       D1 hit each other and "interact" together   *(21VL, page 47)*

The routine is varied flexibly by 21VL first using the two dolls like hand puppets and then using them like finger puppets. This choice is arbitrary and determined only by 21VL's interests and abilities. At the same time, the flexible variations progressively correspond to conventional symbolic usage.

Conventional correspondence between verbal symbols and their referents is commonplace. Most conventional verbal symbolic correspondences, however, are still limited to naming (e.g., "Block") or reiteration (e.g., subject 21KA says "Car" four times as he grasps one car). On the other hand, pluralization just begins to be generated in the context of reiteration (see 21RR protocol fragment on page 212). In reiteration, 21RR combines verbal with gestural reference (Lines 3.5). By pluralizing, 21RR may begin to symbolically mark her addition of another "boat." Indeed, 21RR may be one of only two subjects to generate some form of verbal comparative. To the extent that she is trying to say "Three," 21RR is just beginning to number the objects; but even then she enumerates reiteratively. The other subject (21KM) may have formed the rudiments of a comparative when she names an object "Green."

Infants continue to demonstrate objects by semiconventional forms (e.g., holding something up to another person while vocalizing "Uh"). Other demonstratives, however, are generated that are fully conventional (e.g., "Look at that"). Infants also generate fully conventional demonstrative forms of negation (e.g., "I don't want that," and "I don't like that").

Almost invariably infants make reference to nothing more than present objects and events. Only one infant begins to refer linguistically to what she has just done as well as to what she is doing. This includes the production of some fully formed sentences (irrelevant intervening transactions are omitted):

6.	*RH takes Brush 1 out of mouth*	S:	*"Mommy. I brush teeth, momma."*
10.	*RH lowers B1 from mouth*	S:	*"I. I, done."*
24.	*RH raises B1 to mouth and brushes teeth*	S:	*"I brush teeth, momma."*
33.	*LH lowers Brush 2 from mouth*	S:	*"I brushed my teeth, momma."*

(21SS, pages 26 and 27)

In these ways 21SS begins to extend her verbal reference from present to no longer present events (cf., Antinucci & Miller, 1976; and Bloom, Lifter, & Hafitz, 1980). But the extension is made by one infant only. As also expected at its origin, the first extension is to the immediate past, not to a distant past. Furthermore, the extension is to an actual event and not a potential event. Therefore, actual past events may be expected to be verbalized by infants before they can begin to verbalize potential events, whether past or future.

II. Investigating the Material Properties of Object Identity

Comparative part–whole inspection of single objects is no longer necessary to determine the identity of objects unless they are unusual in some way (e.g., subject 21RR rotates a clover ring around its axis three times while visually examining it). Instead, infants look over the objects presented to them in selecting those that have common properties. After selecting and composing objects, infants may begin to point at and trace their constructions:

22. *RH raises to table and index finger points while resting on table*
23. *RH index finger points and moves toward previously stacked four blocks*
24. *RH moves toward stack and pointing index finger touches subject's side of B2*
25. *RH with index finger pointing moves vertically up stack such that finger touches stack as it moves up from Block 2, to Block 1, to Block 4 to Block 3 and stops on top of B3 with index finger still in a pointing position*   (21AL, pages 2 and 3)

Differentiated tactual inspection traces the general properties of the construction 21AL just made with the objects. Overtly tracing objects' features and their composition marks gestural exploration and representation by infants of part–whole properties of objects and their combination into configuration. This ability is usually not found until at least ages three to four years (e.g., Piaget & Inhelder, 1967; and Zaporozhets, 1965). Yet, as we have just seen, it has its developmental roots in infants' representational tracings at this stage.

Representational preservation of lost objects is no longer a problem. It continues to be expressed in a vocal medium (e.g., "Uh, oh"). Sometimes it is also already expressed verbally (e.g., "Whoops—I dropped it Mom").

One other new element stands out in infants' determination of object identity at this stage. Infants sometimes try to extend mappings that are successful for one kind of object to objects for which these mappings are inappropriate. For instance, subject 21RR tries to pull apart two wooden circular rings, one after the other. Subject 21RR had just finished two PlayDoh tasks when she generated these impossible interactions with wooden rings. She tries to transfer her possible breaking of quasi-continuous PlayDoh rings to discrete wooden rings. Her attempts are selective by class properties. She attempts to break all and only the wooden rings that are similar to (though not identical with) circular PlayDoh rings she has decomposed. She does not attempt to break the other objects presented which comprise two cars.

Negative feedback from interaction with objects, such as that received by 21RR, serves to delimit the material properties of objects. Determining what is empirically possible and what is impossible continues to be tested by infants at this stage and is crucial to their initial construction of physical reality. In particular, it marks infants' construction of causal and spatial functions that is analyzed in Sections III and IV.

III. Differentiating between Possible and Impossible Causes and Effects

Causal instrumentation becomes progressively differentiated and integrated. Objects are selected with which to construct dependent variables. Increasingly, they tend to be different from the object selected as the independent variable for experimenting. To illustrate, the instrument is first prepared by subject 21EN picking up a spoon in his right hand before stacking three cylinders on top of each other. Moreover, the spoon is stored in the right hand while the left hand selects cylinders only and stacks them to form a target for the prepared instrument. This causal routine is repeated again a little further in the task by 21EN. Both affirmation of the dependent variable and its instrumental negation, then, are well-regulated. Control is exercised over both components of the causal construction.

Causal control is apparent in one other development at this stage. The bottom object is targeted both times by 21EN. The bottom object is thereby transformed into a causal intermediary for transitive transmission of the effect (i.e., making all three cylinders fall). Hence, linear causality is progressively differentiated and integrated into three components, namely, agents, intermediaries, and patients, with infants gaining mastery and control over the construction of all three components.

Predicate differentiation also progressively informs infants' causal experimentation that is not instrumental. To illustrate, one infant (21VL) drops all eight presented objects down inside her overalls. First she selects and drops all and only the four brushes. Then she selects and drops all and only the four triangular columns. Still, her control may be semisystematic since she ignores the different colors of the objects (i.e., half of the brushes and half of the columns are blue while the other half are red). To credit 21VL with full systematicity would require assuming that she knows that color is not a relevant independent variable in her experiment.

Much of infants' causal explorations are designed to differentiate between possible and impossible physical conditions. Constructing vehicular instruments that infants can not yet fully control is a primary method of testing physical reality:

4. *LH places Doll and Brush on Plate*
5. *BH pick up P*
5a. *D and B fall off P*   (21JE, page 5)

40. *RH stacks Cylinder 1 upright on Cylinder 3 held upright in air by LH*
41. *LH moves left holding C3 with C1 stacked on C3*
41a. *C1 falls off C3 to table*
42. *RH picks up Cylinder 2 and stacks C2 upright on C3 held in air by LH*
42a. *C2 falls off C3 to table*   (21AF, page 31)

88. *BH reach out slowly to previously stacked*
     Blue Cylinder 1/Red Cylinder 2/Red
     Cylinder 1
89. *RH picks up BC1 with RC2 and RC1 on*
     top

90.5.   RH *holds BC1*
90.5.   LH *holds RC2*
90.5a. RC1 *falls to table*
92.   RH *stacks BC1 upright on Blue Cylinder*
        2 standing upright on table
93.   LH *transfers RC2 to RH which stacks*
        RC2 upright on BC1/BC2
94.   RH *picks up RC1 and stacks RC1 upright*
        on RC2/BC1/BC2
95.   BH *grasp BC1 and RC2 and lift*   (E: *"What's that?"*)
        BC1/RC2/RC1 up
95a.   RC1 *falls off RC2 to floor*   (21EN, pages 16 and 17)

These constructions combine two functions. The first is determining the
spatial dependency relation necessary between objects stacked on top of each
other to make them balance (e.g., the balancing object must be held upright for
the balanced object not to fall off). The second is determining and maintaining
the balance when moving stacked objects by using the lower one(s) as vehicles to
transport the upper ones. In both these functions, resistances by the objects to
infants' still limited psychomotor skills negate infants' attempts to affirm the
dependency relations between the objects. These are impossible empirical conditions at this stage.

Infants also begin to explore some causal conditions that are physically impossible but for which their psychomotor skills are not at issue:

55.   LH *holds Red Cylinder 1 upright on table and leans RC1 to right and then left*
        several times
56.   LH *tilts RC1 too far*
56a.   RC1 *falls to its side*
57.   LH *picks up RC1, starts to but does not completely stand RC1 upright, and*
        releases RC1
57a.   RC1 *falls to its side and onto floor*   (21EN, page 15)

The limits of the possible are tested by 21EN. He exceeds them twice and the
resistance of the object negates his efforts. These replicated experiments provide
definitive feedback that it is impossible to make a tilted cylinder stand upright.
The limits of physical reality have been exceeded; it is this fact which 21EN
begins to determine by replicated experimenting.

In the main, however, infants' explorations of the boundaries between possible
and impossible causal conditions usually confound physical resistance with infants' psychomotor skills (intervening transactions are omitted from the 21CP
protocol fragment):

5.   LH *holding Circular Ring 2 points toward camera*
5a.   CR2 *rolls out of LH and rolls across table*

    9.   *LH picks up CR2, stands CR2 up, holds CR2 steady by keeping a finger on top of CR2, and releases CR2 (as if trying to get CR2 to roll on table like in Line 5a)*

  9a.   *CR2 falls to its side on table*

16.5.   *LH stands CR2 up and holds top of CR2*

16.5.   *RH stands Circular Ring 3 up and holds top of CR3*

18.5.   *LH raises from CR2*

18.5a.   *CR2 falls on its side*

18.5.   *RH raises from CR3*

18.5a.   *CR3 falls on its side*

25.5.   *RH holds CR3 up on table*

25.5.   *LH holds CR2 up on table*

  27.   *RH releases CR3*

 27a.   *CR3 falls on its side*

  28.   *LH releases CR2*

 28a.   *CR2 rolls $\frac{1}{4}$ inch, then falls over on its side*   (*21CP, pages 3 and 4*)

  13.   *RH finger inserts in Blue Circular Ring and twirls BCR around on table*

 13a.   *BCR slips from finger and*   S: "Ahh, uhh,"
        falls to floor   (*21KA, page 45*)

Both infants start by generating possible kinetic conditions; 21CP does so by accident while 21KA does so in a controlled fashion. Many subsequent attempts by 21CP (only some of which are reproduced here) are not successful. In these attempts it is not always clear whether 21CP is exploring the boundaries between possible and impossible balancing and/or rolling conditions. It appears as if 21CP is doing both. In any case, some of his explorations are in parallel and correspondence with each other (Lines 16.5–18.5a and 25.5–28a). This activity instigates investigating equivalence and nonequivalence between possible conditions and between impossible conditions.

While 21KA begins by generating a possible spinning condition, it degenerates into an impossible condition. The resistance of the object is too difficult for 21KA's limited psychomotor skills to overcome, and it negates her construction. Thus, 21KA initiates, but cannot complete, the necessary conditions for determining when spinning is empirically possible and when it is empirically impossible. Indeed, she marks vocally, and perhaps onomatopoetically, when spinning becomes impossible for her.

Causal dependency functions, then, are progressively tested experimentally in order to determine and differentiate the possible from the impossible. This includes exercising and generalizing second-order functions to form new dependency relations:

  3.   *LH slides Racer 3 into Car 3 such that R3 pushes C3 continuously to the table's edge*

> 4. *RH grasps C3 and slides C3 against Car 2 such that C3 pushes C2 continuously,*
>   *while LH holds R3*   (21PG, page 16)

First, 21PG transforms Car 3 into an extended causal patient; after this, he transforms it into its reciprocal: an extended causal agent.

IV. Differentiating between Possible and Impossible Spatial Constructions

Spatial functions are explored extensively. This exploration includes developing coregulative control over spatial dependency relations (irrelevant intervening transactions are omitted in the 21AL protocol fragment):

> 16.   *RH holding Spoon by handle tries to fit cup of S into hole at bottom of Doll 2*
>   *held by LH*   (21PG, page 2)

> 64.3. *RH slides Block 3 toward self about 3 inches and then picks B3 up*
> 64.7. *LH slides Block 1 toward center of table and then releases B1*
> 66.   *RH places and holds B3 on B1*
> 67.   *LH touches B3 and B1 to help align and balance B3 held by RH on B1*
> 68.   *RH releases from B3*
> 68a.   *B3 starts to fall off B1*
> 69.   *RH adjusts B3 so that it is balanced on B1*   (21AL, pages 13 and 14)

In part at least, 21PG is determining possible and impossible spatial fitting functions, that is, when and how objects fit with or into each other. This involves determining the dependency relations between inserting and enveloping spatial features. Both hands are used by 21AL to prepare, adjust, and maintain a balanced stacking relation between objects. While not recorded here, 21AL ends up with a balanced stack of six blocks.

Throughout this stage infants repeatedly affirm and negate possible spatial functions. Infants stack objects, knock the stack over, upright the stack of objects again, and so on; infants upright objects, lie them down, upright them again, and so on. Reversible relations internal to possible spatial functions are thereby generated and generalized by infants.

In Section III we considered constructions in which the resistance of the objects overwhelm infants' attempts to balance them (e.g., 21CP's attempts to upright rings). Physical negation feeds back to infants' constructions such that they begin to take the negations into account. In turn, this new knowledge about the limits of physical possibilities feeds forward to infants' subsequent constructions which are altered as a consequence.

In one routine, for example, subject 21EN attempts to stack spoons on top of cylinders. He seems cognizant of his procedure since he laughs and acts pleased while he is building. However, he observes that it is physically impossible to balance the two spoons on the cylinder. This observation leads him to negate his initial affirmation that this is physically possible. Thus, he no longer requires direct disconfirming movement (i.e., physical resistance) by the object to negate his affirmation, since he no longer attempts to leave the spoons on top of the cylinder. He has found out that this will not work.

Similarly, *21EN* begins by affirming an impossible spatial function in a second routine. He tries to contain a doll in a receptacle space (a car) that is not big enough; this behavior, as we have seen, is typical throughout infancy (e.g., infants try to contain rectangular-shaped receptacles in each other by embedding the long side of the contained over the short side of the container, which is impossible). He does not simply release the to-be-contained doll in the impossible to-be-container car. Rather he removes the doll when he observes that the spatial function he is trying to construct is impossible. Still, he then attempts the same impossible spatial function with the doll and another car that is identical to the first. Finally, taking into account the negative results, *21EN* generates a possible spatial function by placing the doll on a plate.

Possible spatial container–contained functions become progressively reversible; infants affirm and negate them. For instance, regulated sequential reciprocity is generated by subject *21AF* between containing, undoing containing, and containing three cups in each other. This is symptomatic of the development of second-order spatial functions in which dependency relations between containers and contained begin to be covaried.

Generating second-order spatial functions becomes particularly apparent when infants are presented with objects and two receptacles (in procedural phase II of the testing). It is still common for infants at this age to contain all the objects in one receptacle only and then notice that the other receptacle is empty. Typically this leads infants to transform the container into a vehicle of transmission; they move the container to a position over the empty receptacle, overturn the container, and empty its contents into the so far unused receptacle. By now this may be accomplished in smooth and well-regulated routines.

However, it does not always work out so clearly. For instance, transforming Receptacle 2 from a container into a vehicle for transferring contained objects is only partially achieved by subject *21RR*. Still, she goes on to transforming Receptacle 2 from a partially successful vehicle into a successful cover for her substitute container (Receptacle 1). Here, reciprocal spatial functions are generated sequentially by *21RR*; Receptacle 2 is transformed (a) from a container into a vehicle for another container, and then (b) from a vehicle into a cover for the other container.

The spatial functions of receptacles are thereby progressively differentiated by infants. Containers also just begin to have their functions differentiated by infants. For instance, both receptacles are first used by subject *21KA* to contain all and only cylinders. Later they are also used to contain the other objects. Containing is further differentiated by orientation and receptacle. All cylinders are contained upright in one receptacle. To achieve this oriented containment, 21KA corrects herself three times. She uprights a cylinder that she knocked over in the process of uprighting another cylinder in the receptacle; she redirects her placement of a cylinder after beginning to place it in the other receptacle; and she transfers a cylinder that she initially contained upright by itself in another receptacle so that it is contained upright in the receptacle with the rest of the cylinders.

Differentiated containing is elaborated further by negation. All the cylinders are transferred by 21KA from the first to the second receptacle. All the cylinders are also contained by lying them down. In effect, 21KA negates her initial affirmation (i.e., uprighting all and only cylinders in one receptacle) by switching both orientation and container (i.e., lying down all and only cylinders in the other receptacle).

V. Precise Three-Unit Matching and Three-Step Ordering

Correspondences condition infants' spatial constructions. Thus, as noted, first 21KA contains all the cylinders by uprighting them in one container; then she contains all the cylinders by lying them down in the other container. The result is that the second matched spatial orientation negates the first matched spatial orientation.

Sometimes infants begin to be cognizant of the reversible matchings by negation that they are constructing:

9. RH picks up Doll 3 and places
   D3 on its side next to Doll 1 and
   Doll 2
10. RH knocks upright D1 and D2 to
    their sides.
11. RH knocks upright Doll 4 to its   S: "Ha, ha."
    side   (21RR, page 4)

A continuous correspondence is generated by 21RR between the spatial orientation (i.e., lying down) of all four dolls and the causal mappings (i.e., knock over) used to achieve this with three of the dolls. This continuous correspondence negates the initial matched spatial orientation of all four dolls (i.e., upright). When finished, 21RR laughs at what she has done.

Continuous causal correspondences, like spatial correspondences, are progressively differentiated and regulated. For instance, in one task, subject 21AL uses one finger to flick all and only the trucks toward the experimenter. In another task she uses the same finger to flick all and only the dolls toward the experimenter. Some flicks are fairly precisely targeted. Other flicks reflect selective cooperative correspondence. Subject and experimenter reciprocally target the dolls toward each other; but while the experimenter rolls the dolls, the subject flicks the dolls.

Discrete correspondences do not usually exceed matching three units. Only the performance of one infant may have begun to exceed this limit (irrelevant intervening transactions are omitted):

34. *RH taps Yellow Hexagonal Column on table, 6 times, then raises YHC, while LH holds Green Cross Ring (experimenter taps Yellow Cross Ring on table, 1 time)*   (E: *"How about this one?"*)

35. *LH taps GCR on table, 6 times, then raises GCR, while RH holds YHC (experimenter taps YCR on table, 1 time)*

36. *LH taps GCR on table, 5 times, while RH holds YHC*

41. *LH holding Green Hexagonal Column and YHC, taps YHC on table, 5 times*

42. *LH transfers GHC and YHC to RH (experimenter taps YCR on table, 6 times and places YCR on table)*

43. *LH picks up YCR and taps YCR on table, 6 times, then places YCR on table (experimenter taps YCR on table, 4 times)*

44. *LH picks up GCR and taps GCR on table 4 times, then places GCR on table*

45. *LH picks up YCR and taps YCR on table 4 times, then places YCR on table*

46. *LH picks up GCR and taps GCR on table, 5 times*   (21EN, pages 7 and 8)

These constructions are exceptional. Still, they suggest the hypothesis that infants as young as 21 months may begin to generate equivalences between quantities ranging from four to six units as long as they are also matched mappings. In this case the matched mappings are tappings.

In the main, matched equivalences are generated between subjects' own constructions; but some are also cooperatively constructed with the experimenter. Thus, 21EN's series comprises ⟨ 6, (1), 6, (1), 5, 5, (6), 6, (4), 4, 4 ⟩ taps, where the experimenter's taps are given in parentheses. At the beginning of the series, 21EN matches his own number of taps (i.e., 6-to-6 and 5-to-5) but not the experimenter's one unit taps. At the end of the series, 21EN matches the experimenter's number of taps (i.e., 6-to-6 and 4-to-4) as well as his own (4-to-4).

Small number discrete correspondences are well coordinated with continuous correspondences by this stage:

4.5.   *RH pushes at Yellow Rectangular Ring and Yellow Circular Ring 1, 2 times*
4.5.   *LH pushes at Green Rectangular Ring 1 and Yellow Circular Ring, 2 times*
                                                                (21VL, page 21)

Two-to-two discrete correspondences between the number of mappings are coordinated with continuous correspondences between the form of mappings (i.e., pushing at). Actually, they are both also coordinated with two-to-two compositional correspondence since each configuration comprises two objects.

Precise discrete mapping orders do not generally exceed three units. These include generating: (a) unidirectional increasing ⟨ 2, 3 ⟩ orderings such as tap two times followed by three times; (b) unidirectional decreasing ⟨ 3, 2 ⟩ orderings such as tap three times followed by tap two times; and (c) bidirectional ⟨ 2, 3, 2 ⟩ orderings such as a series of two, three, two taps.

When the number of units exceeds three then the series generated are usually imprecise. To illustrate, one infant generates an increasing unidirectional ⟨ 1, 13, 20 ⟩ ordering while another infant generates a bidirectional ⟨ 13, 7, 7, 10 ⟩ ordering. Both probably represent three-step orderings where the first translates into something like ⟨ little, more, many ⟩ and the second into something like ⟨ many, some, some, more ⟩.

Exceptions continue to be generated. These are two-step series in which the largest unit may be six; whereas they are no more than five units at the previous stage. For instance, we have already observed that subject 21EN generates a series of this order (see protocol fragment on page 223). Before cooperating with the experimenter, 21EN taps 6, 6, 5, and 5 times. This part of the series is spontaneous; indeed, it is generated notwithstanding the experimenter's two intervening modeling of single taps.

Some of these series also reflect the continuing coordination of orderings with correspondence. Consider further 21EN's production. If we limit ourselves first to his spontaneous production we observe that he interweaves corresponding six-to-six and five-to-five taps with a decreasing order of six followed by five taps. If we include his cooperative production then he interweaves corresponding six-to-six, five-to-five, (six)-to-six, and (four)-to-four-to-four taps with a bidirectional order of six followed by five followed by six followed by four taps, where the experimenter's taps are given in parentheses.

Precise continuous, like discrete mapping orders, do not exceed three units (e.g., ⟨ touch, tap, hit ⟩). However, continuous orderings are generated less frequently than discrete orderings. This continues a trend noted at the previous stage.

Continuous ordering may be coordinated with discrete ordering. To illustrate, one infant generates an ordered bidirectional ⟨ touch 2 times, hit 4 times, touch 3 times ⟩ series. The continuous order is precise while the discrete order is not. Nevertheless, as one order increases so does the other; and as one order decreases so does the other. This relationship enhances the possibility of infants cognizing and reflecting upon the relations between ordered extensive (discrete) and intensive (continuous) quantities.

Continuous, like discrete orderings, also continue to be coordinated with correspondence. To illustrate, one infant generates the series ⟨ touch, (hit:hit) ⟩. An increasing ordered nonequivalence (between touch and hit) is thereby tied to equivalence (between hit and hit). Such productions foster the varied and growing links that infants are establishing between ordered nonequivalence and unordered equivalence.

11

Progress and Regress in Compositions of Compositions

There is a temporary decrease in set size and increase in the frequency with which infants at this age generate the smallest configurations possible, namely, two-object combinations. In part this decrease in set size is accounted for by an increase in contemporaneous combinations (i.e., two compositions or recompositions generated simultaneously or in partial temporal overlap). Thus, for instance, set size cannot exceed two objects in all the four-object conditions when infants construct two contemporaneous compositions.

Two other developments may also account in part for the decrease in set size. One is increasing attention by infants to coregulate the objects included in their configurations. The other is an increase in the number of objects that infants directly contact in constructing their configurations. Both of these developmental factors may temporarily serve to draw infants away from being concerned with constructing larger combinations of objects.

I. Temporary Decreases in Composing and Recomposing

Composing productivity ranges from a low of 3.44 to a high of 7.19 compositions per minute (Table 11.1, Row 1). This range is a bit narrower but is basically similar to that at age 18 months when productivity ranges between 5.34 and 9.60 compositions per minute (see Table 7.2, Row 3, on page 146). Still, it should not be overlooked that the rate of productivity is always at least a bit lower in each of the seven test conditions at age 21 months. Nevertheless, the decrease with age

TABLE 11.1
Spontaneous Phase I: Mean Composing Productivity at Age 21 Months

	Control	Additive		Multiplicative		Disjoint	
	Class conditions						
	Four-object 1	Four-object 2	Eight-object 3	Four-object 4	Eight-object 5	Four-object 6	Eight-object 7
1. Compositions	9.30[a]	9.83	11.17	13.55[b]	12.22[a]	7.40[a]	7.75
2. Time	2 min 29 sec[c]	1 min 26 sec[a]	1 min 58 sec[a]	1 min 45 sec[d]	2 min 36 sec[e]	1 min 21 sec[e]	1 min 31 sec[a]
3. Productivity per minute	3.44	6.81	6.28	7.19	4.78	5.21	5.27

[a]N = 10 subjects.
[b]N = 11 subjects.
[c]N = 8 subjects.
[d]N = 9 subjects.
[e]N = 7 subjects.

TABLE 11.2
Spontaneous Phase I: Mean Frequency of Composing and Recomposing at Age 21 Months

		Four-object condition			Eight-object condition		
		Thematic 1	Variant 2	% Variant 3	Thematic 4	Variant 5	% Variant 6
1.	Semicontrol	4.10	5.20	56			
2.	Additive	4.00	5.83	59	6.75	4.42	40
3.	Multiplicative	6.73	6.83	50	8.89	3.33	27
4.	Disjoint	4.80	2.60	35	4.92	2.83	36
5.	All conditions	4.91	5.19	51	6.47	3.44	35

is significant in only one of the seven test conditions, the eight-object multiplicative condition (Mann–Whitney $U = 13$, $p < .05$, two-tailed).

As always, the productivity ranges overlap in the four-object and eight-object conditions, though the range is somewhat wider in the four-object conditions. Compositions per minute range from 3.44 to 7.19 in the four-object conditions and from 4.78 to 6.28 in the eight-object conditions. In general, then, productivity is quite uniform.

Also, productivity does not vary as a function of class conditions, with one partial exception. Productivity is significantly lower in the four-object control condition than in the four-object additive condition ($N = 8$, $x = 1$, $p = .035$, sign test), and the four-object multiplicative condition ($N = 7$, $x = 0$, $p = .008$, sign test). Productivity in the four-object control condition is not significantly lower than in the other four class conditions tested. Nor is productivity significantly different when comparing any other conditions to one another.

Constructions are split between compositions and recompositions in the four-object conditions (Table 11.2, Rows 1–5, Columns 1–3). This small decrease from the rate of recomposing at age 18 months (see Table 7.2) is not statistically significant (Mann–Whitney $U = 43$, $p > .10$, two-tailed). Recomposing accounts for only about a third of subjects' constructions in the eight-object conditions (Table 11.2, Rows 1–5, Columns 4–6). This substantial decrease from the 57% rate of recomposing at age 18 months (see Table 7.2) is significant (Mann–Whitney $U = 34$, $p < .05$, two-tailed). Indeed, the rate of recomposing at age 21 months in the eight-object conditions retreats to a level comparable to that generated at age 15 months (see Table 3.2, Rows 1–5, Columns 1–3).

II. Temporary Decreases in Provoked Composing and Recomposing

Provoked composing and recomposing in the phase II procedures (i.e., receptacles, modeled sorting, modeled compositions) do not increase in frequency. If anything, they decrease in frequency as compared with infants' productions at age 18 months. At the same time, provoked, like spontaneous composing and recomposing, progress in articulateness and systematicity. Moreover, infants begin to produce two class consistent sets in the receptacles condition.

Containing still consists primarily of putting objects one at a time into one receptacle at a time. Containing two objects at a time in one receptacle is still unusual, although it is done occasionally by two-thirds of the infants. No infant contains objects in two receptacles at the same time.

Infants rarely take objects out one or two at a time from the receptacles in which they have contained them. Half of the infants take out contained objects by turning the receptacles over and dumping the objects onto the table or into another receptacle (see Chapter 10, Section IV). Transferring objects between containers includes picking up objects that missed (i.e., that fell to the table instead) and placing them into the recipient receptacle. Two infants begin to use two receptacles as both containers and vehicles for transferring objects back and forth (i.e., they dump the objects from one receptacle into a second and then dump the objects back into the first receptacle).

Placing has become the typical mapping used to contain objects in receptacles. Mistakes are quickly corrected and are sometimes even accompanied by expressions such as "Uh, oh." Only two subjects still throw objects in order to contain them in receptacles; and only one subject still drops objects in order to contain them.

The spatial placement arrangement is usually still inarticulate and haphazard. Exceptionally articulate arranging of objects in containers does begin to be generated. Thus, for instance, subject 21KA matches the way she contains objects by uprighting them all in a receptacle (as already considered on page 222).

The pattern of containing objects in two receptacles does not change significantly from that produced at age 18 months (see pages 147–152). In the four-object additive condition, the pattern is almost exactly alike at ages 18 and 21 months. About two-thirds of the subjects contain objects in two receptacles (Table 11.3). All except one subject contain all four objects.

In the eight-object disjoint condition, most infants at age 21 months contain objects in one receptacle only (i.e., 7 out of 12 subjects). In comparison, at age 18 months most infants contain objects in two receptacles (i.e., 7 out of 10 subjects). This apparent reversal is not, however, statistically significant ($x^2 = 0.808$, $df = 1$, $p > .05$). Whether containing in one or two receptacles, almost all 21-month-old infants (i.e., 10 out of 12 subjects) contain the eight presented objects, thus strengthening the tendency to contain all objects that was initiated by a majority of infants at age 18 months (i.e., 6 out of 10 subjects).

Only one infant expresses symbolically any cognizance of completion upon containing all objects. This infant does so by saying "Done" after containing all

TABLE 11.3
Provoked Phase II: Frequency of Containing All or Some Objects at Age
21 Months

	Condition			
	Four-object additive		Eight-object disjoint	
Receptacles	All	Some	All	Some
One	4	0	6	1
Two	6	1	4	1

objects in one receptacle. But other infants already indicate some cognizance by stopping, sitting back, and looking at the experimenter.

Containing in two receptacles is no more flexible than it is at age 18 months. Most 21-month-old infants still do so by containing objects in one receptacle and then switching to containing in a second receptacle, without ever switching back to containing in the first receptacle. This is, of course, the minimal procedure required to contain objects in two receptacles. Only one-third of containing in two receptacles is generated by recursive switching back and forth between receptacles more than once. This is the same rate at which recursion is generated at age 18 months.

Containing in two receptacles tends to produce two equal numbered sets in the four-object additive condition (Table 11.4, Rows 1 and 2). Five infants generate equal sets while two generate unequal sets. This continues the tendency at age 18 months when similar results are found (see Table 7.4, Rows 1 and 2, on page 150). Now, however, containing equal numbered sets are also usually differentiated by class properties (Table 11.4, Rows 1 and 2). At age 18 months, containing equal sets is still associated with mixed predication (see Table 7.4, Rows 1 and 2).

No clear trend emerges in the eight-object disjoint condition (Table 11.4, Rows 3 and 4); this lack of a pattern too, is similar to the findings at age 18 months (see Table 7.4, Rows 3 and 4). If anything, containing in two receptacles at age 21 months is marked by a predominance of generating unequally numbered objects that are mixed in their predicate properties.

Provoked spatial sorting into two sets by predicate properties (initiated and assisted by the tester, who also continuously corrects the subjects' performances, during procedural phase II) remains exceptional. Only one-third of the infants engaged in provoked sorting of objects into two classes. All of these infants are also limited to sorting two sets in only one of the two eight-object tasks (additive and multiplicative) in which this procedure was tested. This limitation contrasts with containing two sets which, as we have just seen, is generated by most infants

TABLE 11.4
Provoked Phase II: Extensive by Intensive Properties of Objects Contained in Two
Receptacles at Age 21 Months

| | Predicate properties | | | | | |
| | Order | | | Enclosure | | |
Quantitative properties	Unmixed 1	Partly unmixed 2	Mixed 3	Unmixed 4	Partly unmixed 5	Mixed 6
Four-object additive:[a]						
1. Equal sets	3		2	4		1
2. Unequal sets	2		0	0		2
Eight-object disjoint:[b]						
3. Equal sets	0	1	0	1	0	0
4. Unequal sets	1	2	1	0	1	3

[a]$N = 11$ subjects.
[b]$N = 12$ subjects.

at this age. It continues a developmental trend observed at ages 15 and 18 months as well.

All sorting into two sets is limited to grouping only some of the objects presented. Still, it begins to be executed systematically:

5. *RH places Doll 3 next to Doll 2 and Doll 1*
6. *RH reaches toward experimenter's hands again (experimenter hands Doll 4 to subject)*
7. *RH takes D4 from experimenter and places D4 on table 2 inches from Half Column 1*
8. *RH reaches toward experimenter (experimenter slides D4 next to D3 and hands Half Column 3 to subject)*
9. *RH takes HC3 from experimenter and stands HC3 up 2 inches from HC1 (experimenter slides HC3 closer to HC1 and hands Half Column 4 to subject)*
10. *RH takes HC4 from experimenter and places HC4 2 inches from HC1*

(21KA, page 14)

Subject 21KA sorts two of the three dolls and two of the three columns presented to him after the experimenter's initial placement of a doll to 21KA's left and a column to his right. The remaining doll and column are not grouped with the other objects.

The predicate constructions by 21KA are as advanced as any generated at this age. Only one of the four objects sorted is misplaced by predicate properties when 21KA places a doll next to a column (Line 7). In most instances, however, infants at this age are limited to no more than correctly assisted sorting of some objects of one class.

Provoked matching (where the tester models two classes and gives the subjects additional exemplars in procedural phase II) induces even more impoverished cooperation. None of the infants match objects to both modeled classes. This is an apparent decrease from age 18 months when infants begin to add objects to both sets systematically. Only a minority of the infants match objects to one of the two modeled classes; when they do so, the matchings are usually class consistent.

III. Temporary Decrease in Size of Compositions

Two-object compositions predominate in both the four-object (Table 11.5, Row 1) and eight-object conditions (Row 4). Still, they are more prevalent in the four-object than the comparable eight-object conditions (Rows 1 and 4, Columns 3–8). This difference approaches statistical significance ($N = 12$, $x = 3$, $p = .073$, sign test) and, as we have seen, it characterizes composing throughout the second year. Apparently, presenting infants with only four objects puts restrictions upon the size of their compositions. This limitation makes inherent sense since any time infants construct two related compositions (e.g., by correspondence), they have no choice but to generate 2 two-object compositions in the four-object conditions. Infants have more objects available to generate the same relation in the eight-object conditions (e.g., by constructing 2 three-object compositions).

There is an unexpected significant increase in the proportion of generating two-object compositions from age 18 months (see Table 7.5, Row 1, on page 155) to 21 months (Table 11.5, Row 1) in the four-object conditions (Mann–Whitney $U = 33$, $p < .05$, two-tailed). The 15% increase with age is due to infants' productions in the additive, multiplicative, and disjoint conditions, but not the semicontrol condition. There is, then, a concomitant 15% decrease with age in the production of three- and four-object compositions.

The proportion of two-object compositions also increases from age 18 months (see Table 7.5, Row 4) to 21 months (Table 11.5, Row 4) in the eight-object conditions; but the 12% increase is not statistically significant (Mann–Whitney $U = 61$, $p > .10$). There is no compensating decrease in production of three- and four-object compositions in the eight-object conditions. They comprise 36% of infants' construction at age 18 months (see Table 7.5, Rows 5 and 6) and 35% at age 21 months (Table 11.5, Rows 5 and 6). Instead, infants construct fewer five- to eight-object compositions. They comprise 17% of infants' constructions at age 18 months (see Table 7.5, Rows 7–10) and only 8% at age 21 months (Table 11.5, Rows 7–10).

Three- and four-object compositions comprise only one-fourth of 21-month-old infants' constructions in the four-object conditions (Table 11.5, Rows 2 and

TABLE 11.5

Spontaneous Phase I: Mean Frequency and Percentage of Compositional Extent at Age 21 Months

	Semicontrol[a]		Additive		Multiplicative[b,c]		Disjoint[a]		Total	
	X̄	%	X̄	%	X̄	%	X̄	%	X̄	%
	1	2	3	4	5	6	7	8	9	10
Four-object condition:										
1. Two-object	3.90	42	8.83	90	11.73	86	5.20	70	7.58	75
2. Three-object	0.70	8	0.00	0	1.36	10	1.20	16	0.79	8
3. Four-object	4.70	51	1.00	10	0.45	3	1.00	14	1.72	17
Eight-object condition:										
4. Two-object			5.92	53	7.00	57	5.08	66	5.73	58
5. Three-object			2.42	22	1.56	13	1.08	14	1.65	17
6. Four-object			2.08	19	2.11	17	1.33	17	1.76	18
7. Five-object			0.42	4	0.44	4	0.25	3	0.35	4
8. Six-object			0.08	1	1.00	8	0.00	0	0.29	3
9. Seven-object			0.00	0	0.11	1	0.00	0	0.03	0
10. Eight-object			0.25	2	0.00	0	0.00	0	0.09	1

[a]N = 10 subjects in semicontrol and disjoint four-object conditions.
[b]N = 11 subjects in multiplicative four-object condition.
[c]N = 9 subjects in multiplicative eight-object condition.

3). They comprise more than a third of infants' constructions in the eight-object conditions (Rows 5 and 6). In addition, almost one-tenth of infants' compositions comprise five to eight objects in the eight-object conditions where this is possible.

There is a concomitant decrease in the proportion of compositions constructed by infants manipulating one object only. This decrease is coupled with an increase in the proportion of compositions constructed by infants manipulating more than one object (Table 11.6). This development follows upon minimal or no change in these proportions from ages 12 to 18 months.

In the four-object conditions, only 23% of compositions are generated by infants manipulating one object (Row 2, Column 1). This represents a 12% decrease from age 18 months (see Table 7.6, Row 2, Column 1, on page 157) which is not statistically significant (Mann–Whitney $U = 47$, $p > .05$). Thus, less than one-fourth of compositions are now constructed by manipulating one object only while more than three-fourths are constructed by manipulating two to four objects (Row 2, Columns 2–4). The main increase is in the proportion of compositions constructed by manipulating all four objects. It doubles from 6% at age 18 months to 12% at age 21 months.

Parallel development marks infants' performances in the eight-object conditions. Only one-third of compositions are constructed by manipulating one object at 21 months (Row 4, Column 1) as compared with almost one-half at age 18 months (see Table 7.6, Row 4, Column 1). The decrease of 13% is not, however, statistically significant (Mann–Whitney $U = 63$, $p > .05$). Two-thirds of infants' compositions are now constructed by manipulating two to eight objects (Row 4, Columns 2–8).

Thus, while the sizes of the compositions tend to decrease from ages 18 to 21 months, the number of objects directly manipulated in order to construct these compositions tends to increase. This trend suggests the hypothesis that more complex constructive procedures (i.e., directly manipulating more objects in

TABLE 11.6

Spontaneous Phase I: Number of Objects Directly Manipulated by 21-Month-Old Subjects to Produce Compositions in All Class Conditions

		Number of objects								
		1	*2*	*3*	*4*	*5*	*6*	*7*	*8*	*Total*
Four-object conditions:										
1.	Frequency of compositions	99	256	23	51					429
2.	% compositions	23	60	5	12					100
Eight-object conditions:										
3.	Frequency of compositions	111	148	41	29	2	2	1	2	336
4.	% compositions	33	44	12	9	1	1	0	1	100

order to compose them) may require a temporary restriction upon the number of objects composed. This restriction is indeed temporary; at age 24 months, infants generate fewer two-object compositions while manipulating more objects to construct larger compositions (see Chapter 15, Section III).

Moreover, infants place increasing emphasis upon getting their compositions right. Infants repeatedly adjust and correct their mapping placement of objects in relation to each other so that they will be aligned in the way they want them to be. For instance, 21AL aligns three blocks on top of each other to form a stack, and then continues as follows:

8.5.	*LH releases and picks up Block 2*
8.5.	*RH releases from Block 1*
10.	*LH holding B2 meets RH in center*
11.	*BH lower B2 onto B1 (previously) stacked in alignment on Blocks 3 and 4*
11a.	*B1 slides out of alignment*
12.5.	*LH releases B2 and starts to adjust B1 back to original position, stacked in alignment with B3 and B4*
12.5.	*RH hold B2 a few inches above B1*
14.	*LH continues to adjust B1 on B3/B4*
15.	*RH places B2 on table to right of B1/B3/B4 stack*
16.5.	*RH adjusts B1, aligning B1 with B3/B4 stack*
16.5.	*LH supports the left sides of B1/B3/B4 stack, helping to align the objects*
18.5.	*RH picks up B2 and lowers B2 onto B1*
18.5.	*LH moves to support left sides of B1/B3/B4 stack in same manner as in second line 16.5*
20.	*RH continuously adjusts B2 slightly to align it with B1, B3, and B4*

(21AL, pages 4 and 5)

After this, 21AL takes off and replaces the top two blocks several times. Each time she replaces blocks in the stack, 21AL carefully coregulates her alignment of the objects very much in the way given in the protocol fragment. This sequence of compositions and recompositions, then, is featured by much coregulative activity. It produces equivalence by replacement (to be considered in Chapter 12).

IV. Temporary Increases in Mobile–Stabile Production

The overall pattern of features marking compositions and recompositions does not change in any significant way from ages 18 to 21 months. Most combinations are stabiles, some are mobiles, and even fewer combine stabiles with mobiles. Still, combined mobiles–stabiles increase in frequency; and stabiles decrease in frequency in the eight-object conditions only. However, both of these changes are temporary. (Chapter 15, Section IV).

The ratio of producing stabiles to mobiles is seven to five in the four-object conditions (Table 11.7, Rows 4 and 8). This difference is not significant ($N = 11$, $x = 4$, $p = .274$, sign test). Stabiles are generated almost twice as frequently as mobiles in the eight-object conditions (Table 11.8, Rows 4 and 8). This difference is significant ($N = 10$, $x = 1$, $p = .011$, sign test).

Stabile compositions are generated with equal frequency in four-object (Table 11.7, Row 4) and eight-object (Table 11.8, Row 4) conditions. The range of production does not vary either. The range is from 39% to 56% in the four-object conditions and from 39% to 54% in the eight-object conditions. This rate maintains a pattern of construction developing throughout infancy.

Stabiles make up roughly half of infants' combinations in the four-object conditions at both 18 months (Table 7.7, Row 4, page 159) and 21 months (Table 11.7, Row 4). While stabiles also make up roughly half of infants' combinations in the eight-object conditions at age 21 months (Table 11.8, Row 4), this is a 13% decrease from age 18 months (Table 7.8, Row 4, page 160). This decrease with age is significant (Mann–Whitney $U = 30$, $p < .01$) though temporary since it is completely reversed by age 24 months.

As always, most stabiles feature contact between the objects composed in all conditions (Tables 11.7 and 11.8, Row 1). Stabiles featured by proximity between the objects composed remain in the minority, though they are more prevalent in the eight-object (Table 11.8, Row 2) than the four-object (Table 11.7, Row 2) conditions. Stabiles marked by both contact and proximity are rare in all conditions (Tables 11.7 and 11.8, Row 3).

Mobile compositions are a substantial minority in both the four-object (Table 11.7, Row 8) and eight-object (Table 11.8, Row 9) conditions. It duplicates infants' production at age 18 months when 37% of their compositions are mobiles in the four-object conditions and 27% are mobiles in the eight-object conditions. Thus, the rate of producing mobiles remains constant.

In all conditions, most mobiles, like stabiles, are the product of contact between the objects composed (Table 11.7 and 11.8, Row 5). Mobiles marked by proximity (Tables 11.7 and 11.8, Row 6) are even rarer than stabiles marked by proximity. Mobiles marked by both contact and proximity are unusual in all conditions (Tables 11.7 and 11.8, Row 7).

Mobile–stabile compositions are generated least frequently in all conditions (Tables 11.7 and 11.8, Row 8), as they are throughout infancy. Still, they are produced a bit more frequently than at age 18 months (Tables 7.7 and 7.8, Row 8). The real increase is in the eight-object conditions; this compensates for the decrease in stabiles since mobiles remain constant. Furthermore, while mobile–stabile compositions are half as frequent as mobiles in the four-object conditions, they are about as frequent in the eight-object conditions. This is a temporary increase, however, since the production of mobile–stabile compositions drops sharply at age 24 months.

TABLE 11.7
Four-Object Conditions, Spontaneous Phase I: Mean Frequency and Percentage of Compositional Features at Age 21 Months

	Class conditions									
	Semicontrol[a]		Additive		Multiplicative[b]		Disjoint[a]		Total	
	X̄ 1	% 2	X̄ 3	% 4	X̄ 5	% 6	X̄ 7	% 8	X̄ 9	% 10
1. Contact stabile	3.60	39	4.00	41	4.27	32	1.80	24	3.46	34
2. Proximity stabile	0.60	6	1.25	13	0.82	6	1.10	15	0.95	9
3. Contact–proximity stabile	0.70	8	0.33	3	0.18	1	0.40	5	0.40	4
4. Total stabile	4.90	53	5.58	56	5.27	39	3.30	44	4.81	48
5. Contact mobile	2.40	26	3.00	31	4.45	33	1.90	26	2.98	29
6. Proximity mobile	0.00	0	0.42	4	0.36	3	0.60	8	0.35	3
7. Contact–proximity mobile	0.10	1	0.00	0	0.55	4	0.30	4	0.23	2
8. Total mobile	2.50	27	3.42	35	5.36	40	2.80	38	3.56	35
9. Mobile–stabile	1.90	20	0.83	8	2.91	21	1.30	18	1.72	17
10. Causal	1.20	13	0.67	7	1.36	10	1.00	14	1.05	10
11. Noncausal[c]	8.10	87	9.17	93	12.18	90	6.40	86	9.05	90
12. Horizontal[c]	1.70	25	2.83	49	3.27	58	2.60	49	2.63	45
13. Vertical[c]	4.00	59	2.00	35	2.27	40	2.30	43	2.60	44
14. Horizontal–vertical[c]	1.10	16	0.92	16	0.09	2	0.40	8	0.63	11

[a]N = 10 subjects.
[b]N = 11 subjects.
[c]Compositions whose spatial dimensions are ambiguous are not scored. Consequently, the dimensional means summate to less than the compostitional means.

TABLE 11.8
Eight-Object Conditions, Spontaneous Phase I: Mean Frequency and Percentage of Compositional Features at Age 21 Months

			Class conditions[i]					
	Additive		Multiplicative[a]		Disjoint		Total	
	X̄ 1	% 2	X̄ 3	% 4	X̄ 5	% 6	X̄ 7	% 8
1. Contact stabile	3.75	34	1.89	15	1.75	22	2.44	25
2. Proximity stabile	2.00	18	2.67	22	1.75	22	2.03	20
3. Contact–proximity stabile	0.25	2	0.22	2	0.16	2	0.20	2
4. Total stabile	6.00	54	4.78	39	3.67	47	4.68	47
5. Contact mobile	2.42	22	2.11	17	1.08	14	1.79	18
6. Proximity mobile	0.50	4	1.11	9	1.08	14	0.85	9
7. Contact–proximity mobile	0.00	0	0.00	0	0.08	1	0.03	0
8. Total mobile	2.92	26	3.22	26	2.25	29	2.68	27
9. Mobile–stabile	2.25	20	4.22	34	1.83	24	2.56	26
10. Causal	1.17	10	1.11	9	0.42	5	0.85	9
11. Noncausal	10.00	90	11.11	91	7.33	95	9.06	91
12. Horizontal[b]	4.75	59	6.00	76	3.92	59	4.65	64
13. Vertical[b]	2.42	30	1.44	18	1.67	25	1.82	25
14. Horizontal–vertical[b]	0.83	10	0.44	6	1.08	16	0.79	11

[a] $N = 10$ subjects.
[b] Compositions whose spatial dimensions are ambiguous are not scored. Consequently, the dimensional means summate to less than the compositional means.

239

Causal combinations decrease sharply; indeed, the ratio is halved from ages 18 to 21 months. They make up one-fifth of infants' constructions at age 18 months (Tables 7.7 and 7.8). They constitute only one-tenth of the compositions generated in all conditions at age 21 months (Tables 11.7 and 11.8, Row 11).

There is one major development in the spatial dimensions in which compositions are constructed. Combinations constructed in the vertical dimension double in frequency in the four-object conditions from ages 18 (Table 7.7, Row 13) to 21 months (Table 11.7, Row 13). Now they are generated as frequently as horizontal compositions (Table 11.7, Row 12) and comprise almost half of infants' constructions.

Otherwise, the pattern of spatial dimensions in which infants construct compositions remains the same. Most combinations are still constructed in a single dimension: either horizontal or vertical (Tables 11.7 and 11.8, Rows 12 and 13). Only one-tenth of infants' compositions are constructed in two combined dimensions (i.e., both horizontal and vertical) in all conditions (Tables 11.7 and 11.8, Row 14).

V. Increase in Contemporaneous Compositions

Compositions constructed in temporal isolation from each other constitute a small fraction of infants' productivity (Table 11.9). They make up one-tenth of infants' constructions in both the four-object (Row 1) and eight-object (Row 5) conditions. Moreover, the proportion of isolate compositions is substantially the same as at age 18 months (see Table 7.9, Rows 1 and 5, on page 163).

Compositions constructed in temporal succession predominate. They make up roughly two-thirds of infants' constructions in both the four-object (Row 2) and eight-object (Row 6) conditions. The proportion of consecutive compositions generated in the eight-object conditions is comparable to that generated at 18 months. In the four-object conditions, the proportion of consecutive compositions decreases from 88% at age 18 months to 68% at age 21 months. However, this 20% drop with age is not significant (Mann–Whitney $U = 65$, $p > .05$).

Decreasing consecutive compositions in the four-object conditions is compensated by increasing production of partially overlapping and simultaneous compositions (Rows 3 and 4). The latter constitute only 6% of infants' productions at age 18 months while they constitute 23% at age 21 months. This 17% increase with age is statistically significant (Mann–Whitney $U = 10$, $p = .001$). As already suggested, this increase in constructing contemporaneous compositions accounts, at least in part, for the concomitant temporary increase in constructing two-object compositions.

Partially overlapping and simultaneous compositions constitute one-fourth of

TABLE 11.9
Spontaneous Phase I: Temporal Relations between Compositions at Age 21 Months

	Class conditions									
	Semicontrol[a]		Additive		Multiplicative[a]		Disjoint[a]		Total	
	$\bar{X}$	%	$\bar{X}$	%	$\bar{X}$	%	$\bar{X}$	%	$\bar{X}$	%
	1	2	3	4	5	6	7	8	9	10
Four-object condition:										
1. Isolate	1.30	14	0.75	8	0.82	6	0.90	12	0.93	9
2. Consecutive	7.80	84	7.42	75	7.64	56	4.30	58	6.84	68
3. Partially overlapping	0.20	2	1.33	14	3.64	27	2.00	27	1.81	18
4. Simultaneous	0.00	0	0.33	3	1.45	11	0.20	3	0.51	5
Eight-object conditions:										
5. Isolate			1.00	9	1.89	15	0.50	6	1.03	10
6. Consecutive			7.42	66	8.78	72	3.67	47	6.24	63
7. Partially overlapping			2.08	19	1.33	11	2.92	38	2.12	21
8. Simultaneous			0.67	6	0.22	2	0.67	9	0.53	5

[a] $N = 10$ subjects in the four-object, semicontrol and disjoint conditions and in the eight-object multiplicative condition.

infants' production in the eight-object conditions (Rows 7 and 8). This proportion is comparable to that generated in the four-object conditions, and it is substantially unchanged from that generated in the eight-object conditions at age 18 months.

Overall, then, the pattern of temporal relations between compositions is remarkably similar under four- and eight-object conditions. The only changes from age 18 months occur in the four-object conditions where consecutive compositions decrease while partially overlapping and simultaneous compositions increase. The result is that the latter constitute one-fourth of infants' constructions under all conditions. The implications of this ever enlarging pool of constant given elements for generating second-order logicomathematical relations will be explored in Chapter 12.

12

Initial Relations upon Relations between Paired Compositions

Structuring coordinate second-order operations is progressively consolidated and elaborated. One-to-one correspondences begin to be extended to more than two contemporaneous compositions. One-to-many correspondences with two contemporaneous compositions begins to be generated in provoked as well as spontaneous transactions. This includes the origins of structuring classification by substitution to produce predicate (intensive) consistency as well as to preserve quantitative (extensive) relations of equivalence and nonequivalence.

I. Exchange between Paired Compositions

Exchange by replacing, substituting, and commuting continues to be generated with two contemporaneous compositions as well as with single compositions. The rate of unambiguous second-order exchanges with two contemporaneous compositions does not increase at this stage, but forms that are ambiguous are generated so the measures may well underestimate the rate at which second-order exchanges are produced. In addition, second-order exchanges are progressively controlled and regulated. They also begin to be used to form intensive (predicate) consistency in contemporaneous compositions.

Replacing is still primarily a first-order proto-operation. Most replacing is generated within single sets (Table 12.1). Replacing objects in two sets remains exceptional. This may well be an underestimation since infants at this stage also

243

TABLE 12.1
Number of Subjects Generating Exchange at Age 21 Months

	One composition						Two compositions
	3-object	4-object	5-object	6-object	7-object	8-object	
Replace	4	6	0	1	0	0	2
Substitute	1	0	0	0	0	0	6
Commute	4	6	0	0	0	0	5
Coordinate exchange	1	2	0	0	0	0	1

generate ambiguous forms of replacing that are likely to be transitional to developing second-order structures.

Ambiguous forms of second-order replacing occur when infants construct a composition comprising two parts. For instance, after placing two cylinders near each other, 21CP continues as follows:

> 32.5.   RH holds Rectangular Ring 1 on Cylinder 1 such that RR1 covers C1
> 32.5.   LH holds Rectangular Ring 2 on Cylinder 2 such that RR2 covers C2
> 32.5a. RR2 slips out of LH
> 34.5.   RH continues holding RR1 on C1 (as in first Line 32.5)
> 34.5.   LH picks up RR2 and holds RR2 on C2 such that RR2 covers C2
>
> (21CP, page 8)

In addition to (or perhaps instead of) replacing one object in a single four-object composition, 21CP may be replacing an object in one of two matching units that he constructs. If the former is true, then he has merely generated equivalence by a first-order replacement. If the latter is true, he has also constructed an equivalence (by replacement within one subset) upon an equivalence (by correspondence between two subsets) or a second-order exchange. If it errs, our coding system is designed to score infants' constructions conservatively; accordingly, 21CP's construction was scored as a first-order replacement within a four-object composition.

Most first-order replacing is generated with four-object compositions. Some are consequences of rectifying accidental occurrences (e.g., 21CP's construction). Some are marked by careful coregulation designed to produce exact compositions (see, for example, the 21AL protocol fragment on page 236). Yet others are under such perfect control that they are essentially automatic forms:

> 72.5.   LH picks up Circular Ring 1
> 72.5.   RH picks up Circular Ring 3
>   74.   LH transfers CR1 to RH, so RH
>   holds CR1 and CR3

75. *LH picks up Circular Ring 4 (off Circular Ring 2) and transfers CR4 to RH, so RH holds CR4, CR1, and CR3*

76. *LH adjusts CR4 held by RH which is also holding CR1 and CR3*

77. *LH picks up CR2, transfers CR2 to RH, and helps RH hold CR2, CR4, CR1, and CR3*

78. *LH takes CR2 from RH, so RH holds CR4, CR1, and CR3*

79. *LH place CR2 on table such that CR2 (accidentally) hits Doll 3, while RH holds CR4, CR1, and CR3*

79a. *D3 rolls off table to floor*

80. *LH picks up CR2 and transfers CR2 to RH, so RH holds CR2, CR4, CR1, and CR3*

           S: *"Ohhh."*

                (21EN, page 36)

This routine (of collecting objects by picking them up and transferring them from one hand to the other) is executed smoothly and efficiently. It is a form that no longer requires any effort or working out of its details. Indeed, it is a flexible reproduction of the same 21EN routine, marked by coregulatory correspondence and self-correction, considered on page 210. We may therefore entertain the hypothesis that such routines are progressively executed for the sake of exercising replacement. If correct, this hypothesis implies that infants are becoming virtuosos at replacing elements in as many as four-object compositions. This hypothesis also implies that these first-order exchanges are becoming pure, albeit still practical, cognitive forms or protological structures.

Only two infants generate second-order replacing in an unambiguous fashion. The production by one infant is particularly unusual because he begins by constructing four pairs of cylinders standing upright on the flat sides of rectangular columns that are lying down on the table (see 21AF protocol fragment on page 251). This correspondence is exceptional for this stage since it already matches four compositions. To this, 21AF adds blowing at one cylinder as if he were trying to either blow it off the column on which it is standing or as if he is pretending that the cylinder is a candle on a cake that he is trying to put out. After this, 21AF lifts this cylinder off the column on which it is standing, inserts the cylinder in his mouth, and then stands the cylinder back upright on the same column. Next 21AF lifts another cylinder off the column on which it is standing, stands the cylinder upright on the table, and then touches the cylinder back upright on the same column for a moment.

Initially, then, *21AF* constructs equivalence between four paired objects. Only two pairs are used to produce equivalences upon equivalences by replacement. Interpolated in between, *21AF* either tests the physical possibility of blowing over a cylinder or playfully pretends to blow out a nonpresent candle flame.

There is no quantitative advance in generating substitution at this stage (Table 12.1). If anything, there is some diminution in the production of first-order substituting as compared with the level of production at the previous stage (Table 8.1). However, half of the subjects generate second-order substituting. Moreover, structuring second-order substitutions progresses. While exceptional, this structuring prefigures developments at subsequent stages.

The most important and exceptional second-order substituting is generated by one infant (*21AL*) only in a countercondition (in test phase III) in which three circular rings are presented grouped together with one rectangular column and three rectangular columns are presented grouped together with a circular ring. Subject *21AL* reorganizes these two groups so as to eliminate the predicate inconsistencies (irrelevant intervening transactions are omitted):

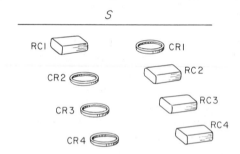

1. *RH picks up CR1, picks up CR2, and carries CR1 and CR2 to left*
2. *RH places CR2 on table, and then places CR1 touching CR2:*

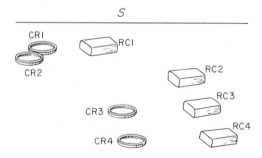

3. *RH slides CR3 and CR4 to self*
3a. *right arm hits CR1 to floor*
4. *RH carries CR3 and CR4 to CR2 and opens hand to release CR3 and CR4*

    4a.   CR3 *drops on top of* CR2, *but* CR4 *sticks to RH thumb*

    5.   *RH shakes* CR4 *off thumb*

    5a.   CR4 *drops to table touching* CR2 *and* CR3 (*mother picks up and replaces* CR1 *with other circular rings*)

8.5–10.5.   *RH holds and rotates* RC2 *and LH holds and rotates* RC4 *such that the* RC2, RC3, *and* RC4 *alignment rotates to the left*

  12–14.   *LH picks up* RC1 *and transfers* RC1 *to RH which places* RC1 *to right of* RC2 (*which is aligned with* RC3 *and* RC4)

    15.7.   *RH picks up* RC2 *and stacks* RC2 *on* RC1

    21.   *RH stacks* RC4 *on* RC2/RC1 *stack*

    24.   *BH hold* RC3 *stacked on* RC4/RC2/RC1 *stack* (21AL, pages 80 and 81)

By substituting the misplaced elements, and only the misplaced elements, from the incorrect groups into their proper classes, 21AL corrects the predicate errors presented in this countercondition. Subject 21AL exchanges elements between the two sets thereby producing second-order substitution. Two substitutions are generated successively, not simultaneously. Each presented group is also reorganized successively even though this is not necessary in order to effect the substitutions. The resultant compositions (an overlapping cluster of rings and a stack of columns) bear little, if any, resemblance to the two presented alignments. In all of this, 21AL gives no indication that he is connecting the two compositions to each other. So while this second-order substitution corrects the predicate groupings and while it foreshadows core features of developed substitution, it still lacks these features.

Still, this is the only predicate reorganization by substitution generated by an infant at this stage that results in correcting classificatory inconsistencies presented in counterconditions. Three other infants correct or partly correct predicate misplacements in counterconditions by reorganizing the presentation (see Section IV for a fuller discussion). But none do so by any substitution of elements between sets.

Commuting is generated at roughly the same rate as at the previous stage (Table 12.1). Most commuting consists of direct first-order exchanges within single compositions comprising three or four objects. Diminution, if any from the previous stage, is in generating first-order commuting with compositions comprising more than four objects and in generating inverse commuting. Any increase from the previous stage comes from infants generating second-order commuting with two compositions. As at all other stages during infancy, then, commuting leads the way for infants' structuring of second-order exchange.

Commuting is marked by progressive, but still incomplete, regulatory control (irrelevant intervening transactions are omitted):

  34.   *RH lies Square Column 1 down*
         on table next to Square Column
         2 lying on table

39. *BH place Cylinder 1 upright on*
    SC1 and Cylinder 2 upright on
    table touching SC1 and C1

44. *RH places and adjusts C1 on*   S: *"Yahh." (a high-pitched*
    SC2 so that C1 stands upright   *shriek of joy; she acts*
    on SC2   *very pleased with herself)*

48. *RH places C2 upright on SC2:*

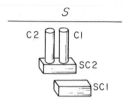

(*21VL,* pages 7 and 8)

Subject *21VL* structures the commutative equivalence relation (SC2, SC1:C1, C2) ↝ (SC1, SC2:C1, C2) by carefully constructing a four-object stabile composition and recomposition. Both stabiles preserve *21VL*'s initial alignment of the square columns (Line 34). Only the placement order of the two cylinders is transformed by *21VL* from an initial 2:1 correspondence with Square Column 1 (Line 39) to a 2:1 correspondence with Square Column 2 (Lines 44 and 48).

Incomplete, though progressive, regulatory control is evidenced by *21VL* not executing exactly equivalent spatial relations in the two stabiles. So while she seems to try to upright both cylinders on Square Column 1 at the same time, only one cylinder ends up there; the other ends up next to it on the table. This may be why she works on one cylinder at a time in constructing her commutative transformation. If so, it also reflects *21VL*'s progressive cognizance of her own actions and their possible (and impossible) interactions with the structure of physical (spatial) relations. Moreover, *21VL*'s vocalization and demeanor suggests some cognizance of her achievement (Line 44). Such cognizance would reflect progressive equilibrium in the regulation of infants' interactions with their environment.

Cognizance by infants of their transformative activity is also revealed in other ways. For instance, subject *21CL* looks and smiles at the experimenter as he commutes a four-object stabile from a vertical–horizontal structure

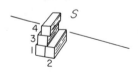

to a vertical structure

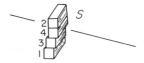

to a horizontal structure.

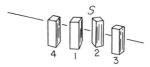

He certainly behaves as if he is communicating about his transformations of the composition's structure as he generates them.

Almost half of the infants generate second-order commuting. Typically, they are direct, not reversible, exchanges. Furthermore, they all remain limited to reordering elements within two compositions. They still do not commute two compositions with each other.

The rate at which coordinate exchange is generated decreases from that generated at age 18 months (see Table 8.1). Still, structural advances are manifest in the application of coordinate exchanges to the resolution of physical difficulties. To illustrate, subject 21AF tries to construct a stack of two blocks topped by a circular ring. The ring falls off. She tries to rectify this (for her, impossible) physical composition by replacing the ring, but it falls off again. She finally transforms this (impossible) composition into one which is physically possible for her by switching from replacing to commuting objects; 21AF places the ring between the blocks (i.e., she changes the order of the stack from block, block, ring to block, ring, block). Sequential coordination of replacing with commuting thereby serves to determine aspects of possible (and impossible) spatial functions (i.e., balanced *vs.* imbalanced dependency relations). So while it only involves preserving quantitative equivalence in 1 three-object composition, coordinate exchange facilitates cognizing progressively complex physical phenomena.

II. Correspondences between Three and Four Very Small Compositions

As they do throughout the second year, all infants at this stage generate minimal correspondences between compositions, that is, one-to-one (bi-univocal) matchings between two sets or subsets comprising two elements each (Table 12.2). All infants thereby produce minimal quantitative equivalence between two collections of two objects. Moreover, three-fourths of the infants generate two matched collections more than once. Most of these correspon-

TABLE 12.2

Number of 21-Month-Old Subjects Generating Matched Compositions and Exchanges on These Correspondences

Units	Objects in each unit			Exchange operations		
	2	3	4	Replace	Substitute	Commute
2	12	2	0	2	1	5
3	1			0	0	0
4	1			1	0	0

dences continue to match two compositions to each other rather than two parts of one composition to each other. Of the total generated by all subjects, 86% match two compositions while only 14% match two parts of one composition.

These correspondences tend to match stabile compositions. Eleven (of 12) subjects match two stabiles in generating the correspondences. Of the total generated by all subjects, 57% match stabiles, 32% involve mobiles, and 16% involve combined mobiles–stabiles. Only 5% match causal compositions, so almost all are noncausal.

Moreover, corresponding compositions (of two elements each) primarily match class consistent collections. Of the total compositions involved, 79% are unmixed, 7% are partly unmixed, and 14% are mixed in order of predication; and 62% are unmixed, 6% are partly unmixed, and 32% are mixed in enclosure. Thus, these equivalence compositions or parts of compositions are usually matched in everything but their class properties, although the sets or subsets tend to be class consistent.

Infants' second-order correspondences tend to be minimal, as they have been up to this age. They match two collections of two objects. Precursory exceptions just begin to be generated at age 18 months when two infants (out of 12) construct two matched collections comprising three objects each. Additional precursors are generated at this stage.

Only two infants construct clear correspondences between 2 three-object compositions (Table 12.2). Exceptional instances are also generated by a few other infants of unclear, though probably compositional prerequisites of correspondences between 2 three-object and 2 four-object collections. So far this is no different than the findings on precursors generated at the previous stage.

Multiple unit correspondences just begin to be generated at this stage (Table 12.2). Their membership is minimal since they comprise two elements only in each set. In this they are no more advanced than the one-to-one correspondences generated between two sets. This is consistent with a general principle of mental development, namely, simplicity. The principle of simplicity states that at its origin, progress is embodied in: (a) the simplest forms possible; and (b) descendant forms that are equal to or less than their progenitor forms (i.e., those out of which they develop). Accordingly, at their outset, the membership of each set of multicorrespondences is always equal to or less than the extent of each collection making up one-to-one correspondences between two sets, never more.

Only two clear instances of multicorrespondences are generated during this stage. One consists of one-to-one correspondences between three sets, each of which comprises two elements; and the other matches four sets, each of which comprises two elements, in one-to-one correspondence (Table 12.2). Interestingly, both correspondences are generated by uprighting cylinders on columns that are lying flat on the table. In this way, subject *21RR* composes correspondences between three vertical stabiles that she pretends are boats (see pages 212 and 213). Also in this way, subject *21AF* composes correspondences between four vertical stabiles:

4. *RH stands Cylinder 1 upright on Rectangular Column 1 lying on table*
5. *LH picks up Cylinder 4 and transfers C4 to RH which stands C4 upright on Rectangular Column 3 lying on table*
6. *LH picks up Cylinder 3 and transfers C3 to RH which stands C3 upright on Rectangular Column 4 lying on table*
7. *LH picks up Cylinder 2 and transfers C2 to RH which stands C2 upright on Rectangular Column 2 lying on table*   (21AF, page 38)

Notwithstanding their adherence to the principle of simplicity, these initial multicorrespondences are immediately enlisted in the service of further cognitive elaborations. The three-set correspondence is used as the structure for symbolic play by *21RR*. The four-set correspondence is used by *21AF* as the given for both (a) second-order replacing and (b) causal exploration and/or symbolic play. Overall, there is some increase in using corresponding sets or subsets as the constant elements of exchange operations (Table 12.2). Still, only one-half of the subjects exchange elements of corresponding collections.

One-to-many (co-univocal) correspondences are not generated as frequently as one-to-one correspondences, as is true throughout the second year of infancy. But they are progressively coregulated and coordinated with other developing operations:

10.5. *RH holds left side of (previously constructed) stack of Cross Ring, Rectangular Ring, Circular Ring, and Triangular Ring (listed from bottom to top) tilted on table*
10.5. *LH slides TR to stack on top of CrR and inserts TR into stack*
12. *BH rotate stack of four rings away from self and toward table such that rings are now stacked CrR, TR, CR, and RR (from bottom to top)*   (21CL, page 2)

Subject *21CL* maps one object and three objects onto each other by simultaneously inserting one ring into three rings and encircling three rings around one ring. This coregulated fitting one-to-three relation is immediately commuted, which preserves equivalence over the transformation.

Second-order one-to-many correspondences originate at this stage. They are marked by constructing 2 one-to-many matchings that are in one-to-one correspondence with each other (irrelevant intervening transactions are omitted):

39. *RH stands Doll 2 upright and in middle of Circular Ring 2*
48. *RH stand Doll 1 upright and in middle of Circular Ring 1*

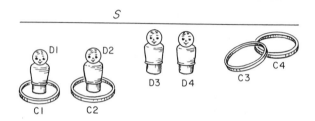

49.5. *RH picks up Doll 3*
49.5. *LH picks up Doll 4*
51.5. *RH releases D3 on and in CR1 (looks like trying to get both D1 and D3 in CR1)*
51.5a. *D3 falls over and lands next to CR1*
51.5. *LH releases D4 on and in CR2 (looks like trying to get both D2 and D4 in CR2)*
51.5a. *D4 falls over and knocks D2 over onto table*   (21JF, pages 12 and 13)

This co-univocal comprises six objects. But it is actually possible to generate second-order co-univocals with a minimum of only five objects (see the 24YM construction on page 337). On the other hand, constructing second-order bi-univocals requires a minimum of only four objects. This difference accounts for the developmental delay of second-order co-univocals as compared with bi-univocals.

As expected, second-order co-univocals are rarely generated at their origins. Also, as expected, initial structuring of second-order co-univocals is labile. Thus, 21JF tries to construct two matched spatial relations of two dolls in one ring. Both are equally physically impossible. Yet, even when they are destroyed, as a consequence, something of the co-univocal is preserved.

Both the constructive procedure and the attempted products are matched. This matching is also expected at the initiation of second-order co-univocals. It relfects initial lack of detachment and differentiation of the structuring process from the structured result. Its positive function, as always, is to reinforce the constructed relation by redundantly instantiating mapping the two co-univocals onto each other in one-to-one correspondence.

III.　Flexible Ordering of Two Very Small Compositions

The frequency with which infants generate second-order series does not change. All infants continue to generate minimal ⟨ 1-, 2- ⟩ object series comprising a single object in relation to two composed objects. Six infants generate an ordered series of ⟨ 2-, 3- ⟩ object compositions where the two compositions are maintained in simultaneity and in relation to each other. Four infants generate an ordered series of ⟨ 3-, 4- ⟩ object compositions. Only one infant generates both ordered series of ⟨ 2-, 3- ⟩ and ⟨ 3-, 4- ⟩ object compositions; so nine infants generate two-step ordered series that exceed minimal ⟨ 1-, 2- ⟩ object series. Infants never generate three step ordered series which at a minimum comprise ⟨ 1-, 2-, 3- ⟩ object collections.

Progress is manifest in articulating two-step orderings (irrelevant intervening transactions are omitted):

52.　*LH stands Half-Cylinder 4 upright on table*
53.　*RH picks Half-Cylinder 1 up and stands H-C1 upright near H-C4*
54.　*RH picks up Doll 4 and stands D4 upright*
59.　*RH stands Doll 2 upright next to D4*
60.　*RH stands Doll 3 upright*
61.　*RH moves D3 next to D2 that is next to D4*　　　　　(21AF, page 32)

7.　*LH picks up Cylinder 2 and transfers C2 to RH which stands C2 upright on Rectangular Column 1 lying on table*
31.　*RH stands Cylinder 1 upright on Rectangular Column 2 lying on table*
32.　*LH picks up Cylinder 4 and stands C4 upright on C1 which is upright on RC2:*

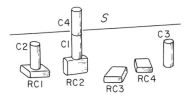

(21AF, pages 38 and 39)

Both ordered series of ⟨ 2-, 3- ⟩ object compositions are stable constructions that are preserved in temporal overlap. Both are marked by spatial correspondence between the compositions. In the first construction, this is accomplished by uprighting the objects in two clusters; one cluster comprises two upright half-cylinders and the other cluster comprises three upright dolls. Vertical stacking provides spatial correspondence in the second construction. The first ordered series, then, comprises two horizontal stabiles while the second ordered series comprises two vertical stabiles. All this is typical at this stage.

The first ordered series, but not the second, is typical of those generated at this stage in one other way. It is unmixed in its predicate class properties, while the second is not. It comprises two separate compositions of half-cylinders and dolls, while the second mixes rectangular columns with cylinders in each composition.

Most ordered series of two compositions are still constructed by generating two sets, one after the other; the two series considered are good illustrations. Some ordered series begin to be produced by decomposing a previously constructed larger whole into two ordered parts. For instance, subject *21AL* first constructs a stack of four rectangular columns lying on top of each other topped by four circular rings lying on top of each other. After this, *21AL* decomposes the stack:

37. *RH grasps Circular Rings 4, 3, and 1 by putting fingers through their holes and slides CR4, CR3, and CR1 off the stack and to the right*
38. *RH places CR4, CR3, and CR1 stacked and to the right*
39. *RH slides Circular Ring 2 off the stack and places CR2 separately to the right*

(21AL, page 76)

Decomposing results in two simultaneous stabile compositions that are in spatial correspondence and are unmixed in predicate class properties. One composition comprises three stacked rings and the other composition comprises four stacked columns. Together they form an articulate two-step ordered series of ⟨ 3-, 4- ⟩ object compositions.

Integrating two compositions into one larger whole and decomposing one larger whole into two derivative compositions does not increase in frequency, nor does their inverse coordination. If anything, there is a decrease at this age (Table 12.3) as compared with the frequency of integrating, decomposing, and reversible coordinated integrating and decomposing compositions at age 18 months (see Table 8.3 on page 185).

Integrating and decomposing usually continues to involve only four objects: this is the minimum necessary to realize these operations. Most integrating and decomposing also continues to involve equal units (i.e., by adding 2 two-object compositions into 1 four-object composition and by dividing 1 four-object composition into 2 two-object compositions). These quantitative equivalences between two units, then, may be inherent to restrictions imposed by infants working mainly with four objects. Even if this is the case, however, it takes nothing

TABLE 12.3
Number of 21-Month-Old Subjects Adding and Subtracting Units

Units	Integrate	Decompose	Integrate & decompose	Decompose & integrate	Total coordinated
Equal	4	2	1	1	2
Unequal	1	2	0	0	0
Total	4	4	1	1	2

away from structuring the form of minimal numerical equivalences between compositions, its potential cognizance by infants, or its usage by infants as given elements for further cognitive operations.

Inherent restrictions of this sort place limitations upon the size of the units with which infants can work at this stage, that is, they may determine the element domain. Only infants' mappings can structure the given elements into a larger composition by integrating them into a whole or into two smaller compositions by decomposing them into smaller parts. Thus, it is the interaction of infants' structuring inherent given elements that results in minimal quantitative equivalence between compositions.

This analysis gains credence from infants' structuring five to eight objects. They do not often integrate and decompose with this many objects at this stage. But when they do, infants usually work with two unequal units. The *21AL* protocol fragment (on page 254) is representative in this regard. Recall that *21AL* first composes an eight-object stack comprising four columns topped by four rings. Thus, *21AL* could have decomposed this whole into two equal parts of four objects at least as easily as what he actually did. Instead, as we have seen, *21AL*'s decomposing produces a stack of four columns and a stack of three rings, that is, ordered nonequivalence.

Protoaddition and protosubtraction with single sets does not progress. The products are mainly two-step ordered series of ⟨ 2-, 3- ⟩ or ⟨ 3-, 2- ⟩ object compositions when they are precise. However, already at age 18 months, infants also sometimes generate precise two-step ordered series that include more objects and precise three-step ordered series of ⟨ 2-, 3-, 4- ⟩ or ⟨ 4-, 3-, 2- ⟩ object compositions. Occasionally, this includes precise bidirectionally ordered series such as ⟨ 2-, 3-, 4-, 3-, 2- ⟩ object compositions.

IV. Class Consistency between Paired Compositions

Predication is mainly a matter of infants classifying objects belonging to single collections since most of their compositions are still composed consecutively (see Table 11.9, Rows 2 and 6, on page 241). Nevertheless, infants now compose one-fourth of their collections in partial temporal overlap or simultaneously (see Table 11.9, Rows 3, 4, 7, and 8). This increasing pool of contemporaneous compositions makes it increasingly possible for infants to classify objects within multiple collections that are linked to each other spatiotemporally, if nothing else. Usually, these include two compositions. In exceptional constructions, infants begin to generate three or four very small contemporaneous compositions (see, for example, the *21AF* protocol fragment on page 251).

This enlarged pool also makes it possible to statistically evaluate infants' predicate classification of contemporaneous compositions in half of the tasks where the frequencies are sufficient. These tasks are the four-object multiplicative and disjoint conditions, and the eight-object disjoint condition. In the tasks where the frequencies are still not large enough to permit statistical analyses, the trends seem to be toward unmixed classification when infants generate contemporaneous compositions. Almost all these collections are unmixed in both predicate order and enclosure properties (see, for illustrative purposes, the 21AF and 21AL protocol fragments on pages 253 and 254). Contemporaneous collections that are mixed in their predicate order and/or enclosure properties are rare (for an illustration see the second 21AF fragment on page 253).

In the four-object multiplicative condition, contemporaneous compositions are unmixed in their predicate enclosure properties ($N = 5$, $x = 0$, $p = .031$, sign test). Only four subjects generate predicate order properties in constructing contemporaneous compositions. While not sufficient for statistical analyses, they are invariably unmixed or class consistent. In the four-object disjoint condition, both order and enclosure properties do not achieve statistical significance (for order $N = 5$, $x = 1$, $p = .188$, and for enclosure $N = 6$, $x = 2$, $p = .344$, sign tests). Effectively, predication is random in this condition. In the eight-object disjoint condition, the predicate enclosure properties of contemporaneous compositions are unmixed ($N = 5$, $x = 0$, $p = .031$, sign test). Only three subjects generate order properties in constructing contemporaneous compositions, but those are almost entirely unmixed or class consistent.

In addition to progress in constructing contemporaneous compositions that are class consistent, infants begin to correct compositions that are presented to them in class inconsistent groupings (administered as counterconditions in phase III of the testing). As expected at its origins, transforming class inconsistent into class consistent compositions is partial. It is generated by only one-third of the infants. Furthermore, two of these four infants only rectify one, not both, of the two class inconsistent compositions with which they are presented. These two subjects either leave the other objects alone or eventually manipulate the objects in ways that do not correct the remaining class inconsistency.

A third subject's, 21CL's, restructuring of two separate alignments of objects lying on the table is more complex. One alignment grouped together three square columns with one cylinder while the other alignment grouped together three cylinders with one square column. After about a minute of manipulating all the objects, they are in this disposition on the table:

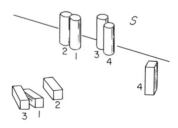

(21CL, page 104)

At this point in his transformations, *21CL* has partially corrected the classification by collecting together all the cylinders. In addition, however, his rearrangement of the groupings is beginning to lose any resemblance to the initial presentation. Not finished, *21CL* continues to manipulate the objects so that in about another half minute he produces the following two groupings:

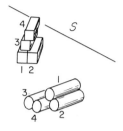

(21CL, page 105)

By this point in his transformation of the original presentation, *21CL* has completely corrected the original class inconsistency. But he has also completely changed the original arrangement of two alignments. He does not simply substitute the misplaced cylinder and square column for each other. Thus, while he ends up correcting both predicate misplacements, the two classes are treated as separate sets and not as related classes that are different but complementary.

Complete correction by substituting the two misplaced objects for each other is produced by subject *21AL* only; it has already been considered on pages 246 and 247. As noted there, the corrections are not performed simultaneously but successively and with intervening transactions. Moreover, the substitutions are not simple and direct. The result is that the two original alignments are completely reorganized into a heap and a stack, and are also made class consistent. As with the *21CL* reconstruction, this raises questions about the likelihood that the subjects are classifying two collections in relation to each as different but complementary sets (see Sugarman, 1983).

Some classification, as we have seen, increasingly applies to contemporaneous compositions, whether or not they are intensively related to each other by predicate properties. As noted at the outset of this section, most classifying still applies to individual compositions only. Most, but still not all, of this is class consistent.

Predication of single compositions is class consistent in both additive conditions. In the four-object additive condition, the order of handling objects to compose them is about ten-to-one favoring identical objects (Table 12.4, Row 1, Columns 1–3), while the random probability ratio is two-to-one favoring complementary objects. The difference is statistically significant ($N = 12$, $x = 2$, $p = .019$, sign test). For enclosure, the found ratio is about four-to-one favoring composing identical objects (Row 1, Columns 4–6) for the same random probability ratio. This difference, too, is statistically significant ($N = 12$, $x = 2$, $p = .019$, sign test).

TABLE 12.4
Spontaneous Phase I: Mean Frequency of Class Consistent Composing at Age 21 Months

	Order			Enclosure		
	Unmixed 1	Partly unmixed 2	Mixed 3	Unmixed 4	Partly unmixed 5	Mixed 6
Four-object condition:						
1. Additive	7.25	0.08	0.75	7.75	0.17	1.92
2. Multiplicative[a]	7.54	0.18	1.73	10.00	0.09	3.45
3. Disjoint[b]	4.20	0.20	1.30	4.80	0.40	2.20
Eight-object condition:						
4. Additive	5.92	0.08	1.42	8.50	0.42	2.25
5. Multiplicative[c]	2.44	5.56	1.11	3.78	6.56	1.89
6. Disjoint[b]	4.80	0.00	0.80	5.90	0.10	3.30

[a]$N = 11$ subjects.
[b]$N = 10$ subjects.
[c]$N = 9$ subjects.

In the eight-object additive condition, order is about four-to-one favoring composing identical objects (Row 4, Columns 1–3), while the random probability ratio favors complementarity by four-to-three. The difference is not statistically significant ($N = 12$, $x = 3$, $p = .073$, sign test). For enclosure, the found ratio favoring identical objects is about three-to-one (Row 4, Columns 4–6) for the same random probability ratio. The difference is statistically significant ($N = 12$, $x = 2$, $p = .019$, sign test).

Predication varies in the multiplicative condition as a function of the number of objects: four vs. eight. In the four-object condition, predication is not quite class consistent, although it may approach it. The random probability ratio is two-to-one favoring composing complementary rather than disjoint objects. For order, the found ratio favoring predication by complements is almost five-to-one (Row 2, Columns 1–3). Nevertheless, the difference from the random probability ratio is not statistically significant ($N = 11$, $x = 3$, $p = .113$). For enclosure, the found ratio is about three-to-one favoring composing by complements (Row 2, Columns 4–6), but the difference from the random probability ratio is not statistically significant ($N = 11$, $x = 4$, $p = .274$).

The eight-object multiplicative condition has a random probability ratio of five-to-two favoring composing ummixed (identical) and partly unmixed (complementary) objects over composing mixed (disjoint) objects. For order, the found ratio is about six-to-one (Row 5, Columns 1 and 2 vs. 3), which is significantly different from the random probability ratio ($N = 9$, $x = 1$, $p = .020$, sign test). For enclosure, the found ratio is more than five-to-one (Row 5, Columns 4 and 5 vs. 6). The difference between the found and the random probability ratio is not statistically significant ($N = 9$, $x = 2$, $p = .090$, sign test).

Overall, then, infants compose multiplicative classes of eight objects by their complements, that is, on one dimension by either form or color as if the presentation consisted of additive rather than multiplicative classes of objects. This mode of composition is reflected in the measures labeled partly unmixed (Row 5, Columns 2 and 5) which contain the highest mean scores.

Identical objects are usually composed together into single collections in the disjoint conditions, though the effect is clearest when infants are presented with eight rather than four objects. In the four object condition, the random probability ratio is two-to-one favoring composing disjoint rather than identical objects. For order, the found ratio is more than three-to-one favoring composing identical objects (Row 3, Columns 1–3), which is significantly different from the random ratio ($N = 7$, $x = 0$, $p = .008$). For enclosure, the found ratio is about two-to-one favoring composing identical objects (Row 3, Columns 4–6), but the difference from the random ratio is not statistically significant ($N = 10$, $x = 6$, $p = .828$).

The eight-object disjoint condition favors composing disjoint rather than identical objects by a random probability ratio of four-to-three. For order, the found ratio is six-to-one favoring composing identical objects (Row 6, Columns 1–3) and is significantly different from the random ratio ($N = 10$, $x = 0$, $p = .001$). For enclosure, the found ratio is almost two-to-one favoring composing identical objects (Row 6, Columns 4–6) and is significantly different from the random ratio ($N = 10$, $x = 1$, $p = .011$).

Together, these findings indicate continuing progress toward composing identical or similar objects into single collections, as does the tendency for order of handling to be at least as class consistent as the enclosure properties of these single compositions. This development occurs notwithstanding a third continuous trend during the second year. Order and enclosure properties are linked where order applies. They correspond in 92% of the compositions in the four-object conditions, 94% in the eight-object conditions, and 93% overall.

It is no longer the case that composing is more class consistent in the condition presenting the fewest objects (i.e., in the four- rather than the eight-object conditions). If anything, composing is equally class consistent in the four- and eight-object additive conditions, while it is more class consistent in the eight-object than in the four-object multiplicative and disjoint conditions.

Causal compositions are less frequently class consistent than noncausal compositions, as they are at age 18 months (see pages 189 and 190); but the differential is decreasing. The predicate enclosure properties of noncausal compositions are 68% unmixed, 9% partly unmixed, and 23% mixed. Causal compositions are 56% unmixed, 22% partly unmixed, and 21% mixed. Thus, this is the first age at which more causal compositions are unmixed than not. This trend suggests the hypothesis that embodying agents and patients in different classes of objects is becoming unnecessary, or at least less necessary, for infants to construct causal compositions.

13

Elaborating Relations within Paired Compositions of Malleable Objects

Development in interacting with quasi-continuous objects and with combined discrete and quasi-continuous objects continues to parallel that with discrete objects. Most importantly, the organization of second-order structures are progressively filled in, consolidated, and generalized. This includes the origins of structuring many-to-one correspondences by reversibly coordinating composing with its inverse, redecomposing. It also includes the origins of structuring one-to-many correspondences by reversibly coordinating decomposing with its inverse, recomposing.

These two counivocal structures are correlative to each other. Composing followed by redecomposing couples affirmation with negation of the part–whole structures of collective objects (one) with collective sets (many). Decomposing followed by recomposing couples negation with affirmation of the part–whole structures of collective sets (many) with collective objects (one).

The stage is thereby set for the organizational integration of these structures. As also expected at their origins, their instantiation is partial. They are primarily restricted to structuring extensive counivocal relations between collective objects (one) and collective sets (many). Intensive counivocal (one-to-many) relations await much further intervening structural development.

I. Coordinating Experimenting with Transforming

Infants continue to examine, as they do throughout the second year, the part–whole structure of objects before, during, and after transforming them by combinativity operations of deforming, reforming, decomposing, etc. This coordinate examine-and-transform procedure also continues to be applied comparatively to sets of objects as long as the membership is small.

One new feature of examine-and-transform that only begins to develop is tactilomotor examining of the inside as well as the outside properties of rings. This examination may include gross tracing by hand of the inside shape of rings. To illustrate, upon initial presentation of a large circular PlayDoh ring, subject 21AF immediately deforms it into less of a circular and more of an elliptical shape. To reform its initial circular shape the

5. *RH taps at the Large Ring*
5a. *LH becomes rounder*
6. *RH(fisted) moves counterclockwise around inside of LR, repeatedly*
7. *RH raises from middle of LR and one finger touches LR, five times*

(21AF, page 16)

Here tactilomotor tracing of the inside shape (Line 6) is followed by what is by now standard tactual examination (Line 7). A bit later, tracing the inside of a different object is not accompanied by another mode of tactile examination (irrelevant intervening transactions are omitted):

10. *RH (fisted) moves counterclockwise around inside of Small Ring 1, repeatedly*
15. *RH (fisted) moves counterclockwise around inside of SR1, repeatedly*

(21AF, pages 17 and 18)

At its initiation, all inside tactilomotor tracing is limited to gross examining, such as by a fist moving round-and-round the inner part of a ring. As expected, both the organ usage (e.g., a fist instead of the tip of a finger) and the action (e.g., continuous circular instead of punctate touching motions) are undifferentiated. Inside tracing begins to be differentiated at the next stage (see page 350). Still, even gross inside tracing extends infants' determination of the comparative part–whole structure of objects. Moreover, they can coordinate this extended knowledge about objects with their transformations of these same objects.

Experimental examination of objects' causal properties continues to be generated as it has at the previous stage, for instance, by rolling objects around in infants' hands and dropping them from different heights to see what happens. In addition, at this stage, experimenting with the causal properties of objects begins to be linked clearly to transforming their part–whole structure, particularly by deforming them. Such experimenting-and-transforming is essential to determining the relations between the predicate and causal properties of objects.

Coordinate experimenting-and-transforming is most apparent when they are repeatedly intertwined temporally (irrelevant intervening transactions are omitted):

2.	BH roll Ball around in hands	
2a.	B rolls out of BH onto table	
8.	BH roll B around in hands	
8a.	B rolls out of BH onto table	
10.	RH taps/hits B on table, 1 time	
11.	RH holds B shoulder high to right	
11a.	B rolls out of RH and fall to floor	
13.	BH roll B around in hands for about 15 seconds	
13a.	B rolls out of BH onto table	S: "Tee, hee." (laugh)
21.	BH (perpendicular to table) hold B between palms	
22.	BH rotate flat (so that they are parallel to table)	
22a.	B rolls out of hands onto table and continues rolling toward experimenter	
24.	RH holds B in palm and then lets B roll out of hand onto table	
25.	RH flicks B back toward self	
25a.	B rolls into subject's stomach at edge of table	
27.	BH roll B between hands	
28.	BH lower B to table and, while on top of B, roll B up and back about 2 inches	
31.	RH grasps B and hits B on table, 4 times	
32.	RH lets B roll out of hand	
32a.	B rolls onto table and continues rolling toward experimenter	(21JF, pages 15 and 16)

This coordinate experimenting-and-transforming sequence is even more extensive than that presented in this fragment. The sequence begins and ends with semisystematic experimenting; in between 21JF both transforms and experiments with the ball of PlayDoh. Thus 21JF generates extensive conditions for determining the effects of changing the shape of the ball upon its motile behavior. By laughing at some of his experimenting he also evidences cognizance of his manipulation of the object.

Still infants rarely symbolize their transformations of objects. When they do, the communication is ambiguous and global:

2.	BH hold Large Ball while visually inspecting LB	
3.	RH thumb presses into LB held by LH	S: "Op. Open. Opp, Open."
3a.	indentation in LB	(M: "Open it.")
4.	BH extend LB to mother	S: "Open."
5.	BH move LB back to center of table	(M: "Open it.")
6.	RH fingers press into LB held by LH	S: "Open it, Momma."
6a.	multiple, not deep, indentations in LB	(M: "You do it.")

7.	*RH releases LB held by LH*	S: *"Do it, Momma."*
8.	*LH extends LB to mother*	(M: *"Uh, uh. You do it."*)
9.	*LH moves LB back to center of table*	S: *"Do it."*

(21SS, page 24)

Subject 21SS reproduces her mother's verbal expansion of "Open" to "Open it." She also contracts her mother's imperative "You do it" to "Do it." None of this specifies whether 21SS wants the large ball of PlayDoh to be deformed, broken, or decomposed.

Infants are more prone to point at objects and name them appropriately ("Balls" and "Clay") and inappropriately though perhaps playfully ("Apple" and "Cookie"). Subject 21SS even counts "One, two, tree, two" as she hands five PlayDoh balls one by one to the experimenter.

II. Articulating Instrumental Deforming

Deforming continues to dominate infants' transformations of objects (Table 13.1). Frequency of deforming does not vary systematically as a function of the number of objects presented or whether they are formed into balls or rings. For instance, it may seem as if deforming is generated more frequently when infants are presented with one object (Row 1, Column 1) than when they are presented with three objects (Row 1, Column 4). However, a small but substantial proportion (mean of 1.57) of the deformations are multiple in the three object condition while none are in the one-object condition. This difference probably cancels out the higher frequency of individual deformations in the one-object condition.

The highest frequency of deforming occurs in the spontaneous phase of the combined discrete and quasi-continuous condition (Row 1, Column 7). It is accounted for by the tendency that infants have to use the tongue depressor stuck in a ball like a drumstick. They use the tongue depressor as a handle with which to repeatedly beat the attached PlayDoh ball on the tabletop. The result is a high frequency of instrumental and contingent deforming of the attached PlayDoh balls.

Almost all infants (10 of 12 subjects) generate multiple contingent deforming. Most of these are the product of banging PlayDoh objects on the tabletop. An increasing proportion of contingent deformations are instrumental. Most instrumental deforming is still global, particularly when it is the product of using a tongue depressor to bang an attached PlayDoh ball on the tabletop. But some instrumental deforming is already more articulate in form and precise in product:

  6. *RH pokes Tongue Depressor 1 into Ball 1*   (21JF, page 39)

111. *RH saws Tongue Depressor 1 back and forth on top of Ball 1 held by LH*
(21AL, page 104)

TABLE 13.1
Mean Frequency of Combinativity Proto-Operations Generated by 21-Month-Old Subjects in Quasi-Continuous and Discrete–Quasi-Continuous Conditions

	One object			Three objects			Discrete–quasi-continuous	
	Phase I 1	Phase II 2	Phase III 3	Phase I 4	Phase II 5	Phase III 6	Phase I 7	Phase II 8
1. Deform	10.30	5.14(0.57)[a]	6.34(0.09)	7.14(1.57)	1.88(1.00)	4.33(0.78)	13.40(0.80)	4.09(0.54)
2. Reform	0.20(0.10)	0.00	0.18(0.18)	0.00	0.00	0.00	0.00	0.00
3. Break	0.00	0.14	0.91	0.43	0.25	0.33	0.30	0.18
4. Reconstruct	0.00	0.00	0.00	0.00	0.00	0.00	0.00	0.09
5. Decompose	2.70	0.57	3.82(0.09)	3.00(0.14)	1.38	6.11	1.30(0.10)	1.00
6. Recompose	0.20[0.30][b]	0.00	0.09	0.00	0.00	0.00	0.00	0.00
7. Compose		0.00	1.00	0.28	0.00	0.55(0.11)	0.00	0.09
8. Redecompose		0.00	0.54[0.09]	0.00	0.00	0.11	0.00	0.09
9. Attach							2.10[0.10]	1.45[0.45]
10. Redetach							1.30	1.00
11. Detach							1.10	0.82
12. Reattach							0.50[0.40]	0.27
13. Number of subjects	10	7	11	7	8	9	10	11
14. Mean duration	1 min 49 sec[c]	0 min 33 sec[d]	1 min 54 sec[c]	1 min 42 sec[c]	0 min 37 sec[e]	1 min 52 sec[f]	1 min 56 sec[c]	1 min 6 sec[c]

[a]Mean frequency of multiple transformations are given in parentheses.
[b]Mean frequency of attempted but not successfully executed transformations are given in square brackets.
[c]Based on duration for 9 subjects.
[d]Based on duration for 5 subjects.
[e]Based on duration for 6 subjects.
[f]Based on duration for 7 subjects.

The local causes of such articulate instrumental deforming are not obvious. Thus, 21JF's instrumental deforming may actually be a biproduct of trying to attach a tongue depressor to a PlayDoh ball rather than trying to use it to deform the ball, and 21AL's may actually be a biproduct of trying to decompose a PlayDoh ball by cutting it. Be this as it may, the result is precise instrumental deforming. Indeed, 21AL immediately proceeds to generate multiple gestural representations:

112. *LH picks up Ball 1 while RH holds Tongue Depressor 1*
113. *RH saws TD1 back and forth, about 10 times, over but not on top of B1 held by LH*   (21AL, page 104)

Although only a conjecture, it is not improbable that 21AL is reflecting pragmatically upon the instrumental transformation she has just generated (see Piaget, 1951, for similar symbolic activity during this age period). Practical reflection enhances the probability that instrumental deforming will become progressively articulate and precise means of part–whole transformation.

Reforming objects previously deformed does not progress (Row 2). If anything it is generated even less frequently than at age eighteen months (see Table 9.1, Row 2, on page 194). At age eighteen months, six infants clearly reform objects, and the objects include ball shapes as well as rings. Only one infant at age twenty one months clearly reforms objects (see the first 21AF protocol fragment on page 262 for an illustration of this subject's reforming). While this infant re-reforms objects more than four times, the objects are always ring shapes and never ball shapes.

III. Comparing Matched with Ordered Sets of Deformations

Corresponding deformations of single objects are commonplace and are becoming well-differentiated and regulated procedures:

2. *BH slightly squeeze Large Ball as feeling LB*   S: *"Ohhhh."*
3. *BH rotate LB around while visually inspecting LB*
4. *BH fingertips squeeze the middle of LB*   (21RR, page 18)

11.5. *RH pinches right side of Large Ball*
11.5. *LH pinches left side of LB*   (21RR, page 19)

Two mapping forms are used by 21RR to produce corresponding deformations within a single object: squeezing and pinching. Both are fine-grained performances that produce relatively precise matched deformations in the part–whole structure of the object. In addition, squeezing is coordinated with tactile and visiomotor inspection of the object and the transformations 21RR is generating.

Instrumental production of corresponding deformations within single objects are also becoming well-differentiated and regulated procedures. They are usually generated successively. For instance, one infant reproduced the following transformation nine times in a row to produce nine similar indentations:

    30.   *RH pushes edge of Tongue Depressor 1 on top of Ball 1 and then slides TD1 down onto table*
    30a. *shallow slit indentation made in B1*   (21CL, page 145)

Occasionally, two instruments are used to produce two similar deformations at the same time. Infants do this by each hand pushing the tip of a tongue depressor into a side of a PlayDoh ball. The result is two shallow indentations on opposite sides of the ball. Essentially, then, these infants are doing two of 21CL's consecutive transformations at the same time. Their matched mappings produce simultaneous equivalent deformations within a single object.

Matched deformations are also produced consecutively on a set of objects. These productions are well-regulated, but some (e.g., 21CL) are more differentiated and fine-grained than others (21AL):

    37.   *RH index finger pushes down on Ball 4*
    37a. *shallow indentation made in B4*   (21CL, page 60)

    27.   *RH open palm presses down on Small Piece 4, 1 time*
    27a. *SP4 is flattened out*   (21AL, page 48)

While only one instance is presented for illustration, 21CL uses an index finger to correspondingly deform eight objects, and subject 21AL uses a palm to correspondingly deform four objects. Most corresponding deformations (e.g., 21AL) still apply to small sets of objects, but some (e.g., 21CL) already apply to sets comprising an intermediate number of objects.

Corresponding deformations of two objects at the same time is generated by 8 of 12 subjects. Almost all these subjects do this more than once. Almost all use both contingent and noncontingent procedures to produce matched deformations of two objects. Furthermore, an ever-increasing assortment of contingent forms are generated:

    1.5. *RH taps top of Ball 1, 3 times*
    1.5. *LH taps top of Ball 2, 3 times*
    3.5. *RH picks up B1 and immediately slams B1 down on table*
    3.5. *LH picks up B2 and immediately slams B2 down on table*
    5.5. *RH rolls and presses B1 on table by pressing top of B1 while rolling it*
    5.5. *LH rolls and presses B2 on table by pressing top of B2 while rolling it*
                               (21JF, pages 16 and 17)

The seriated aspect of this sequence of corresponding deformations will be considered later in this section. Here it should simply be noted that this fragment reflects the range of contingent deforming generated at this stage. Subject *21JF* generates three forms of corresponding deformations in a row that he applies to two objects at the same time. The first corresponding deformations, produced by tapping the top of two balls, are ambiguously contingent. The second, slamming the two balls down on the table, is a relatively unarticulated form of contingent deforming. They are repeated many more times by *21JF* later in the task, and they are still the most typical form of contingent deforming generated at this stage. The third corresponding deformations by combined rolling while pressing the two balls on the tabletop are the most complex and articulate contingent forms generated at this stage. As such, the procedures used by *21JF* to produce corresponding deformations are still relatively novel and unusual.

Corresponding instrumental deforming of two objects simultaneously also progressively varies when infants interact with tongue depressors and PlayDoh balls. The most typical deformation is unarticulated (i.e., successive or simultaneous pounding of two balls on the tabletop by manipulating tongue depressors to which the balls are attached). Several forms are more articulate and differentiated. These include using tongue depressors to deform PlayDoh balls and using one combined tongue depressor–ball to hit down on another. The latter form is a reciprocal as well as a simultaneous way of deforming two objects. Another form extends the part–whole structure of the combined objects:

17.5.   *RH lowers Tongue Depressor 1/Ball 1 so that B1 touches table and then pushes TD1 further into B1*

17.5.   *LH lowers Tongue Depressor 2/Ball 2 so that B2 touches table and then pushes TD2 further into B2*

19.5.   *RH raises TD1/B1 and touches B1 end to B2 end, 2 times*

19.5.   *LH raises TD2/B2 and touches B2 end to B1 end, 2 times*

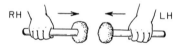

(*21VL*, page 53)

The overall structure of the combined objects are not changed by *21VL*. Indeed, the corresponding deformations are apparently intended to strengthen the attachment between the two tongue depressors and their respective PlayDoh balls (Lines 17.5). In addition, the corresponding deformations are immediately coordinated with inspection; only the deformed parts, the balls, are matched up end-to-end against each other two times (Lines 19.5). Comparison by repeatedly aligning the deformed parts of the two combined objects permits rough determination of whether the transformed part–whole structure of the two objects are congruent.

Pairs of corresponding deformations are also sometimes coordinated with playful and expressive routines:

24.5.   RH *hits Ball 1 on tabletop, 1 time, then raises B1 to shoulder*
24.5.   LH *hits Ball 2 on tabletop, 1 time, then raises B2 to shoulder*

(21JF, page 17)

28.5.   RH *holding TD2 of Tongue Depressor 2/Ball 2 taps B2 on tabletop, 8 times*
28.5.   LH *holding TD1 of Tongue Depressor 1/Ball 1 taps B1 on tabletop, 8 times*

(21PG, page 46)

Subject *21JF* repeats his routine immediately and exactly (not reproduced here). In contrast, subject *21PG* continues by detaching the combined objects and then trying unsuccessfully to reattach them. He accompanies these transformations by saying "Walk. Walking. Eh, eh, Mom." Thus, his expressive behavior is more labile and difficult to interpret.

Two of 12 subjects also correspondingly deform three objects at the same time. One subject uses a noncontingent procedure (i.e., *21KA* squeezes three PlayDoh balls in the same way at the same time). The other subject uses a contingent procedure (i.e., *21JF*'s right hand slams two PlayDoh balls down onto the tabletop at the same time as his left hand slams one PlayDoh ball down on the tabletop). Neither subject repeats this procedure with three objects. Hence, these are still exceptional and nonregulated constructions.

Ordered deformations figure prominently in infants' transformations. Many are coordinated with corresponding deformations. A good illustration is provided by the *21JF* protocol fragment on page 267. Two balls are increasingly flattened out, forming a coseriated ⟨ tap, slam, press ⟩ ordering of deformations.

At each step, the corresponding deformations are produced by identical mappings (e.g., pressing both balls). This sameness is typical. Successive steps in the coseriated ordered deformations, however, are produced by different mappings (e.g., tapping *vs.* slamming *vs.* pressing). This difference is becoming typical. When different mapping forms are used to produce successive steps within ordered series then it becomes increasingly possible to detach the constructed orders from the particular pragmatic ways by which they are constructed. This detaching furthers the possibilities already developed for abstracting and representing ordering operations of addition and subtraction.

Since coseriated deforming transforms two objects at the same time, it permits infants to directly observe, compare and record two ordered series of additions and subtractions, which they are generating. At least two other means of generating ordered deformations that also foster this comparison continue to develop. One consists of consecutively generating ordered deformations in two or more objects (e.g., transforming a ball into a flatter and flatter pancake, and then doing the same thing to several other balls). The other is possible with a single object:

12.   RH *index finger digs into Large Ball*   S: "Ball."
12a.   *a crevice is dug into top of LB*

13.3.   RH index finger continued digging
       into crevice in LB
13.3a. *crevice in top of LB becomes bigger*
13.7.   *RH other fingers press into LB*
13.7a. *four indentations are made in LB*   (*21PG*, pages 25 and 26)

Two orderings (within a crevace, and between a crevace and four indentations) plus a set of one-to-one correspondences (between four indentations) are contained within this one object. Also, the mappings generating the ordering between the crevace and the indentations are different (i.e., respectively, digging and pressing). Thus, comparing and abstracting both ordered nonequivalence and unordered equivalence become possible at the same time within the part–whole transformations of this one object. At the same time, *21PG* names repeatedly the object ("Ball") of his transformations, but not the transformations themselves or their products.

IV. Progressive Coordination of Decomposing with Other Transformations

Breaking objects so that their form but not their number changes (e.g., a ring into a strand) does not increase in frequency. The rate of production is a bit higher in three test conditions at age 21 months (Table 13.1, Row 3, Columns 2, 3 and 4) than at age 18 months (see Table 9.1, Row 3, Columns 2, 3 and 4, on page 194). But they are also a bit lower in five test conditions at age 21 months (Table 13.1, Row 3, Columns 1, 5, 6, 7 and 8) than at age 18 months (Table 9.1, Row 3, Columns 1, 5, 6, 7 and 8). On balance, then, breaking remains stable at a low but fairly substantial rate of production.

Breaking is progressively regulated and coordinated with examining:

3.   *BH move back and forth while holding Large Ring*
3a. *LR is broken open into one long strand*
4.   *BH hold LR still while looking at LR*
5.   *LH holding one end of LR wraps part of LR around RH which is holding the other end of LR*
6.   *LH holding one end of LR shakes LR back and forth, while RH holds the other end of LR*
6a. *LR breaks into a big and a small strand (one in each hand)*   (*21KA*, page 19)

The product of transforming the ring into a strand is examined visually (Line 4) and by determining what can be done with a strand (Lines 5–6a). Thus, breaking is followed-up with experimentally deforming the strand. Ultimately this results in decomposing the strand into two parts.

Reconstructing is almost nonexistent (Table 13.1, Row 4), and is generated even less frequently than at age 18 months (see Table 9.1). It is generated once only by one infant:

3. *LH pushes Tongue Depressor 2 all the way through* Ball 2
3a. *TD2 raises a flap on B2*   S: *"Uh, oh."*
4. *LH places TD2 on table, while RH holds B2*
5. *LH pushes flap of B2 back down on B2 held by RH*   (21SS, page 44)

Thus, while exceptional, controlled reconstruction of a break is possible, and 21SS expresses some vocal cognizance (Line 3a) of this fact.

The rate of decomposing does not change from age 18 months (see Table 9.1, Row 5) to 21 months (Table 13.1, Row 5). When compared with transformations at age 18 months, the rate of decomposing by 21-month-old infants is higher in three test conditions, lower in three conditions, and equal in two conditions.

Rate of decomposition does not vary as a function of the number of objects presented when they are all made out of PlayDoh. In the comparable initial spontaneous testing phases I, the mean rate is 1.49 decompositions per minute in the one object condition (Row 4, Column 1) and 1.76 decompositions per minute in the three object condition (Row 4, Column 4). This small difference is not statistically significant ($N = 5$, $x = 2$, $p = .50$, sign test).

Rate of decomposing is lower in the two combined discrete and quasi-continuous conditions (Row 4, Columns 7 and 8) than in all the six pure quasi-continuous conditions (Row 4, Columns 1–6). In the most directly comparable initial spontaneous testing Phase I, the mean rate is only 0.67 decompositions per minute in the combined condition (Row 4, Column 7). Still this rate is not significantly lower than the mean productivity of 1.49 in the one object condition and of the mean productivity of 1.76 in the three object condition (sign tests). Thus, the rate of producing decompositions is actually remarkably stable across object conditions.

Decomposition is progressively regulated and coordinated with other transformations. To illustrate, infants easily break a PlayDoh ring open, stretch it out into a straight strand, and then decompose it into two or more parts. Alternatively, the sequence of coordinated transformations may begin with decomposing a piece off a PlayDoh ball and rubbing it into the table. For instance, subject 21AF did this repeatedly and thereby also generated an extended set of one-to-one correspondences between decompositions coupled with deformations. The product is a fairly extended equivalence class of transformed but matched elements.

Routines coordinating decomposing with other transformations are expanded and progressively refined:

3. *LH presses down on Small Ball 5*
3a. *SB5 is flattened out on table*

   4. *RH index finger runs through flattened SB5*
   4a. *SB5 is cut into two halves*   (21PG, 29)

Later in the same task 21PG repeats this routine with another small ball. The coordinated procedures, then, are in one-to-one correspondence with each other. Each product comprises two roughly equivalent derivative elements. Further, they constitute two equivalent sets of two elements. The latter product, however, is still labile because the production of the two sets are not consecutive and are not placed in direct relation to each other on the table (that is, other objects are transformed and placed on the table between these two sets).

Contingent decomposing is also marked by controlled expansion of instrumental procedures:

   29. *RH, holding Tongue Depressor 1/Ball 1 by TD1, runs B1 along length of the edge of Tongue Depressor 2 held at end by LH*
   29a. *TD2 pulls a small part of B1*   (21SS, page 44)

The ball is decomposed by 21SS manipulating two instruments; the ball itself is not directly manipulated by 21SS. Further, the cutting instrument (Tongue Depressor 2) is used as a passive agent with which to decompose the patient object (Ball 1), which is manipulated actively by a vehicular instrument (Tongue Depressor 1). This agent-to-patient relation is novel and is the reciprocal of the usual relation constructed up to this stage. Usually, the agent is active, and the patient is passive (e.g., decomposing a PlayDoh ball by poking a tongue depressor into it).

Exceptional second-order decomposing continues to be generated, but even these remain labile constructions. For instance, corresponding decomposing of two objects into two matched sets of two equal elements by 21PG, presented above, is still an unusual and labile construction. While half of the subjects generate such labile sets by decomposition, the sets are almost always not matched with each other.

Similarly, exceptional pairs of geneological sets are constructed by decomposing two objects into two collections of smaller and smaller parts. Only two subjects do this and their constructions are also labile. Most geneological decomposition is still applied to single objects only; these are generated by half of the subjects. Overall, then, there is no increase in the rate of generating second-order equivalence or ordered nonequivalence at this stage.

There is little, if any, apparent advance in the linguistic behavior that accompanies infants' decomposing. Usually, infants still do not accompany decomposing with any verbalizations. On exceptional occasion they say something like "Pizzas" while decomposing (subject 21CP) as if they are expressing the playful object or product of their decomposing.

V. Negation between One-to-Many and Many-to-One Transformations

Recomposing objects previously decomposed is infrequent (Table 13.1, Row 6). Recomposing or attempted recomposing is generated by only one-third of the subjects. All these subjects recompose the original extent of the whole object. No subject recomposes the original intensity (form) of the whole object by putting the decomposed parts back together again.

Still, the structure of the inverse relation between decomposing and recomposing begins to be extended in two ways (irrelevant intervening transactions are omitted in the 21PG fragment):

15. *RH index finger and thumb pull a piece (P1) off Large Ball*
21. *RH index finger and thumb stick P1 back on LB*
27. *RH picks P1 off LB*   (21PG, pages 26 and 27)

26.5. *RH squeezes Medium Piece 1 against Large Strand*
26.5. *LH squeezes Small Piece 1a against Large Strand*   (21CP, page 18)

Fine sensorimotor manipulation by 21PG indicates that these coordinated transformations are controlled and directed. Thus, the initial decomposition is inverted into a recomposition which, in turn, is inverted into a decomposition. The product is extensive, but not intensive, identity by negation.

The second way in which the inverse relation between decomposing and recomposing is elaborated is initiated by 21CP. He tries to recompose two parts at the same time. These parts are geneological derivatives of the large strand to which he is recomposing them. Before this, 21CP first broke open a large ring into a strand, decomposed the strand into a large strand and a medium piece, and then decomposed the medium piece into a medium piece 1 and a small piece 1a. His recomposition efforts constitute a many-to-one correspondence that inverts the one-to-many decompositions of the large strand. As usual, reversibility remains restricted to negating extensive but not intensive (form) transformations.

Composing is still not generated by all infants. A majority of subjects (7 out of 12) generate composing at a relatively low rate (Table 13.1, Row 7). This is similar to the pattern that obtains at age 18 months (Table 9.1, Row 7, page 194), although perhaps at a slightly reduced rate.

Many-to-one correspondences begin to condition composing, as we have seen, just as they do recomposing:

36. *RH sticks Ball 1 on Large Ball sitting on table, while LH holds Balls 3 and 5*
37. *RH takes B5 from LH and sticks B5 on LB, while LH holds B3*
38. *RH takes B3 from LH and sticks B3 on LB*

39. *RH picks up B4 and sticks B4 on LB*
40. *RH picks up B2 and sticks B2 on LB*   (21VL, page 33)

By sticking all the small balls on the big ball 21VL uses a many-to-one correspondence to compose the collection of many objects (B1, B2, B3, B4, B5 and LB) into one collective object (B1/B2/B3/B4/B5:LB). She follows this by redecomposing one ball (B4) from the collective object which is thereby reduced to B1/B2/B3/B5:LB, composing B4 with the collective object to reform it into B1/B2/B3/B4/B5:LB; deforming the collective object into an unarticulated object; and finally redecomposing three pieces from the unarticulated object.

Total composing, then, is partially inverted by redecomposing; redecomposing is inverted by composing; and composing is inverted by partial redecomposing. This sequence of linked reversible operations forms a many-to-one correspondence by composition which is partially rendered back into a one-to-many correspondence by redecomposing. This reversible co-univocal structure (from many-to-one to one-to-many correspondences) is the inverse of that which negates one-to-many correspondences by decomposing into many-to-one correpondence by recomposing. The latter structure, we have seen (i.e., the 21CP construction analyzed above), also originates at this stage.

Thus, the complete reversible structure of counivocal correlation of composable and decomposable elements is initiated at this stage. It is, of course, rarely manifest at its origin. Indeed, no single infant manifests the entire structure. Moreover, although redecomposing (Table 13.1, Row 8) is, as always, generated more frequently than recomposing (Row 6), redecomposing remains an infrequently generated transformation produced by only one-fourth of the infants.

While rare, the reversible structure linking composing and redecomposing begins to be coordinated with the reversible structure linking attachment and detachment of conglomerate objects:

54. *RH sticks Piece 2 onto Tongue Depressor 1 (held by LH which also holds Tongue Depressor 2/Ball 1 throughout this sequence)*
55. *RH picks up Piece 2b and sticks P2b on TD1*
56. *RH picks up P2a and sticks P2a on TD1 and P2b*
57. *RH pulls P2, P2a and P2b off TD1*   (21CP, page 49)

Many-to-one correspondence by composing combined with attaching (Lines 54–56) is negated by one-to-many redecomposing combined with redetaching (Line 57). The initial collection of discrete and quasi-continuous objects is composed and attached into a collective object. In turn, the collective object is negated into a collection. The product of this reversible co-univocal structure is again an identity operation.

Attaching, detaching and their inverses, redetaching and reattaching, are already robust transformations (Table 13.1, Rows 9–12, Columns 7 and 8) that are generated by most infants. As always, negating attaching by redetaching is generated more frequently than negating detaching by reattaching, This parallels the advance of negating composing by redecomposing over negating decomposing by recomposing.

Tongue depressors and PlayDoh balls are attached to each other such that both the procedures and the products are in one-to-one correspondence. The matched products begin to be checked as to whether they are congruent shapes. The procedure is very much like that which infants begin to use in order to check corresponding deformations that they have produced in the PlayDoh part of conglomorate objects (see 21VL's construction considered on page 268).

The inverse relations, attaching–redetaching and detaching–reattaching, are also sometimes applied sequentially to two combined objects. The result is structuring one-to-one correspondence between these inverse transformations. In this way, they further mark the development of second-order operations with combined objects.

Seriated attaching and seriated reattaching has become relatively commonplace. The sequence may include pushing a tongue depressor into a Play-Doh ball as many as three or four times so that the attachment will be deeper and deeper while infants visually monitor what they are doing. Occasionally, this sequence of ordered attachments is repeated with two conglomorate objects in a row. The result is coseriated attachment, that is, equivalent ordered transformations of conglomorate objects.

IV

STAGE 8 AT TWENTY-FOUR MONTHS

14

Subroutines within Routines

Infants elaborate their routines or pragmatic propositions by constructing subroutines within them. Subroutines are partially separate pragmatic propositions that infants incorporate into the overall structure of their routines. Typically, this incorporation requires both anticipatory planning and regulatory coordination for the subroutines to fit as proper parts of the whole routine.

This advance is apparent in infants' symbolization in action, including their playful pretense. It is not yet apparent in their linguistic symbolization, which is not yet marked by any forms of subphrasing. Still, linguistic development catches up with and outstrips symbolization in action in other important respects, including further developments in symbolizing the nonpresent, initiated at the previous stage. It also includes the formation of comparatives, including rudimentary counting and scalars.

This advance in planning and coordinating constructions is also apparent in the development of second-order functions. One important consequence of more advanced planning by infants is that they progressively structure causes and effects into circular dependency relations. Another important consequence of more advanced coordinating is the initiation of reciprocally integrating two instruments into a single regulated causal means.

I. Transition to Planned Subroutines

Infants plan and correct their routines (e.g., when objects are knocked over accidently by infants while they are aligning them upright in a row, infants

279

carefully replace them in exactly the same position and orientation). Planning and correcting provide the regulatory bases for constructing more complex routines that include differentiated and coordinated subroutines. For instance, first subject 24SG prepares a set of two circular rings. She holds the first set in abeyance while she constructs a second stacked set with the other two circular rings. When the second set is ready she stacks the first, prepared set on the second. The product is an integrated stack of all four rings.

Subroutines are still rudimentary at their inception. First, they are generated by only 5 of the 12 infants. Second, and crucially, subroutines are elementary constructions as compared with the routines in which they are embedded. Nevertheless, these elementary subconstructions begin to condition composing to form more elaborate routines. To illustrate, eleven consecutive steps make up subject 24EH's elaborate stack of all eight objects that include four circular rings (labeled R) and four rectangular blocks (labeled B):

1. Coregulatively stacks R4 on R1 by careful and precise edge matching to form a stabile construction R4/R1.
2. Adds R4/R1 onto B2 which increases the stabile stack to R4/R1/B2.
3. Touches R3 on B1 forming a momentary mobile composition R3/B1.
4. Adds R3 onto R4/R1/B2 which increases the stabile stack to R3/R4/R1/B2.
5. Adds B1 onto R3/R4/R1/B2 which increases the stabile stack to B1/R3/R4/R1/B2.
6. Displaces R2 in preparation for substituting R2 for B1.
7. Subtracts B1 from B1/R3/R4/R1/B2 which decreases the stabile stack to R3/R4/R1/B2 once again as in step 5.
8. Adds prepared R2 onto R3/R4/R1/B2 which increases the stabile stack to R2/R3/R4/R1/B2.
9. Adds B1, subtracted in step 7, to R2/R3/R4/R1/B2 which increases the stabile stack to B1/R2/R3/R4/R1/B2.
10–11. Successively adds B4 then B3 to B1/R2/R3/R4/R1/B2 which increases the stabile stack to its completed stack form B3/B4/B1/R2/R3/R4/R1/B2.

This is the second of three times, during one task, that 24EH constructs the identical stack composition of three blocks on top of four circular rings on top of one block. After each time, she dismantles the stack and says "Do dat again." Then she reproduces the exact same stack twice. Thus, there are good indications, including 24EH's verbally stated intention to "Do dat again," that this complex stabile composition is a well-regulated and planned production and reproduction. In addition, for the first time, the bare precursory outlines of subproductions begin to be generated, but only in this anticipatory context.

Thus, *24EH*'s repeated constructions outstrip the usual direct composing that still comprises most combinativity at this stage. Her constructions go beyond directly adding objects to each other to compose, for example, a stack. She begins to generate indirect or branching procedures, that is, subconstructions or subroutines. Step 1 by *24EH* constitutes a minimal subroutine that generates a subcomposition. This subcomposition anticipates part of the composition into which it is assembled in step 2.

A second subroutine is already a bit more elaborate and comprises steps 6–9. It consists of coordinate substitution and replacement as a subproduction within the composition. This involves self-regulatory correction of a classificatory feature of the composition. After stacking a block on top of the three rings in step 5, *24EH* notices that one ring is left unstacked. Instead of directly stacking the last ring on top of the block, she alters or corrects her construction. She anticipates her correction by: (a) moving the last ring over to the stack; (b) removing the top block; (c) substituting the last ring so that all four rings are stacked together; and finally, (d) replacing the same block before adding the two other remaining blocks to complete her reconstruction.

Repeating compositions indicates that infants' reproductions of their own constructions extend to relatively elaborate and complex self-generated protosyntactic routines. In comparison with infants' self-generated routines, imitation of modeled routines, while beginning to develop, is relatively primitive. For instance, while subject *24YK* reproduces the modeled vocalization ("Hop, hop") and compositional product (aligned columns) by the experimenter with fidelity, she does not imitate the modeled "hopping" mapping; she simply moves her object over to the others. One possibility is that *24YK* is too young to grasp the modeled intermodal correspondence between the mapping and the representational vocalization.

Protosyntactic routines, as we have just seen, expand in two major ways at this stage. The scope of the routines are extended to exact reproductions by infants of their own complex and long compositional structures. The most complex performance at this stage, that by *24EH*, includes all eight objects as elements. It is constructed three times in a row, and it always takes the same vertical form of one block, four rings, and three blocks.

Protosyntactic routines are also expanded by introducing subconstructions that are sometimes coupled with self-regulation (i.e., correcting and planning). Infants already interrupt their routines without disrupting them at earlier stages, as we have seen. But now infants begin to be able to interrupt the overall routines they are generating in order to construct subroutines in the service of properly executing their overall composition. This may include correcting any mistakes they have made in constructing their protosyntactic routines; sometimes this correction is expressed verbally but elliptically by exclamations such as "No!" While these protosyntactic routines are generally marked by planning, anticipation is increasingly clear when infants reproduce their routines exactly and when they verbally indicate their intentions by comments such as "Do dat again."

These routines are infant's own creations. They make no reference to and are apparently unrelated to conventional routines or systems of syntactic construction. Other routines are conventional or semiconventional and involve playful symbolization. For instance, subject 24EH brushes, slides, and taps her hair with a traingular column while looking at this in the one-way mirror and saying "I brush my hair." A little later she watches herself repeatedly bite the triangular column, smiles, puts the column to her mother's mouth, and says "Apple."

Three additional advances mark protosyntactic routines. One is increasing substitution of arbitrary for realistic objects (e.g., columns are used by 24EH as pretend instruments and food). Such pretense begins to be extended to verbal substitutions. For instance, different names ("boat" and "two crackers") are given to red triangular columns in succession by subject 24SH as she slides them around. Both involve substituting playful names for the pretense objects in the place of an actual name of the object that 24SH knows since she later calls some columns "blocks." This entails varying the substitute names from an initial symbolic transformation ("boat") to a second symbolic transformation ("two crackers"). Thus, the symbolic transformations include the rudiments of second-order verbal substitutions.

Such playful substitution may be fairly extended. For instance, 24EJ says "Ducks," both as he places a cross ring on an overturned cup and as he picks up a spoon. Then he emits related strings of "Quack, quack" as he slides the spoon toward and along an edge of a receptacle, slides the spoon up the side of the receptacle, slides the spoon up the side of the overturned cup, and finally moves ("flies") the spoon in the air. Both arbitrary and realistic objects are used as playful substitutes for the same objects (e.g., both a cross ring and a spoon are used by 24EJ to stand for "Ducks"). Additionally, arbitrary objects are used as substitutes for the object of the play as well as for the subject of the play (e.g., subject 24WW brushes the top of a square column with a brush and subject 24SH [see page 332] uses a spoon to eat from a two column stack treated as an ice cream cone).

On the surface at least, symbolic substitution has been extended from one-to-one mappings to one-to-many mappings in three ways. First, one object may be different things (e.g., 24SH uses a column as both a boat and a cracker). Second, two different objects may be the same thing (e.g., 24EJ uses a ring and a spoon as ducks). Third, one object may be "plural" things (e.g., 24EJ pretends that a single ring and a single spoon are each "Ducks").

A second advance marking protosyntactic routines is more full verbal symbolization of the playful pretense (e.g., 24EH declares "I brush my hair"). Occasionally, infants' conventional routines are accompanied by verbal questions that involve other persons in their playful routines. For instance, 24LM repeatedly dips a spoon in a cup, holds the spoon to her mother's lips, and says "Want some more?" or "Want more?"

A third, important advance is that extended protosyntactic routines are progressively informed by operations and functions:

4.	RH *beats Doll on top of Car,* *then Plate*
5.	LH *picks D up from P*
6.	RH *picks up P and rotates P* *around on top of D held by LH,* *as looks at experimenter*
7.	*looks at P held by RH and D* *held by LH*
8.	RH *puts P down, LH puts head* *of D on P, then lays D down on* *P*

      S: "Doll is hurt . . . lie down."

                    (24SH, pages 6 and 7)

13.5.	LH *rubs Doll 2 against Doll 1* *held by RH*
13.5.	RH *rubs D1 against D2 held by* *LH*

      S: "Hi, how are you today?
            I'm just fine."

                    (24SH, page 12)

9.5.	RH *places and holds Doll 4* *upright inside Rectangular Ring* *2*
9.5.	LH *places and holds Doll 1* *upright inside Rectangular Ring* *1*
11.	RH *rotates D4 inside RR2 so* *that D4 faces right, as LH holds* *D1 inside RR1*
12.	BH *release dolls inside rings*
13.	RH *rotates D4 inside RR2 so D4* *faces self*
14.	RH *places Doll 3 upright inside* *Rectangular Ring 3*
15.	RH *slides Rectangular Ring 4 to* *left and about 1/2 inch in front* *of Doll 2*
16.	RH *places D2 upright inside RR4*
17.	BH *grasp and lift RR4 slightly,* *and BH knock D2 flat and out of* *RR4 as releases from RR4*

      S: "Boat. In boat."

      (M: "In boat?")
      S: "Yes."

      S: "He in boat. Sailing in
            boat." (sing-songy)

19.	RH lifts and places D2 upright inside RR4 held by LH	S:	"Fall down. Hurt itself."
20.5.	LH releases from RR4 and grasps D2		
20.5.	RH rotates D2	S:	"Hurt itself."
22.5.	LH releases D2		
22.5.	RH continues to rotate D2 as moves D2 about 3/4 inch to right		
22.5a.	bottom of D2 pushes RR4 to right a little		
24.	RH touches RR4 for a moment, as RH holds D2		
25.	RH releases D2 upright inside RR4 with D2's face oriented away from self		
26.	LH grasps and rotates head of D1 so D1's face is oriented away from self		
27.	LH rotates D4 around a bit and D4 falls flat inside RR2		
27a.	D4 displaces RR2		
28.	LH lays D1 flat inside RR1	S:	"Go to bed."
28a.	D1 displaces RR1		
29.	RH lies D2 flat in RR4 and LH touches D2 for a moment		
30.	RH lies D3 flat in RR3		(24EH, pages 68 and 69)

The first *24SH* routine is marked by substitution (Lines 4 and 5), while the second *24SH* routine is marked by reciprocity. Both routines by *24SH* are accompanied by linguistic symbolization of second-order semantic relations. For instance, "Doll is hurt . . . lie down" encodes the consequences of the results of *24SH*'s pretend causal routines. The result of beating the doll on a car and a plate is that the doll is hurt and, as a consequence, lies down on a plate (which most likely is a symbolic substitute for a bed). Still missing is any verbal symbolization by causatives (such as "so") of the causal relation between the result and the consequence.

Playful substitution readily incorporates one-to-many symbolic correspondences. Rectangular rings are used by *24EH* to stand for both a boat and a bed. Present and relatively arbitrary objects are now often used to stand for nonpresent and familiar objects.

Spatial and causal dependency relations are verbally symbolized by both infants. At its most sophisticated level during this stage, second-order causal and spatial transitive dependencies are constructed in action and are expressed linguistically by *24EH*:

1. A doll is placed upright in a rectangular ring (Lines 15 and 16). The present spatial relation of doll in ring is represented by the locative phrase, "He in boat." The additional nonpresent pretense of sailing embellishes the relation between doll and ring to include causal as well as spatial dependencies. These are represented by both a causative and a locative, "Sailing in boat."
2. The rectangular ring is raised slightly (perhaps in an attempt to pretend to sail it) and the doll is knocked over (Lines 17 and 18). The first-order dependency—resultant causal and spatial transformation—is represented by a transitive causative phrase ("Hurt itself") that is repeated twice (Lines 19 and 20.5).

Linguistic expressions, then, may symbolize nonpresent, that is, not-here (e.g., sailing) as well as present (e.g., insertion) dependency relations. The social implications are enhanced symbolic communication. For instance, subject 24EJ follows up her loss of a car that she dropped to the floor with the causative phrases "Car fall. Go?," as she watches it. The experimenter retrieves the car for her. In a second instance, 24EJ follows up pretending to drop a spoon (but actually hides it under the tabletop in her hand) with the combined causative–locative phrase "Fall down," coupled with looking at the experimenter. Both experimenter and mother laugh at 24EJ's game-like joke construction.

Finally, it should not be overlooked that symbolic and playful pretense rarely applies to more than single small sets of two objects or referents. This constraint still applies to the most sophisticated routines produced. For instance, subject 24EH generates causal dependencies that are reciprocal. Two dolls are pushed, pressed, wiggled, and rotated against each other, face to face, to produce symmetrical and transitive causal dependencies. Each object is used simultaneously as a causal means and as a causal end. The expressions (growling "Roww!" and exclaiming "Eat him up!" two times) accompanying the routine are of an asymmetrical and transitive causal dependency. Thus, while causal transitive dependency is expressed, its potential symmetrical feature is not marked linguistically. We have already observed that reciprocal dependency may already be marked linguistically (in the 24SH protocol fragment, page 12, Lines 13.5, presented on page 283, subject 24SH imputes an asymmetric polite dialogue to the two dolls that he manipulates symmetrically against each other).

Linguistic expressions still usually symbolize referents that are present in subjects' transactions. Reference to the nonpresent increases, however. For instance, subject 24SG repeatedly refers to nonpresent "Toothpaste," while tactually and visually inspecting the toothbrush she is holding. She addresses her verbalization to the experimenter. This verbalization is coupled with nonverbal communication. She looks at the experimenter and the cabinet as if she is requesting that the experimenter get some toothpaste for her from the cabinet where the rest of the test objects are kept.

Gestural and verbal reference have become fully directive as well as demonstrative. For instance, subject 24DM points continuously at an object while looking back and forth between it and the tester. On the other hand, subject 24SH says "Bring me the boys," as she waits for the tester to extend a male doll. Then she takes it and places it between two cross rings instead of with the other dolls.

The developmental trend is toward coordinating gestural and verbal reference into conventional communication:

7.5.	RH index finger points toward something on experimenter's side of table	S:	"That one." (quietly)
7.5.	LH holds Blue Cylinder 1 tilted upright on table for a moment (experimenter takes BC1 from subject and places it with Blue Triangular Column 1)		
9.	simultaneous with experimenter's action, subject leans forward and RH index finger continues to point while looking toward what she's pointing at (experimenter extends Red Triangular Column 2 to subject)	S: (E:	"That one." (quietly) "This one?")
10.	looks at RTC2 for a moment, as BH extend toward object		
11.	immediately BH withdraw from RTC2 and RH index finger points toward object as looking toward object (experimenter shakes RTC2 in air a little)	S:	"No. (shakes head 'no') Dat one."
12.	looks at RTC2 as BH extend toward RTC2		
13.	LH grasps RTC2 as looks up at experimenter		
14.	LH immediately releases RTC2		
14a.	RTC2 falls to table		
15.	looks quickly at RTC2		
16.	looks toward objects she's spotted as RH index finger points toward them (simultaneous with Line 16, experimenter places RTC2 with RTC1; experimenter extends Blue Triangular Column 2 toward subject)	S: (E:	"Right deh. Dat one." "this one.")
17.5.	LH touches BTC2		

17.5.	*RH points toward objects on*	S:	*"Ri hea." (quietly)*
	experimenter's side, as looks first toward		
	them and then at		
	experimenter		(24SG, page 26)

Referring to and denoting not immediately present but desired objects is now possible. To that extent, reference and denotation are becoming detached symbolic processes or mappings of mappings. Moreover, these two fundamental symbolic processes are becoming differentiated and integrated syntactic forms. Infants convey in expressive forms the objects to which they are referring at the same time as they refer to the objects they are denoting.

Two additional features, present in some of these constructions, are worth comment. The first is that symbol and concept formation need not be coextensive. Subject *24SH* asks for "the boys." Yet, when the experimenter gives him a boy doll, *24SH* groups it with the rings, not with the other boy doll.

The second feature is that symbol formation is progressively regulating social interactions. Infants begin to enter into dialogues with others about the objects of their reference and expression. These dialogues include repeatedly correcting another person by providing positive, negative, and combinations of positive and negative symbolic feedback (e.g., the 24SG protocol fragment). Infants' social regulative symbolization complements their self-regulative symbolization considered on page 279–282.

Symbols in words are still not as advanced as symbols in actions in some important respects. Symbols in actions are marked by extended and complex protosyntactical routines. They also begin to be marked by embedded subconstructions or clause-like subroutines.

Symbols in words have already caught up with and outstripped symbols in action in other important respects. These include the formation of rudimentary comparative phrases. One form is marked by one-to-one correspondence. However, it is produced by only one subject (*24LM*) who generates quantitative and predicate two-to-two correspondence between two sets (see protocol fragment on page 326). His symbolic expressions of his constructions are more primitive. Each phrase is limited to naming one object only; he does not pluralize. However, he correctly qualifies the referent object by its color name. In this way, *24LM* produces the necessary conditions for producing syntactic forms of comparatives. Indeed, he gets as close as using both a connective phrase ("And the yellow one.") and several demonstrative phrases (e.g., "That's the red one.") to potentially mark comparing the different colors of the two objects. One other subject (*24EH*) does not construct corresponding sets, but marks her verbal denotation of the objects with the appropriate plural form and the connective "and." The subject remarks "boys and cars" as the experimenter presents a task comprising two male dolls and two cars.

This infant is also the only subject to produce another protosyntactic form of denoting comparative class (predicate) properties. After stacking all four rings by chained similarity (i.e., yellow rectangle, green rectangle, green cross, yellow cross), subject 24EH expresses the similarity by a nondifferentiated comparative phrase, "There—like this." Shifting criteria of resemblance, characteristic of figural or graphic collections (Inhelder & Piaget, 1964), is matched by global verbal denotation of resemblance.

Symbolizing comparative class properties is outstripped by subjects' symbolization of comparative seriation (ordinal) properties. The range of symbolic forms is already relatively wide. Thus, rudimentary pluralization (in the Stern and Werner sense defined on page 116) begins to be used by subject 24EH in order to mark ordinal addition and one-to-one correspondence between symbolic units and units of objects. The same semiconventional phrase is applied to different exemplars of different classes. Subject 24EH couples "and one truck," "and one truck there," and "and one truck," with consecutive placing while grasping individual rings of different shapes and colors. In this way, the phrases constitute only precursors of pluralization since true pluralization requires consistent application to different exemplars of the same class.

Primitive scalars also begin to be generated to mark ordinal or vectorial relations (see Sinclair, 1967). Subject 24LM is most typical. He uses "more," which is the qualifier usually employed by infants at this stage when expressing ordinal adding (e.g., "More combs." and "More toys.") In this regard, the scalar form produced by another subject, 24EJ, is unusually advanced:

16.	LH brings VW1 to subject's face, while RH holds VW4	S:	"Cars."
17.	LH places VW1 on table, while RH holds VW4	S:	"Faster car."
32.	looks at Racer 4 held by RH on table, while LH holds Racer 2 on table	S:	"Two faster cars."
33.	RH pushes R4 and LH pushes R2, up and back, slowly, 2 times		
44.	LH raises VW1 and points to Racer 3 on table, while RH holds VW2	S:	"This faster."
48.	RH pushes VW3 slightly, while LH holds VW1	S:	"Not faster."
49.	RH releases VW3, while LH holds VW1	S:	"S-s-s-s- . . . ."
61.	looks at VW1 held by RH, while LH holds R2		
62.	looks at R2 held by LH, while RH holds VW1	S:	"Faster car."
	(experimenter points to Racer 1)	(E:	"What's that?")
63.	LH places R2 on table, while RH holds VW1	S:	"Faster . . .car!"

64. *LH picks up R1, while RH holds VW1*	
68. *LH pushes R1 forward on table, while RH holds VW1*	(E: *"Where are the other faster cars?"*)
69. *LH releases R1, while RH holds VW1*	
70. *LH picks up R3, while RH holds VW1*	S: *"There!"*
	(24EJ, pages 11–14)

However primitively, *24EJ* is already beginning to denote one-way vectorial or functional properties of motion when speed is scaled ordinally. Moreover, he negates (Line 48) as well as affirms (e.g., Line 44) ordinal speed.

Comparatives that represent numerical order also just begin to be produced by a few infants. For instance, subject *24SH* hands two cylinders to the experimenter and says "Two blocks" as she gives the second cylinder to the experimenter. The most advanced form, generated only once by one subject (*24EJ*, Line 33 above), coordinates scalar and numerical comparatives to produce the phrase "Two faster cars."

Less advanced, but more typical of this stage, is rudimentary counting. Their semiconventional manifestations apply to small numbers only and are generated rarely. To illustrate, subject *24SH* consecutively pushes Car 1, Car 2, Car 3, Car 2, Car 4 on the table. Then he pushes Car 1 off the table while saying "Two cars . . . Three cars." Very small number counting begins to be marked by the conventional feature of iterative sequencing. But even counting very small numbers is not yet marked by the conventional feature of one-to-one correspondence between numerals (symbols) and units (referents), as is evident in *24SH*'s counting. This correspondence does not develop until at least the third or fourth year of childhood (e.g., Gelman & Gallistel, 1978; Saxe, 1977).

Anything more than very small number counting is primitive. At most, the numbers "1, 2, 3" are marked by both minimal conventional sequencing and partial one-to-one correspondence. In effect, comparative numbering again applies to small empirical number series only:

8.	*RH holds Car 3 in Yellow Circular Ring*	S: *"1, 2 . . . "*
9.	*RH takes C3 out of YCR*	
10.	*RH puts C3 in YCR*	S: *"3, 10 . . . "*
11.	*RH picks up Car 5 and holds C5 end in RCR*	S: *"10, 4, 10, 8."*
12.	*RH takes C5 out of RCR*	
13.	*LH picks up Red Car while RH holds C5*	S: *"10, 8, 2, 14."*
14.	*LH puts RC in RCR, while RH holds C5*	S: *"10, 2 . . . "*
15.	*RH puts C5 in RCR, parallel to and touching RC*	S: *". . . and 'nother one . . ."*

16. *RH picks up Car 4 and puts C4*   S: *". . . and 'nother one . . ."*
     in YCR next to C3
16a. *C4 tips*
17. *RH adjusts C4*
18. *RH picks up Car 2 and tries to*   S: *". . . and 'nother."*
     wedge that into YCR as well   (24LM, pages 55 and 56)

This is the most advanced performance found. Still, conventional sequencing does not exceed the number "3" and correspondence is not maintained beyond matching the numbers "1, 2" with two units. Yet they may be expected to constitute global antecedents for developmental articulation. This hypothesis is plausible if global, and even very small number semiconventional, counting actually expresses minimal iterative addition. This hypothesis is consistent with 24LM's performance that begins with semiconventional counting (Lines 8 and 9), degenerates into global counting (Lines 9–14), and culminates in minimal pluralization (Lines 15–18).

II. Object Identity as a Class Element

Comparative inspection of individual objects is still used on occasion to determine the identity of objects, particularly when they are not familiar. But the primary function of comparative inspection is shifting to determining the identity of objects as elements of sets. If preservation of objects is still at issue for infants at this stage, it is becoming a minor issue. Representational identity or class membership is becoming the main issue with which infants grapple when they investigate and determine new things about objects and their properties.

Infants' cognizance of objects as class elements is manifest in two important ways. The first extends comparative inverse inspection, by now a well-established procedure for determining the intensive part–whole structure of objects, that has its developmental roots at least as early as age six months (Langer, 1980). Now infants also clearly link up this procedure with the intensive operation of selecting objects by their predicate properties that has been developing in parallel.

Consider the most advanced coordinate form of comparing and selecting objects found at this stage:

4. *RH picks up and brings Mirror 2 to face, while LH holds Mirror 1*
5. *RH rotates M2 over and back and over, looking (front-back-front) at M2, while*
    LH holds M1
6. *LH rotates M1 over and back and over, looking (front-back-front) at M1, while*
    RH holds M2
7. *RH rotates M2 over and back and over, looking at M2, while LH holds M1*
8. *LH rotates M1 over and back and over, looking at M1, while RH holds M2*

9. *RH rotates M2 over and back and over, looking at M2, while LH holds M1*
10. *LH rotates M1 over and back and over, looking at M1, while RH holds M2*
11. *RH puts M2 down face up on table, while LH holds M1* (24LM, page 7)

Several features mark infants' determination of objects as class elements. Inverse visiomotor transformations may be applied to all the objects with which infants transact. In this production, of which only the beginnings are reproduced here, the transformations are reproductive. Precisely the same visiomotor inverse transforms (i.e., looking at front-back-front rotations) of each object are generated consecutively by *24LM*. The reproductive transforms are applied to six of the eleven objects presented to *24LM*. They are applied first to all objects of one class with multiple membership (i.e., four mirrors). Then they are applied to two of the three singular objects presented (i.e., one spoon and one brush). They are not applied to the third singular object (i.e., one car), nor are they applied to any of the members of the other class presented (i.e., four dolls). Reproductive inverse transforms, then, are coupled with selecting all the mirrors followed by the spoon and the brush. Flat instrument-like objects only are included for consideration. All doll objects are ignored. Moreover, inclusion begins first with class consistent selection of all the mirrors.

The second way in which infants determine the representational identity of objects as elements of a class also consists in coordinating two cognitive constructions. These too, as we have seen, have been developing in parallel since at least age six months. They consist of (a) composing objects with each other to form collections and (b) comparing the properties of objects. The result of interweaving these two constructions is overt manifestation of cognitive conflict. The conflict begins to happen at this stage when infants are faced with objects having partially disjoint and partially conjoint properties in the intersective (anomalous) class condition (see Langer, 1980, page 420). To illustrate, infants are presented with an alignment of two red spoons and an alignment of two yellow cylinders and given a yellow spoon:

1. *LH picks Yellow Spoon up* (M: *"Ooo, look at that."*)
2. *looks at Red Spoons 1 and 2, as RH touches YS held by LH*
3. *BH hold YS, as looks at YS*
4.5. *RH reaches close to Yellow Cylinder 2 such that RH is posed in loose grasp gesture about 1 1/2 inches in front of YC2, as looks at Yellow Cylinders 1 and 2*
6.3. *RH reaches very quickly toward YC1 and then RH withdraws toward self*
6.7. *LH extends YS toward experimenter,* (S: *"I don't want . . ."*)
     as looks at RS 1 and 2

8.5.   *LH withdraws YS toward self in air*
       to left
8.5.   *RH picks up RS 1 and 2, looking at*   S: *(mumbles something)*
       RS 1 and 2   (24SG, pages 79 and 80)

Visual and tactual comparison of the anomalous yellow spoon with the red
spoons (Lines 2 and 3, 6.7–8.5) and the yellow cylinders (Lines 4.5–6.3) is
interwoven with virtual but nonactualized grasping of the yellow cylinders (Lines
4.5–6.3), holding the anomalous yellow spoon above the red spoons (second
line, 4.5), and holding the red spoons in the other hand (second line, 8.5).
When objects begin to be compared for both their similar and different properties, then there is no fully satisfactory way of composing the anomalous object
with either class with which it partially intersects. The result is interrupted
nonconsummated composing. The cognitive conflict may even begin to be
expressed symbolically (Line 6.7).

III. Consolidating the Circular Aspects of Causality

Two basic forms of causal constructions continue to be exercised at this stage.
One form consists of anticipating and observing effects that are dependent upon
causes. To illustrate, the trajectory of a toy racer that the experimenter rolls
across the table toward subject 24WW is anticipated precisely by his left hand.
His prediction enables him to catch the racer as it approaches him. Coordinate
anticipation and catching compensates for the trajectory of the racer. Thereby, it
negates the racer's movement by an exactly reciprocal blocking movement. The
causal end is anticipated by the causal means, as well as dependent upon it.

The structure of this first-order function is so well-developed that 24WW
follows it up by pushing the racer right back to the experimenter accompanied by
onomatopoeic vocalization ("Boom"). As a whole, the causal interaction is also
marked by precise cooperative, asymmetrical correspondence. The subject reproduces, in a reciprocal form, the performance of the experimenter.

A second basic form of causality involves constructing, replicating, and observing effects that are directly dependent upon causes. The causal variables are
still only manipulated semisystematically at this stage. Thus, they remain semivariables. Yet, they are progressively systematic:

6–9a.   *RH picks up Clover Ring 4, places CR4 in mouth, body leans over left arm of*
         chair, mouth releases CR4, and watches as CR4 falls to floor
10–17a. *LH releases Clover Ring 2 over left arm of chair such that CR2 falls to floor,*
         as watches
18–20a. *replication of Lines 6–9a with Rectangular Ring 3*
21–24a. *replication with Rectangular Ring 2*

The routine is kept constant throughout the series of causal replications (i.e., releasing one object at a time over the chair's left arm). Only one minor modification occurs when the left hand, instead of the mouth, releases an object. The objects are varied. All objects are dropped to the floor and all the resultant effects are monitored by 24LM. These causal constructions still constitute first-order functions because 24LM drops the objects in the order CR4, CR3, RR2, RR1, CR1, CR3, RR4. He shifts classes three times when only one shift is necessary to test the differential effect of dropping clover and rectangular rings. Thus, all factors are almost kept constant while object class is varied semisystematically and the results are observed.

First-order causal experimenting with dropping objects by the mouth is elaborated into repeated second-order causal functions by this infant on a later task. Releasing objects one at a time by the mouth is altered to spitting out objects by the mouth. Additionally, and significantly, each object is projected toward a target that the infant constructs prior to "bombing" it (nonrelevant transactions are omitted from the protocol fragment)

4. *RH places and centers Square Column 1 upright on Cylinder 1 which is upright on table*

16. *mouth spits out Cylinder 2 at SC1/C1 stack*

16a, C2 hits stack and knocks SC1 off C1

17. *RH picks up C2*

18. *LH picks up SC1, turns SC1 upright, and uprights SC1 back on C1, while RH holds C2 (experimenter replaces Square Column 2 upright to right)*

19. *RH puts C2 in mouth which spits C2 out at SC1/C1 stack*

19. *C2 lands upright against C1 part of stack*   S: (laughs)

21. *looks at this*

24. *RH uprights SC2 on table near SC1*

25. *LH picks up C1 and pluts C1 in mouth which spits out C1 at objects*

25a. *C1 lands on its side beyond other
objects on table
(experimenter returns C1 upright)*

26. *RH picks up C1 and puts C1 in
mouth which spits out C1 at
objects on table*

26a. *C1 hits C2 and they both roll
away*

27. *RH picks up SC2 and puts SC2
in mouth which spits out SC2 at
objects on table*

27a. *SC2 lands in front of and near
C1 and C2 (which experimenter
has replaced upright)*   (24LM, pages 71–73)

While the causal constructions and replications are still only semisystematic, they are already marked by significant coordination of independent and dependent semivariables. Both are constructed by the subject. Both "missiles" and "targets" are thereby determined or controlled by the subject. Indeed, the independent semivariable is a function of the dependent semivariable.

Causes or means are increasingly structured as functions of effects or ends, as well as effects being structured as dependent functions of causes. This structuring extends infants' cognition to the circular aspect of causality in which effects may feedback to causes and causes feedforward to effects. This circular (cybernetic) aspect of causality is a control feature of second-order functions. It incorporates both feedforward and feedback causal features in coordinate constructions. Its developmental roots are to be found in infants' covariations of means and ends (or causes and effects) that we have seen is the hallmark of second-order functions and which, as we have also seen, originates at stage 5.

First-order physical functions are linear constructions. Goals depend upon means such that effects are direct functions of causes. Means depend upon goals such that causes are direct functions of effects. A fundamental structural development that produces second-order physical functions is the transformation of linear into circular dependencies. Goals depend upon means and means depend upon goals. Effects are direct functions of causes and causes are direct functions of effects. The transformational mechanism, then, consists of the developing proportional-like coordination (by covariation) of first-order functions to each other.

A feature of second-order functions that parallels second-order operations is that they may each include related application to two compositions. When the functions are causal, then the contemporaneous compositions constructed by infants are invariably mixed by predicate properties; and each composition comprises two objects only: one agent and one patient. Thus, the agent and patient objects are usually different. Motion is typically transmitted from the agent to the patient object via propulsion, but entrainment is also increasingly possible (see the protocol fragment by the same subject, 24LM, on page 326):

54.5.   RH pushes Block 1 forward into Brush 2
54.5a. Br2 moves forward
54.5.   LH pushes Block 2 forward into Brush 1
54.5a. Br1 moves forward
56.5.   RH pushes B1 up and to right
56.5a. Br2 is pushed to right
56.5.   LH pushes B2 up and to left
56.5b. Br1 is pushed to left   (24LM, page 15)

Second-order causal functions are becoming progressively well-regulated. The same infant, 24LM, generates all types analyzed (i.e., targeting, propelling, and entraining). Each type is repeated, often many times. Each type may be systematically varied (e.g., from pushing forward to pushing diagonally or pulling back). Some are accompanied by symbolic expressions that are still primitive when compared to the causal functions that they accompany. The symbolic accompaniments consist of onomatopoetic expressions of event features (e.g., "Wee, wee, wee.") or some but not all object names (i.e., "Red car." and "And the yellow one.").

As expected, first-order causal functions with single compositions include more objects than in each of the paired sets to which second-order functions apply. While causality with two sets is still limited to two objects each, causality with single sets extends to as many as five members (e.g., in a causal chain). First-order causal transmission with single sets.are well-regulated. They are often repeated in succession. Second-order functions may also apply to single sets when they coordinate two types of causal transmission (e.g., entrainment and propulsion) within a single construction:

55.   RH pushes Yellow Hexagonal Column 1 inside Blue Circular Ring 1 which pushes BCR1 into Blue Circular Ring 2
55a.   BCR1 pushes BCR2 to left   (24WW, page 81)

Single instruments begin to be used as two differentiated but integrated, simultaneous causal means in such second-order functions.

Two instruments also just begin to be coordinated by reciprocity into a single regulated causal means at this stage. To begin with, the execution is already persistent, if primitive. It is marked by continuous feedback since infants already take into account variations in the effects that they are producing using two instruments at the same time. It is also marked by feedforward since infants modify their causal manipulations of the two instruments in order to achieve the effects they are trying to produce.

These second-order functions, then, are marked by continuous and ongoing retroactive and anticipatory regulation. They are planned covarying dependency relations that now extend to relatively complex and delicate causal phenomena. Only a small sample of one subject's efforts follows:

72.5.   RH *slides Green Cross Ring tilted to left till RH is to immediate right of Green Hexagonal Column*

72.5a.   GCR *contacts GHC*

72.5.   LH *slides Yellow Cross Ring approximately upright to right till LH wrist is to immediate left of GHC*

74.   *lifts GHC between GCR held by RH and LH wrist, while LH holds YCR and places GHC tilted upright on table*

75.   RH *removes GCR from GHC, while LH wrist gently pushes GHC to full upright position*

76.5.   RH *lowers GCR flat on top of GHC, touching fingers through GCR on top of GHC*

76.5a.   GHC *tips and wobbles*

76.5.   LH *holds YCR in air to left of GHC*

78.   RH *holds GCR on GHC tilted upright, while LH touches YCR to side of GCR*

79.5.   LH *holds YCR immediately behind GHC (it may touch GHC, but only barely)*

79.5.   RH *holds GCR on GHC, with fingers going through GCR and touching GHC*

79.5a.   GHC *continues to wobble*

81.   RH *removes GCR from GHC*

81a.   GHC *falls flat*   (24SG, pages 14 and 15)

53.   RH *holding Spoon 2 by handle pushes S2 such that bowl end of S2 is under Cylinder 1, pushing C1 against LH, while LH holds Spoon 1*

53a.   C1 *lifts partly off table all the while touching LH*

54.   RH *lifts S2 under C1 and lowers S2 again, while LH holds S1*

54a.   S2 *pushes C1 about 2 inches toward subject*

55.   LH *lifts S1 off table and withdraws S1 to the back of C1, while RH holds S2 under C1:*

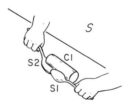

56.6.   RH *pushes S2 against back of C1 toward subject*

56.5a.   C1 *moves closer to subject*

56.5.   LH *pushes S1 against back of C1 toward subject*

56.5a.   S1 *pushes C1 to right a bit rotating C1 such that opposite (left) end rests on S2 as in Line 55:*

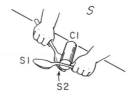

58.5. *RH lifts S2 out from under C1*
58.5. *LH lifts S1*
  60. *LH immediately lowers handle part of S1 onto C1 and pushes handle against C1, also pushing LH thumb against C1, while RH holds S2*
60a. *C1 moves about 2 inches away from subject*
61.5. *RH raises S2 several inches in air*
61.5. *LH lifts C1 along with S1 such that S1 is on top of C1*
63.5. *RH lowers S2 a few inches in air*
63.5. *LH raises S1/C1 a little higher (above S2)*
  65. *LH lowers S1/C1 on top of S2 (holding S1 on top of C1, so it doesn't contact S2) held by RH*
65a. *S1/C1 slowly pushes S2 down onto table*   (24SG, pages 73 and 74)

Two differentiated causal sources are rudimentarily coordinated in order to produce a single synchronous effect. Structuring this coordination is only possible if infants simultaneously covary two causal functions with each other such that they summate effectively. Infants are thereby structuring advanced second-order causal functions, if only barely as we have just seen.

Reciprocal causal coordination of two objects, which originates at least as early as stage 1 at age 6 months (Langer, 1980, pages 63 and 64), are progressively regulated. For instance, two objects are first oriented so that they face each other and then they are crashed into each other repeatedly by subject 24EH. First, the two objects are identical cars; then a doll is substituted for one of the cars. Again, accompanying symbolic expressions are limited to an event feature "Eeeeeeeee-crash") or an object ("Fire truck").

Regulated usage of an object as a causal instrument permits infants to construct progressively differentiated and increasingly extended experimenting. It permits observation and replication of different results with both the same patient object and with varying patient objects while holding the agent object constant. Thus, experimental semivariables are becoming progressively differentiated. Fine distinctions in causal results become increasingly possible when, for instance, a doll is used to bang consecutively on three different parts of the same plate.

Determining which dependent relations are possible and which are impossible is progressively coordinated with negation. Infants continuously and repetitively try to negate what are usually still impossible balancing conditions for them, such as stacking four columns upright on each other. When successful, this is typically followed immediately by negating the constructed possible dependency relation, such as by knocking over the stack or by pulling out the bottom object in the stack.

Infants also continuously replicate possible balancing conditions together with their causal negation. Replacement conditions these experiments. For instance, the same stack is constructed four times in succession by subject 24SE. Each time it is destroyed in precisely the same way. The results are thereby consistently reproduced by 24SE.

IV. Expanding Possible Spatial Constructions

Spatial coregulation progressively marks possible balancing conditions in which infants repeatedly attempt to overcome physical resistances. The dependency relations infants construct are difficult to achieve at this stage because they require coordinating spatial functions (here, one object supporting another) with movement functions (here, vehicular transmission of one object by another). The goal is a balanced trajectory (e.g., subject 24SG using a spoon to transport a cylinder across the table).

Fully executing such second-order spatial functions successfully is still beyond infants' capacities at this stage. Overcoming the physical resistances due to the shapes of the objects and gravity requires more mature sensorimotor coordination than most children have developed by this age. Still, the task they are setting themselves is clear, if not yet fully achievable. The repeated aim is to use an object as a vehicle with which to both balance and displace another object.

Progressive spatial coregulation marks infants' containing operations. Infants become increasingly adept at rotating receptacles so that they will fit spatially into each other. This includes nesting receptacles in each other, as well as inverting receptacles to form covers. All the while infants contain objects in these receptacles. Sometimes this includes containing objects in two receptacles, particularly when the receptacles are nested in each other. The preferred mode, however, remains to contain objects in one container only.

Containing is transformed by infants into intermediary functions for transmitting contained objects. In typical fashion, one subject (24SE) begins by putting all eight objects together in Receptacle 2 such that the objects are mixed. When his attention is drawn to the other, empty Receptacle 1 by the experimenter, 24SE transfers all eight objects by hand from Receptacle 2 to Receptacle 1 such that the objects are still mixed. When the experimenter models partial sorting into the two receptacles by unmixed predicate properties, 24SE follows up by containing objects such that each receptacle contains three objects that are again mixed by predicate properties. Then he transfers the three objects from Receptacle 2 to Receptacle 1 by using Receptacle 2 as a vehicle. He continues to use

Receptacle 2 as a vehicle to transmit first the remaining car and then the remaining spoon to Receptacle 1. The final result is that all the objects are once again contained together in one receptacle and are mixed by predicate properties. In this way containment is used as a means for immediate transitive transmission of contained objects as well as an end (to contain objects in a container).

Constructing subroutines (see Section I) begins to be extended to containing. To illustrate, after almost nesting Receptacle 3 in Receptacle 2, subject 24EJ inverts the nesting by embedding Receptacle 2 in Receptacle 3. He complicates his routine by intercollating a subconstruction, consisting of placing a cross ring in Receptacle 3, between preparing for and completing nesting the two receptacles in each other. Thus 24EJ interrupts embedding or containing receptacles in each other by containing an object in a receptacle. He continues by containing six objects in the topmost, Receptacle 2. Finally, he inverts a third receptacle with which he attempts to cover Receptacle 2.

Progressive coregulation is marked in this performance by detour behavior. When he meets resistance, 24EJ does not continue the direct trajectory of his behavior, as younger infants do. Rather, he takes into account the spatial obstacle by changing the direction of his behavior in order to avert the obstacle and, as a result, is successful in overcoming its resistance.

Both containers and contained objects can now be coordinated by correspondence as long as the number of elements are small. Thus, for instance, three forms of spatial correspondence are generated by subject 24GA. First, she places brushes face up in two receptacles such that their orientations match. Second, she aligns three objects in one receptacle such that their positions match. Third, she aligns both receptacles such that their positions match, twice in a row.

These three forms of spatial correspondence are coordinate with each other. They overlap in time. The orientations of the objects and the receptacles are matched: they are all placed upright. Also, the position of the objects and the receptacles are matched: they are all placed in parallel alignment. As a result, contained objects are coordinated with their containers by correspondence. Once constructed, this linkage is negated by a single transformation. Subject 24GA re-aligns the two receptacles' long edges in parallel. Throughout, then, spatial congruence relations are constructed by various correspondences.

V. Possible and Impossible Correspondences

Continuous correspondence of spatial dependency involving differentiated balancing of objects takes many forms at this stage, We have already considered one in which infants try to make taller and taller stacks of objects, negate them by knocking over the stack, try to reconstruct the stacks, and so on. Another form that originates as early as age 18 months consists of uprighting rings on one of their edges. Usually, though not always, uprighting rings is still too difficult for infants to achieve without help from another person. Infants often express non-verbal requests for help when having difficulty uprighting or stacking objects (e.g., by pointing).

Sometimes infants initiate cooperative correspondence for playful purposes, not because they need help. Finely differentiated and coordinated spatial dependency relations often mark these cooperative correspondences. These may be initiated by infants (e.g., banging rings on the index finger of one of their own hands, then their mothers', and finally the experimenter's). Infants are also increasingly willing to engage in cooperative correspondences initiated by others, but they remain selective (irrelevant transactions are omitted):

32. *LH taps Triangular Column 2 horizontally on table, not really looking at TC2, 2 times (experimenter taps Brush 1, 2 times)*
33. *RH taps Cylinder almost vertically on table, 2 times*
36.5. *RH taps C rapidly and vertically on table*
36.5. *LH taps TC2 rapidly and vertically on table, as looks back and forth between C and TC2*
38. *RH and LH tap C and TC2 alternatingly, continuing rapid pace and looking back and forth between C and TC2 (experimenter taps Triangular Column 1 on table)*
39. *RH and LH tap C and TC2 simultaneously and in time with experimenter's tapping*
40. *pauses and looks at experimenter and TC1, as RH and LH hold C and TC2 on the table, semi-upright (experimenter pauses, picks up B1, holds B1 vertically, taps TC1 and B1 simultaneously, and then pauses again; subject does not move)*
41. *LH index rubs on table edge while holding TC2 and RH holds C, as watches experimenter*
42. *RH moves C and LH moves TC2 to lap and holds them there*

(24GA, pages 62 and 63)

These discrete correspondences are precise. They are initiated by 24GA. At first 24GA is willing to engage in cooperative correspondence, but eventually she stops participating.

Most discrete correspondences, including those executed with precision, are not generated in a cooperative context. For instance, subject 24SH aligns four cars such that they all face in the same direction. The cars are matched precisely in their spatial orientation. The self-generated task 24SH has set for himself consists of forming discrete correspondence between all and only the cars. Similarly, precision of execution marks continuous correspondence as well. For instance, subject 24DM slides a rectangular column until it hits the seam created by two tables pushed together. Then he slides the column up and down the seam a few times. After this he turns the column over on its narrow side and slides it up and down the seam a few times.

The outstanding development at this stage in additive and subtractive mappings is that they begin to be coordinated with expressive symbolization and playful pretense. For instance, subject 24YK generates a continuous increasing then decreasing ⟨ pretend push, push, push/ throw, attempt push, push ⟩ bidirectional series. The increase but not the decrease is accompanied by onomatopoetic vocalization ("Brmm . . .").

15

Progressively Stable Compositions
of Compositions

Combining objects into compositions and recompositions progresses markedly. Constructing combinations in isolation virtually disappears. While most are still generated consecutively, two contemporaneous compositions and recompositions constitute from one-fifth to one-third of infants' combinations, depending upon the condition. Thus, infants increasingly construct elements with which to structure second-order functions and operations.

Most combinations are stabile constructions by this stage. They are also increasingly constructed by infants directly manipulating most of the objects included in the combinations. In addition, they are increasingly constructed in the vertical as well as the horizontal dimension. Moreover, their membership increases. Two-fifths of infants' combinations comprise three or four objects. Still, it should not be overlooked that even by age 24 months most of infants' combinations do not exceed two objects. Combinations comprising as many as five to eight objects are an increasing but very small proportion of infants' constructions.

The "regressive" features of combining found at age 21 months are temporary. They are all reversed by age 24 months. Thus, rate of production and proportion of recomposition increases at age 24 months while generation of two- object combinations and mobiles–stabiles decreases.

I. Increases in Composing and Recomposing

After a small, partial, and temporary decrease at age 21 months, the range of mean composing productivity at age 24 months rises again. The range is 5.43–

9.97 compositions per minute at age 24 months (Table 15.1, Row 3); 3.44–7.19 at age 21 months (Table 11.1); and 5.34–9.60 at age 18 months (Table 7.1). The increase from ages 21 to 24 months is significant in two of the seven test conditions. Composing productivity increases significantly in the eight-object multiplicative condition (Mann–Whitney $U = 11$, $p = .027$) which is the only condition in which productivity decreases significantly from ages 18 to 21 months (see pages 228 and 229). The four-object disjoint condition is the only other one in which composing productivity increases from ages 21 to 24 months (Mann–Whitney $U = 14$, $p = .032$). Compositional productivity, then, is basically invariant from ages 12 to 24 months, with a small temporary dip at age 21 months. The means rarely differ much by either class or number of objects conditions.

Fewer compositions are generated in the eight- than in the four-object conditions (Table 15.1, Row 3, Columns 2–7); this difference is statistically significant (Mann–Whitney $U = 16$, $p = .052$). On the other hand, we shall see that compositions include more objects in the eight-object conditions (Table 15.6). Obviously, it takes longer to construct compositions that include more objects. This accounts, at least in part, for the decrease in productivity per unit of time.

Duration of individual compositions increases from ages 12 to 24 months, even though productivity rate remains constant, with the exception already noted. Some of the factors at play are the same at age 24 months as they are at earlier ages. These factors are (a) the preservation of one composition while constructing another, (b) the construction of compositions that are used as the props for protosymbolic and playful routines, and (c) the construction of compositions that include more objects. A new factor that increases the duration of some compositions at age 24 months is the introduction of subconstructions within routines (as seen, for instance, in the 24EH routine presented on pages 280 and 281).

After a small, partial, and temporary decrease at age 21 months, the proportion of recomposing to composing at age 24 months returns to the level to which it progresses by age 18 months. More than half of infants' combinations are the result of recomposing in the four-object conditions. The proportions are 60% at age 18 months (Table 7.2), 51% at age 21 months (Table 11.2), and 57% at age 24 months (Table 15.2, Rows 1–5, Columns 1–3). Any variations with age, then, are insignificant.

The temporary decrease in proportion of recompositions that infants generate occurs in the eight-object conditions. The proportions are 57% at age 18 months (Table 7.2), 35% at age 21 months (Table 11.2), and 48% at age 24 months (Table 15.2, Rows 1–5, Columns 4–6). The increase from ages 21 to 24 months is significant (Mann–Whitney $U = 42$, $p < .05$) as is the decrease from ages 18 to 21 months (see page 229). Thus, the dip at age 21 months is effectively reversed by age 24 months.

TABLE 15.1
Spontaneous Phase I: Mean Composing Productivity at Age 24 Months

	Control	Additive		Multiplicative		Disjoint	
	Four-object 1	Four-object 2	Eight-object 3	Four-object 4	Eight-object 5	Four-object 6	Eight-object 7
1. Compositions	13.00[a]	11.90[b]	9.83	15.00	16.00	11.64[c]	9.70[b]
2. Time	2 min 17 sec[d]	1 min 28 sec[a]	1 min 59 sec[e]	2 min 28 sec[e]	2 min 26 sec[e]	1 min 21 sec[e]	2 min 0 sec[e]
3. Productivity per minute	5.71[d]	8.26[a]	5.43[e]	7.39[e]	7.94[e]	9.97[e]	5.75[e]

Class conditions

[a]N = 6 subjects.
[b]N = 10 subjects.
[c]N = 11 subjects.
[d]N = 3 subjects.
[e]N = 8 subjects.

TABLE 15.2
Spontaneous Phase I: Mean Frequency of Composing and Recomposing at Age 24 Months

		Four-object condition			Eight-object condition		
		Thematic 1	*Variant* 2	*% Variant* 3	*Thematic* 4	*Variant* 5	*% Variant* 6
1.	Semicontrol[a]	5.83	7.17	55			
2.	Additive[b]	5.00	6.90	58	5.08	4.75	48
3.	Multiplicative	6.42	8.58	57	8.33	7.67	48
4.	Disjoint[c,b]	5.18	6.45	55	4.90	4.80	49
5.	All conditions	5.62	7.33	57	6.18	5.79	48

[a]N = 6 subjects.
[b]N = 10 subjects in the additive four-object condition and in the disjoint eight object condition.
[c]N = 11 subjects in the disjoint four-object condition.

Most remarkable is the almost total absence of variation. Perfect quantitative uniformity characterizes infants' recomposing operations at age 24 months. The range of recomposing is between 55% and 58% in the four-object conditions (Table 15.2, Rows 1–4, Column 3), and between 48% and 49% in the eight-object conditions (Table 15.2, Rows 1–4, Column 6).

II. Progressively Flexible Provoked Composing and Recomposing

Provoked composing and recomposing progresses significantly. Containing two compositions becomes increasingly flexible. Sorting two compositions becomes substantial, begins to be recursive, and is marked by self-correction. It already tends to produce quantitative equivalence between two sets coupled with unmixed predication. Only modeling two pre-existing sets does not yet provoke substantial composing with both sets by infants at this stage. Instead, infants systematically integrate the two sets into one larger composition.

All subjects continue to compose by containing objects in receptacles (during procedural phase II). All subjects tested contain all objects in the four-object additive condition (Table 15.3); but this is already the case by age 18 months (Table 7.3). Five out of nine subjects contain all the objects in the eight-object condition (Table 15.3). This number is less than at age 21 months when 10 out of 12 subjects contain all objects (Table 11.3).

There is no change with age in the pattern of containing objects in two receptacles. As at age 21 months, half of the subjects generate two overlapping sets by containment in two receptacles (Table 15.3). They do so in both the four- and eight-object conditions.

TABLE 15.3
Provoked Phase II: Frequency of Containing All or
Some Objects at Age 24 Months

Receptacles	Four-object additive		Eight-object disjoint	
	All	Some	All	Some
One	3	0	2	3
Two	3	0	3	1

Containing still usually involves adding objects one-by-one. But adding more objects than one at a time is not unusual. Three subjects contain two objects at a time, two subjects contain three and four objects at a time, and one subject even contains eight objects at a time. However, when more than one object is added at a time, containment is global and placements are haphazard. Thus, these compositions usually take the form of a heap. While often still global, one-by-one adding is more likely to produce articulate containment. For instance, after containing two brushes and two mirrors in one container, subject 24SH carefully rearranges the two mirrors so that their placements are matched in parallel alignment.

Seven contemporaneous compositions by containment in two receptacles are generated (Table 15.3). Four are constructed by a recursive procedure (as defined on page 148). Of these four recursive constructions, three are generated in the eight-object condition where there are sufficient numbers of elements to make recursion a plausible procedure. Three of the four subjects who generate contemporaneous containment in the eight-object condition, then, use recursion. To the extent that contemporaneous containment is generated at this age, it is marked by flexible switching two or more times between receptacles:

1. *RH places Doll 3 in Receptacle 2, while LH holds Rectangular Ring 3*
2. *RH takes RR3 from LH and lowers RR3 into Receptacle 2 without releasing RR3*
3. *RH raises RR3 out of R2 and touches RR3 into Receptacle 1*
4. *RH raises RR3 out of Receptacle 1*
5. *LH picks up and places Doll 2 in Receptacle 1, while RH holds RR3*
6. *RH places RR3 in Receptacle 1*
7. *RH picks up Doll 1 and extends D1 toward Receptacle 1*
8. *RH moves D1 to right and places D1 in Receptacle 2*
9. *RH picks up Doll 4 (experimenter removes D2 from Receptacle 1 and holds D2 to subject)*
10. *RH places D4 in Receptacle 2, as looks quickly at D2 held by experimenter*
11.5. *RH picks up Rectangular Ring 2 and places RR2 in Receptacle 1*
11.5. *LH picks up Rectangular Ring 4 and places RR4 in Receptacle 1*

13.　*RH picks up Rectangular Ring 1 and places RR1 in Receptacle 1*
14.　*RH takes D2 from experimenter and places D2 in Receptacle 1*

(24EH, pages 70 and 71)

The final product comprises two contained compositions with unequal (5, 3) numbers of elements. The order in which objects are contained is mixed by predicate properties while their enclosure is almost unmixed by predicate properties, except that 24EH insists upon containing Doll 2 with the rectangular rings. She replaces it (Line 14) even after the experimenter removes Doll 2 from Receptacle 1 in which 24EH had placed it with the rectangular rings (Line 5).

Flexible contemporaneous composing by containment begins to be marked by three other features as well as recursion at this stage. Flexibility is marked by subconstructions. For instance, 24EH tries out Rectangular Ring 3 in both receptacles and then holds it outside of both receptacles (Lines 2–5) while containing Doll 2 in Receptacle 1 (Line 5). After this, she contains Rectangular Ring 3 in Receptacle 1 such that it is grouped with Doll 2 (Line 6).

Flexibility is marked by trying out different possible containments before final placements. This is an early form of self-correction. We have just noted one instance of this in 24EH' performance (Lines 2–6). Immediately after this, 24EH goes through the same self-corrective procedure with another doll (Lines 7 and 8). This repetition indicates that self-correction is becoming regulated.

In contrast, infants at this stage do not cooperate with and profit from the attempts by others to correct objects that are misplaced by predicate properties. This behavior has already been pointed out in the 24EH containment, and it is true for all the other subjects as well. For instance, not only does another subject (24SG) not profit from the experimenter's corrections, which she nevertheless carefully monitors, but she actively negates them. Thus, she replaces a mirror in the wrong receptacle while verbally "correcting" the experimenter by saying "No, dat one dere."

Flexibility also just begins to be marked by infants reorganizing their initial composing by containment. Hence, two infants recombine two contained compositions into one. To illustrate, subject 24TK generates two contained sets by recursion, then she unites the two compositions into one by taking out the two objects she had just contained in Receptacle 2 and adding them to the two objects already placed in Receptacle 1 to form a single four-object set.

One infant (24SE) transforms one contained set into another singular contained set. First she contains all objects, consisting of four brushes and four cars, in one receptacle in a mixed order. Then she takes them all out and contains them in the other receptacle, again in a mixed order. Not only is this a rare form of reorganization at this stage, but it is also primitive, that is, undifferentiated and unarticulated. The procedure used to contain objects is global and undifferentiated.

Insufficient data was generated on contemporaneous containment in two re-

TABLE 15.4
Provoked Phase II: Extensive by Intensive Properties of Objects in Two Receptacles at Age 24 Months

	Predicate properties					
	Order			Enclosure		
	Unmixed	*Partly unmixed*	*Mixed*	*Unmixed*	*Partly unmixed*	*Mixed*
Quantitative properties	1	2	3	4	5	6
Four-object additive:[a]						
1. Equal sets	0		1	0		1
2. Unequal sets	2		0	0		2
Eight-object disjoint:[b]						
3. Equal sets	0	1	0	0	1	0
4. Unequal sets	1	1	1	1	1	1

[a]$N = 6$ subjects.
[b]$N = 9$ subjects.

ceptacles to determine any developments at this age in their quantitative and predicate properties (Table 15.4). At most, the data support the impression of a heightened concern by infants to group one set by identical or similar predicate properties. Typically this is the first composition infants contain. Then they usually disregard the predicate properties of the objects comprising the second composition they contain.

For the first time, provoked spatial sorting by predicate properties (initiated by experimental modeling and correcting during test phase II) results in substantial contemporaneous composing (Table 15.5). Sorting objects into two sets is provoked at least as frequently as sorting objects into single sets only. Moreover,

TABLE 15.5
Provoked Phase II: Frequency of 24-Month-Old Subjects Sorting All or Some of the Objects into One or Two Compositions

	Condition			
	Four-object additive		*Eight-object multiplicative*	
	All	*Some*	*All*	*Some*
One set	1	4	0	4
Two sets	4	1	3	2

7 out of 9 subjects sort objects into two sets in either the additive or multiplicative condition and 2 out of 9 subjects sort objects into two sets in both the additive and the multiplicative conditions.

Infants rarely sort all eight objects when composing single sets. Only 1 out of 5 subjects sorts all eight objects into a single set in the additive condition (Table 15.5). No subject sorts eight objects into one composition in the multiplicative condition.

Infants use two procedures to sort objects into single sets. Most frequently infants override the experimenter's modeled sorting into two sets by combining the two sets. They repeatedly transform the two sets that the experimenter keeps trying to construct into a single set. Correlatively, the experimenter's modeled sorting of objects by predicate properties into unmixed sets is usually transformed by the subjects into single sets that are mixed by predicate properties. Only one exception was found. This infant also produces a single composition. However, both the order of composing and the enclosure property of the single configuration are unmixed by predicate properties.

The other, less frequent, procedure used by infants to sort objects into single compositions consists of adding objects to one of the two sets that the experimenter is constructing while disregarding the other set. Usually this procedure also entails composing different objects within a single set so that the predication is mixed. Two exceptions occur in which subjects sort only identical or similar objects within single sets. They either refuse to transact with the different objects or they discard them. The only objects they include in their single sets are unmixed by predicate properties.

While assisted sorting into single sets rarely includes all eight objects, assisted sorting into two sets is usually exhaustive. Four out of 5 subjects sort all eight objects into two compositions in the additive condition (Table 15.5). Three out of 5 subjects sort all eight objects into two sets in the multiplicate condition.

Assisted sorting into two sets usually results in unmixed or partially unmixed sets. Too much should not be made of this finding since the experimenter initiates the unmixed sorting and partially or totally corrects mixed sorting by the subjects. More significant are self-corrections generated by three infants.

One infant (24YK) stacks all four rectangular rings together; this includes 24YK overriding the experimenter's placement of the initial ring. Then 24YK collects all four racers in his left hand; again, this includes 24YK overriding the experimenter's placement of the initial racer. In the course of constructing the set of racers, 24YK mistakenly picks up a rectangular ring but he immediately discards the ring while looking at a racer. Then he picks up the ring he discarded and places it with the other three rings.

Overriding the experimenter's initial spatial separation of two different objects is typical. A second infant (24SE) is unusual in this regard since he maintains the experimenter's initial placements as the location for his subsequent grouping of two unmixed sets. This includes self-correction of one misplacement by substitution.

The most extensive self-correction is generated by a third subject (*24LM*) who is also unusual because he maintains the experimenter's initial placements. Three times *24LM* misplaces objects in terms of their predicate properties and three times he corrects himself by substitution. Once *24LM* even pauses and holds an object before placing it correctly instead of immediately grouping it, as though he might be considering where it belongs. His final product is two simultaneous complete sets of (4,4) objects.

Self-correction, then, begins to be coupled with recursive assisted sorting. Like recursive containing, recursive sorting entails repeated alternation in order to construct two sets. Unlike recursive containing, which originates as early as stage 6 at age 18 months, assisted recursive sorting does not originate until this stage at age 24 months.

Assisted recursive sorting is generated by one-third of the subjects. Generating it twice in a row is exceptional and is produced by one subject only (*24SE*). He first sorts objects recursively when presented with an array in which four of the eight objects are presorted into two unmixed classes. He immediately repeats assisted recursive sorting on a second trial when presented with a minimal array in which only two of the eight objects are presorted into two unmixed singular classes.

The predicate properties of *24SE*'s assisted recursive sorting is typical. On the one hand, the order in which he classifies the objects is mixed by predicate features since he alternates between the two classes in his constructive procedure. On the other hand, the enclosures into which he classifies the objects are unmixed by predicate features. The final constructed products are two separately and consistently classed compositions.

Assisted spatial sorting, whether it results in unmixed predication or not, is not accompanied by descriptive verbal marking. Only one exception is generated once by one infant (*24SG*) naming a ring "Circle." But *24SG*'s naming is an immediate reproduction of his mother's verbal interference (in violation of the instruction given to all parents before the testing session). Thus, verbal expression is not yet spontaneously produced by infants at this age when they are engaged in provoked sorting by predicate properties. Its single manifestation is a direct reproduction of verbal modeling.

With few exceptions, sorting into two compositions is marked by numerical equivalence between two sets. For instance, one infant constructs two piles of four identical objects each. In this way, he generates quantitative equivalence and spatial correspondence between the two sets as well as unmixed predicate sorting. The necessary conditions are thereby generated for coordinating extensive with intensive relations. These conditions augment the coordination begun at the previous stage when infants compose two sets by containment (page 231).

While provoked containing and sorting results in substantial contemporaneous composing, provoked matching does not. (Provoked matching during phase II testing is initiated by the experimenter presenting two alignments presorted by predicate properties plus two to four extra objects belonging to the two classes modeled in the alignments.) Most infants (a) add objects to one presorted set only, or (b) combine the two presorted sets and add objects to form one set only. Two infants add objects to both presorted sets; one infant does not add objects to either set.

Unmixed predication is typically preserved. For instance, when presented with an alignment of two dolls and an alignment of two cars plus an extra doll and an extra car, subject 24EH slides the three cars together into a bunch and ignores the dolls. The result is matching by predicate properties for one set while ignoring the other. Four out of five subjects generate such unmixed single set matching in the control conditions. Five out of seven subjects generate unmixed or partially unmixed single set matching in the four-object disjoint condition. Two other subjects added objects to both presorted sets in this condition. One subject generates unmixed matching and the other partially unmixed matching.

When combining two alignments into a single composition and adding extra objects, infants begin to generate figural or graphic collections (Inhelder & Piaget, 1964):

2.   *RH places Cross Ring 6 halfway between Cross Rings 3 and 4 but closer to self, while LH holds Cross Ring 5*

3.   *LH places CR5 between Cross Rings 1 and 2 but closer to experimenter*

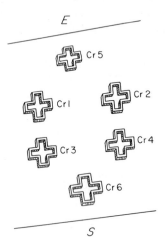

4.   *looks at experimenter, RH points at the array, looks at experimenter again*
                                                    (24TK, pages 2 and 3)

The product of 24TK adding two extra objects is one symmetrical configuration of all six objects. She transforms the two presented alignments into one set by her symmetrical addition of the two extra objects. In this way she groups all the objects together, as they should be in terms of their identical predicate properties, instead of the two presented sets. This is a deliberate violation or control condition that is part of the experimental test. When finished, 24TK refers the experimenter to her symmetrical and unifying transformation of the experimenter's construction (Line 4). This nonverbal communication seems directed toward making the experimenter cognizant of the corrective transformation.

Many other forms of reforming presorted compositions are also introduced by infants at this stage. These reformations become progressively differentiated and articulate. Systematic reorganizations are generated by more than one-half of the infants though, typically, they are still restricted to reconstructing two presented compositions into one. Since they often involve operational transformations, such as correspondence and commutativity, they are analyzed in detail in the appropriate sections of Chapter 16.

Here we will limit ourselves to pointing out two general features of the systematic reformations that begin to be generated at this stage. Recomposing plus adding objects is used by infants to transform two unmixed presorted sets presented to them into three mixed subsets of a single composition. For instance, subject 24SE produces a graphic three-part arrangement of dolls lying down in rectangular rings. While mixed by predicate properties, the three parts are matched by spatial arrangement and quantitative equivalence. The arrangement, moreover, suggests that it has playful symbolic meaning for 24SE, although he manifests no further signs of this. Instead, he consecutively pushes each part away from himself and to the experimenter.

Sometimes, recomposing is more clearly marked by playful symbolization. To illustrate, a pre-existent alignment of two cylinders is transformed into a stack of three cylinders by subject 24SH which he calls "Ice cream." Then he takes away a spoon from the other pre-existent alignment and uses it to pretend to eat from the stack. He repeats the theme of this playful routine two more times.

III. Re-Establishing the Gradual Increase in Size of Compositions

The increase in producing two-object compositions at age 21 months is transient. By age 24 months, two-object compositions are no longer in the majority in the eight-object conditions (Table 15.6, Rows 4–10) although they still are the mode. Two-object compositions remain in the majority in the four-object condi-

TABLE 15.6
Spontaneous Phase I: Mean Frequency and Percentage of Compositional Extent at Age 24 Months

	Semicontrol[a]		Additive[b]		Multiplicative		Disjoint[b,c]		Total	
	$\bar{X}$ 1	% 2	$\bar{X}$ 3	% 4	$\bar{X}$ 5	% 6	$\bar{X}$ 7	% 8	$\bar{X}$ 9	% 10
Four-object condition:										
1. Two-object	8.67	67	7.90	66	8.08	54	7.91	68	8.08	62
2. Three-object	1.17	9	1.30	11	1.92	13	2.45	21	1.79	14
3. Four-object	3.17	24	2.70	23	5.00	33	1.27	11	3.08	24
Eight-object condition:										
4. Two-object			3.25	33	8.33	52	4.50	46	5.41	45
5. Three-object			2.42	25	2.92	18	1.60	16	2.35	20
6. Four-object			1.92	20	2.92	18	3.00	31	2.59	22
7. Five-object			0.50	5	1.08	6	0.00	0	0.56	5
8. Six-object			0.50	5	0.25	2	0.10	1	0.29	2
9. Seven-object			0.25	3	0.00	0	0.20	2	0.15	1
10. Eight-object			1.00	10	0.50	3	0.30	3	0.62	5

[a] $N = 6$ subjects.
[b] $N = 10$ subjects in additive four-object and disjoint eight-object condition.
[c] $N = 11$ subjects in disjoint four-object condition.

tions, however (Table 15.6, Rows 1–3). The difference in rate of generating two-object compositions in comparable four-object (Row 1, Columns 4–8) and eight object conditions (Row 4, Columns 4–8) is significant ($N = 12$, $x = 2$, $p = .019$, sign test). This continues a trend found throughout the second year; its probable cause has already been considered (page 233).

The proportion of compositions comprising two-objects only decreases exactly 13% in both the four- and eight-object conditions from ages 21 months (Table 11.5, Rows 1 and 4, respectively) to 24 months (Table 15.6, Rows 1 and 4, respectively). This decrease is significant in both the four-object (Mann–Whitney $U = 39$, $p < .05$) and eight-object conditions (Mann–Whitney $U = 39$, $p < .05$). Thus, the increase in producing two-object compositions from ages 18 to 21 months is completely reversed by age 24 months.

Indeed, the figures on producing two-object compositions are alike at ages 18 (Table 7.5, Rows 1 and 4) and 24 months. The proportions are also alike for rate of producing three- to eight-object compositions at ages 18 (Table 7.5, Rows 2, 3, and 5–10) and 24 months. This means that there is no increase in the size of individual compositions constructed over this 6 month age span. Instead, there are other developments. The most notable is increasing construction of contemporaneous compositions (see Section V). This increase has crucial consequences for structuring second-order operations. In comparison, the consequences of increasing set size are peripheral.

The 13% decrease in producing two-object compositions in the four-object conditions is compensated by equal increases in generating three- and four-object compositions (Table 15.6, Rows 2 and 3). The latter constitute almost four-tenths of infants' combinations in the four-object conditions. But most of these comprise four objects. This is, of course, the biggest combination it is possible to construct in these conditions.

The 13% decrease in producing two-object compositions in the eight-object conditions is compensated by proportionate increases in generating three- to eight-object compositions (Table 15.6, Rows 5–10). The latter constitute 55% of infants' combinations. Most of these are split about evenly between three- and four-object compositions. Still, more than one out of infants' ten combinations comprise an intermediate number of objects, that is, five to eight objects.

While the size of compositions does not increase from ages 18 to 24 months, the operations upon them become progressively complex (as already suggested and detailed in Chapter 16). This trend is made immediately evident by the continuing change during this age period in the proportion of compositions generated by direct transactions with one to eight objects. We have already examined the increasing proportions of compositions generated by directly manipulating more than one object from ages 18 to 21 months (pages 235 and 236). Now we consider the development from ages 21 to 24 months.

The percentages of compositions constructed by manipulating one to four

TABLE 15.7

Spontaneous Phase I: Number of Objects Directly Manipulated by 24-Month-Old Subjects to Produce Composition in All Class Conditions

		Number of objects								
		1	2	3	4	5	6	7	8	Total
Four-object condition:										
1.	Frequency of compositions	130	296	25	54					505
2.	% Compositions	26	59	5	11					101
Eight-object condition:										
3.	Frequency of compositions	109	147	72	60	5	6	0	8	407
4.	% Compositions	27	36	18	15	1	1	0	2	100

objects remains constant in the four-object conditions from ages 21 months (Table 11.6, Row 2) to 24 months (Table 15.7, Row 2). There is also no change in the percentage of compositions generated by manipulating five to eight objects in the eight-object condition from ages 21 to 24 months (Row 4, Columns 5–8, Tables 11.6 and 15.7). Such constructions remain rare.

On the other hand, the percentages of compositions generated by manipulating one and two objects decreases from ages 21 to 24 month in the eight-object conditions (Row 4, Columns 1 and 2, Tables 11.6 and 15.7). Their combined decrease is 14%. This decrease is compensated by a 12% increase in compositions that infants construct by manipulating three and four objects. Together they now comprise one-third of infants' constructions while they only comprised one-fifth of infants' constructions at age 21 months.

The percentage of compositions constructed by directly transacting with three and four objects increases from ages 21 to 24 months in the eight-object, but not the four-object, conditions. They now constitute one-sixth of the compositions in the four-object conditions and one-third of the compositions in the eight-object conditions. The relative difference between four- and eight-object conditions is maintained with increasing age throughout the second year. Thus, the more numerous the number of objects presented and combined, the more numerous the number of objects infants directly manipulate in constructing their compositions.

IV. Predominance of Stabile Production

The proportion of stabile to mobile compositions continues to shift in the direction of producing stabiles. The increase in producing combined mobiles–stabiles in the eight-object conditions at age 21 months is only a temporary change that is reversed by age 24 months. The overall pattern, then, is a predominance of stabiles, a substantial minority of mobiles, and infrequent mobiles–stabiles.

Stabiles are produced almost twice as frequently as mobiles in the four-object conditions (Table 15.8, Rows 4 and 8) but the difference is not significant ($N = 12$, $x = 4$, $p = .194$, sign test). Stabiles are generated more than twice as frequently as mobiles in the eight-object conditions (Table 15.9, Rows 4 and 8). This difference is significant ($N = 10$, $x = 1$, $p = .011$, sign test).

Stabiles constitute roughly six out of every ten combinations generated by infants. This proportion does not vary from the four-object (Table 15.8, Row 4) to the eight-object conditions (Table 15.9, Row 4). Furthermore, the range does not vary. The range is 47–62% in the four-object conditions and 52–69% in the eight-object conditions. This is a developing pattern throughout infancy.

Stabiles are generated ever more frequently. There is a 10% increase in constructing stabiles in the four-object conditions from ages 21 months (Table 11.7, Row 4) to 24 months (Table 15.8, Row 4). This increase with age is significant (Mann–Whitney $U = 42$, $p = .05$). There is a 15% increase in producing stabiles in the eight-object conditions from ages 21 months (Table 11.8, Row 4) to 24 months (Table 15.9, Row 4). This significant increase with age (Mann–Whitney $U = 31$, $p = .01$) reverses the temporary 13% decrease in generating stabiles from ages 18 to 21 months.

Most stabiles continue to be featured by contact between the member elements. The percentages are 67 and 62 in the four- and eight-object conditions, respectively (Tables 15.8 and 15.9, Rows 1). Unlike mobiles, proximity is more likely to mark stabiles. The percentages are 21 and 26 in the four- and eight-object conditions, respectively (Tables 15.8 and 15.9, Rows 2). If we add to this compositions marked by both contact and proximity (Tables 15.8 and 15.9, Rows 3), then we find that one-third of stabile compositions continue to be marked by proximity relations between their member objects.

Mobile production does not change substantially from ages 21 months (Tables 11.7 and 11.8, Row 8) to 24 months, although the rate decreases a bit. Mobiles make up about one-third of infants' combinations in the four-object conditions (Table 15.8, Row 8) and one-fourth of their combinations in the eight-object conditions (Table 15.9, Row 8). While much less frequent than stabile production, mobile production is more variable. The ranges of producing mobiles barely overlap in the four- and eight-object conditions. They range from 10% to 28% in the eight-object conditions and 28% to 41% in the four-object conditions.

Most mobiles, like stabiles, continue to be featured by contact rather than proximity. This feature does not vary with the number of objects presented. Contact marks 76% of mobiles in the four-object conditions (Table 15.8, Row 5) and 79% of mobiles in the eight-object conditions (Table 15.9, Row 5). Proximity marks only 17% of mobiles in the four-object conditions (Table 15.8, Row

TABLE 15.8
Four-Object Conditions, Spontaneous Phase I: Mean Frequency and Percentage of Compositional Features at Age 24 Months

	Class conditions									
	Semicontrol[a]		Additive[b]		Multiplicative		Disjoint[c]		Total	
	X̄ 1	% 2	X̄ 3	% 4	X̄ 5	% 6	X̄ 7	% 8	X̄ 9	% 10
1. Contact stabile	5.00	38	5.10	43	6.08	41	4.09	35	5.10	39
2. Proximity stabile	0.83	6	1.70	14	1.33	9	2.18	19	1.59	12
3. Contact–proximity stabile	0.33	3	0.60	5	1.92	13	0.27	2	0.87	7
4. Total stabile	6.17	47	7.40	62	9.33	62	6.55	56	7.56	58
5. Contact mobile	4.50	35	2.30	19	3.42	23	2.82	24	3.13	24
6. Proximity mobile	0.83	6	0.90	8	0.50	3	0.64	5	0.69	5
7. Contact–proximity mobile	0.00	0	0.40	3	0.33	2	0.27	2	0.28	2
8. Total mobile	5.33	41	3.60	30	4.25	28	3.73	32	4.10	32
9. Mobile–stabile	1.50	12	0.90	8	1.42	9	1.36	12	1.28	10
10. Causal	4.00	31	0.50	4	3.75	25	2.64	23	2.64	20
11. Noncausal	9.00	69	11.40	96	11.25	75	9.00	77	10.31	80
12. Horizontal[d]	4.17	33	4.00	55	3.67	38	4.18	57	3.97	45
13. Vertical[d]	7.17	57	2.60	36	3.42	35	2.64	36	3.56	40
14. Horizontal–vertical[d]	1.17	9	0.70	10	2.58	27	0.45	6	1.28	15

[a] N = 6 subjects.
[b] N = 10 subjects.
[c] N = 11 subjects.
[d] Compositions whose spatial dimensions are ambiguous are not scored. Consequently, the dimensional means summate to less than the compositional means.

TABLE 15.9
Eight-Object Conditions, Spontaneous Phase I: Mean Frequency and Percentage of Compositional Features at Age 24 Months

		Class conditions						
		Additive[a]		Multiplicative		Disjoint[a]		Total	
		X̄ 1	% 2	X̄ 3	% 4	X̄ 5	% 6	X̄ 7	% 8
1.	Contact stabile	4.08	42	6.50	41	3.00	31	4.62	39
2.	Proximity stabile	1.67	17	2.42	15	1.70	18	1.94	16
3.	Contact–proximity stabile	1.00	10	1.17	7	0.30	3	0.85	7
4.	Total stabile	6.75	69	10.08	63	5.00	52	7.41	62
5.	Contact mobile	1.92	20	2.42	15	2.60	27	2.29	19
6.	Proximity mobile	0.42	4	0.58	4	0.00	0	0.35	3
7.	Contact–proximity mobile	0.33	3	0.33	2	0.10	1	0.26	2
8.	Total mobile	2.67	10	3.33	21	2.70	28	2.91	24
9.	Mobile–stabile	0.42	4	2.58	16	2.00	21	1.65	14
10.	Causal	1.25	13	1.58	10	1.70	18	1.50	13
11.	Noncausal	8.58	87	14.42	90	8.00	82	10.47	87
12.	Horizontal[b]	4.25	53	4.83	56	2.40	38	3.91	50
13.	Vertical[b]	2.67	33	3.08	36	3.30	52	3.00	39
14.	Horizontal–vertical[b]	1.08	14	0.75	9	0.70	11	0.85	11

[a]N = 10 subjects.
[b]Compositions whose spatial dimensions are ambiguous are not scored. Consequently, the dimensional means summate to less than the total compositional means.

5) and only 12% of mobiles in the eight-object conditions (Table 15.9, Row 6). Combinations of contact and proximity features mark less than 10% of mobiles in both four- and eight-object conditions (Tables 15.8 and 15.9, Row 7).

Mobile–stabile combinations decrease in frequency in both the four- and eight-object conditions to about one out of every ten combinations produced by infants (Tables 15.8 and 15.9, Row 9). This reverses the temporary increase in their production at age 21 months to about one-fifth of infants' combinations (Tables 11.7 and 11.8, Row 9). Effectively, the rate of generating mobiles–stabiles returns to that established by age 18 months (Tables 7.7 and 7.8, Row 9).

As they are at ages 18 and 21 months, the proportions of mobiles–stabiles continue to be a bit greater in the eight-object (Table 15.9, Row 9) than in the four-object (Table 15.8, Row 9) conditions. Also, the range is much wider in the eight- than in the four-object conditions. It is only 8–12% in the four-object conditions and 4–21% in the eight-object conditions.

Causal compositions remain a small minority of infants' constructions. The rate does not change from ages 21 to 24 months in the eight-object conditions (Table 15.9, Row 10). It increases to one-fifth of infants' productions in the four-object conditions (Table 15.8, Row 10). The low rate of producing causal combinations does not, of course, imply arrest of or regression in the structural development of causal constructions. Quite the contrary, we have already seen that the causal relations become progressively elaborate functions.

The main dimensional development from ages 18 to 24 months is a decrease in the frequency of constructing compositions in the horizontal dimension and a corresponding increase of compositions constructed in the vertical dimension. The distribution is becoming bimodal. This trend began at age 21 months in the four-object conditions and is still most evident in these conditions (Table 15.8, Rows 12 and 13). Although less strong, the same bimodal distribution begins to be established at this age in the eight-object conditions (Table 15.9, Rows 12 and 13). Two-dimensional horizontal–vertical combinations remain infrequent (Tables 15.8 and 15.9, Row 14).

V. Continuing Increase in Contemporaneous Compositions

Isolated compositions become ever rarer by age 24 months. The proportion of compositions that are constructed in isolation from other compositions decreases from 9% at age 21 months (Table 11.9, Row 1) to almost none at age 24 months (Table 15.10, Row 1) in the four-object conditions. Indeed, for the first time isolated compositions are never generated by any of the subjects in one of the conditions, the four-object disjoint condition (Table 15.10, Row 1, Columns 7 and 8). In the eight-object conditions, isolated compositions are also now almost

TABLE 15.10
Spontaneous Phase I: Temporal Relations between Compositions at Age 24 Months

| | Class conditions | | | | | | | | | |
| | Semicontrol[a] | | Additive[b] | | Multiplicative | | Disjoint[c,b] | | Total | |
	X̄	%	X̄	%	X̄	%	X̄	%	X̄	%
Four-object conditions:										
1. Isolate	0.33	3	0.20	2	0.33	2	0.00	0	0.21	2
2. Consecutive	12.67	97	10.10	85	11.25	75	8.18	70	10.28	79
3. Partially overlapping	0.00	0	1.40	12	2.25	15	2.36	20	1.73	13
4. Simultaneous	0.00	0	0.20	2	1.17	8	1.09	9	0.72	6
Eight-object conditions:										
5. Isolate			0.42	4	0.75	5	0.70	7	0.62	5
6. Consecutive			7.42	75	8.92	56	5.60	58	7.41	6
7. Partially overlapping			2.00	20	5.83	36	3.20	33	3.71	3
8. Simultaneous			0.00	0	0.50	3	0.20	2	0.24	2

[a]N = 6 subjects.
[b]N = 10 subjects in the additive four-object condition and in the disjoint eight-object condition.
[c]N = 11 subjects in the disjoint four-object condition.

nonexistent (Table 15.10, Row 5). The effective consequence is that almost all compositions are now generated in some temporal relation to each other.

Consecutively constructed compositions still predominate. In the four-object conditions the proportion increases from 68% at age 21 months (Table 11.9, Row 2) to 79% at age 24 months (Table 15.10, Row 2). In the eight-object conditions, the proportion at age 24 months (Table 15.10, Row 6) is the same as at age 21 months.

Two contemporaneous compositions are constructed ever more frequently. Most of the increase is in partially overlapping combinations since simultaneous constructions are still unusual. Furthermore, all the increase is in the eight-object conditions where contemporaneous compositions now make up a full third of infants' constructions (Table 15.10, Rows 7 and 8). While the proportion of contemporaneous compositions do not increase from ages 21 to 24 months in the four-object conditions, they continue to constitute one-fifth of infants' constructions (Table 15.10, Rows 3 and 4).

Overall, 11 out of 12 subjects generate contemporaneous compositions. One-fifth of the compositions in the four-object conditions and one-third of the compositions in the eight-object conditions are constructed in partial or total temporal overlap. These constructions provide an enlarging pool of constant given elements necessary to progressively develop second-order operations analyzed in Chapter 16. These constructions also provide elements for second-order functions (analyzed in Chapter 14, Section II).

16

Elaborating Relations upon Relations between Paired Compositions

Second-order structuring is extended to all relational and conditional operations. Exchange structures of this power are also progressively coordinated with other operations, functions, and symbolic constructions. The implications are particularly powerful for the development of second-order substitution. This includes the origin of mapping one-to-one correspondences upon substitution as well as major advances in mapping substitution upon correspondence which was initiated at previous stages.

Progress is also made by infants in constructing correspondences and in classifying objects in more than one composition. In general, this stage is marked by significant elaboration of the organization of second-order structures. The products are progressive intensive (predicate) consistency as well as extensive (quantitative) equivalence and ordered nonequivalence.

I. Expanding Exchange between Paired Compositions

Structuring second-order exchanges develops in numerous ways. They are increasingly coordinated with each other, with other operations and functions, and with symbolic constructions. Most significant are developments in second-order substituting that increasingly approaches the form of true substitution with small numbers. This trend has cognitive implications for constructing second-order correspondence and classification.

Replacing is progressively becoming a second-order operation. Almost half of the subjects replace objects within two contemporaneous compositions (Table 16.1). Still, most replacing is within single compositions, thus, first-order. Most first-order replacing, however, includes three- to five-object compositions, whereas at age 21 months they include only three- and four-object compositions (Table 12.1). A few infants only replace objects within somewhat bigger, six- to eight-object compositions. Thus, these remain exceptional constructions as late as the end of the second year.

As many as three or four elements may be replaced within single sets by this stage. The replacements are progressively marked by coregulation of the objects composed together. For instance, subject 24YK stacks four cylinders on top of each other. She marks completion of her composition by sitting down, placing her hands in her lap, smiling, and saying "Bah." She proceeds to decompose the stack by taking off the topmost cylinder, but this inadvertently makes the middle two cylinders topple off the bottom cylinder. Hence, she systematically replaces the three objects that have fallen off the stack. This includes adjusting cylinders on top of each other so that they will be well-aligned with each other and not fall off. The product is recomposition of a four-object stack by replacing three objects.

Replacing is progressively coordinated with other cognitive developments, such as causal experimenting (already considered in Chapter 14). It is also progressively coordinated with playful symbolic routines. To illustrate, subject 24SH constructs compositions and repeated recompositions with three objects by stacking two square columns on each other; touching, tapping, and stroking a spoon on top of the stack; repeatedly putting the spoon in and out of his mouth, and saying: "Ice cream cone. Good ice cream cone."

The spoon is replaced two times in this playful three-object combination before it results in a disruption by the third replacement in which 24SH strokes the spoon on the topmost cylinder. Immediately, 24SH reconstructs his playful three-object construction. But now this involves replacing two objects (a spoon and a column) instead of one object (a spoon) to produce quantitative equivalence within the three-object set:

$$[(SC1, SC2) \pm S1] \sim [(SC1, SC2) \pm S1] \sim [(SC1, SC2) \pm S1] \sim$$
$$[SC1 \pm (SC2, S1)] \tag{16.1}$$

The changed bracketing leaves the quantity constant; thus replacing becomes increasingly associative.

Second-order replacing is generated by almost half of the infants. Almost all of these, however, consist of exchanges in which subjects replace objects in only one of two compositions that they have constructed in relation to each other.

TABLE 16.1
Number of Subjects Generating Exchange at Age 24 Months

	One composition						Multiple compositions
	3-object	4-object	5-object	6-object	7-object	8-object	
Replace	6	8	6	0	2	1	5
Substitute	7	1	2	0	1	0	7
Commute	7	9	4	1	1	2	5
Coordinate exchanges	4	2	2	0	1	1	4

The most advanced form links spontaneous replacing in one of two compositions with provoked substituting in both (irrelevant intervening transactions are omitted):

20.	*RH places Yellow Car in Yellow Circular Ring held by LH*		
21.	*RH reaches for Red Car across table*	S:	*"Want that car."*
22.	*RH picks up RC and extends RC toward Red Circular Ring*	S:	*"That's the red one."*
23.	*LH index finger points at YC/YCR, while RH holds RC*	S:	*"That's the yellow one!"*
24.	*RH places RC in RCR*	S:	*"Red. Red one."*
25.5.	*RH pushes RC forward which moves RCR forward with RC*		
25.5	*LH pushes YC forward which moves YCR forward with YC*	S:	*"Wee wee wee wee"*
27.	*RH pushes RC which pushes RCR further forward, while LH holds YC*	S:	*"Wee Wee . . ."*
28.	*RH pulls RC back which pulls RCR back, while LH holds YC*	S:	*"Wee."*
29.	*BH release cars*		
29a.	*YC slips onto edge of YCR*		
30.	*LH places YC back in YCR*	S:	*"Wee wee wee."*
32.5.	*repeat of Lines 25.5*	S:	*"Wee wee wee."*
	(E picks up both cars and places RC in YCR and YC in RCR)	(E:	*"Watch this."*)
36.	*LH picks up RC and RH picks up YC*		
37.	*LH places RC in RCR, while RH holds YC*	S:	*"Red car."*
38.	*RH puts YC in YCR*	S:	*"And the yellow one."*
			(24LM, pages 52 and 53)

First 24LM matches the colors of cars to rings so that the two sets are in predicate and quantitative correspondence. Then he matches their spatial placements and movement displacements as well. An accidental consequence is that the Yellow Car slips out of the center of the Yellow Ring. Subject 24LM replaces the Yellow Car in the center of the Yellow Ring. Replacing reconstructs the exact spatial placement, unmixed predication, and quantitative equivalence by one-to-one correspondence.

The experimenter tests this interpretation by a countercondition in which she exchanges the placements of the cars by substitution. This exchange maintains quantitative and spatial but not predicate correspondence. Subject 24LM immediately substitutes the cars back into their original ring positions. He thereby constructs predicate matching by identical colors accompanied by demonstrative and comparative color naming, as well as maintaining quantitative and spatial equivalence. He then goes on (not reproduced here) to construct both spatial and movement correspondence between the two sets as well by exactly reproducing the mappings generated in Lines 25.5–28.

Second-order substituting is generated by more than half of the subjects (Table 16.1). Furthermore, most subjects generate first-order substituting with compositions comprising three objects. This reverses the apparently temporary decrease at age 21 months (Table 12.1). Still, substituting in compositions comprising more than three objects remains exceptional.

Structuring second-order substituting progresses. Three subjects begin to produce quantitative equivalence between two contemporaneous compositions by exchanging elements between two sets. Prior to this stage, elements are substituted within sets only. Still, between set substituting is prefigured at the previous stage in exceptional productions (see pages 246 and 247).

The production of one infant, that of 24LM (considered on page 311), is transitional in this regard. Three times 24LM holds an object to the wrong set and corrects himself by substituting each object in the other set. The deliberative character of 24LM's placements within and exchanges between sets is corroborated by his hesitation before placing one of the objects. The final product is two equivalent (4,4) contemporaneous compositions.

In the process, 24LM also constructs two equivalent (2,2) and (3,3) compositions. The entire sequence constructed by 24LM then constitutes two ordered ⟨2-,3-,4-⟩ element compositions. Such developments at this stage in coseriation, and their coordination with exchange structure, is analyzed further in Section III.

In another sequence already considered (page 326), 24LM generates full-fledged second-order substituting between two contemporaneous compositions. So do two other subjects:

D1	HC1
D2	HC2
D3	HC3
HC4	D4

S

1. *RH picks up Doll 4 and places D4 behind Doll 1*
2. *LH picks up Half Column 4 and transfers HC4 to RH which places HC4 to right of Half Column 1* (24TK, page 12)

1. *RH picks up Square Column 4 and LH picks up Cylinder 4*
2. *LH places C4 so C4 is in line with the other three cylinders, while RH holds SC4*
3. *RH places SC4 so SC4 is in line with the other three square columns* (24SE, page 47)

Let the two sets be labeled X and Y, then X = Y in number of elements. Both infants systematically exchange one element between X and Y. The two infants consecutively substitute one element from set X into set Y and one element from set Y into set X. The product is conservation of quantitative equivalence in the 2 four-element sets so that X and Y remain equal.

This new level of extensive operations is fused with infants' intensive operations. Moreover, it is generated only when infants group objects by their predicate properties into two classes by proximity (between identical elements) and separation (of nonidentical elements). Obviously, intensive operations of classification cannot produce extensive operations of quantification. Intensive operations, however, can stimulate substituting elements between compositions of classes. In turn, substituting may lead to producing quantitative equivalence between compositions.

The procedures used by these infants are now relatively systematic and well-regulated. Their enactments differ, however. Even in the sequence in which he is initially provoked into spatial sorting, 24LM constructs two compositions. His procedure involves alternating back and forth between the two sets, making three initial predicate errors of placement, and comparing the objects so that he can self-correct his predicate errors. In the process, as we have seen, 24LM generates both coseriated extensive (quantitative) equivalence between two compositions and consistent intensive classification of two compositions. The other two infants only rectify countercondition presentations (administered in test phase III). They do not construct the initial two sets. Still, both 24SE and 24TK consecutively substitute single elements between the two sets. This substitution produces intensive identity within two classes. It also preserves extensive equivalence between two sets.

Moreover, 24TK does not simply construct equivalence by second-order substitution. She coordinates it with trying to form quantitative equivalence between the two sets by one-to-one correspondence. Thus, she does not stop after substituting the two misplaced objects for each other, but continues on immediately to integrate the two sets by correspondence:

3. *RH picks up Half Column 3 and places HC3 to right of Half Column 4*
4. *RH picks up Half Column 2 and places HC2 to right of HC3 forming:*

D4				
D1				
D2	HC1	HC4	HC3	HC2
D3				

(24TK, page 12)

The rest of 24TK's reconstruction is directed at standing the dolls on top of the half columns. She doesn't succeed at this only because she cannot get all of the dolls on top without accidentally knocking one or two down. Part of the reason for this is her insistence on using a symmetrical procedure. First she puts a doll on the left end column, then one on the right end column. When she goes to fill in the middle, her hand is too big and she knocks the first two uprighted dolls down.

The initial constructive impetus may have come from intensive (predicate) operations. The final attempt is to form spatial and extensive (quantitative) correspondence within one larger whole that integrates the two preceding compositions. Along the way (Lines 3 and 4) 24TK generates relatively complex successive coordination between different operational relations. Two classes, unmixed in predicate properties and equal in quantitative membership that are initially produced by substitution, are immediately transformed by correspondence into two sets that are still equal in quantitative membership but more ambiguous (or mixed) in predicate relations.

Thus, 24TK sequentially coordinates equivalences upon equivalences. Up to this stage, this coordination has been limited to initial equivalences by correspondences being transformed by subsequent exchanges. Exchanges upon correspondences continue to develop, as we shall see in Section II. The reciprocal form, correspondences upon exchanges, originates at this stage. This form is well illustrated by 24TK's transformations upon transformations. First, she substitutes objects between compositions, producing equivalence between them. Then she places the objects in correspondence, producing secondary equivalences upon the initial equivalence.

Such coordinative constructions greatly expand the structure of second-order operations since the coordinations begin to be constructed in both directions. Infants already begin, at earlier stages, to generate substitutions upon correspondences. Now they also begin to generate correspondences upon substitutions. Both are operations to the second power that produce equivalences upon equivalences.

First-order commuting is generated at substantially the same rate from ages 18 through 24 months. Most of these exchanges still do not exceed commuting five-object compositions; so commuting six- to eight-object compositions remains exceptional (Table 16.1). But the frequency of reversible commuting becomes substantial, and the transformations are progressively well-regulated.

Commuting, including that featured by reversibility, begins to be well-coordinated with other operations. As always, it is often coordinated with correspondence (irrelevant intervening transactions are omitted):

11. *LH picks up Mirror 1 by handle, transfers M1 to RH by handle, and adjusts RH grip on M1 with aid of LH*
12. *RH picks up Mirror 4 by handle while holding M1*
13. *LH takes M4 out of RH by face and puts M4 back in RH so M4 is more parallel to M1 in RH*
14–15. *RH picks up Mirror 3, then Mirror 2 so holding M1, M2, M3, and M4 in RH all face up and parallel*
16. *LH groups 4 mirrors by faces and BH turn 4 mirrors over so that they are held by faces by LH only*
24. *RH takes M1 from LH, holds M1 on table face down and horizontal, turns M1 face up and releases M1*

25. *RH takes M2 out of LH face up and places M2 face up and to right of M1 but not quite touching M1*
26. *RH takes M3 out of LH face up and places M3 face up and to right of M1 and M2*
27. *RH takes M4 out of LH face up and places M4 face up and to right of M3*

(24GA, pages 9 and 10)

Only the initial correspondence and first two commutings by 24GA is reproduced here. In this she forms a spatially corresponding alignment of all and only the mirrors by holding them in parallel with their faces up (Lines 11–15). She commutes this corresponding alignment into a second one by turning all four mirrors over such that she still holds them in parallel but in inverse order and with their faces down. She commutes the second spatially corresponding alignment into a third one by placing all mirrors with their faces up again. All her transformations are well-regulated constructions.

After these initial two well-regulated commutings coordinated with correspondences, 24GA generates four more that are not reproduced in the protocol fragment. She commutes the third spatially corresponding alignment into a fourth one by holding all mirrors in parallel. She commutes the fourth spatially corresponding alignment into a fifth one by inverting all mirrors before giving them to and taking them back from her mother. She commutes the fifth spatially corresponding alignment into a sixth one by inverting all mirrors so that they face down. Finally, she reversibly commutes the sixth spatially corresponding alignment into a seventh one by inverting all mirrors so that they face up.

The sequence of successive recompositions forms the reversible commutative structure,

$$\langle M1,M4,M3,M2\rangle \rightsquigarrow \langle M2,M3,M4,M1\rangle \rightsquigarrow \langle M1,M2,M3,M4\rangle \rightsquigarrow \langle M1,M2,M3,M4\rangle \rightsquigarrow$$
$$\langle M4,M3,M2,M1\rangle \rightsquigarrow \langle M1,M2,M3,M4\rangle \rightsquigarrow \langle M4\ M3,M2,M1\rangle. \quad (16.2)$$

The relations between objects are decreasingly that of transformations and increasingly that of logical constants, since they are formed by collecting objects together. This new relation is therefore represented by a comma between the elements collected that are becoming logical constants.

Second-order commuting is generated by almost one-half of the subjects (Table 16.1), but only one infant conditions it by inverse reversibility. Still, there are other signs of structural progress. All second-order commuting is with two compositions that are quantitatively equal. Furthermore, one infant (24EH) begins to commute as many as four corresponding compositions (analyzed in Section II). For now, let us consider the more typical commuting of two corresponding compositions:

31.7. *RH holds Red and Yellow Cars on table, while LH holds Red and Yellow Circular Rings*

33. *LH places RCR and YCR on the table such that RCR is stacked on YCR as looking at this, while RH holds RC and YC on table*
34. *LH takes RCR off YCR and places RCR to left of YCR, while RH holds RC and YC on table*
35. *LH takes YC from RH and places YC upside down on table, while RH holds RC*
36. *RH places RC upright off to right*
37. *BH takes YC and turn YC upright*
38. *RH takes YC and places YC upright to right of RC*
39. *RH picks up YCR*
40. *LH picks up RCR and transfers RCR to RH turning RCR to be against YCR*
41. *LH adjusts RCR in RH which also holds YCR*
42. *LH picks up RC, then YC, so LH holds RC and YC, while RH holds RCR and YCR*   (24GA, pages 18 and 19)

The two sets are in quantitative two-to-two correspondence. They are also in spatial correspondence, both by being held and by being aligned on the table. Only the elements within each set are commuted.

By commuting correspondences, 24GA produces equivalences upon equivalences. Commuting is within both compositions, never between them. This is typical at this stage. Infants never commute two compositions with each other. Thus, the structure of second-order commuting is more primitive than second-order substituting. The latter, as we have seen, already begins to include substituting elements between as well as within two compositions.

At least one reason for this developmental delay is that substituting between two compositions can be accomplished by minimal exchange. Only one object from each composition need be displaced to change their element relation. In contrast, commuting between two compositions can only be accomplished by maximal exchange. Both compositions must be displaced to change their order relation.

Coordinate exchanges do not increase in overall frequency (Table 16.1). Also, they usually still comprise replacing and commuting which are generated consecutively. Coordinate exchange structures that include substituting remain less frequent. But coordinate exchanges with multiple compositions are now generated by one-third of the subjects.

The constructive procedures used to generate coordinate exchange structures are increasingly complex and regulated:

10. *RH inserts Oval Ring 5 through the middle of the just stacked six rings*
11. *RH takes OR5 out and stacks OR5 on top of the other six stacked rings*
11a. *stack falls over into a pile*
12. *LH picks up OR5 and Clover Ring and transfers OR5 and CR to RH which places OR5 and CR on top of the pile of five rings*
13. *BH picks up and turns the pile of seven rings over, dropping some of the objects onto the table*   (24YM, page 4)

The initial commutative relation within a seven-object composition is gener-ated by 24YM transforming (a) a stable stack of six rings with one ring inserted into them into (b) an unstable stack of seven rings. When the stack tumbles it is immediately and partially reconstructed by replacing two rings to form a pile of seven rings. In turn, this seven-object composition is commuted (unstably) by inverting it. This coordinated structure of commuting followed by replacing followed by commuting generates consecutive quantitative equivalence in a set of seven objects.

Self-correction progressively marks regulated coordinate exchange structures. For instance, commuting is coordinated consecutively with replacing, which in turn, is coordinated consecutively with reversible commuting of a stack of four cylinders by 24SG. In addition to self-monitoring, this coordinated equivalence structure is marked by two important symptoms of progressive self-regulating. First, coregulative adjustment is generated throughout. It serves to preserve the balance between the objects in the stack constructions. Second, predicate rela-tions govern selection and rejection of objects to be stacked by 24SG. This process serves to produce stacks and alignments that comprise (a) one set of cylinders only and (b) two subsets of blue cylinders and red cylinders only.

Regulation just begins to be accompanied by verbal expression of aspects of the regulation by one infant only (24SE). Replacing is coordinated consecutively with commuting an eight-object well-regulated alignment in which he adjusts objects in relation to each other. At one point 24SE verbally marks his regulative efforts by saying "This right." Such expressiveness is still unusual since it is generated by only one infant. More typical are coordinated exchange structures marked by playful pretense coupled with verbal naming such as "Boat" and "Good ice cream."

Coordinate exchanges of one of two contemporaneous compositions, or of two potential subsets of one composition, are generated by at least a third of the subjects (Table 16.1). Typically they involve numerically corresponding two-to-two or three-to-three element compositions. Usually, they are coordinated with other spatial correlations within the compositions. Thus, for instance, subject 24SG coordinates commuting with replacing two objects in a four-object com-position that comprises two corresponding subsets of two objects.

II. Expanding Correspondences between Three and Four Very Small Compositions

Infants are quite preoccupied with constructing correlational structures. Much of their interactions with objects are directed toward generating progressively complex one-to-one correspondences between compositions. They also pro-gressively construct second-order one-to-many correspondences.

Almost all one-to-one correspondences generated at age 21 months are still limited to matching two compositions or subcompositions; and almost all of these include only two objects per unit (Table 12.2). By age 24 months, most subjects generate one-to-one correspondences between two units in which each comprises three or four objects (Table 16.2). Also, almost half of the subjects, 5 out of 12 infants, construct correspondences between three or four compositions or subcompositions.

Only one infant, 24DM, does not generate minimal correspondences between two units of two objects each. But 24DM does generate two corresponding sets, once of three objects each and at another point of four objects each:

9. *RH stacks Rectangular Column 3 flat on Rectangular Column 2, which was previously stacked flat on Rectangular Column 1*
10. *RH makes little adjustments so that RC3/RC2/RC1 are well-aligned (experimenter hands subject Rectangular Column 4)*
11. *RH takes RC4 and gives RC4 to Mother (experimenter places Square Columns 1, 2, 3, and 4 randomly about on the table)*
12. *RH grabs SC1 and SC2 and sets them down in front of self and immediately next to RC3/RC2/RC1 stack*
13. *RH stacks SC1 flat on SC2 (experimenter picks up and holds SC3 to subject)*
14. *RH takes SC3 and stacks SC3 flat on top of SC1/SC2 (mother extends RC4 back to subject)*
15. *RH takes RC4 and begins to stack RC4 on SC3/SC1/SC2, hesitates, and does not stack RC4 on SC3/SC1/SC2*
16. *(instead) RH stacks RC4 flat on RC3/RC2/RC1 (experimenter holds SC4 to subject)*
17. *RH takes SC4 and stacks SC4 flat on SC3/SC1/SC2*

(24DM, pages 15 and 16)

This illustrative construction of two matched stacks of four objects each by 24DM indicates that even though he does not generate any two-to-two equivalence structures during the testing session, it is not for lack of competence to produce corresponding compositions. The level of construction is quite advanced. First, it is marked by coregulative adjusting rectangular columns to each

TABLE 16.2
Number of 24-Month-Old Subjects Generating Matched Compositions and Exchanges on These Correspondences

	Objects in each unit			Exchange operations		
Units	2	3	4	Replace	Substitute	Commute
2	11	7	8	6	2	4
3	4			0	0	0
4	3			1	0	1

other so as to straighten out a stack of three. Second, it is marked by self-correction and substitution. Third, self-correction is part of constructing predicate equivalence within compositions as well as quantitative equivalence between them. Fourth, the two compositions are matched spatially by 24DM stacking both sets of columns horizontally. Fifth, and this we shall return to further in this section, second-order correspondence is marked by alternating construction between the two stacks 24DM is composing. This includes 24DM storing a rectangular column with his mother while stacking three square columns. Finally, the two matched stacks are stabile compositions.

By age 24 months, 79% of the correspondences between compositions generated by infants comprise stabile compositions; only 8% are mobiles; and the remaining 13% are mobile–stabiles. The main shift is from 28% mobiles at age 18 months and 32% mobiles at age 21 months. Moreover, by age 24 months all subjects construct equivalence between compositions by matching two stabiles, as well as any they produce by matching two mobiles or two mobiles–stabiles.

Most correspondences between compositions continue to be class consistent, such that each of the two units are unmixed in their predicate enclosure properties (e.g., 24DM's corresponding stacks). Of the total production, 64% are unmixed, 16% are partially unmixed, and 19% are mixed. The main development is the decrease from 34% mixed enclosure at age 18 months and 32% mixed enclosure at age 21 months.

The proportion of correspondences that match causal mobiles remains small: only 15%. What we have just observed about the predicate properties marking correspondences also begins to apply to those that are causal. Correspondences between causal mobiles are just as likely to be unmixed as mixed in classification. The actual number of causal correspondences produced are small. Thus, while the trend is toward unmixed causal correspondences it is not possible to evaluate the trend statistically.

While no longer exceptional, one-to-one correspondences between three or four sets and subsets are still in the minority (Table 16.2). They are never generated at age 18 months and rarely at age 21 months. Now, three infants generate correspondences between three compositions once only; the fourth does so twice. Two of the infants who generate correspondences between three compositions once also generate correspondences between four compositions once only.

The other infant who generates correspondences between four compositions does not construct correspondences between three compositions. Yet he is the only infant who generates more than one correspondence between four compositions. He does so five times. In apparent preparation for constructing four one-to-one correspondences he selects all four spoons out of the presented random array of spoons and cups. He collects the spoons in his right hand:

10. *LH takes Red Spoon 1 out of RH and puts RS1 in Red Cup 1, leaning over RC1 and looking in at RS1 and RC1*
11. *LH takes Yellow Spoon 1 out of RH*
12. *RH places Red Spoon 2 in front of Red Cup 2, while LH holds YS1*
13. *RH puts Yellow Spoon 2 in Red Cup 2, leaning over RC2 and looking in at YS2 and RC2, while LH holds YS1*
14. *RH takes YS1 back from LH and puts YS1 in Yellow Cup 2, leaning over YC2 and looking at YS1 and YC2*
15. *RH picks up RS2 and leans further over YC2 looking in*
16. *looks to left in direction of Yellow Cup 1, while RH holds RS2*
17. *RH puts RS2 in YC1*   (24GA, page 29)

Three times in a row 24GA decomposes and then recomposes this four-composition correspondence. These three reconstructions are well-regulated. They are not interrupted, as is this initial construction, by any potential errors and self-corrections. The first two reconstructions reproduce with fidelity the predicate distribution of the initial construction. Two compositions are unmixed by color (i.e., a red spoon in a red cup and a yellow spoon in a yellow cup) and mixed by form. Two compositions are mixed (disjoints) by both color and form (i.e., a red spoon in a yellow cup and a yellow spoon in a red cup). The last reconstruction changes the predicate distribution so that all four compositions are unmixed by color (i.e., the colors of the spoons-in-cups are matched) and mixed by form.

Much later in the same task 24GA reproduces his final correspondence with fidelity:

11. *RH starts to put Red Spoon 1 in Red Cup 1 but withdraws RS1 from RC1 and puts RS1 in Red Cup 2*
12. *RH picks up Red Spoon 2 and pauses with RS2 over and directly behind RC2*
13. *RH withdraws RS2 from RC2 and puts RS2 in RC1*
14. *RH picks up Yellow Spoon 2 and puts YS2 in Yellow Cup 2*
15. *RH picks up Yellow Spoon 1 and puts YS1 in Yellow Cup 1* (24GA, page 37)

The first two insertions are marked by hesitation. Still, he constructs four corresponding units that are unmixed by color and mixed by form.

Even though correspondences between three or four units are not yet generated frequently, infants already begin to regulate their constructive procedures:

9. *RH stands Green Square Column upright in middle of Yellow Circular Ring 1 such that GSC and YCR1 do not touch*
10. *RH picks up Yellow Hexagonal Column 1 and touches end of YHC1 to inside edge of Blue Circular Ring 2, in attempt to stand YHC1 upright in BCR2*
11. *RH stands YHC1 upright in BCR2 such that YHC1 and BCR2 do not touch*
12. *RH picks up Yellow Hexagonal Column 2 and taps YHC2 on side of Blue Circular Ring 1*

13. *RH holds YHC2 upright in BCR1 but partially on top of edge of BCR1*
14. *RH tips YHC2 a little such that YHC2 still touches side of BCR1*
15. *RH tips YHC2 90° so that YHC2 lies flat on one edge of BCR1*
15a. *BCR1 is displaced to right*   (24WW, page 87)

In each of the first two insertions, 24WW uprights a column in a ring such that the objects do not touch. This is a difficult achievement which he does not manage in the third insertion.

Two-thirds of the still infrequent correspondences between three and four sets feature spatial dependencies of insertion. Some, like those generated by 24GA, compose spoons in cups; others compose dolls or columns in rings (e.g., 24WW). The remaining one-third feature spatial relations of horizontally (e.g., columns next to brushes) or verticality (e.g., stacks). Thus, objects that permit spatial inserting functions may facilitate infants constructing correspondences between as many as three and four compositions. But correspondences between multiple sets are possible, and infants begin to construct them, whatever the spatial functions between objects.

Stabile composing marks three- and four-set correspondences. Only one construction involves mobile as well as stabile composing. While less frequent than two-unit correspondences, when produced, multi-unit correspondences are more stable than two-unit correspondences.

To the degree that stable construction of multi-unit correspondences develop at this stage, such matches facilitate structuring more advanced part–whole transformations. This includes second-order operations in which multi-unit equivalences serve as constant given elements. Thus, while still rare, this permits expanding the power of second-order structuring (Table 16.2).

Consider, for instance, the 24EH protocol fragment presented on pages 283 and 284. Replacing (Lines 18 and 19) within one of the four matched couples (Lines 9.5–16) is generated as soon as the correspondence is disturbed by 24EH trying to lift one of the matched couples (Line 17). The entire construction and self-regulative rectification is accompanied by elaborate story-like representation. A bit later 24EH generates precursory rudiments of commuting the four compositions by lying down all the dolls in all the rings (Lines 27–30). The initial correlation is thereby transformed into a modified but still one-to-one correspondence that preserves the equivalence relation between four couples. These operational elaborations are accompanied by symbolic elaboration as well (Line 28a).

Corresponding compositions are progressively structured as elements for exchange operations. Replacing within two or more corresponding compositions is generated by half of the subjects at this stage (Table 16.2). The numbers, however, remain constant from age 21 months for substituting and commuting corresponding compositions. Still, when generated, all exchange operations are now also applied to corresponding units that include three and four objects in each composition.

The pattern of relations between bi-univocal (one-to-one) and co-univocal (one-to-many) correlating, set at earlier stages, continues to progress during the present stage. Bi-univocals predominate; the ratio is at least six bi-univocals for every co-univocal generated by 24 month old subjects. Most co-univocals continue to comprise one-to-two or two-to-one correspondences; but one-to-three or -four and three- or four-to-one matching are also generated with some frequency.

Fairly typical is an extensive one-spoon-to-three-cups construction by subject 24LM. Throughout, it is coordinated with reversible substitution and replacement. It is also marked by corrective self-regulations, plus pretend (e.g., mock licking of the spoon) and verbal play (e.g., "Do want some?" and "Want some more?"). A three-rings-to-one-column construction by 24WW is marked by corrective self-regulations and coregulations between objects that are as advanced and complex as any generated at this stage:

37. *RH begins to lift Yellow Circular Ring 1 up and over (previously constructed) Green Square Column standing upright in Yellow Circular Ring 2*

37a. *GSC totters and almost falls*

38. *LH grabs GSC to keep it from falling and lifts GSC off the table as RH holds YCR1 around middle of GSC*

39. *LH places and holds GSC in middle of YCR2 on table as RH releases YCR1 on top of YCR2*

40. *LH transfers GSC to RH as LH tilts GSC into side of YCR1/YCR2*

40a. *YCR2 pushes into Blue Circular Ring 1*

41. *RH straightens GSC to upright position as LH picks up BCR1*

42.2. *RH holds GSC as LH drops BCR1 around GSC and on top of RH*

42.3. *RH releases GSC upright on table inside YCR1/YCR2*

42.3a. *BCR1 falls on top of YCR1 pretty much aligned* (24WW, page 89)

Second-order one-to-many correspondences continue to develop:

23.5. *RH stands Cylinder 1 upright on left end of Square Column 2 lying flat on table*

23.5. *LH stands Cylinder 2 upright on right end of Square Column 2*

25. *LH picks up Cylinder 3 and stacks C3 upright on C1*

27. *RH picks up Cylinder 4 and stacks C4 upright on C2* (24YM, page 20)

This is still a fairly rudimentary second-order co-univocal. The "many" term is minimal since each comprises only two objects forming a one-to-two-and-two correspondence. Moreover, the infant's regulative functioning is not yet equal to the structural requirements for constructing this advanced form of co-univocals. The result is that 24YM generates a very labile version of the co-univocal he is trying to construct; it takes the intended form for only a moment:

Thus, as is also to be expected early in the development of a new operational structure, even rudimentary second-order co-univocals are generated infrequently at this stage. This continues the general trend that we have observed beginning at age 6 months in which development in co-univocal matching lags behind development in bi-univocals (Langer, 1980). Second-order bi-univocals, as we have seen, are already commonplace constructions.

Interweaving co-univocals with bi-univocals just begins to include ordered transformations. The most advanced seriated coordination of bi-univocals with co-univocals is generated by subject 24GA. He begins with four one-to-one bi-univocal correspondences between spoons-in-cups considered on pages 334 and 335. Then he takes three spoons out of three cups and consecutively constructs an ordered series of ⟨ 1:1 ⟩, ⟨ 2:1 ⟩, ⟨ 3:1 ⟩, and ⟨ 4:1 ⟩ spoons-in-cups:

33.3.   *RH puts Red Spoon 2 and Yellow Spoon 2 back into Yellow Cup 1*

33.7.   *leans up to look at YC1 as releases RS2 and YS2*

35.   *RH touches, almost grasps, then releases Red Spoon 1 (previously put) in Red Cup 1*

36.   *RH slowly removes YS2 and RS2 from YC1, as steadily watches RS1 in RC1*

37.   *RH puts YS2 and RS2 in RC1 with RS1*

38.   *RH takes YS2, RS1 and RS2 out of RC1*

38a.   *RC1 wobbles (experimenter steadies RC1)*

39.   *LH grasps then releases bowl ends together of YS2, RS1 and RS2 held together by handles by RH*

40.   *RH reaches for but doesn't pick up Yellow Spoon 1, while holding YS2, RS1 and RS2*

41.   *LH picks up YS1, turns YS1 upright and transfers YS1 to RH, turning YS1 so that the bowl end of YS1 is pointing the same way as the other three spoons held by the RH*

42.   *RH transfers YS1 to LH which puts YS1 in YC1, while RH holds YS2, RS1 and RS2*

43.   *RH puts YS2, RS1 and RS2 in YC1 with YS1*   (24GA, pages 38 and 39)

It should not be overlooked that 24GA substitutes Red Cup 2 for Yellow Cup 1 in progressing from ⟨ 2:1 ⟩ to ⟨ 3:1 ⟩ co-univocals. He inverts the substitution back to Yellow Cup 1 in the final step of the series in order to construct his highest ⟨ 4:1 ⟩ co-univocal.

After this ordered series of co-univocals 24GA takes out all four spoons and continues on as follows (not reproduced in the above protocol fragment). He stacks all four cups in each other but begins by looking in the bottom cup to make sure it is empty of spoons even though he previously emptied it. After stacking the cups he inserts all four spoons in the uppermost cup. The result is a four-to-four bi-univocal which matches all the spoons to all the cups by pragmatic and exhaustive insertion of all objects.

This lengthy sequence of pragmatic correlations serves to construct and coordinate basic forms of second-order bi-univocals with co-univocals. The initial one-to-one correspondence between four couplings are transformed into three many-to-one correspondences. The latter are marked by reversible substitution of the single element. More significant still, they are generated in an increasing order: ⟨ 2:1 ⟩ ⟨ 3:1 ⟩ ⟨ 4:1 ⟩. In turn this seriated many-to-one correspondence is transformed into a one-to-one correspondence (4:4) between two subcompositions.

Progressively, then, a pragmatic operator, a correlator, develops that maps transformations between bi-univocal and co-univocal correspondences into each other. This correlator progressively establishes and structures the extensive relations between unordered equivalences, and ordered equivalences. This correlator, then, begins to coordinate adding and subtracting with one-to-one correspondences.

III. Articulating the Order Relations between Paired Compositions

Adding and subtracting become progressively self-regulated. Relatively stable contemporaneous compositions are generated that serve as constant given elements for ordinal seriation and for integration and decomposition. Infants monitor their constructed elements, transform them into ordinal relations in a controlled fashion, and engage in directed corrective maneuvers, as is evident, for instance, in the intercollative integrations generated by subject 24SE (see protocol fragment on pages 342 and 343). Moreover, infants pay increasing attention and respect to the predicate properties of their constructed (two set) elements; as is also evident, for instance, in the same 24SE protocol fragment.

The main developments are in the progressive formation of second-order adding and subtracting. First-order constructions of ordered series of single sets do not progress beyond the level already achieved at age 21 months. Thus, they do not require further consideration at this point.

The proportion of infants generating ordered compositions of compositions remains about the same from ages 18 to 21 to 24 months. Five infants construct paired units forming the discrete order ⟨2-,3-⟩ elements; four infants generate ⟨3-,4-⟩ element paired units; and two infants generate both ⟨2-,3-⟩ and ⟨3-,4-⟩ element paired compositions. Thus, 7 of the 12 subjects generate precisely ordered paired compositions. Four subjects generate imprecisely ordered paired compositions. Most comprise ⟨2-, many-⟩ element paired compositions.

The form of paired orderings remains fairly constant as well. While still relatively transient, second-order adding and subtracting is progressively marked by regulative control and operational coordination:

8. *LH aligns Square Columns 3 and 4 upright on table one behind the other as RH holds SC3 and SC4*
9. *BH place SC3 and SC4 on table aligned*
10. *looks at experimenter, looks at objects, looks at experimenter, looks away at cabinet, and looks back at objects*
11. *LH picks up Square Column 2 by its top and touches SC2 upright on top of Cylinder 1*
11a. *C1 totters a little*
12. *LH transfers SC2 to RH*
13. *LH pushes Square Column 1 to right, touching and aligning SC1 with C1, while RH holds SC2*
14. *RH places SC2 to right and touching C1 so that SC2, C1 and SC1 are aligned:*

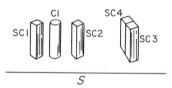

(24WW, pages 1 and 2)

First 24WW constructs two ⟨2-,3-⟩ element sets by manipulating the two-element composition. After looking this over, he commutes this paired ordering. In this way, the sequence of manipulations transforms the two-part ⟨2-,3-⟩ ordering while preserving it.

Part of the predicate properties of this ordering are unmixed (i.e., the two-object unit) and part are mixed (i.e., the three-object unit). Other two-part orderings generated at this stage are marked by unmixed predication:

47. *LH grasps Red Rectangular Ring 2 and brings it in RH to align it with RR1 in RH*
48. *BH align Red Rectangular Rings 1 and 2 and transfer RRR1/RRR2 to LH*
49. *RH picks up Yellow Rectangular Ring 1 and places YRR1 aligned on RRR1/RRR2 held by LH*
50. *RH quickly picks up Yellow Rectangular Ring 2 and aligns YRR2 on YRR1/RRR1/RRR2 held by LH*
51. *LH transfers YRR2/YRR1/RRR1/RRR2 to RH as looking at cars*
52. *LH Picks up Yellow Car 2 then Yellow Car 1 and then Red Car 1, while RH holds YRR2/YRR1/RRR1/RRR2* (24YK, page 12)

Both parts of this ⟨3-,4-⟩ element ordering are unmixed in predicate properties with three cars in one hand and four rings in the other. Unmixed predication is augmented by 24YK's subsequent construction. She hands the three cars to her sister. Then she retrieves the remaining fourth car and gives it to her sister so that it goes with the three other cars. All the while she holds on to the four rings.

A further consequence of this construction is that two ⟨3-,4-⟩ element-ordered compositions are transformed by 24YK into two ⟨4-,4-⟩ element-equivalence compositions. This form of elaborating ordered nonequivalent into equivalent compositions, like that analyzed in the previous section, is one of the various ways by which infants already transform their quantitative structures into each other. These different coordinative transformations serve to insure that powerful structural relations are forged between equivalence and nonequivalence of ever increasing magnitudes.

Symbolic expressions produced by infants while constructing two ordered compositions are still comparatively primitive. The most advanced symbolic productions are reiterative in form. For instance, some infants repeatedly say "Cars" while constructing two ordered compositions made up of cars. None of these symbolic reiterations are marked by one-to-one correspondence between the number of cars composed and the number of symbolic reiterations. Also, none of the subjects count or express numerals while constructing two ordered compositions, even though they begin to count in other contexts and they begin to use scalars such as "more" in the context of their ordinal constructions (see pages 288–290).

Integrating two compositions into one larger whole and decomposing one larger whole into two compositions continues to be generated by almost all subjects (Table 16.3). Predominance of integration over decomposition also continues. Almost all integrations and disintegrations of compositions are applied only to units that comprise equal numbers of elements. This quantitative equivalence restriction upon integration and disintegration is already manifest by age 18 months. The restriction is almost total by age 24 months.

Decomposing always produces quantitatively equivalent sets, whether it is followed by integration or not (Table 16.3). Almost all decomposing is still limited to disintegrating a four-object composition into 2 two-object parts. There are only two exceptions that are the products of single integrations by two subjects (Table 16.3). These two infants integrate a composition of two objects together with a composition of three objects to produce a larger composition of five objects. Otherwise, these two infants, like the rest of the subjects, only integrate sets comprising equal numbers of objects.

The main structural development in adding and subtracting compositions of objects is the shift to generating inverse coordination. For the first time, more subjects integrate and decompose sets than simply integrate sets (Table 16.3).

TABLE 16.3
Number of 24-Month-Old Subjects Adding and Subtracting Units

Units	Integrate	Decompose	Integrate & decompose	Decompose & integrate	Total coordinated
Equal	5	2	6	4	7
Unequal	2	0	0	0	0
Total	5	2	6	4	7

Also, for the first time, more subjects decompose and integrate sets than simply decompose sets.

Without exception, all inverse coordinations between addition and subtraction are applied to units comprising equal numbers of objects (Table 16.3). This regularity even exceeds the almost total uniformity of infants' noncoordinate addition or subtraction. Quantitative equivalence is always maintained by subjects at this stage when they negate additions by subtractions of sets of objects and vice versa.

Integrating and decomposing is limited to relating two compositions each of which comprise two objects. Only two exceptions are produced that foreshadow developments expected during the third year. Both exceptionally advanced productions are generated by the same infant (24SE). In one instance, 24SE consecutively decomposes a larger whole he has constructed into three constituent parts. The three parts correspond with each other since they each comprise a doll lying in a ring. Also, the consecutive decomposing procedures correspond with each other since they are each generated by the same mappings, namely, grasping each ring in turn and pushing it to the experimenter.

In the other instance, 24SE tries to integrate 2 four-object compositions into one larger whole:

4. *RH pushes VW4 sideways across table back and forth, then releases VW4*
5. *LH grasps VW3, slides VW3 across table toward VW4, and turns VW3 sideways so VW3 points in the same direction as VW4*
6. *LH grasps VW2, slides VW2 across table to VW3 and VW4, and turns VW2 so VW2 points in the same direction as VW3 and VW4*
7. *LH grasps VW1 and aligns it next to VW2, VW3, and VW4*
8. *RH picks up Spoon 4, while LH touches Spoon 2*
9. *RH transfers S4 to LH*
10. *RH picks up Spoon 3 and transfers S3 to LH which now holds S3 and S4*
11. *LH transfers S3 and S4 to RH*
12. *LH picks up Spoon 2 and transfers S2 to RH which now holds S2, S3, and S4*
13. *LH picks up Spoon 1 and transfers S1 to RH which now holds S1, S2, S3, and S4*
14. *RH transfers S1, S2, S3, and S4 to LH, while turning toward mirror*

15. *LH transfers S1 to RH which places S1 on table*
16. *LH transfers S2 to RH which places S2 aligned with S1*
17. *LH transfers S3 to RH which places S3 aligned with S1 and S2*
18. *LH places S4 aligned with S1, S2, and S3:*

VW4
VW3   S1   S2   S3   S4
VW2
VW1

19. *LH picks up VW1 and places VW1 between S1 and S2*
20. *LH picks up VW2, places VW2 between S2 and S3, and turns VW2 around so it points toward self (same as VW1)*
21. *LH picks up VW3, and places VW3 between S3 and S4*
22. *LH picks up VW4 and starts to place VW4 between two spoons but can't find a place to put VW4, so holds VW4 out toward mother (who does not react)*
23. *LH places VW4 on table*
24. *LH picks up VW3*
25. *RH picks up VW4 and places VW4 between S3 and S4 (where VW3 had been), while LH holds VW3*
26. *LH places VW3 next to VW2 and between S2 and S3, but more toward the experimenter's side of the alignment*   (24SE, pages 51–53)

Attempted integration of 2 four-object compositions by 24SE may initiate relating cardinal and ordinal quantitative values. Concrete operational relations between cardinal and ordinal values do not, of course, develop until about age seven years (Piaget, 1952b). Their precursory roots may be found during this stage, but only in rare constructions, such as that by 24SE, as is to be expected at their origins.

To begin with, 24SE constructs two compositions of four objects each, so they have equivalent cardinal values. Then he tries to integrate the two compositions by repeatedly intercollating one VW between two spoons. The first three inter-collations are successful since the number of seriated spatial steps or the ordinal value between four object points is three. The extensive relation between cardinal values (n) and ordinal values ($n-1$) is not yet grasped by 24SE. This leads him to the necessarily impossible intercollation of the fourth VW between two spoons (Lines 22 and 23).

The unsuccessful, because necessarily impossible, fourth intercollation immediately leads to two further part–whole transformations. First, 24SE substitutes VW4 for VW3 in the seven-object integrated composition (Lines 24 and 25). Then he constructs a "compromise" solution where VW3 is placed with VW2 which is already intercollated between two spoons; but he places VW3 so that it is not properly aligned with the other objects (Line 26).

Of course, none of these maneuvers can solve the necessarily impossible pragmatic relation between cardinal and ordinal values that 24SE tries to construct. We may therefore propose the structural developmental hypothesis that 24SE has generated a fruitful new cognitive problem even though he can not solve it with the second-order operations available to him at this stage. This new opening provides the form of structural disequilibrium necessary to the development of the only possible logicomathematical solution. Even in pragmatic constructions there are specifiable distinctions and relations between cardinal and ordinal quantifications; only three things can be placed between four objects when the relation is one-to-one. The relations are necessary.

IV. Expanding Class Consistency within and between Paired Compositions

Classifying is still predominately a matter of predicating single compositions.[1] Yet it is increasingly becoming a property of contemporaneous compositions as well, since the rate of composing in partial or total temporal overlap continues to increase at a steady pace. This increase is now manifest in both four-object and eight-object conditions (Table 15.10, Rows 3, 4, 7, and 8).

Consequently, it is possible to evaluate statistically the predicate properties of infants' contemporaneous compositions in half of the tasks. In the other tasks, infants still do not generate contemporaneous compositions at a sufficient rate for statistical evaluation. In these latter tasks the trend appears to be toward unmixed predication.

Contemporaneous compositions are generated by six subjects in the eight-object additive task. Both order ($N = 6$, $x = 0$, $p = .016$, sign test) and enclosure ($N = 6$, $x = 1$, $p = .109$, sign test) properties of these compositions tend to be unmixed. In the eight-object multiplicative task, seven subjects generate contemporaneous compositions. The order properties are random ($N = 5$, $x = 3$, $p = .812$, sign test). The enclosure properties are not clear. If they tend to be consistent, then it is by negation (differences) rather than by affirmation (similarities) between the objects in each of the contemporaneous compositions ($N = 6$, $x = 1$, $p = .109$, sign test). In the four-object disjoint task, eight subjects generate contemporaneous compositions. Both order ($N = 7$, $x = 3$, $p = .50$, sign test) and enclosure ($N = 8$, $x = 4$, $p = .637$, sign test) properties are random.

Infants just begin to reorganize pre-existent compositions (presented to them

---

[1]For analyses of comparable findings in the provoked prcedural conditions of containing in two receptacles, assisted sorting into two sets, and matching two modeled classes, see Chapter 15, Section II.

in phase III counterconditions) according to their predicate properties.[2] Four infants recompose one of the two mixed compositions so that it is no longer mixed by class properties. Two infants move a misplaced object only. The other two infants move several objects in order to form one unmixed recomposition. Two infants recompose both mixed compositions so that they are no longer mixed by class properties. Both infants substitute the two misplaced objects for each other by moving those two objects only (see pages 327–329 for the subjects' protocols and for their analysis).

Infants continue to combine identical objects in their individual compositions in the additive conditions. In the four-object condition, the order of handling objects to compose them is a little under four-to-one favoring identical objects (Table 16.4, Row 1, Columns 1–3) while the random probability ratio is two-to-one favoring complementary objects. The difference is significant ($N = 9$, $x = 1$, $p = .02$, sign test). For enclosure the found ratio is a little over three-to-one favoring identical objects (Row 1, Columns 4–6) for the same random probability ratio. The difference for enclosure, although in the same direction as that for order, is not statistically significant ($N = 9$, $x = 2$, $p = .09$, sign test).

In the eight-object additive condition, order is almost entirely by identical properties (Row 4, Columns 1–3) when the random probability ratio favors complementarity by four-to-three. The difference is significant ($N = 12$, $x = 1$, $p = .003$, sign test). The ratio difference for enclosure, while smaller, is still overwhelming (Row 4, Columns 4–6) and significant ($N = 12$, $x = 2$, $p = .019$, sign test).

Predication in multiplicative conditions varies somewhat as a function of the number of objects presented. In the four-object condition, the random probability ratio is two-to-one favoring complementary over disjoint properties. For order, the found ratio favors complementarity by over four-to-one (Row 2, Columns 1–3). The difference from the random ratio is not statistically significant ($N = 12$, $x = 3$, $p = .073$, sign test). For enclosure, the found ratio favors complementarity by three-to-one (Row 2, Columns 4–6). The difference from the random probability ratio is significant ($N = 12$, $x = 2$, $p = .019$, sign test).

The eight-object multiplicative condition has a random probability ratio of five-to-two favoring unmixed and partly unmixed (identical and complementary) over mixed (disjoint) predication. For order, the found ratio favors unmixed and partly unmixed predication by more than four-to-one (Row 5, Columns 1–3) and is significant ($N = 12$, $x = 2$, $p = .019$, sign test). For enclosure, the found

---

[2]These reorganizations are a bit more advanced than those reported by Sugarman (1983, Table 6.2). The more advanced earlier age reorganizations found in the present research may be accounted for by (a) the larger sample of subjects and (b) the more numerous counterconditions tested in the present investigation.

TABLE 16.4
Spontaneous Phase I: Mean Frequency of Class Consistent Composing at Age 24 Months

	Order			Enclosure		
	Unmixed	Partly unmixed	Mixed	Unmixed	Partly unmixed	Mixed
Four-object condition:						
1. Additive[a]	8.00	0.20	2.20	8.60	0.60	2.70
2. Multiplicative	8.75	0.33	1.92	10.67	0.83	3.50
3. Disjoint[b]	6.09	0.00	2.00	6.73	0.36	4.55
Eight-object condition:						
4. Additive	7.08	0.17	0.75	7.00	1.33	1.50
5. Multiplicative	3.83	3.42	1.67	4.92	6.42	4.67
6. Disjoint[a]	4.80	0.10	2.40	5.80	0.80	3.10

[a]N = 10 subjects.
[b]N = 11 subjects.

ratio is a bit less than five-to-two (Row 5, Columns 4–6) and is not significant ($N = 12$, $x = 4$, $p = .274$, sign test).

Predicating tends to be by identical properties in the disjoint conditions; but, as at ages 18 and 21 months, more so in the eight- than in the four-object condition. In the four-object condition, the random probability ratio is two-to-one favoring predication by disjoint over identical properties. For order, the found ratio is three-to-one favoring identical properties (Row 3, Columns 1–3) but the difference from the random ratio is not significant ($N = 11$, $x = 3$, $p = .113$, sign test). For enclosure, the found ratio is three-to-one favoring identical properties (Row 3, Columns 4–6) but the difference from the random ratio is not significant ($N = 11$, $x = 4$, $p = .274$, sign test).

The eight-object disjoint condition has a four-to-three random probability ratio favoring disjoint over identical properties. For order, the found ratio is two-to-one favoring identical properties (Row 6, Columns 1–3). The difference between the found and the random ratio is significant ($N = 9$, $x = 1$, $p = .02$, sign test). For enclosure, the found ratio is almost two-to-one favoring identical properties (Row 6, Columns 4–6). The difference between the found and the random ratio is significant ($N = 10$, $x = 2$, $p = .055$, sign test).

This picture continues the trend to predication by similarities throughout the second year of infancy; but it is still not complete even for small single compositions as late as age 24 months. Moreover, order and enclosure properties of infants' compositions are still not dissociated. In the four-object conditions, order and enclosure correspond in 89% of the compositions where order applies. In the eight-object conditions, they correspond in 86% of the compositions where order applies. For all object conditions combined, the correspondence between order and enclosure totals 87%.

Causal compositions also continue to be differentiated from noncausal compositions in their predicate structure, as they have been throughout infants' second year. Causal compositions are less likely to combine similar or identical objects (i.e., 42% unmixed, 15% partly mixed, and 42% mixed enclosure) than are noncausal compositions (i.e., 62% unmixed, 14% partly unmixed, and 24% mixed enclosure).

On the other hand, the effects of order vs. enclosure and four-object vs. eight-object conditions are disappearing toward the end of the second year. As we have seen, the enclosure properties of compositions are becoming almost as class consistent as the order properties. Thus predication is also becoming as class consistent in intermediate number (eight-object) conditions as in small number (four-object) conditions.

17

Representational Transformations of Malleable Objects

Representational identity of the intensive part–whole structure of quasi-continuous objects is increasingly the subject of infants' transformational constructions. Accordingly, the structure of infants' reversible coordination between the combinativity operations of deforming and reforming progresses. So does infants' reversible coordinations between breaking and reconstructing. The latter includes a substantial proportion of virtual as well as actual reconstructing of the initial form of the broken objects.

One other, a new form of representational identity of the intensive structure of objects originates at this stage. It is the product of infants' coordinating three combinativity operations. First they decompose a longer object into smaller parts (e.g., a ring into two pieces). This act is followed by deforming one of the decomposed parts, perhaps to get it into good working condition (e.g., straightening out the piece into a strand). The decomposed and deformed part is then reconstructed into a smaller version of the initial object (e.g., a small ring). This may already include virtual reconstructing into a smaller version of the initial version.

The products, then, are clearly representations instead of presentations of the intensive identity of the initial object from which they are derived. These and other representational transformations constructed at this stage are the products of progressive structural coordination of combinativity operations with each other. They reflect progressive development of second-order operations that usher in the transformation of prerepresentational cognition into representational cognition.

I. Coordinating Symbolization with Transformation

Carefully examining malleable objects still precedes, accompanies, and follows transforming them; this includes examining and transforming individual objects and sets of a small number of objects. Examining rings by tracing their inside borders is progressively differentiated out of the rough form initiated at the previous stage (see page 262):

1.5. *RH finger touches inside of Ring 3*
1.5. *LH finger touches inside of Ring 1*
3.5. *RH finger twirls around inside edge of R3*
3.5. *LH finger twirls around inside edge of R1*

(24WW, page 52)

This sequence is followed by multiple deformations to be considered in Section III.

Experimenting continues to mark infants' examination of malleable objects. It includes extensive semisystematic causal manipulations with all the objects presented as long as the number is small. Thus, for instance, in one experimental sequence that he generates, subject 24SE repeatedly drops and only drops all three small PlayDoh balls presented to him. His only variation is to drop anywhere from one to three objects at a time. In this way, 24SE generates the necessary conditions for determining differential effects due only to his variations in the number of objects that he drops at a time.

Smiling at and social demonstration of transformations may accompany examining them. Some social demonstration includes well-coordinated motoric components such as appropriate spatial placements and displacements of the objects of communication. These components may be coupled with linguistic, verbal, and intonational components such as "Look!," and gestures such as smiling at the other person. They may also include rudimentary questions about the objects being transformed, such as "What that?"

Various comparative object properties are also expressed verbally, though not necessarily accurately. The list of comparative constructions is much augmented as compared with the previous stage. It includes: "Ball, anotha one," while pushing one PlayDoh ball into another one; "Big PlayDoh," while deforming a large PlayDoh ball; "More balls," while grabbing a PlayDoh piece; "Nother ball. . . . Big ball!," while picking up a large PlayDoh ring; and "Ballie," "Baseball," "Not a football," "Not football," and "A play ball," while variously interacting with three small PlayDoh balls.

Transforming objects is also now accompanied by full-fledged playful pretense with and fanciful naming of the constructed products. The constructions include repeated and corresponding decomposing pieces that are coordinated with repeated and corresponding deforming of the pieces. Each deformation is accompanied by saying "Snake," and squeezing a ring together accompanied by "Water." Two deformations of a ball are accompanied by saying "Starfish," each time followed by pushing the sausage-shaped object and saying "Snake crawl—this a snake! Snake crawl." In turn, these iterations are followed by pushing the object harder and saying "Spider!," then finally demonstrating the object again saying "Spider," and composing two pieces together while saying "Egg! Egg!."

Linguistic expressions of infant's cognizance of and practical reflection upon their own constructive activity progresses and is an important feature of developing self-regulation. Verbal descriptions of deforming become only fairly frequent (e.g., "Squeeze it."). Other transformations are rarely, if ever, marked linguistically.

Verbally denoting and demonstrating the products of all forms of transforming are generated fairly frequently, particularly by the one-word utterances "There," "Look," and "See." One infant only (24EH) generates a more advanced, comparative representation of what she has just produced. After decomposing a strand into a big and a small piece, 24EH says "That piece like that." It is not clear whether 24EH is comparing the two pieces produced by her decomposition since her verbalization accompanies both the right hand placing the smaller strand next to a ring and the left hand holding the longer strand. Assuming that she is comparing the products of her decomposition suggests that she is merely likening their form to one another (i.e., that they are both strands) and not their size.

Linguistic expression of planful cognizance by infants of their own constructive activity is generated unambiguously by only one infant, the same 24EH who says "Gonna make PlayDoh." Her statement accompanies multiple deformations embedded in a long sequence of many deformations not given in the protocol fragment. Even here, the intended action ("Gonna make") and product ("PlayDoh") remain obscure and nondifferentiated symbolic particles.

At its origins, symbolic planning of transformations does not precede the planned transformations (see Werner, 1948, on older children). Rather, it is a by-product of transformations. Initially symbolic planning is therefore hypothesized to be generated after and/or co-occurring with its related construction. The performance by 24EH is consistent with this hypothesis, as are those of other subjects, some of which are presented in this section. For instance, subjects never say "Snake" before constructing a snake-like shaped object. To the extent that such figurative naming may express planful cognizance, they always accompany or follow upon the transformational products which they name as depicting some fanciful object. They are yet to be elaborated into anticipatory expressions of planful cognizance.

II. Further Expansion of Reforming to Construct Form Identity

Deforming dominates transformation of malleable objects as late as age 24 months. It is still the most frequently generated transformation (Table 17.1). As always, many include multiple deformations such as continuously kneading PlayDoh (Row 1).

Reforming increases sharply so that 90% of the subjects reform the initial shape of objects that they have deformed previously. The rate of generation also increases (Row 2). As compared with deforming, however, reforming remains subordinate. While applied to solid as well as ring objects, only the simplest curvilinear shapes are reformed. Neither deforming nor reforming generates rectilinear or more complex curvilinear features throughout the first two years of life (cf., Langer, 1980; Piaget & Inhelder, 1967).

Folding solid objects progresses and is marked by pragmatic reversibility. To illustrate, in quick succession subject 24EH deforms (folds over) and reforms (unfolds) two balls. These two corresponding inverse functions are preceded by corresponding repeated preparatory deforming of (progressive flattening) the two objects. They are followed by a sequence of interactions that include (a) tactile and visual inspection of both balls, (b) seriated preparatory deformation (progressive flattening) of one, and (c) corresponding inverse deformation (folding over) and reformation (unfolding) of both balls.

Two objects are deformed and reformed in one corresponding way by 24EH. One object is deformed and reformed in two different ways by another subject, 24LM. First he repeatedly flattens and pinches up an object. Immediately afterwards he bends and straightens out the same object. Such sequences make it clear that the reversible structure of deforming and reforming simple solid objects has become a well-regulated function.

The reversible structure of deforming and reforming simple rings has also become a well-regulated function (irrelevant transactions are omitted):

13. *BH squash Large Ring together*
14. *BH pull LR out again the other way*
16. *BH squash LR together again*
17. *BH break LR into strand*
18. *BH puts two ends of LR back together again without making them stay together*
                                                                    (24SE, page 25)

These reversible transformations are preceded by repeated visual inspection of the ring and by yet another type of inverse deforming and reforming (not in-

TABLE 17.1
Mean Frequency of Combinativity Operations Generated by 24-Month-Old Subjects in Quasi-Continuous Conditions

	One object			Three objects		
	Phase I 1	Phase II 2	Phase III 3	Phase I 4	Phase II 5	Phase III 6
1. Deform	14.60 (2.50)[a]	12.67 (2.00)	15.78 (4.67)	9.13 (2.88)	9.57 (1.14)	8.00 (0.75)
2. Reform	0.80 (0.20)	2.17	1.00 (0.11)	0.50	0.43 (0.29)	0.13
3. Break	0.60 [0.10][b]	0.83	0.67	0.63	1.00	1.13
4. Reconstruct	0.00 [0.20]	0.17 [0.67]	0.11 [0.89]	0.00 [0.13]	0.00 [0.29]	0.00
5. Decompose	1.20	2.00 (0.17)	1.78	4.13	4.57	6.00
6. Recompose	0.10	0.17	0.00	0.00	0.00	0.25 (0.25)
7. Compose		0.00	1.00	0.75	0.00	1.38
8. Redecompose		0.00	0.22	0.50	0.00	0.25
9. Number of subjects	10	6	9	8	7	8
10. Mean duration	1 min 35 sec[c]	2 min 28 sec[d]	1 min 50 sec[e]	1 min 45 sec[f]	1 min 35 sec[g]	1 min 46 sec[f]

[a]Mean frequency of operations involving multiple transformations are given in parentheses.
[b]Mean frequency of attempted, but not successfully executed, transformations are given in square brackets.
[c]Based on duration for 8 subjects.
[d]Based on duration for 4 subjects.
[e]Based on duration for 7 subjects.
[f]Based on duration for 6 subjects.
[g]Based on duration for 5 subjects.

cluded in the protocol fragment). They are followed by inverse transformations between deforming, reforming, and deforming. The sequence culminates with 24SE breaking the ring, followed by inversely deforming and reforming it. The latter two transformations constitute virtual but not actual reconstruction of the break 24SE just produced in the ring. (Virtual reconstructing, reforming, and their coordination with reforming are analyzed at the end of Section IV.)

This productive sequence, then, includes two forms of reforming. It begins with twice repeated negating of pressing or squashing the ring together by pulling the ring out. It ends with negating of stretching the ends of the former ring out by putting the ends together without actually reconstructing the ring.

III. Progressive Coordination of Matched with Ordered Sets of Deformations

Contingent deforming that produces corresponding transformations of several objects in a row are generated with ease. To illustrate, subject 24EH reproduces the following transformation on four objects:

48. *BH lower Large Strand 1 to table so it's basically flat and perpendicular to edge with RH end bent sticking up and LH bending left end down over table edge.*

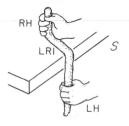

(24EH, page 37)

Corresponding contingent deforming is becoming well-regulated. In each instance the table edge is used by 24EH as an instrument upon which to deform a PlayDoh strand. This act is repeated precisely four times on four strands of differing lengths within a short time span. Each time, the result is a right angle-like form. The product is one-to-one correspondence between the shapes of four deformed objects. Moreover, 24EH's declarative statement ("Get it to go like this.") about what she is doing on her fourth deformation indicates some cognizance that she is constructing corresponding transformations.

Noncontingent corresponding deformations, both in number and form, are applied just as easily to solids as to rings. For instance, subject 24WW does the following to three rings in a row:

7. *LH holds Ring 1 as RH pushes one side of R1 in contact with other side and folds R1 over so that it becomes sausage-shaped*   (24WW, page 52)

Two, then three small solid balls are also simultaneously and repeatedly deformed in one-to-one correspondence by 24WW in another task. The result is that all five small balls are deformed from balls into flat shapes within a short time span. Two balls are reciprocally and contingently deformed twice in a row by 24SH. The result is that four small balls (out of the five presented in this condition) are deformed in one-to-one correspondence within a short time span.

Coseriated deforming of two and of three objects is common. For instance, as already indicated, two and then three small balls are deformed simultaneously and repeated in one-to-one correspondence by 24WW. The result is equivalent progressive deformation of two objects followed almost immediately by equivalent progressive deformation of three objects.

Progressive coordination between correspondence and order constructions continues to be generated in one other important way at this stage:

34.	*RH index presses 5 times into Slab, in 5*	*S:* "*Pink (vocalize).*"
	different places	
34a.	*5 indentions*	
35.	*BH peel S off table*	*S:* (*vocalize*)
		(*M:* "*Mmmmm?*")
36.	*BH flip S onto other side toward self*	
36a.	*back edge of S is curled under a bit*	
37.	*RH palm lightly pats S*	*S:* (*vocalize*)
37a.	*S resembles a turnover*	
38.	*RH thumb presses into S, 6 times, in 6*	
	different places mostly near edges	
38a.	*6 indentations*	(24EH, page 21)

Five indentations are made on one side followed by six indentations on the other side. At the same time, then, 24EH generates two sets of deformations. Their intensity (predicate form) is in one-to-one correspondence with each other. But their extensity is ordered in number of deformations comprised by each set forming a ⟨ 5, 6 ⟩ series of corresponding indentations.

Regulated deformations are used to generate ordered series. The construction may or may not be contingent. To illustrate, subject 24SH pounds a big ball on the table top harder and harder three times in a row. The result is progressive flattening of the ball. Subject 24EH generates a decreasing order by both reducing the number and intensity of her deformations from hitting down on a slab three times to just patting it very lightly two times.

IV. Virtual and Actual Reconstruction of Form Identity

All infants break objects, but most breaking is still confined to opening up rings. The rate of breaking is increasing continuously and, for the most part, gradually (Table 17.1, Row 3). Corresponding breaking just begins to be generated by a few infants. To illustrate, both subjects 24SE and 24WW break open three rings within a brief time interval. They both construct equivalent transformations of rings into strands by repeated corresponding breaking. The difference between them is that 24SE's repetitions are consecutive, while 24WW's are also interwoven with decomposing the broken rings.

The origin of corresponding coordinations between breaking and decomposing is accompanied by the initiation of corresponding coordinations between breaking and deforming. Precisely corresponding coordinated breaking and deforming originates at this stage and is still an exceptional construction. Such complex second-order coordinations begin to produce precisely interwoven equivalences. To illustrate, subject 24YM deforms three broken rings in the same way so as to transform them into three equivalently straight strands. After this, he tries unsuccessfully to reconstruct the last broken ring by connecting the two ends of the strand.

Coordinated breaking and deforming is constructed by infants to transform rings into straight line segments that are congruent with each other. This is not yet the case with coordinated breaking and decomposing. It is not yet used by infants as a means to produce congruent straight line segments.

Coordinating breaking with reconstructing rings is generated by 60% of infants. While the rate of reconstructing is still low it is increasing gradually (Table 17.1, Row 4). Most reconstructions at this stage are like that produced by 24YM. They consist of nonconsummated but precise reconstructions. Some reconstructions are nonconsummated because they are difficult for infants to accomplish. Apparently, this is so for 24YM who tries, gives up, and then gives the broken ring to his father to reconstruct.

Other nonconsummated reconstructions may not be unsuccessful attempts but, rather, deliberately virtual instead of actual:

23. *BH pick up, break Ring 1, and put broken R1 on the table*
24. *BH pick up and put the two broken ends of R1 together again but without pinching together the ends, then drop R1 to table*
25. *BH pick up (previously) broken Ring 3 and put the two ends of R3 together but without pinching them together, then drop R3 to table*
26. *does the same as Line 25 with (previously) broken Ring 6*
27. *does the same as Line 25 and 26 with (previously) broken Ring 2, only this time BH also try to pinch together the two ends of R2*
28. *BH break R2 into two pieces (P1 and P2)*
29. *BH grasp P1 and put together its two ends*
30. *BH grasp P2 and put together its two ends*   (24SE, page 30)

Three times in a row, and within a brief time span, 24SE generates precise virtual reconstructions of three strands back into rings. They are virtual because 24SE does not pinch the ends together. Indeed, he makes no attempt to actually reconstruct the rings; he seems content with his three virtual reconstructions. All three correspond to each other such that 24SE is constructing representational equivalences, that is, correlations between "fictional" transformations.

Immediately afterward, 24SE actually and precisely reconstructs a ring from a fourth strand. This ring serves as a control finding since it demonstrates that 24SE has the sensorimotor capacity to generate actual reconstructions. His preceding three virtual reconstructions are not for want of ability to generate actual reconstructions of rings. In this way, they constitute virtual mappings of actual transformations, and they construct representational correspondences.

This construction is compounded by 24SE's subsequent transformations. After reconstructing Ring 2, 24SE decomposes it into two pieces. Immediately, he constructs two consecutive virtual reconstructions. First, he puts together the ends of one piece without pinching them together. Then he does the same with the other piece. The products are two more corresponding virtual, not actual, ring reconstructions. The total and final result of this sequence of coordinated transformations is the construction of numerous representational correspondences. This includes the production of one more virtual ring than the number of actual rings with which the infant started out.

Coordinations upon coordinations originate at this stage. They consist of coordinating deforming–reforming with breaking–reconstructing (see 24SE protocol fragment on page 352). Almost invariably these second-order coordinations involve virtual rather than actual reconstruction (subject 24SE, Line 18, is typical in this regard). The result is coordination of actual (deforming–reforming) with virtual (breaking–reconstructing) transformation coordinations. In all instances the resultants, while different, are identity operations. In addition, they begin to coordinate actual with virtual (representational) identities.

V. Reforming Decomposed Parts to Construct Form Identity

The rate of decomposing does not change from ages 21 to 24 months (Table 17.1, Row 5). But decomposing has become well-regulated. For instance, subject 24WW uses his right hand index finger to carefully pick up a piece out of a ball held by his left hand. Subject 24WW evinces cognizance of and control over decomposing this object by several behaviors. He names ("A ball.") and demonstrates the object (shows it to the experimenter) before bringing it to himself; he visually monitors his fine-motor decomposing and its object; and, finally, he physically and verbally ("Here.") gives the resultant product to his mother.

Regulated decomposing permits forming coordinated routines:

33.   *BH pull Piece 1 in two (P1a and P1b)*
34.   *RH presses P1a into table, smearing P1a*

35. LH presses P1b into table, smearing P1b
36. BH pick up and pull Piece 2 in two (P2a and P2b)
37. RH presses P2a into table, smearing P2a
38. LH presses P2b into table, smearing P2b
39. RH picks up Piece 3 and together with LH pulls P3 in two (P3a and 3b)
40. LH presses P3a into table, smearing P3a
41. RH presses P3a into table, smearing P3b
42. BH pick up and pull Piece 4 in two (P4a and P4b)
43. RH presses P4a into table, smearing P4a
44. LH presses P4b into table, smearing P4b
45. LH picks up Large Piece
46. RH pulls bit (B1) off LP held by LH and presses B1 into table, smearing B1
47. RH pulls bit (B2) off LP held by LH and presses B2 into table, smearing B2
48. RH pulls bit (B3) off LP held by LH and presses B3 into table, smearing B3
49. RH pulls bit (B4) off LP held by LH and presses B4 into table, smearing B4
50. RH pulls bit (B5) off LP held by LH and presses B5 into table, smearing B5
51. RH pulls bit (B6) off LP held by LH and   S: "There!"
     presses B6 into table, smearing B6
52. RH takes bit (B7) remaining of LP from LH   S: "See? See?"
53. RH presses B7 into table, smearing B7   S: "There!"

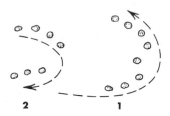

2   1

(24EJ, pages 36 and 37)

This coordinated routine comprises two parts. In the first part, 24EJ decomposes four small pieces of PlayDoh into two equal portions. Both portions are then correspondingly and contingently deformed by being pressed into the table top. The result is eight smears of PlayDoh. Thus, corresponding decompositions become the constructed constant givens or elements for corresponding deforming.

A variant of these second-order correspondences is generated in the second part of the routine. Now 24EJ decomposes a larger piece of PlayDoh into seven equivalent bits. After each decomposition he correspondingly and contingently deforms each bit by pressing it into the table top. Finally, he correspondingly and contingently deforms the remaining bit as well by pressing it into the table top.

These two parts of 24EJ's routine produce two sets of deformed decompositions that are in rough one-to-one correspondence with each other (as can be seen from the diagram of the whole produced by 24EJ). The products of the first part (labeled 1 in the diagram) are placed so as to form an arc, as are the products of the second part (labeled 2). The arrows indicate the directions in which 24EJ works in each arc. While the first arc comprises eight smears, the second arc comprises seven smears. As a whole, then, 24EJ has constructed two imprecisely equivalent alignments of deformed decompositions. His verbalizations at the end (followed by sitting back in his chair, not reproduced in the fragment) suggest that he is cognizant of and wishes to show his construction.

Decomposing objects into (a) single sets of matching derivative elements and (b) two sets of derivative elements in one-to-one correspondence with each other is no longer unusual. Indeed, as we have seen, corresponding decompositions are beginning to be coordinated with other operations such as deforming and breaking. Thus, 24EJ generates two imprecisely equivalent alignments of seven elements matched to eight elements.

Corresponding decomposing by 24EJ produces two stable matched sets. They are preserved for some time and are even the subject of some cognizance and social communication by 24EJ. However, this is not yet typical of this stage; most corresponding decomposing still results in labile compositions. More typical is the transformational sequence generated by subject 24EH. Three times in a row 24EH decomposes a ring into two parts such that the resultant pieces are all roughly matched to each other in size and shape. However, 24EH does not form separate configurations with the dismembered parts. He merely collects them into one undifferentiated configuration.

Geneological decomposing of a whole into parts decreasing in size is generated by almost all infants. For the most part, infants still generate single geneological series. Eight of 10 subjects generate single geneological series. Three of these 8 subjects also generate pairs of geneological series.

While most geneological decomposing is still limited to producing single series, these series are becoming precise progressions:

  5. *BH pull Large Ring apart into two pieces (P1 and P2)*
  6. *RH puts P1 on table*
  7. *BH pull P2 into two pieces (P21 and P22)*
  8. *RH puts P21 on table*
  9. *BH pull P22 into two pieces (P221 and P222)*
 10. *RH puts P221 on table*
 11. *BH pull P222 into two pieces (P2221 and P2222)*   (24SH, page 20)

This geneological series is precise in the decreasing order of derived parts into which the whole ring is decomposed. Each new part is half of its predecessor.

Deforming coordinated with reconstructing begins to be applied to the products of decomposing. This coordination generates a derivative of the initial object. The intensive part–whole structure of the derivative object is both a transformation of and is similar to its progenitor. Thus, the coordinated construction constitutes a second-order (i.e., a reformation of a decomposition) and symbolic (i.e., a reproductive transform) identity operation.

To illustrate, subject 24SG decomposes a ring into two parts, one large and one small. She works with the larger part only. She deforms it from a curvilinear into a straight line strand which makes it easy to transform it further in a fairly precise and controlled way. After this, she reconstructs the strand into a virtual, not actual, ring. Finally, she deforms the virtual ring back into a straight line strand. Throughout, the transformations are marked by regulation, self-monitoring, and cognizance. Transformative mappings are coordinated with and are adjusted to each other. The transformational mappings and their products are examined visually. Moreover, 24SG's verbal remarks upon (e.g., "Look!") and smiling at her transformations indicate a measure of cognizance.

The origins at this stage of deforming and reconstructing (whether actual or virtual) decomposed parts may account, at least in part, for the lack of progress in recomposing (Table 17.1, Row 6). Recomposing is generated by only 30% of the subjects. In part, these figures may be small because infants are just beginning to reform one decomposed part only. Thus, for instance, the performance by 24SG includes virtual reforming of one decomposed part into a ring, which thereby shares the intensive but not extensive properties of the original whole. Since such constructions cannot properly be counted as coordinated decomposing–recomposing, the measure necessarily underestimates the development of recomposing at this stage.

Recomposing consists of putting back together decomposed parts to form the whole out of which they are decomposed. Because of this, it always involves generating extensive identity and may or may not include intensive identity. Reforming decomposed parts, in contrast, is necessarily restricted to intensive identity since the extent of the parts are smaller than the whole from which they are decomposed.

Recomposing remains a pragmatic extensity operation throughout infancy as it has been since its origin:

58–59.   *BH push together several small pieces as LH picks them up and places them in experimenter's hands*

60–64.   *BH push together some other small pieces, BH lift glob from table transferring it to RH which drops it into experimenter's hands*   (24WW, page 64)

Even when well-regulated and directed toward social interaction, recomposing has not yet developed into a pragmatic intensity operation since it is not featured by qualitative identity.

Composing is still not a dominant transformation, although the rate of production increases a bit from age 21 months. Composing continues to lag behind deforming, decomposing, and even breaking. Even as late as age 24 months, composing is generated by only 50% of infants and at a relatively low rate (Table 17.1, Row 7).

Redecomposing, like recomposing, is also still a subordinate transformation. It is generated by only 30% of subjects and at a low rate (Table 17.1, Row 8). A consequence is that coordinated composing–redecomposing, like decomposing–recomposing, remains a subordinate reversible construction.

Redecomposing, like recomposing, is a pragmatic extensity operation. Unlike recomposing, redecomposing is just beginning, in rudimentary ways, to constitute a pragmatic intensity operation (irrelevant intervening transactions are omitted):

  6.7. *LH picks up Balls 1 and 2 together*
   8. *RH picks up Balls 3, 4, and 5 together*
   9. *RH transfers B3, B4, and B5 to LH as LH squeezes all five balls*
  9a. *balls merge together some*   S: *"Look!" (laughs)*
 21.5. *LH pulls away 4 stuck balls from a 5th ball, and raises them a few inches in air*
                                            (24SG, pages 33 and 34)

Five small balls are composed together while preserving their basic shape. Later one of these balls is redecomposed and the resultants are demonstrated physically and verbally. Thus, 24SG's redecomposing produces imprecise and partial extensive and intensive identity of one of the five composed balls. At its origin, then, intensive identity is not the result of transformations directed toward reconstructing an object's initial form. It is merely the residue of the initial form that has not been fully wiped out by composition.

V

CONCLUSION

Representational Cognition

18

Cognition becomes bileveled, combining first- with second-order functional structures, during infants' second year. At the same time, the power of this bileveled organization is transformed developmentally stage by stage. The structural developmental model of cognition that emerges is complex and, as hypothesized, recursive (i.e., multileveled, multidirectional, and multistructural).

Cognition develops in power and expands in extent during infants' second year. Initially infants raise only part of their proto-operational and protofunctional structuring to the second degree. They complete the organization of these second-order structures during the remainder of their second year. Thus, second-order logicomathematical and physical cognition co-exists with the first-order cognition out of which it develops and which originates during infants' first year. The power of both first-order cognition and its structural developmental derivative, second-order cognition progresses during infants' second year and, it is expected, beyond. But the dominance gradually shifts toward second-order cognition, while the products of developing first-order constructions progressively serve as elements for second-order cognitions (e.g., increasing set size of individual compositions).

Cognition becomes bileveled while it progresses in power stage by stage. This includes three structural developmental transformations. At first only first-order cognition develops stage by stage. Second-order cognition only begins to be constructed by infants when the structures of first-order cognition are completed toward the end of their first year. These partial second-order structures are not completed until the end of infants' second year. Second-order cognition does not simply replace first-order cognitions; rather, both first- and second-order cognition continue to develop in power, stage by stage. These conditions provide both the organizational equilibrium and disequilibrium for structural development.

The present findings extend the initial evidence (Langer, 1980) for the constructivist thesis about the origins of cognition. The basic proposition is that infants' proto-operations and protofunctions are the initial source of their logicomathematical and physical cognition beginning in their first year. The findings also extend the initial evidence for the structural model of the base components of logicomathematical cognition. They comprise combinativity, relational, and conditional proto-operations that produce pragmatic equivalence, ordered nonequivalence, and reversibility. Finally, the present findings provide initial evidence for the claim that the structural developmental transformation of first- into second-order operations and functions produces the origins of representational cognition during the second half of infancy.

I. Operations

The initial organization of logicomathematical cognition is unileveled and consists of first-order operations and products. Its development during infants' first year, when it exclusively marks logicomathematical cognition, has already been reviewed in Chapter 1. The present findings confirm the hypothesis that the power of first-order operations continues to develop during infants' second year when their organization of structures is already completed and when logicomathematical cognition is no longer exclusively first-order.

Recall, for instance, that infants' individual compositions of objects become progressively stable and increase in size during their second year. These more constant and enlarged elements are exploited by infants to construct more advanced first-order conditional and relational operations. This includes progressively elaborated extensive features. To illustrate, quantitative equivalence by exchanging objects is increasingly constructed within increasingly large and stable single collections, as is ordered nonequivalence by adding and subtracting objects (so that ordering as many as six seriated objects by age 24 months was found by Hetzer, 1931, and comparable results were found by Greenfield, Nelson, & Saltzman, 1972; Mounoud & Bower, 1974; Nicolopoulou, 1979; and Sugarman, 1983).

The advances include progress in the intensive features of first-order operations as well. Notably, increasing classification by similarities marks infants' single compositions during the second year. As in other studies (e.g., Nelson, 1973; Ricciuti, 1965; Sugarman, 1983; Woodward & Hunt, 1972), we found that infants extend their composing by similarities to ever larger compositions of objects during the second year. But we also found that this generalization must be qualified in at least two ways. First, the limit is three- to four-object compositions. Random classification still marks five- to eight-object compositions (which is consistent with observations by Inhelder & Piaget, 1964), Second, the generalization does not yet fully apply to all class conditions. For instance, it does not apply to the four-object disjoint condition in which random classification marks infants' composing at age 24 months.

Such advances in structuring discrete quantities are complemented by advances in structuring continuous quantities with first-order operations. This includes the extensive features of continuous quantities. To illustrate, quantitative equivalence by one-to-one correspondence is extended to more numerous matched deformations within single malleable objects, as is ordered nonequivalence by geneological decomposing of single malleable objects. It also includes the intensive features of continuous quantities. Most notably, infants increasingly reform the (shape) identity of single malleable objects they have deformed and they increasingly reconstruct the (shape) identity of malleable objects they have broken.

While first-order operations dominate infants' logicomathematical cognition during their first year, they no longer do so during their second year. Some second-order operations originate toward the end of infants' first year. Their organization is completed during infants' second year but their progressive development is not.

Second-order operations are developmental derivatives of infants' mapping their first-order operations and products upon each other. Thus, second-order logicomathematical cognitions are integrative constructions. They grow out of or are produced by infants coordinating the first-order cognitions that they developed during their first year. These integrations form structures of logicomathematical operations and products to the second degree.

The full organization of second-order operations is completed during the second year. Though still not predominant even by age 24 months, infants' constructions of second-order operations begin to balance the advances in their first-order operations. This shift in developmental level and structural power is paced by progress in combinativity operations necessary to construct second-order cognition.

Most important to infants developing second-order cognition is the origin of forming compositions of compositions of objects. This new structural development is initiated toward the end of infants' first year when they begin to compose two collections of objects in temporal overlap. It is augmented by the continuous increase in generating contemporaneous compositions during infants' second year.

This development in constructing contemporaneous compositions is crucial. It enables infants to open up more frequent and advanced possibilities for constructing new and more powerful cognitions. Generating numerous contemporaneous collections produces a rich source of potential compositions of compositions of objects. In turn, compositions of compositions serve as the elements for constructing second-order relational and conditional operations.

Consider part of the present findings on how infants progressively construct second-order one-to-one correspondence, substitution, and classification. One-to-one correspondence is a fundamental way by which infants begin to construct equivalence between their contemporaneous compositions. It is also their first way. Initial manifestations are found at age 12 months when more than half of the infants generate minimal matchings between pairs of compositions that contain no more than two objects each (Langer, 1980). Minimal matched compositions are commonplace by age 18 months (as also found by Sinclair, *et al.*, 1982; and Sugarman, 1983). In addition, a few infants begin to expand their one-to-one correspondences to more than minimal compositions which include three or four objects.

One-to-one correspondences begin to be extended to matching more than two compositions by age 24 months (see also Sinclair, *et al.*, 1982, who report somewhat more precocious development of correspondences; and Sugarman, 1983). Multiple compositions of compositions by correspondence begins to extend constructing equivalence between more than two collections but where the membership of each collection is again minimal, that is, two objects only. On the other hand, when infants of this age construct two corresponding compositions, then the membership is no longer minimal; most infants generate two compositions of three or four objects each.

Constructing equivalence by second-order exchange operations originates between ages 15 and 18 months. Infants construct two contemporaneous compositions and substitute objects within them such that they transform the membership of the two collections while preserving the initial quantitative relation between them (whether of equality or inequality). No infants this age substitute objects between two contemporaneous compositions. So by age 18 months, infants' second-order substitutions still do not fully meet the criteria for true substituting between two collections.

Still, about half of these second-order substitutions already produce elementary equivalences upon equivalences. Infants first construct equivalence between two compositions of objects by one-to-one correspondences. Then they use these equivalent compositions as the elements for constructing equivalence within the two compositions by substituting objects in them. So by mapping substitution upon correspondence, infants begin to produce equivalences upon equivalences.

The major new development in second-order substitution between ages 21 and 24 months consists of exchanges that fully meet the criteria for true substituting between two compositions of objects, but no more than two very small compositions. Infants just begin to exchange objects between as well as within two contemporaneous compositions.

Infants build two logicomathematical extensions with this advance. One is extensive and completes infants' structuring of equivalences upon equivalences that they initiate at age 18 months. Now, too, infants begin by constructing equivalence between two compositions of objects by one-to-one correspondence. But now infants use these equivalent compositions as the elements for constructing equivalence between the two compositions by substituting objects between them. The structure of equivalence to the second degree or true equivalence upon equivalence is being completed.

The second logicomathematical extension infants build with this advance in second-order exchange is intensive. Infants begin to structure the classificatory properties of contemporaneous compositions by substituting objects between them. This includes beginning to correct counterconditions presented to them. Recall that these conditions present infants with two parallel alignments properly classified except for one class error in each. A few infants now correct the classificatory errors by exchanging the two misplaced objects for one another. The result is proper (i.e., unmixed) classification of two compositions related to each other by substitution.

It should not be overlooked, however, that the result is also quantitative (i.e., equivalence between two compositions by substitution). The structural developmental implications are therefore twofold. On the one hand, structuring the extensive features of discrete quantities, such as by substituting equal numbers of objects in two compositions, may feedforward to or have positive implications for structuring the intensive features of discrete quantities, such as composing the objects in each of two contemporaneous collections by similarities. On the other hand, structuring the intensive features of discrete quantities, such as by composing similar objects together in each of two contemporaneous collections, may feedforward to or have positive implications for structuring the extensive features of operations, such as producing quantitative equivalence in two contemporaneous compositions.

Classification by substitution between two compositions indicates that infants begin to classify more than single compositions of objects between ages 18 and 24 months (as also found by Denney, 1972; Nelson, 1973; Ricciuti, 1965; Roberts & Fischer, 1979; Starkey, 1981; Sugarman, 1983; and Woodward & Hunt, 1972). Still, we found that as late as age 24 months, infants construct class consistent contemporaneous compositions by similarities in only one of six class conditions tested. It is the eight-object additive condition which is one of the simplest possible.

As with the development of first-order logicomathematical cognition, progress in structuring discrete quantities with second-order operations is complemented by progress in structuring continuous quantities. Structuring the extensive features of continuous quantities progresses. This includes quantitative equivalence by one-to-one correspondence between two sets of deformations, each of which is in one-to-one correspondence with the other deformations. It also includes ordered nonequivalence in two coseriated collections by geneological decomposing of two malleable objects. Structuring the intensive features of continuous quantities also progresses. This includes beginning to integrate both reforming with reconstructing and reforming with recomposing to construct identity operations (e.g., to make two small circular rings out of one large circular ring) which may initiate the formation of intensive tautology.

The organization of logicomathematical cognition, then, has become bileveled and is complete by the end of infants' second year. All the structures of second-order combinativity, relational, and conditional operations with both discrete and continuous quantities are in place. Nevertheless, their development is not over; they are expected to progress, stage by stage, beyond infants' second year (Langer, in preparation).

II. Functions

The structural development of physical cognition continues to parallel that of logicomathematical cognition during infants' second year. The initial organization of physical cognition is unileveled and includes first-order causal and spatial protofunctions, as reviewed in Chapter 1. Thus, its initial structural development parallels that of infants' logicomathematical development during the first year. In addition, the organization of infants' physical cognition, like their logicomathematical cognition, becomes bileveled during the second year.

First-order functions are not simply replaced when infants develop second-order functions. Instead, infants' first-order functions continue to develop during their second year. The structural developmental result is that first- and second-order functions become coextensive during infants' second year. In this, too, the structural development of infants' physical cognition parallels that of their logicomathematical cognition.

Causal means–ends functions continue to be central to the cognition of physical phenomena during infants' second year. This includes infants' first-order causal constructions which are nothing more than direct one-way functions from means to ends. At first infants'causal constructions are relatively labile since both their means and their ends fluctuate from moment to moment. The causal dependencies they generate change constantly; they do not yet manifest the elementary stability introduced by repetitive mappings, that is, semiconstancy and semisystematicity. Hence to begin with, infants' first-order functions are nothing more than segregated pragmatic dependencies

$$\mathcal{X} \to \mathcal{Y} \tag{18.1}$$

where $\mathcal{X}$ represents different means or causes that are not related to each other and $\mathcal{Y}$ different ends or effects that are not related to each other. All functions are different and isolated one-way physical dependencies that are not related to each other. We may illustrate these minimal causal functions with two well-known common causal relations constructed by infants early in their first year. They are "shaking is dependent on swatting" and "noise is dependent on banging." These elementary functions are unconnected. Thus, there are no structural, developmental, or formal links between the elements or dependency relations in these segregated functions.

The development of regulated, initially repetitive, mappings begins to stabilize the causal dependencies infants construct by age 6 months (Langer, 1980). First-order functions are thereby transformed developmentally from Eq. (18.1) into

$$\mathcal{X} \rightarrow \mathcal{Y} \tag{18.2}$$

In this protofunction $\mathcal{X}$ stands for particular means or causal semivariables such as "pushing" and $\mathcal{Y}$ for particular ends or effect semivariables such as "rolling." The causal couplings are already semisystematic one-way direct physical dependencies that are, however, restricted to repeater functions that replicate particular relations without variation. To illustrate, one common construction by infants during the second half of their first year takes the form of "Repeated Rolling is dependent upon Repeated Pushing." The replicated effect is a particular function of or specifically dependent on the repeated cause.

Neither the independent nor the dependent semivariables are ordered or classed. The semivariables are unordered particular elements. In the illustration, the independent semivariable Repeated Pushing is a particular element as is the dependent semivariable Repeated Rolling. These semivariables are reproducible elements that do not vary by either order or class. The functional dependency that is thereby constructed is a particular direct one-to-one relation; it is nothing but a repeater function.

Infants' first-order causal functions, represented by Eq. (18.2), are transformed developmentally beginning at the end of their first year and continuing during their second year into

$$\mathbb{X} \rightarrow \mathbb{Y} \tag{18.3}$$

where $\mathbb{X}$ and $\mathbb{Y}$ represent oriented independent and dependent semivariables, respectively. This includes two progressively developing features that are not yet integrated with one another, however. On the one hand, semivariables are partly ordered. To illustrate, a construction that becomes common during infants' second year takes the form of "Rolling Further is dependent on Pushing Harder." On the other hand, semivariables are partly classified, if only by single consecutive classes. To illustrate, another common construction takes the form of "Rolling Objects is dependent on Pushing Cylinders." This is the product of infants' experimenting that eventually leads them to selectively push cylinders only and to stop pushing square columns. In effect, they are beginning to constructively differentiate possible from impossible causal phenomena. Clearly missing is any attempt by infants to construct any two-place functions that intersect partly ordered with partly classified semivariables (e.g., "Rolling Objects Further is dependent on Pushing Cylinders (only) Further").

Two major advances, then, mark this structural development in first-order functions. First, their elements progress from particular to oriented semivariables (i.e., partly ordered or partly classified). Second, and consequently, the causal relations constructed with these elements progress from direct repeated one-to-one dependencies to more indirect variable dependencies. The form of the linkage has become a pragmatic ratio-like function.

At their most advanced, infants' first-order causal functions, represented by Eq. (18.3), are transformed developmentally during their second year into

$$\mathbb{X} \rightarrow \mathfrak{H} \rightarrow \mathbb{Y} \tag{18.4}$$

where $\mathfrak{H}$ is an intermediary means or semivariable. To illustrate, causal chains based upon intermediary means become common constructions and take forms such as "Rolling Further is dependent on Moving Harder which is dependent on Pushing Harder." The pragmatic ratio is becoming increasingly indirect because of the introduction of transitive transmission of the dependency relation (i.e., overt transitive transmission of motion in the illustrative construction) via an intermediary semivariable.

Two developments mark the increasing power of infants' transitive dependencies. First, infants begin to construct intermediary semivariables as well as adopting those already presented to them. For instance, infants construct a four cylinder stack; then with another object they strike the bottom cylinder in order to topple the cylinders on top of it. Second, infants incorporate increasing numbers of objects into their intermediary semivariables (e.g., motion may be transmitted through as many as three objects by age 24 months). Nevertheless, the intermediary semivariable remains particular in all first-order functions (i.e., it is not ordered or classified).

All forms of first-order causal functions, including those represented by Eqs. (18.1) to (18.4), are nothing more than one-way relations. The means–ends dependencies are always oriented in one direction only. The significance of this structural limit will become apparent as we take up next the developmental transformation of first- into second-order functions.

While first-order causal functions vary independent semivariables only, second-order functions vary both independent and dependent semivariables. Furthermore, and this is the crucial structural development, they covary the independent and dependent semivariables with each other. Infants initiate their second-order structuring by covarying causal means and ends.

Recall, for illustrative purposes, the cat-and-mouse game that infants play during their second year. First they push an object to make it roll; when it rolls they block it or make it stop; when it stops they push it again to make it roll once again, and so on. Let $\mathcal{X}$ represent the independent semivariables and $\mathcal{Y}$ represent the dependent semivariables, such that $\mathcal{X}_1$ is the initial "pushing" means or independent semivariable, $\mathcal{X}_1$ the initial "rolling" end or dependent semivariable, $\mathcal{X}_1'$ the initial complementary "blocking" means or independent semivariable, and $\mathcal{Y}_1'$ the initial complementary "stopping" end or dependent semivariable. Then

$$\mathcal{X}_1 \rightarrow \mathcal{Y}_1 \rightarrow \mathcal{X}_1' \rightarrow \mathcal{Y}_1' \rightarrow \ldots \rightarrow \mathcal{X}_n \rightarrow \mathcal{Y}_n \rightarrow \mathcal{X}_n' \rightarrow \mathcal{Y}_n' \quad (18.5)$$

Eq. (18.5) states that "stopping," from the first to the last, is dependent on "blocking," from the first to the last, which is dependent on "rolling," from the first to the last, which is dependent upon "pushing," from the first to the last.

Thus, the means infants construct are changed and determined by the ends they produce. In turn, the ends infants produce are changed and determined by the means they construct. The functional dependencies between means and ends, between independent and dependent semivariables, begin to be constructed analogically. Thus, in the cat-and-mouse game the initial stopping is dependent on the initial blocking as the initial rolling is dependent on the initial pushing. But, also, the second pushing is dependent on the initial stopping as the initial blocking is dependent on the initial rolling. It can be seen from this that the form of the analogy is general.

Since the functional dependencies covary analogically and the analogy is general, Eq. (18.5) may be rewritten as the protoproportion

$$\frac{\mathcal{Y}_1}{\mathcal{X}_1} \overset{.}{\approx} \frac{\mathcal{Y}_1'}{\mathcal{X}_1'} \overset{.}{\approx} \ldots \overset{.}{\approx} \frac{\mathcal{Y}_n}{\mathcal{X}_n} \overset{.}{\approx} \frac{\mathcal{Y}_n'}{\mathcal{X}_n'} \quad (18.5a)$$

or more generally

$$\frac{\mathcal{Y}}{\mathcal{X}} \overset{.}{\approx} \frac{\mathcal{Y}'}{\mathcal{X}'} \quad (18.5b)$$

The structure of second-order causal functions is a protoproportion ($\overset{.}{\approx}$). It comprises analogical dependencies between means and ends that covary. From this perspective, protoproportional functions are developmental precursors of preproportional functions (formalized by Grize, 1977).

Structural development from first- to second-order causal functions is both continuous and discontinuous. In first-order functions, ends or effects vary with means or causes $(X \rightarrow Y)$, such as "Rolling is dependent on Pushing." Or, means or causes vary with ends or effects $(X \leftarrow Y)$ such as "Blocking is dependent on Rolling." But the dependencies are directed one way only $(X \rightarrow Y$ or $X \leftarrow Y)$, not both ways. The structure of one-way pragmatic dependencies is a protoratio at most. With the development of second-order functions, means or causes and ends or effects covary $(X \rightarrow Y$ and $X \leftarrow Y)$. First-order dependencies are mapped onto each other so that they are directed two ways ($X \rightleftarrows Y$). The structure of two-way pragmatic dependencies is a protoproportion.

Second-order dependencies are not yet true functions for a number of reasons. One important structural deficiency is that second-order causal functions, unlike true causal functions, are restricted to establishing dependencies between particular elements. The elements are not oriented; neither independent nor dependent semivariables are partly ordered or partly classed. The elements are nothing more than unordered pragmatic equivalences. So in our illustrative example, "pushing" and its complement "blocking" are not varied on a continuum or by class. Accordingly, these independent semivariables and their respective effects, "rolling" and its complement "stopping," are invariant. Both means and ends are nothing but particular elements.

On the other hand, both means and ends are transformed discretely by negation into their complements. By negation, independent semivariables are transformed successively into their discrete complements (e.g., "pushing" into "blocking" into "pushing" or $\mathcal{X}_1$ into $\mathcal{X}_1'$ followed by $\mathcal{X}_1'$ back into $\mathcal{X}_1$). Thus, too, dependent semivariables are transformed successively into their discrete complements (e.g., "rolling" into "stopping" into "rolling" or $\mathcal{Y}_1$ into $\mathcal{Y}_1'$ followed by $\mathcal{Y}_1'$ back into $\mathcal{Y}_1$). Both means and ends are no more than particular elements that are transformed by negation into their complements.

We may then view protoproportions as fundamental to negation or the passage from one particular element into its complement by a constant transformation. In the illustrative function the particular elements are transformed by infants from "pushing" into "blocking" independent semivariables, and then back into "pushing," and so on. The particular elements are also transformed by infants from "rolling" into "stopping" dependent semivariables, and then back into "rolling," and so on.

Second-order functions are integrative constructions. They coordinate elementary first-order means–ends dependencies with each other. This coordination produces a second level of more powerful and representational functions. A fundamental structural developmental difference is that first-order functions do not exceed direct ratio-like dependencies between means and ends while second-order functions are indirect proportional-like or analogical relations between means and ends.

Second-, like first-order causal functions, develop in power, stage by stage, during infants' second year. Most notable is the construction and use of intermediaries. Hence, both levels of causality continue to develop beyond the organizational completion of their structures.

It should not be overlooked that there is parallel progress in the development of spatial protofunctions. We shall not belabor the point by reviewing our findings so far on spatial functions which, like those on causal functions, are still preliminary and partial only. Infants' spatial dependencies, such as alignments, envelopments and translations, develop from first- to second-order functions during their second year. Both levels of spatial construction also coexist and develop during this age period.

III. Necessity and Possibility

Precursory logicomathematical necessity is constructed by infants as soon as they generate part–whole transformations or first-order proto-operations. From this perspective, the multiplicity of extensive and intensive relations infants already generate during their first year (Langer, 1980) are the structural developmental source of constructing necessary inferences that do not, of course, develop fully until adolescence and adulthood. To illustrate, from this perspective substituting objects within single compositions by infants during their first year is precursory to constructing aspects of necessary extensive equivalence. In addition, infants classifying objects into individual compositions by negation or affirmation during the same age period is precursory to constructing aspects of necessary intensive identity.

The thesis is that infants of this age are already constructing the basic and primitive cognitive elements that issue after a long process of developmental transformations in the construction of necessary inferences starting in adolescence (Piaget, 1981, 1983). The data reported in this volume support the further claim that the first major developmental step in this direction, in transforming precursory into true necessity, is taken by infants during their second year. Then they raise both their extensive and intensive logicomathematical constructions to the second power. For instance, infants generate extensive equivalences upon equivalences by substituting objects between corresponding compositions. Such mappings of operations upon operations (or part–whole transformations upon part–whole transformations) initiates the representational cognition of necessary relations. Thus, the transitional developmental stages in the construction of logicomathematical necessity are beginning to be filled in.

None of this process requires cognizance by infants of their logicomathematical constructions nor of the necessary features of these constructions. Nonetheless, we may hypothesize that infants begin to be cognizant of aspects of this activity during their second year by virtue of their constructions becoming representational. On this hypothesis, infants' second-order representational constructions provide them with minimal necessary conditions for beginning to reflectively abstract the logicomathematical properties of their constructions (see Piaget, 1977a, 1977b). Second-order operations are mappings upon mappings. Thus, they begin to detach operations from their initial objects of application. They also begin to coordinate two operations with each other (potentially by negation to form hierarchically integrated and reversible group structures when fully developed during adolescence and adulthood). Detachment and coordination of operations are, according to this hypothesis, the minimal necessary conditions for reflective abstraction of logicomathematical relations and their necessary features.

Precursory physical contingency is constructed in parallel by infants' means–ends transformations or first-order protofunctions during their first year. The first major transition in the developmental transformation of precursory into true physical contingency is initiated by the growth of second-order representational functions. So while the structures, origin, and development of physical contingency are different from that of logicomathematical necessity, the formal parallels are evident.

The development of physical contingency includes progressive differentiation and coordination of possible and impossible constructions. By age 8 months infants already anticipate, verify and replicate possible physical constructions (Langer, 1980). To illustrate, subject 8CC leans over the right arm of the chair in which she is sitting and holds a ring out over the floor with her right hand while looking down at the floor on the right. Then she drops the ring and looks at it when it lands on the floor. This simple physical function is repeated and confirmed twice by 8CC.

Empirical disconfirmation is taken into account and leads to differentiating possible from impossible contingent relations at least as early as age 12 months. To illustrate, subject 12BG drops a block to the floor while looking down at the floor but because he does not extend his hand out far enough, the block lands on the table instead. Subject 12BG looks surprised, picks the block up again, extends his hand out far enough this time, and drops the block to the floor. The physical contradiction, then, is taken into account by 12BG such that he modifies the physical function that he constructs. Thereby he begins to differentiate possible contingent constructions from impossible ones.

Differentiating and coordinating possible and impossible physical constructions become experimental with the development of second-order representational functions. As already noted, for instance, infants begin by pushing objects that will and will not roll away and end up by pushing only those that will roll away. They also upright objects that will and will not stand up easily; they stack objects that will and will not stand on each other easily; and so on.

Progressively, infants differentiate and coordinate possible and impossible functions even within the same composition. Recall, for instance, that at age 18 months subject 18ML successfully stacks two cylinders on each other. After this he tries unsuccessfully to balance a ring on the stack. But he does not let the ring fall and he does not give up easily. He holds the stack together with one hand so that it will not fall over. At the same time he makes painstaking lengthy adjustments with the other hand in the way it grips the ring and in the way in which it repeatedly changes the placement position of the ring on the stack.

Symptoms of cognizance also progressively mark infants' differentiation and coordination of possible and impossible physical constructions. By age 21 months, for instance, subject 21EN stacks two cylinders on each other, laughs, and acts pleased. After this he tries unsuccessfully to place two spoons on the stack. But he does not simply let the spoons go. Instead he takes them off the stack when it does not work.

Making such differentiations between and coordinations of possible and impossible physical conditions opens up the possibility of cognizing new physical differentiations and coordinations. One illustration should suffice. The same subject, 21EN stands a cylinder upright on the table. After this he tilts the cylinder and lets go such that it falls over. Then he repeats the entire routine from uprighting to tilting the same cylinder. Thus, once infants determine some possible conditions, they begin to construct and test the possible and impossible parameters of these conditions.

Logicomathematical necessity and physical contingency do not simply develop in parallel. There is continual developing interaction between them such that progress in one has implications for and informs the progressive construction of the other. According to this hypothesis, logical necessity introduces the element of certainty into physical cognition. On the one hand, this includes the origins of a logic of experimentation (e.g., ordering and classifying causal semivariables) whose precursors we have traced back to infants' first year and their construction of first-order proto-operations (Langer, 1980). On the other hand, this includes the formalization of causal functions whose precursors we have traced back to first-order ratio-like functions during infants' first year. According to this hypothesis, then, these are the initial constructive roots of hypotheticodeductive reasoning that begin to develop in adolescence (Inhelder & Piaget, 1958). Their initial developmental transformation in this direction has been traced in this volume to the growth of second-order operations and proportion-like functions. Hence, we are beginning to determine both the precursors of and developmental stages in the formation of hypotheticodeductive reasoning.

At the same time as logical necessity provides analytic certainty to physical cognition, physical contingency introduces the element of factual uncertainty into logicomathematical cognition. Recalling one protocol fragment should suffice to make the latter point. At age 18 months, 18BB's right hand places all four presented spoons in a cup. Then the right hand takes out together all four spoons from the cup and holds them together. Subject 18BB looks in the cup while her right hand continues to hold all four spoons. Finally, 18BB says "No-mor" while her right hand continues to hold all four spoons. Subject 18BB acts as if some remainder may be found in the cup even though she has taken out (subtracted) all four spoons (the same quantity) she put in (added). Thus, uncertainty is introduced into this simple necessity (that there can be no remainder) by negation. The source of the uncertainty is the apparent intrusion of incomplete differentiation by 18BB between physical possibility and impossibility.

The original ontogenetic sources, then, of necessity and contingency are different. From the present perspective they are, respectively, the first-order part–whole and means–ends transformations already generated by infants during their first year. But, in addition, the initial source of certainty about contingent relations is the product of infants' proto-operations informing their protofunctions. And the initial source of uncertainty about necessary relations is the product of infants' protofunctions informing their proto-operations.

This two-way interaction develops continuously through childhood and adolescence until it is manifest in adult cognition (e.g., Kahneman, Slovic, & Tversky, 1982; Osherson, 1975; Pieraut–LeBonniec, 1980; Wason & Johnson–Laird, 1972). This two-way interaction between necessity and contingency even marks the history of science, including contemporary science. Here we have found that the first major ontogenetic transformation in this two-way interaction occurs when infants develop second-order operations and functions. When they begin to construct second-order or representational cognition, then infants can begin to be cognizant of necessity and possibility.

IV. A Proposed Recursive Model and Its Relations to Other Theories

Representational cognition is a structural developmental transform of elementary cognition. Second-order operations and functions are developmental transforms of first-order proto-operations and protofunctions; and routines are developmental transforms of mappings. While early infancy is characterized by first-order elementary cognition, the developmental shift is toward second-order cognition during late infancy. Even though the latter is a novel development it is still a transformational derivative of the former. This transformational aspect of our model is consistent with Piaget's (e.g., 1970) claim that each stage of cognitive development is a structural transform of a preceding stage.

Nevertheless, Piaget's model is primarily linear while ours is recursive (Langer, in press). Linearity characterizes most contemporary models of cognitive development. Linear models are unileveled since they emphasize successive single orders or levels of cognition only. Linear models are also usually unidirectional since their focus is on progress from lower to higher orders of cognition.

Linear models are unileveled and unidirectional whether they conceptualize cognition as structural or functional (see Beilin, 1983, for an analysis that seeks to integrate structuralism with functionalism), development as stage-like or dimensional, and developmental transitions as transformational or additive. Consequently, linear models are unileveled and unidirectional whether they conceptualize cognitive development as discontinuous, continuous, or both. Beginning at least with Vygotsky (1962), functional descriptions of cognitive development tend to be linear (e.g., Bruner *et al.*, 1966) or partly linear (e.g., Fischer, 1980) and include those that seek to incorporate information processing (e.g., Siegler, 1983; and Sternberg, 1977). The Neo-Piagetian trend begun by Pascuale–Leone (1970) has also generated linear models that attempt to couple structural descriptions of cognitive development with information processing (e.g., Case, 1984; Halford, 1982; and Klahr & Wallace, 1976).

Our recursive model of cognitive development is multileveled, multidirectional, and multistructural. So while it shares much with Werner's (1948) branching tree model (see also Langer's, 1970, analysis of Werner's model) there are significant differences, as we shall see. Our recursive model posits progenitor structures that do not disappear, are not lost, when they spawn their descendent transforms. Rather, both progenitor and descendant cognitive structures continue to develop, although eventually progenitor structures do so less than their descendent structures. Progenitor structures serve as progressively powerful elements for descended structures. They, in turn, progressively integrate their progenitors. This integration permits first- and second-order cognition to co-exist during late infancy.

Two further specifications of this recursive model require mention. They are specifications about the course and form of development. Both are consistent with our earlier claim that a comprehensive portrayal of the longitudinal axis of development takes the form of an inverted obtuse pyramid that is multileveled, multidirectional, and multistructural (see Langer, 1969a, pages 172–176, for details).

This recursive model specifies that the form of development is governed by simplicity. At their origins, second-order like first-order cognitions are expected to take the most rudimentary or primitive forms possible. Accordingly, we found that during their early stages, second-order cognitions take simpler forms than first order cognitions when both are manifest by infants. This is because first-order cognitions are already in the midst of their development when second-order cognitions are just beginning to develop. In this way the recursive model also accounts for the relations between developmental progress and regress that we have dealt with elsewhere (Langer, 1969a, pages 178–180, 1970, 1982b; cf., Bever, 1982, and Strauss, 1982).

The recursive model also specifies that the course of elementary cognition in infancy develops in power stage by stage even as part of it is transformed into representational cognition. Once it arises, representational cognition also develops in power stage by stage. According to this view, structural development is continuous as well as discontinuous (while only functional development of assimilation and accomodation is continuous according to Piaget, 1952a; for further analyses and distinctions see Langer, 1969a, pages 169–172, and 1974). This necessarily includes ontogenetic continuity as well as discontinuity with phylogenetically adapted structures and their functions by genetic transmission.

This claim that the structural development of cognition is both continuous and discontinuous is the theoretical basis for numbering the stages of cognitive development during infancy seriatim as one sequence from stage 1 to stage 8. The theoretical sequence of stages is continuous, discontinuous, and integrative even though: (a) there are no second-order structures early in infancy; (b) second-order structures are derivative transforms of first-order structures; (c) first- and second-order structures coexist during late infancy; and(d) second-order structures progressively integrate first-order structures.

Structural continuity in this recursive model is provided by the mappings, part–whole transformations, and means–ends transformations generated from earliest infancy on through all of cognitive development. These structural developmental invariants are the basic constructive elements of all concept and symbol formation. They are material determinants or causes of logicomathematical operations, physical functions, and symbolic expressions. In this aspect, our recursive model differs sharply with other theories of cognitive development, including those of Piaget, Vygotsky, and Werner.

Structural discontinuity in this recursive model is generated by infants mapping their initial prerepresentational mappings onto each other, mapping their initial prerepresentational operations onto each other, and mapping their initial prerepresentational functions onto each other. These structural developmental transformations are the basic constructive sources of all concept and symbol development. They are formal determinants or causes of the development of representational cognition. In this, too, our recursive model differs sharply with other theories of cognitive development.

Hence, symbolic routines and language during late infancy are both continuous with and discontinuous from protosymbolic mappings during early infancy. In addition, second-order operations and functions during late infancy are both continuous with and discontinuous from first-order operations and functions during early infancy. Advanced conceptual and symbolic forms progressively integrate the very progenitor forms of which they are derivative transforms. The cognitive offspring incorporate their progenitors.

Constructive development marked by structural continuity, discontinuity, and integration is facilitated by the coexistence of developing elementary and representational cognition during late infancy. This coexistence produces progressive equilibrium (e.g., coherence and completeness) in the organization of cognition. At the same time, this coexistence produces progressive disequilibrium (e.g., imbalances between levels of cognition, opening of new possibilities and impossibilities, and introduction of uncertainty) in its organization. We have proposed that both are basic structural sources of cognitive development (Langer, 1969b, 1980, 1982b). They are efficient determinants or causes of cognitive development.

This proposal shares much with Piaget's (1977) equilibration mechanism of development. One difference is important, however. In Piaget's linear model, development is produced by progressive decrease in disequilibrium which is directly coupled with, and is the inverse of, progressive increase in equilibrium. The recursive model is an open dialectical model (Langer, 1974, 1982b) in which (a) progressive disequilibrium is a source of progressive equilibrium, and (b) progressive equilibrium is a source of progressive disequilibrium. Thus, development is produced by both progressive equilibrium and disequilibrium. Recall, for one illustration, the 18 month-old infant who is able to go on to experimenting with the limits of tilting an upright cylinder once he has become a virtuoso at balancing it upright.

This proposal also shares much with structure-dependent models of development (e.g., Chomsky, 1980; Kohler, 1929; and Lorenz, 1965). Here too, however, the differences are significant. A crucial difference is that the recursive model, like Piaget's and many but not all linear models, and Werner's branching tree model, assumes constructive development. Structure-dependent models assume preformism, whether in its genetic (continuity) and/or maturational (discontinuity) guises that have given rise to a wide spectrum of instantiations (e.g., Freud, 1930, 1958; Gesell, 1946; Jung, 1959; and recently Gibson, 1979; Kagan, 1982; and Keil, 1981, 1984). Thus, structure-dependent models leave no room for constructive development (continuity, discontinuity, and integration) of cognition. In contrast, constructive development is the cornerstone of our recursive model.

Cognition, from the present perspective, is a developmental construction; it is not performed genetically or maturationally. The ontogenetic antecedents of cognitive development are elementary but already constructive mappings. Specifically, part–whole transformations are the sources of logicomathematical operations and the production of necessary equivalence, nonequivalence, and reversibility; and means–ends transformations are the sources of physical functions and the production of contingent possibility and impossibility.

It is not possible to derive the structures of logicomathematical and physical cognition from single related, even important, structures. It is even less possible to derive the structures of cognition from single related, even important, psychological functions. Sensorimotor circular reactions, first proposed by Baldwin (1894/1970) and then elegantly expanded by Piaget (1952a), are appropriate candidates as constructive ontogenetic antecedents of cognitive procedures (e.g., Inhelder & Piaget, 1979; Karmiloff–Smith & Inhelder, 1977). They can not be ontogenetic antecedents of the cognitive structures of logicomathematical and physical knowledge. Even less plausible candidates, based on the present account, are functions such as perceptual discrimination and generalization and memory encoding. The serious problems involved in getting from infant functioning (e.g., perceptual categorization) to childhood cognition (e.g., conceptual classification) as a developmental account are increasingly recognized (e.g.,

Cohen & Younger, 1983), and are one of the factors that already prompted Werner's (1948) branching tree model.

Cognition is not unitary. It includes, at least, logicomathematical, physical, and social structures. This view is shared by Piaget (e.g., Piaget & Inhelder, 1969) and Werner (1948), among many others (e.g., Fodor, 1984), although not all others (e.g., classical Gestalt Psychology). In addition, we have found it necessary to distinguish between substructures such as those of spatial and causal functions within physical cognition. Hence Turiel (1983) also distinguishes between the domains of conventional, moral, and personal reasoning within social cognition.

It follows that the structural ontogenetic antecedents of cognition are not unitary. To illustrate, sensorimotor groupings of pragmatic spatial relations proposed by Piaget (1954) are appropriate candidates as constructive ontogenetic antecedents of spatial cognition. From the present perspective however, they cannot even be antecedents of other physical cognition such as causal cognition, let alone logicomathematical cognition.

This implication is not shared by Piaget (1952a) or Werner (1948). Both posit undifferentiated sensorimotor activity as the original global source of cognition. Sensorimotor activity is progressively differentiated and hierarchically integrated with development (into logicomathematical, physical and social structures, according to Piaget).

According to the present perspective, part–whole transformations are the structural ontogenetic antecedents of necessary logicomathematical operations. Different structures, means–ends transformations are the ontogenetic antecedents of contingent physical functions. Furthermore, we have found different means–ends dependencies that are structural antecedents of causal and spatial functions (i.e., dependent energy relations and dependent placement relations, respectively).

These differentiated structures and substructures develop in parallel. They do not necessarily develop at precisely the same rates; and they do not necessarily develop to the same extent within any given individual (Langer, in press). Parallelism is only expected to mark the sequences in which the structural (and substructural) stages of logicomathematical and physical cognition develop. Precocious and more extended development in particular cognitive domains within a given individual is commonplace. Precocious and more extended development in particular cognitive domains is also commonplace in the history of mathematics and science. It is even beginning to be found in nonhuman primates (Antinucci, 1982; Premack, 1976).

The initially differentiated structures and substructures of elementary cognition are further differentiated with development. But they also progressively interact by informing one another. Consequently, their development is marked by both progressive differentiation and coordination into a hierarchically integrated organization. The first major, but still transitional, transformation toward hierarchic integration is the development of representational cognition.

In Section 3 we considered how part–whole and means–ends transformations progressively differentiate and coordinate. This included the proposal that informational interaction during infancy between logicomathematical operations and physical functions initiates the hierarchic integration of necessary and contingent knowledge. Progressively integrated knowledge is primary to infants' developing organization of differentiated and coordinated representational cognition.

Representational cognition, from this perspective, is not a direct product of symbol, including language, development during late infancy (as assumed, for example, by Bruner *et al.*, 1966; Vygotsky, 1962; and Werner & Kaplan, 1963). Nor is representational cognition the indirect product of applying symbolization to sensorimotor development (which is an important part of but not the complete claim made by Piaget, 1951, 1952a). Instead we have proposed that representation constitutes second-order cognition produced by infants mapping their elementary first-order cognitions (i.e., mappings, proto-operations, and protofunctions) onto each other. Chapter 19 elaborates this perspective to account for the structural development of symbol formation and its relation to concept formation.

19

Language and Thought

Pragmatic propositions or routines are the products of infants combining their mappings. By mapping onto their mappings (e.g., virtual and anticipatory gestures), infants begin the process of detaching their constructive applications from their objects of reference. In this way, infants initiate symbol formation during the latter half of their first year (Langer, 1980).

With the formation of routines, the process of symbol formation accelerates rapidly during infants' second year. Without reviewing the details of our findings, it may be recalled that the main line of development is from mappings (e.g., uprighting cups, inserting spoons, etc.) to phrase-like routines that combine mappings (e.g., uprighting a cup and inserting spoons into the cup) to sentence-like routines that combine phrase-like routines (e.g., uprighting a cup then inserting and stirring a spoon in the cup followed by licking the spoon).

Even phrase-like routines generated as early as age 15 months begin to be marked by syntactic regularity, arbitrariness, substitution, conventionalization, and detachment. Thus, some phrase-like routines already partially stand for and communicate nonpresent events. To illustrate, some infants of this age already pretend to feed a doll with a spoon or pretend but do not actually brush their own teeth with a brush.

Routines have the form of pragmatic propositions with fairly demarcable subjects or agents, actions, and objects or patients. They are already featured by the predicted initial construction of equivalence classes of agents (e.g., substituting brushes or spoons for each other), actions (e.g., substituting virtual for actual brushing), and patients (e.g., substituting a doll for the self as an object of brushing). In effect, subjects, actions, and objects begin to be differentiated from

385

each other and integrated with each other. Syntactic interchangeability, differentiation, and integration are entirely serial, not hierarchical. Yet the routines that infants thereby produce are sufficient to evoke and symbolize aspects of nonpresent events.

Sentence-like routines or pragmatic propositions that stand for and communicate nonpresent events may be quite complex by age 24 months. They are becoming planful, impervious to interpolations or interruptions, and syntactic to the point of integrating differentiated subroutines into the structure of the overall routines. Syntactic rules, arbitrariness, and conventionalization progressively govern the generation of these routines. Thus, as expected, infants elaborate expanded equivalence classes of subjects, actions, and objects that are increasingly interchanged and permuted. This rapidly increasing combinatorial power permits infants to generate many new forms of propositional routines.

The development from mappings to routines, then, provides the necessary conditions for the origin and development of symbolization. As expected, this development is marked by three ingredients that are essential to symbol formation. These are standing-for relations by substitution that include playful pretense, arbitrary relations by syntactic combinativity, and conventionalization necessary to social communication.

This development from mappings to routines raises two important questions about the origins and development of representation. One, which we will take up now, is the developing relation between symbol formation in routines and symbol formation in language. The other, which we will take up later, is the developing relation between symbol formation (including both routines and language) and concept formation (including both logicomathematical and physical cognition).

I. Symbol Formation

Semantic and syntactic aspects of symbolization are already being established in infants' routines or pragmatic propositions by age 15 months, as we have just noted. They ontogenetically precede the semantic and syntactic development of language up to this age. At most, by age 15 months infants are at the one word stage (e.g., Brown, 1973). The meaning or referents of these isolated words tend to be particular (e.g., when picking up a car and saying "Auto") or holophrastic and undifferentiated (e.g., Beilin, 1975, and Werner & Kaplan, 1963). Two-word utterances at this age (e.g., "Whaz-zis?" and "Mommy, here.") are rare. When they are generated, two-word utterances begin to afford some further opportunities for semantic and syntactic development (see Maratsos, 1983, for a recent review).

The comparative development of routines and language leads to the conclusion that infants' generation of routines initiates the formation of the expressive and communicative features of symbolization. Even the still-primitive syntactic and semantic structure of routines is missing entirely or almost entirely from infants' language up till at least age 15 months and probably quite a bit older. Hence, ontogenetically routines precede or lead language in forming expressive and communicative symbolization, thus making it possible for routines to lead language into forming expressive and communicative symbolic features.

The hypothesis is that the semantic and syntactic development of language begins by "piggybacking" on more advanced routines. The features of pragmatic propositions (i.e., arbitrariness, substitution, conventionalization, etc.) that mark the symbolic medium of routines are generalized or transferred to the medium of language. This hypothesis accounts for how language becomes symbolic at its origins in infancy.

This hypothesis may also account for much of the subsequent semantic and syntactic development of language during infancy. The symbolic advance of routines over language is maintained in most instances up to age 18 months. Routines stand for nonpresent events (e.g., pretend to give a drink from an empty cup to a doll and to pour water from it on a doll) more completely and conventionally than infants' linguistic productions at this age. Routines are also progressively differentiated and integrated syntactically. In contrast, subjects, actions, and objects are still rarely differentiated and integrated in infants' language at this age (a conclusion echoed by Maratsos, 1983, based on his review of the literature on early speech). This differentiation and integration remains hardly possible when infants' mean length of utterances still does not exceed about one word.

Thus, both the syntax and semantics of language remain meager in comparison to those of routines at age 18 months. The syntactic complexity and semantic power of routines is clearly more developed in most instances than those of language. Still, some significant exceptions are developing. Recall the most advanced linguistic behavior found at age 18 months. While it was generated in the context of our nonverbal tasks that are not designed to elicit any linguistic behavior by subjects, it is nevertheless at least as advanced and complex as any typically reported in the literature for this age (e.g., Braine, 1963; Brown, 1973). This subject accompanied decomposing PlayDoh balls and rings with variants of three basic expressions, "I broke it," "Peeling," and "Doo. Ball." This still exceptional level of verbal expression begins to match the syntactic and semantic structure of infants' routines at this stage.

The development of symbolic routines continues to lead that of language in some ways as late as age 24 months (e.g., routines include differentiated subroutines that are integrated into their overall pragmatic propositions). In other respects, however, the syntactic and semantic structure of infants' language catches up with and begins to outstrip that of their routines. This includes the ability to progressively symbolize the nonpresent and to barely symbolize comparative (e.g., time and color) and quantitative (e.g., number) properties.

The piggyback hypothesis, then can account for how language gets going developmentally as a symbolic (syntactic and semantic) medium. It can also account for how language develops some further essential syntactic and semantic features (e.g., integration of subclauses, and interchangeability of subjects, actions, and objects). Hence, the hypothesis also accounts for how language catches up developmentally to routines.

This hypothesis can not account, however, for how language begins to develop symbolic features by age 24 months that outstrip the syntactic and semantic capacities of routines. The latter development indicates that language begins to develop into an autonomous symbolic medium toward the end of infants' second year and the beginning of their third year (see Bickerton, in press). Its syntactic and semantic development is decreasingly or is no longer dependent upon further development of propositional routines. Then language can rapidly develop symbolic features that far outstrip and exceed the limits of routines (e.g., abstract linguistic notation that stands for potential events).

II. Concept and Symbol Formation

Determining the initial and developing relations between symbol and concept formation, between language and thought, is a problem for all major cognitive developmental theories of representation (Piaget, 1951; Vygotsky, 1962; Werner, 1948; Werner & Kaplan, 1963; see Beilin, 1975, and Mandler, 1983, for reviews). Unlike previous theories, however, our proposals about representation are not based on data that confound concept with symbol development. They are based on our data on infants' conceptual constructions. These are data on infants' developing logicomathematical operations such as extensive equivalences upon equivalences by substituting between two corresponding compositions and intensive identity of an object by negating deforming by reforming. They are also data on infants' developing physical functions such as causal covariation by proportional or analogical dependency. These data on concept formation are independent from our data on infants' developing symbolic productions, such as their pretend routines or verbal utterances.

Concept development is equal to or greater than symbolic development during infancy. This comparative proposition takes into account data on language development generated in this study and that reported in the literature (e.g., Bloom, 1970; Bowerman, 1978; Braine, 1963; Brown, 1973; Maratsos, 1983; Piaget, 1951; and Werner & Kaplan, 1963). Strictly speaking, it is of course not possible to compare quantitatively the development of symbolization with that of conception since there is no common developmental metric that can measure both. Nevertheless, the findings on concept and symbol formation during infancy are rich enough to already extract a set of qualitative generalizations (for detailed expositions see Langer, 1982a, 1983).

First-order operations and functions are well-developed during the second half of infants' first year when their production of symbolic routines and language is still practically nonexistent or is, at most, extremely rudimentary. Second-order operations and functions originate toward the end of infants' first year when they just begin to generate some substantial symbolic routines and language. Second-order operations and functions are well-developed by the second half of infants' second year when routines are becoming well-developed and langauge is just beginning to develop some power and autonomy from other symbolic media such as routines.

Four interactive relations are possible in principle between symbol and concept formation during infancy. Two relations are symmetrical and extreme. At one pole, concept and symbol formation may be dependent structural developmental systems that influence each other mutually and equally. At the other pole, concept and symbol formation are totally independent structural developmental systems that do not influence each other at all. Between these two extremes are two asymmetric relations that are most consistent with the qualitative comparative generalizations that can be drawn from our data on concept and symbol formation. In both these intermediate possibilities, conception and symbolization are independent structural developmental systems during infancy. But concept formation may have implicatory consequences for symbol formation and/or symbol formation may have implicatory consequences for concept formation.

As independent systems, they cannot cause each other's development. To symbolize events cannot cause infants to conceptualize their potential logicomathematical and physical properties. Nor can conceptualizing events cause infants to symbolize their potential semantic properties in syntactic forms. The structural development of one can, however, have implications for the structural development of the other.

To the extent that concept and symbol formation have implications for each other during infancy, the predominant influence is that of conception upon symbolization. Since it leads developmentally, conception can inform and constrain symbolization. Conversely, since it lags behind developmentally during most of infancy, it is less possible for symbolization to have structural developmental implications for conception. As symbolization catches up to conception toward the end of infancy, it begins to be able to influence conception.

This proposal applies to both the semantics and syntax of developing symbolization. It applies equally to the development of language as to the development of propositional routines. At the same time, it should be recognized that the influence of conception on the development of propositional routines may be more direct than its influence on the development of language. The influence of conception on language may be mediated by conception's influence upon propositional routines. This expectation is consistent with our proposal that until language development begins to become autonomous, toward the end of infants' second year, it is dependent in large part upon the development of symbolic routines.

First- and second-order operations and functions provide a rich and developing conceptual foundation for the initial stages of symbol formation in various media, ranging from routines to language. The conceptual organization of knowledge is more developed and therefore richer and more complex than the semantic organization of routines and language during most and perhaps all of infancy. At most, then, infants exploit only part of their organization of logicomathematical and physical conceptions as significant semantic features for symbolization.

The conceptual foundation produced by their operations and functions serves as infants' background of significant knowledge. Their independently developing semantic structures select from these background significances a subset and make this selected subset of significances figural in transformed expressive symbols. The rules governing selection of significances out of infants' conceptual background and their figural expression are inherent properties of symbolic systems. As such, the semantic structures of symbolic systems develop independently. Furthermore, the semantic rules of selection and expression are autonomous, since they vary from one symbolic medium to another. The subset of selected significances and their expression in different media, such as routines and language, are less than isomorphic with each other.

The organization of conceptual significances, then, is expected to inform and constrain the semantic organization of symbolization. But the interactive effect is a structural figure-ground effect. Infants' background conceptual significances have implications for how infants' structure their figural symbolic expressions in different media (e.g., routines, gestures, imagery, and speech). The interactions between figure and ground are structural and implicatory (i.e., formal), not causal (i.e., mechanical).

The development of infants' causal cognition serves particularly well to analyze the expected implicatory relation for one reason: The semantics of both their causal conceptions and their causal symbolization necessarily involve structuring relations between subjects or agents for actions, acting by agents, and objects or patients of actions. For the sake of brevity we will restrict the analysis to comparing infants' protoproportional causal constructions with their production of symbolic causatives at age 18 months.

Causal functions constructed by infants at age 18 months already include covarying dependencies between the actions of agents and patients such that their roles as causes and effects become interchangeable. They form proportional-like or analogical structures (expressed in Eq. 18.5b on page 373). These are relatively complex second-order causal conceptions produced by infants mapping their first-order construction of causal ratio-like functions (expressed in Eq. 18.3) onto each other.

Causal expressions produced by infants at age 18 months are limited by comparison. Infants' causatives are usually holophrastic or particular. When the causatives are holophrastic, they symbolize events in which the causal features of the referents are not differentiated (e.g., saying "Boing" while knocking over several objects and "Vroummmm" while pushing a car around). When the causatives are particular, they symbolize only partial or individual features of the causal referents (e.g., "Car" for a subject and "Drop" for an action). These causatives are typical since infants' productions do not usually exceed onomatopoeic or one-word utterances at this age.

The most advanced causatives produced by one infant only at age 18 months is quite precocious (i.e., "I broke it," "Peeling," and "Doo. Ball," while decomposing PlahDoh objects). Even these precocious causatives do not approach or exploit as semantic elements for symbolization the complexity of infants' conceptual significances that include second-order causal functions. Infants' linguistic causatives make figural, in symbolic form only, part of their causal knowledge.

Throughout, we have found that infants generate more complex cognitions than one could determine by investigating their symbolic, including linguistic, productions. This accounts at least in part for the expectation that infants' symbolic comprehension always exceeds or at least equals their symbolic production. This expectation applies to all symbolic media, including language. The basic reason is that infants can only select and express part of their conceptual knowledge. It is therefore easier, or at least as easy, for infants to understand symbolic communications than it is for them to produce symbolic expressions of conceptual significance. This generalization applies equally to causality as it does to their other logicomathematical and physical cognitions. Infants generate more complex causal cognitions than one could determine by investigating their symbolic causative productions.

The initiation and early development of syntax parallels that of semantic development. First- and second-order operations and functions constitute a developing structural grammar of elementary cognitions. It prepares infants for producing and comprehending arbitrary but conventional rules by which symbols stand for and communicate referents. In this way, it provides the required grammatical foundations for and may facilitate the acquisition of symbolic syntax. Only part of this foundational grammatical knowledge, however, is exploited by the syntax of any given symbolic medium, such as language, at its inception and early development during infancy.

Recalling two structural features of infants' developing logicomathematical cognition should suffice to make the point. One is the combinatory operation of composing that progressively includes elaborating equivalence classes that are arbitrary because they are the products of infants uniting elements such that they are equivalent or dimensionally continuous under certain functions or conditions of dependency. It also includes infants elaborating predicate classes that are progressively realistic and conventional since they increasingly comprehend identical or similar elements.

The second structural feature is infants' developing conditional operation of substitution. Infants progressively exchange elements within and between sets and classes. The products we have seen begin to include forming predicate identity as well as quantitative equivalence.

Development of composing and substituting are necessary but not sufficient conditions for infants to generate symbolic forms in which the parts or elements are progressively combinable and interchangeable. They are also necessary but not sufficient for infants to generate symbolic forms where the configurational wholes increasingly stand for or are notations of nonpresent as well as present referents or significances. Composing, substituting, and the other features comprising infants growing cognitive structures are the generative grammatical foundations that enable infants to increasingly permute the syntactic structure of symbol forms. This structure enables infants to produce and comprehend more numerous and varied symbolic combinations, whether they take the form of mapping routines or linguistic sentences.

Consider only two points in infants' productive linguistic development. By age 18 months infants begin to generate sets of phrase forms (e.g., the set of "Broke it," "I broke it," "I broke" and the set of "Peel," "Peeling"). Each set of phrases is already the product of generative structures that relate, syntactically and semantically, phrase forms and their elements that are increasingly different and varied. By age 24 months infants' generative grammatical structures are much more advanced. They enable infants to begin to produce varied but related sets of phrase and sentence forms (e.g., the set of "Boat," "In boat," "He in boat," and "Sailing in boat," and the set of "Cars," "Faster cars," "This faster," and "Not faster").

Infants' developing cognition provides the foundational grammatical abilities for generating progressive syntactic as well as semantic symbolic forms. In this way, they have implications for or provide the necessary developing parameters of and constraints upon the development of syntactic linguistic production, comprehension and, for that matter, appreciation. The developing grammars governing the generation of syntactic forms within each symbolic medium are autonomous and unique (e.g., the generative grammar proposed for language by Chomsky, 1965).

Symbolic development has implications for concept formation as well. Symbolization may be exploited by infants to facilitate and expand the elements of operations and functions. For instance, playful routines permit substitution of present and arbitrary (e.g., a wooden triangular column) for nonpresent and prototypic objects (e.g., a brush). Symbolization thereby extends the computational range of operations and functions.

This begins to be particularly true of language around age 24 months. At this age, infants begin to use language as a notational medium in relatively powerful ways to symbolize the nonpresent, comparative values, amounts, and so on. Thus, language begins to expand the computational range of thought in at least three ways. Language begins to multiply the constant given elements of operations and functions. Language increases the problem space to which operations and functions apply. Language also provides operations and functions with a progressively abstract and flexible notational symbolic system of elements that are increasingly detached from their objects of reference.

Language remains the most abstract, powerful, and flexible symbolic medium available to children until their cognitive development enables them to begin to acquire mathematical forms of notation. In turn, the development of mathematical symbolization expands the potential elements and power of logicomathematical operations and physical functions. Mathematical notation completes the detachment of symbols from their objects of reference. It thereby facilitates the process by which the elements of thought, at least logicomathematical and physical thought, become progressively transparent (Cassirer, 1953, 1957).

Symbolic, including linguistic development, does not cause concept formation. This is made plain by the ontogenetic facts. As we have found here during infants' second year, and as we previously found during infants' first year (Langer, 1980), their conceptual development generally outstrips their symbolic development. Some symbolic productions are precocious, powerful, and complex for their age (e.g., "Broke it. I broke it." by an 18-month-old subject and, "He in boat. Sailing in boat," by a 24-month-old subject). These precocious linguistic constructions are at least as advanced as any and more advanced than most utterances found at these early ages. Still, even these precocious linguistic productions do not exceed the power and complexity of infants' productions of second-order operations and functions at the same ages.

The conceptual development of subjects producing precocious language may be compared profitably with that of subjects who do not produce precocious language. There is no difference in the respective conceptual productions of these two groups that differ in their linguistic precocity. Subjects producing precocious language do not produce precocious operations and functions. Some subjects not producing precocious language do produce precocious second-order operations and functions (e.g., true equivalences upon equivalences by substituting objects between corresponding compositions by age 24 months).

Hence, linguistic development is not even a necessary condition for conceptual development up to at least age 24 months, let alone a sufficient condition.

Whether language development is necessary to the development of thought after infancy in early childhood will have to be taken up in a subsequent volume (Langer, in preparation). Conceptual development could be a necessary but not sufficient condition for language development during infancy. As we proposed earlier in this analysis, however, the necessary relation is that of structural implication between figure and ground where conception informs symbolization; the relation between them is not that of necessary causation.

Language, and symbolization in general, is certainly not an initiating cause of the development from first- to second-order cognition during infancy. At most, language may facilitate expanding second-order cognition once it has been initiated by infants mapping first-order operations onto each other and first-order functions onto each other. The predominant influence is that of thought upon language. Second-order cognition is necessary, but certainly not sufficient, for the development from relatively primitive symbolization in routines to more advanced symbolization in language.

The development from first- to second-order operations and functions during infancy is consistent with the thesis we proposed at the outset about the development of representation. The main cognitive development during infancy is structural. First-order operations that originate early in infants' first year are precursors of their developing logicomathematical cognition; and first-order functions that originate early in infants' first year are precursors of their developing physical cognition. The main cognitive development during infants' second year is the evolution of second-order operations and functions. Second-order operations and functions develop out of infants integrating their first-order operations and functions. By mapping operations upon operations and functions upon functions, they form representational, logicomathematical and physical cognition.

The development of second-order operations and functions initiates the structural transformation of elementary into representational thought. This consists of infants integrating their first-order coordinations into new second-order coordinations. By mapping their first-order cognitions onto one another, infants begin to construct representation.

Appendix

I. Subjects

Twelve subjects, evenly divided by sex, were tested at ages 15, 18, 21, and 24 months, for a total of 48 subjects. All the subjects were drawn from the nursery school enrollment application lists of the Harold Jones Child Study Center, University of California, Berkeley. By and large, these children are from middle-class families.

II. Discrete Object Tasks

The research design was varied and controlled for (a) object type, (b) class conditions, (c) complexity conditions, and (d) procedural conditions.

A. Object Conditions

Three kinds of discrete objects were presented to subjects. All are of the ordinary kind children play with:

1. *Solid geometric* forms, such as square and circular columns.
2. *Geometric ring* forms, such as square and circular rings.
3. *Realistic* objects, such as miniature cars and dolls.

All three types of objects are made out of nonflexible and nonbreakable materials (at least as far as infants are concerned) such as masonite and wood.

B. Class Conditions

Sets of discrete objects that represent six class conditions were presented to the subjects. Three conditions (A, B, and C) embody three well-delineated class structures, respectively. These are additive (e.g., two VW cars and two racer cars), multiplicative (e.g,. one blue circular ring, one red circular ring, one blue square ring, and one red square ring), and disjoint (e.g., two green rectangular rings and two red dolls) class structures. Three conditions (D, E, and F) embody ambiguous class structures which serve as semicontrol conditions. These are collections of all identical objects (e.g., four blue square blocks), all different objects (e.g., one racer, one doll, one plate, and one brush), and both identical and different objects (e.g., two square, one circular, and one clover ring). Two subsidiary class conditions (G and H) were administered in test phase III (see Procedure Conditions). One involves a singular odd class (e.g., two VWs, two racers, and one singular sedan). The other involves intersective anomalous classes (e.g., two green rectangular rings, two red dolls, and one red rectangular ring); one property but not the other is shared with each of the disjoint classes.

C. Complexity Conditions

Two levels of difficulty were built into the discrete tasks. The task levels range from the simplest possible to a slightly more complex version. To illustrate, for condition A (additive classes) the simplest level consists of two classes with two members of each class (e.g., two VW cars and two racer cars). The next difficulty level consists of two classes with four members of each class (e.g., four VW cars and four racer cars).

D. Procedural Conditions

The procedure consists of three consecutive phases. The techniques used consist of nonverbal probes for eliciting manipulatory activities. In the first phase, subjects engage in spontaneous activity with the objects. The second phase is designed to provoke grouping activity in subjects (e.g., containing objects in two receptacles). These first two procedural phases are used in class conditions A–F. The third phase includes administering the subsidiary class conditions G and H and specific counterconditions (e.g., presentation of two alignments of objects sorted by class properties but with a predicate error in each alignment).

III. Quasi-Continuous Object Tasks

The research design varied and controlled for: (a) object type, (b) complexity conditions, and (c) procedural conditions, that is, spontaneous free play, followed by provoked decomposing or uniting, followed by counterconditions (e.g., presentation of objects that are all the same except for their size).

A. Object Conditions

The form conditions are the same in all major respects as those used in the discrete object tasks, but with one exception. The exception is that it is not feasible to use realistic forms with PlayDoh or clay material that will hold their form yet be malleable enough for infants to be able to deform, decompose, or unite them. Consequently, only two form conditions were used: solid and ring objects.

B. Complexity Conditions

Two conditions (I and J) were tested, one (a singular well-formed object, such as a large circular ring) and many (up to six) objects.

IV. Discrete and Quasi-Continuous Object Tasks

One main condition (K) was tested. Combined sets of discrete, quasi-continuous, and conglomerate discrete–quasi-continuous objects are presented (a big PlayDoh ball, a wooden tongue depressor, and another identical big PlayDoh ball with an identical wooden tongue depressor firmly stuck into one end of the PlayDoh ball). The conglomerate object looks very much like a base drum beater.

As always, testing began with phase I of spontaneous transaction in which the subjects were encouraged to engage in free play with the objects. It was followed by test phase II, designed to provoke attaching and detaching transformations.

V. Design

The research design was the same for all age groups in order to insure comparability between their performances. Furthermore, the testing procedures were always nonverbal in all their relevant features.

Two orders of testing the main task conditions were used at each age level. Half the subjects in each age group were tested in the order: D or E or F, A, I, J, B, C, K. The other half were tested in the order: D or E or F, B, I, J, A, C, K. To facilitate performance, the levels of complexity within conditions A, B, and C were always administered in the order of simplest level first. Otherwise, the two orders are designed to insure an adequate mix of different tasks and objects to maintain young children's interest in transacting with the objects.

VI. Transcribing and Coding

While the subjects were tested in one room, their entire performance was video- and audio-taped from an adjacent room through a one-way mirror. Systematic and comprehensive methods were developed for transcribing all subjects' transactions with objects into sequential logs, and for coding the data logs. The system of transcription records, in spatiotemporal order, the subjects' actions, relations between the subjects' actions, object transformations produced by the subjects' action, relations between object transformations, and relations between the subjects' action and object transformations. Transcribing and coding reliability ranges between .77 and .98.

Glossary

Combinativity structures: Comprised of composing, decomposing, and reforming (plus derivatives such as recomposing and attaching) operations that produce elements and sets. To illustrate, reforming a malleable ring alters its intensive properties (e.g., the shape of the ring) while keeping its extensive properties (e.g., its quantity) constant.

Composition: Any configuration, collection or grouping of objects.

Conditional structures: Comprised of exchange, correlation, and negation operations that transform the extensive and intensive properties of elements, sets and series. For instance, subjects may exchange one object from each of a set of three circular and one square ring and a set of three square and one circular ring by substituting the odd square and circular rings for each other. This transformation preserves the quantitative equivalence (i.e., two sets of four objects) and produces classificatory consistency (i.e., a set of square rings and a set of circular rings). So the intensive relation is altered but the extensive relation is not.

Correlational structures: A subset of conditional structures comprising one-to-one (bi-univocal) and one-to-many (co-univocal) correspondence or matching operations. Bi-univocals map equivalence relations and co-univocals map multiplicative relations within and between sets and series.

Exchange structures: A subset of conditional structures comprising replacement, substitution, and commutativity. All three operations preserve the initial extensive properties of sets and series while transforming them (e.g., substituting a square for a circular ring in a composition of circular rings conserves the quantity of elements making up the set). Replacement also preserves the initial intensive properties of sets and series (i.e., taking away and putting back the same elements in the same place results in identity). But substitution and commutativity may preserve or alter the intensive properties of sets and series (e.g., substituting one circular ring for another in a composition of circular rings preserves the classificatory relation by similarity while substituting a square ring alters it).

Extensive: The quantitative properties (e.g., equivalence) of logicomathematical relations.

Function: A mapping form that constructs a contingent dependency relation (i.e., if x, then y). The reference is restricted to physical functions that include both causal dependencies (i.e., contingent energy relations such as propulsion by pushing one object with another) and spatial dependencies (i.e., contingent placement relations such as alignment by lining up objects in a row).

Intensive: The qualitative predicate properties (e.g., identity) of logicomathematical relations.

Mapping: A relation that expresses the transformational consequence of applying an action to the environment, with or without objects. The relation represents the interactive transformation in both the subject's and the environment's processes and products. So a mapping is a unit of interaction that relates a set A to a set B such that any element a in A is related exactly to an element b in B. If subjects' constructive processes are a source set A and their constructed products are a target set B, then a mapping relates a constructive process a (e.g., placing objects next to one another) to a constructed product b (e.g., a collection of objects). The term mapping is generally used to refer to the part–whole and means–ends transformational relations involved in operations, functions, and symbols.

Means–ends transformation: A basic mapping form by which subjects structure their interactions with the environment to construct physical cognition. These transformations comprise physical dependency relations, including contingent spatial (e.g., stacking objects on top of each other) and causal (e.g., propelling one object with another) relations. Thus, these transformations are the source of functions that produce contingent (possible and impossible) relations.

Mobile: A composition in which the member elements are in kinetic relation to one another (e.g., two objects moving together).

Negation structures: A subset of conditional structures comprising inverse and reciprocal operations that produce reversibility. They preserve the intensive and extensive properties of elements, sets and series.

One-way function: A subset of functions in which the dependency relation is oriented in a single direction only, from means to ends or from ends to means, but not both. Thus, means vary with ends or ends vary with means and the relation is linear.

Operation: A mapping form (e.g., composing, substituting, adding, and negating) that constructs a logicomathematical relation (e.g., set, equivalence, order, and reversibility).

Part–whole transformation: A basic mapping form by which subjects structure their interactions with the environment to construct logicomathematical cognition. These transformations are the source of operations (e.g., composing and negating) that produce necessary extensive (e.g., equivalence) and intensive (e.g., identity) relations.

Protofunction: The name given to the initial ontogenetic manifestations of a function (e.g., causal dependency) in its elementary, pragmatic and presentational form (e.g., pushing one object with another).

Proto-operation: The name given to the initial ontogenetic manifestations of an operation (e.g., commuting) in its elementary, pragmatic and presentational form (e.g., exchanging the position of two objects in a two-object composition).

Relational structures: Comprised of addition, subtraction, division, and multiplication operations that transform the extensive and intensive properties of elements, sets, and series. For instance, subtracting an object from 1 of 2 three-object compositions results in ordered nonequivalence (i.e., a series comprising a set of two objects and a set of three objects) so the extensive relation is altered from quantitative equivalence to nonequivalence.

Routine: The term given to a combination of two or more mappings that take pragmatic proposition-like forms marked by agents, actions, and objects. Typically, routines are sequences of mappings that subjects combine both in parallel and in series (e.g., one hand picks up and stores an object while the other hand uprights another object which is then knocked over with the stored object). Routines may be reproduced, varied systematically, articulated to include subroutines, and so on.

Stabile: A composition in which the member elements are in static relation to each other (e.g., one object stacked on another).

Two-way function: A subset of functions in which the dependency relation is oriented in two directions, from means to ends and from ends to means. Thus, means and ends covary and the relation is circular.

References

Antell, S. E., & Keating, D. P. Perception of numerical invariance in infants. *Child Development*, 1983, 54, 695–701.

Antinucci, F. Cognitive development in a comparative framework. In L. Camaioni (Ed.), *La Teoria di Jean Piaget*. Florence: Barbera, 1982.

Antinucci, F., & Miller, R. How children talk about what happened. *Journal of Child Language*, 1976, 3, 167–189.

Baldwin, J. M. *Mental Development in the Child and the Race*. New York: Wiley, 1894/1970.

Bates, E. *The Emergence of Symbols*. New York: Academic Press, 1979.

Beilin, H. *Studies in the Cognitive Basis of Language Development*. New York: Academic Press, 1975.

Beilin, H. The new functionalism and Piagets program. In E. K. Scholnick (Ed.), *New Trends in Conceptual Representation*. Hillsdale, NJ: Erlbaum, 1983.

Beilin, H., & Klein, A. *Strategies and structures in understanding geometry*. NSF Final Project Report (SED 7912809), 1982.

Bever, T. G. R. (Ed.), *Regression in Development*. Hillsdale, NJ: Erlbaum, 1982.

Bickerton, D. Evidence for a two-stage model of language evolution from ontogeny and phylogeny. In S. Strauss (Ed.), *Ontogeny and History*. Norwood, NJ: Ablex, in press.

Bloom, L. *Language Development: Form and Function in Emerging Grammars*. Cambridge, MA: MIT, 1970.

Bloom, L. M., Lifter, K., & Hafitz, J. Semantics of verbs and the development of verb inflection in child language. *Language*, 1980, 56, 386–412.

Bornstein, M. Two kinds of perceptual organization near the beginning of life. In A. Collins (Ed.), *Minnesota Symposium on Child Psychology* (Vol. 14). Hillsdale, NJ: Erlbaum, 1981.

Bower, T. G. R. *Development in Infancy*. San Francisco: Freeman, 1977.

Bowerman, M. Structural relationships in children's utterances: Syntactic or semantic? In L. Bloom (Ed.), *Readings in Language Development*. New York: Wiley, 1978.

Braine, M. D. S. The ontogeny of English phrase structure: The first phrase. *Language*, 1963, 39, 1–13.

Brown, R. A *First Language: The Early Stages*. Cambridge: Harvard University Press, 1973.

Bruner, J., Olver, R. S., & Greenfield, P. M. *Studies in Cognitive Growth*. New York: Wiley, 1966.

Case, R. The process of stage transition: A Neo-Piagetian view. In R. J. Sternberg (Ed.), *Mechanisms of Cognitive Development*. New York: Freeman, 1984.

Cassirer, E. *Philosophy of Symbolic Forms: Vol. 1. Language*. New Haven: Yale University Press, 1953.

Cassirer, E. *Philosophy of Symbolic Forms: Vol. 3. Phenomenology of Knowledge*. New Haven: Yale University Press, 1957.

Chomsky, N. *Aspects of the Theory of Syntax*. Cambridge, MA: MIT Press, 1965.

Chomsky, N. On cognitive structures and their development: A reply to Piaget. In M. Piattelli–Palmarini (Ed.), *Language and Learning*. Cambridge, MA: Harvard, 1980.

Cohen, L. B., & Younger, B. A. Perceptual categorization in infants. In E. K. Scholnick (Ed.), *New Trends in Conceptual Representation*. Hillsdale, NJ: Erlbaum, 1983.

Davidson, P. M. *The development of numerical reasoning in children: The role of classes, relations, and functions*. Unpublished doctoral dissertation, University of California, Berkeley, 1983.

Denney, N. W. A developmental study of free classification in children. *Child Development*, 1972, 43, 221–232.

Epstein, R., Lanza, R. P., & Skinner, B. F. "Self-awareness" in the pigeon. *Science*, 1981, 212, 695–696.

Fischer, K. W. A theory of cognitive development: The control and construction of hierarchies of skills. *Psychological Review*, 1980, 87, 477–531.

Fodor, J. A. *Modularity of Mind*. Cambridge, MA: MIT, 1984.

Forman, G. E. A search for the origins of equivalence concepts through a microanalysis of block play. In G. E. Forman (Ed.), *Action and Thought*. New York: Academic Press, 1982.

Franklin, M. B. Metalinguistic functioning in development. In N. R. Smith & M. B. Franklin (Eds.) *Symbolic Functioning in Childhood*. Hillsdale, NJ: Erlbaum, 1979.

Freud, S. *Three Contributions to the Theory of Sex*. New York: Nervous and Mental Disease Publishing Co., 1930.

Freud, S. Instincts and their vicissitudes. In *Collected Papers* (Vol. 14). London: Hogarth Press, 1958.

Gelman, R., & Gallistel, C. R. *The Child's Understanding of Number*. Cambridge, MA: Harvard, 1978.

Gesell, A. The ontogenesis of infant behavior. In L. Carmichael (Ed.), *Manual of Child Psychology*. New York: Wiley, 1946.

Gibson, J. J. *The Ecological Approach to Visual Perception*. Boston: Houghton Mifflin, 1979.

Goodson, B. D., & Greenfield, P. M. The search for structural principles in children's manipulatory play: A parallel with linguistic development. *Child Development*, 1975, 46, 734–746.

Gratch, G. The development of thought and language in infancy. In J. D. Osofsky (Ed.), *Handbook of Infant Development*. New York: Wiley, 1979.

Greenfield, P. M. Structural parallels between language and action in development. In A. Lock (Ed.), *Action, Gesture, and Language: The Emergence of Language*. London: Academic Press, 1978.

Greenfield, P. M., Nelson, K., & Saltzman, E. The development of rule bound strategies for manipulating seriated cups: A parallel between action and grammar. *Cognitive Psychology*, 1972, 3, 291–310.

Grize, J. B. Analyses to aid in the epistemological study of the notion of functions. In J. Piaget, J. B. Grize, A. Szeminska, & Vinh Bang (Eds.), *Epistemology and Psychology of Functions*. Dordrecht: Reidel, 1977.

Halford, G. S. *The Development of Thought*. Hillsdale, NJ: Erlbaum, 1982.

Halverson, H. M. An experimental study of prehension in infants by means of systematic cinema records. *Genetic Psychology Monographs*, 1931, 10, 107–286.

Hetzer, H. *Kind und Schaffen*. Jena: Gustav Fildner, 1931.

Inhelder, B., & Piaget, J. *The Growth of Logical Thinking from Childhood to Adolescence*. New York: Basic Books, 1958.

Inhelder, B., & Piaget, J. *Early Growth of Logic in the Child: Classification and Seriation*. New York: Harper & Row, 1964.

Inhelder, B., & Piaget, J. Procedures et structures. *Archives de Psychologie*, 1979, 47, 165–167.

Jacobsen, T. A. *The construction and regulation of early structures of logic: A cross-cultural study of infant cognitive development*. Unpublished doctoral dissertation, University of California, Berkeley, 1984.

Jung, C. G. The archetypes and the collective unconscious. In *Collected Works* (Vol. 9). New York: Pantheon, 1959.

Kahneman, D., Slovic, P., & Tversky, A. *Judgement Under Uncertainty*. New York: Cambridge, 1982.

Kagan, J. *The Second Year*. Cambridge, MA: Harvard, 1982.

Kaplan, E. *Gestural representation of implement usage: An organismic developmental study*. Unpublished doctoral dissertation, Clark University, 1968.

Karmiloff–Smith, A. Micro- and macrodevelopmental changes in language acquisition and other representational systems. *Cognitive Science*, 1979, 3, 91–118.

Karmiloff–Smith, A., & Inhelder, B. If you want to get ahead, get a theory. *Cognition*, 1977, 3, 195–212.

Keil, F. C. Constraints on knowledge and cognitive development. *Psychological Review*, 1981, 88, 197–227.

Keil, F. C. Mechanisms of cognitive development and the structure of knowledge. In R. J. Sternberg (Ed.), *Mechanisms of Cognitive Development*. New York: Freeman, 1984.

Klahr, D., & Wallace, J. G. *Cognitive Development: An Information Processing View*. Hillsdale, NJ: Erlbaum, 1976.

Kohler, W. *Gestalt Psychology*. New York: Liveright, 1929.

Langer, J. *Theories of Development*. New York: Holt, Rinehart & Winston, 1969a.

Langer, J. Disequilibrium as a source of development. In P. H. Mussen, J. Langer, & M. Covington (Eds.), *Trends and Issues in Developmental Psychology*. New York: Holt, Rinehart & Winston, 1969b.

Langer, J. Werner's comparative organismic theory. In P. H. Mussen (Ed.), *Carmichael's Manual of Child Psychology*. New York: Wiley, 1970.

Langer, J. Interactional aspects of mental structures. *Cognition*, 1974, 3, 9–28.

Langer, J. *The Origins of Logic: Six to Twelve Months*. New York: Academic Press, 1980.

Langer, J. Logic in infancy. *Cognition*, 1981, 10, 181–186.

Langer, J. From prerepresentational to representational cognition. In G. Forman (Ed.), *Action and Thought*. New York: Academic Press, 1982a.

Langer, J. Dialectics of development. In T. G. R. Bever (Ed.), *Regression in Development*. Hillsdale, NJ: Erlbaum, 1982b.

Langer, J. Concept and symbol formation by infants. In S. Wapner & B. Kaplan (Eds.), *Toward a Holistic Developmental Psychology*. Hillsdale, NJ: Erlbaum, 1983.

Langer, J. Necessity and possibility during infancy. *Archives de Psychologie*, 1985, 53, 61–75.

Langer, J. A note on the comparative psychology of mental development. In S. Strauss (Ed.), *Ontogeny and History*. Norwood, NJ: Ablex, in press.

Langer, J. *The Origins of Logic: Two to Five Years*. In preparation.

Leslie, A. M. The perception of causality in infants. *Perception*, 1982, 11, 173–186.

Leslie, A. M. Spatiotemporal continuity and the perception of causality in infants. *Perception*, 1984, 13, 287–305.

Lewis, M., & Brooks–Gunn, J. *Social Cognition and the Acquisition of Self*. New York: Plenum, 1979.

Lorenz, K. *Evolution and Modification of Behavior*. Chicago: University of Chicago Press, 1965.

Luria, A. R. *The Role of Speech in the Regulation of Normal and Abnormal Behavior*. New York: Liveright, 1961.

Mandler, J. M. Representation. In P. H. Mussen (Ed.), *Handbook of Child Psychology*. New York: Wiley, 1983.

Maratsos, M. Some current issues in the study of the acquisition of grammar. In P. H. Mussen (Ed.), *Handbook of Child Psychology*. New York: Wiley, 1983.

Mounoud, P., & Bower, T. G. Conservation of weight in infants. *Cognition*, 1974, *3*, 29–40.

Mounoud, P., & Hauert, C. A. Development of sensorimotor organization in young children: Grasping and lifting objects. In G. E. Forman (Ed.), *Action and Thought*. New York: Academic Press, 1982.

Nelson, K. Some evidence for the primacy of categorization and its functional basis. *Merrill–Palmer Quarterly*, 1973, *19*, 21–39.

Nicolopoulou, A. *Seriation in action by eighteen-month-olds*. University of California, Berkeley, unpublished manuscript, 1979.

Osherson, D. N. *Logical Abilities in Children. Vol. 3. Reasoning in Adolescence*. Hillsdale, NJ: Erlbaum, 1975.

Overton, W. F., & Jackson, J. J. The representation of imagined objects in action sequences: A developmental study. *Child Development*, 1973, *44*, 309–314.

Pascuale–Leone, J. A mathematical model for the transition rule in Piaget's developmental stages. *Acta Psychologica*, 1970, *32*, 301–345.

Piaget, J. *Play, Dreams and Imitation in Childhood*. New York: Norton, 1951.

Piaget, J. *The Origins of Intelligence in Children*. New York: IUP, 1952a.

Piaget, J. *The Child's Conception of Number*. London: Routledge & Kegan Paul, 1952b.

Piaget, J. *The Construction of Reality in the Child*. New York: Basic Books, 1954.

Piaget, J. Piaget's theory. In P. H. Mussen (Ed.), *Carmichael's Manual of Child Psychology*. New York: Wiley, 1970.

Piaget, J. *Essai de Logique Opératoire*. Paris: Dunod, 1972.

Piaget, J. *Understanding Causality*. New York: Norton, 1974.

Piaget, J. *Equilibration of Cognitive Structures*. New York: Viking Press, 1977.

Piaget, J. *Recherches sur L'Abstraction Réfléchissante: Vol. 1. L'Abstraction des Relations Logico-arithmétiques*. Paris: PUF, 1977a.

Piaget, J. *Recherches sur L'Abstraction Réfléchissante: Vol. 2. L'Abstraction de L'Ordre des Relations Spatiales*. Paris: PUF, 1977b.

Piaget, J. *Recherches sur les Correspondances*. Paris: PUF, 1980.

Piaget, J. *Le Possible et le Nécessaire. Vol. 1. L'Évolution des Possibles Chez l'Enfant*. Paris: PUF, 1981.

Piaget, J. *Le Possible et le Nécessaire. Vol. 2. L'Évolution du Nécessaire Chez l'Enfant*. Paris: PUF, 1983.

Piaget, J., Grize, J. B., Szeminska, A., & Vinh Bang. *Epistemology and Psychology of Functions*. Dordrecht: Reidel, 1977.

Piaget, J., & Inhelder, B. *The Child's Conception of Space*. New York: Norton, 1967.

Piaget, J., & Inhelder, B. *The Psychology of the Child*. New York: Basic Books, 1969.

Pieraut–LeBonniec, G. *The Development of Modal Reasoning*. New York: Academic, 1980.

Premack, D. *Intelligence in Ape and Man*. Hillsdale: Erlbaum, 1976.

Reifel, S., & Greenfield, P. M. Structural development in a symbolic medium: The representational use of block construction. In G. E. Forman (Ed.), *Action and Thought*. New York: Academic Press, 1982.

Riccuiti, H. N. Object grouping and selective ordering behavior in infants 12 to 24 months old. *Merrill–Palmer Quarterly*, 1965, *11*, 129–148.

Roberts, R. J., & Fischer, K. W. A developmental sequence of classification skills. Paper presented at the Society for Research in Child Development meetings, 1979.

Rubin, K. H., Fein, G. G., & Vandenberg, B. Play. In P. H. Mussen (Ed.), *Handbook of Child Psychology*. New York: Wiley, 1983.

Saxe, G. B. A developmental analysis of notational counting. *Child Development*, 1977, 48, 1512–1520.

Siegler, R. S. Information processing approaches to development. In P. H. Mussen (Ed.), *Handbook of Child Psychology*. New York: Wiley, 1983.

Sinclair, H. *Acquisition du Langage et Developpement de la Pensée*. Paris: Dunod, 1967.

Sinclair, M., Stambak, M., Lezine, I., Rayna, S., & Verba, M. *Les Bébés et les Choses*. Paris: PUF, 1982.

Slotnick, C. *The organization and regulation of block constructions: A comparison of autistic and normal children's cognitive development*. Unpublished doctoral dissertation, University of California, Berkeley, 1984.

Starkey, D. The origins of concept formation: Object sorting and object preference in early infancy. *Child Development*, 1981, 52, 489–497.

Starkey, P., & Cooper, R. G. Perception of numbers by human infants. *Science*, 1980, *210*, 1033–1035.

Starkey, P., Spelke, E. S., & Gelman, R. Detection of intermodal numerical correspondences by human infants. *Science*, 1983, 222, 179–181.

Stern, C., & Stern, W. *Die Kindersprache*. Leipzig: Barth, 1927.

Sternberg, R. J. *Intelligence, Information Processing, and Analogical Reasoning*. Hillsdale, NJ: Erlbaum, 1977.

Strauss, S. (Ed.), *U-Shaped Behavioral Growth*. New York: Academic, 1982.

Strauss, M. S., & Curtis, L. E. Infant perception of numerosity. *Child Development*, 1981, 52, 1146–1152.

Sugarman, S. *Children's Early Thought: Developments in Classification*. New York: Cambridge University Press, 1983.

Turiel, E. *The Development of Social Knowledge*. Cambridge: Cambridge University Press, 1983.

Turiel, E., & Davidson, P. Heterogeneity, inconsistency and asynchrony in the development of cognitive structures. In I. Levin (Ed.), *Stages and Structure*. Norwood: Ablex, 1985.

Vereeken, P. *Spatial Development: Constructive Praxia from Birth to the Age of Seven*. Gronigen: Walters, 1961.

von Wright, G. H. *Norm and Action*. London: Routledge & Kegan Paul, 1963.

Vygotsky, L. S. *Thought and Language*. Cambridge, MA: MIT Press, 1962.

Wason, P. C., & Johnson–Laird, P. N. *Psychology of Reasoning*. Cambridge, MA: Harvard, 1972.

Werner, H. *Comparative Psychology of Mental Development*. New York: International Universities Press, 1948.

Werner, H., & Kaplan, B. *Symbol Formation*. New York: Wiley, 1963.

Woodward, W. M., & Hunt, M. R. Exploratory studies of early cognitive development. *British Journal of Educational Psychology*, 1972, 42, 248–259.

Zaporozhets, A. V. The development of perception in the preschool child. *Child Development Monographs*, 1965, 30, No. 2, 82–101.

Author Index

Subject Index

413